Religion in the American South

Religion

in the

Protestants and Others in History and Culture

American South

EDITED BY

BETH BARTON SCHWEIGER

AND DONALD G. MATHEWS

The University of North Carolina Press

Chapel Hill and London

Designed by April Leidig-Higgins
Set in Ehrhardt by Copperline Book Services, Inc.

The paper in this book meets the guidelines for per-
manence and durability of the Committee on Produc-
tion Guidelines for Book Longevity of the Council
on Library Resources.

Portions of this book have been reprinted with per-
mission in slightly different form from the follow-
ing works: Emily Bingham, *Mordecai: An Early
American Family* (New York: Hill and Wang, 2003)
‹www.fsgbooks.com›; Anthea D. Butler, *Making a
Sanctified World: Women in the Church of God in
Christ* (Chapel Hill: University of North Carolina
Press, forthcoming); Paul Harvey and Philip Goff,
eds., *Themes in Religion and American Culture*
(Chapel Hill: University of North Carolina Press,
2004); and Jerma Jackson, *Singing in My Soul:
Black Gospel Music in a Secular Age* (Chapel Hill:
University of North Carolina Press, 2004).

Library of Congress Cataloging-in-Publication Data
Religion in the American South: Protestants and
others in history and culture / edited by Beth Barton
Schweiger and Donald G. Mathews.
p. cm.   Includes bibliographical references and index.
ISBN 0-8078-2906-4 (cloth: alk. paper)
ISBN 0-8078-5570-7 (pbk.: alk. paper)
1. Southern States—Church history.   2. Protestant
churches—Southern States—History.   I. Schweiger,
Beth Barton.   II. Mathews, Donald G.
BR535.R42 2004
277.5—dc22   2004008916

cloth   08 07 06 05 04   5 4 3 2 1
paper   08 07 06 05 04   5 4 3 2 1

CONTENTS

Religion in the American South

DONALD G. MATHEWS

Introduction

These essays represent work in progress; invitations to write them were ambiguous enough to encourage varied responses, and we were not disappointed.
The common concern was to be "religion and the South," but "the South"
could be either the source or the site of a particular investigation. People coming from life experiences in which religion, expressiveness, aspiration, and public performance could not be contained within southern boundaries or places
originally imagined in their youth would be as important as those wrestling with
the compelling and yet forbidding anguish of salvation within the South. With
all of the essays, we hoped to move forward conversations about the ways in which
the South and religion, as imagined by historians, revealed something about religion in America as well as something about the region. Besides, it has been
fifteen years since the last collection of essays on religion in the South appeared,
and much has happened since then.[1] Despite efforts to the contrary, we arrived
at a manuscript about Protestantism and southern culture without working
from a definition of either. We do have to confess that themes identified with
the South—lynching, revivalism, conversion, the Civil War experience, African
American faith, charismatic expressiveness, gender and religion, religion and
race—are also American themes. This fact is not surprising to students of the
South, unless they are among those who study the region as the best, or worst,
or most peculiar area of the United States. And yet, even though the list above
can refer to American phenomena, it is actually derived from the interests of
those who have engaged southerners in varied but frequently tortured religious
experiences of race, gender, identity, solidarity, oppression, and violence.

The author of each essay, of course, has his or her own message about the
nature of southerners' experience and practice of religion, but collectively we
hope that readers will appreciate the importance of including in their understanding of American religion the travails of faith born of peoples from the
South who engaged each other across the wastes and boundaries of difference,
subordination, hatred, violence, shame, and exclusion. If they did so in flawed,

fragmentary, hateful, and grotesque ways, they also tried to do so in healing and life-affirming ways that remind us that southern religion is necessarily interracial. Moreover, faith does not always obey sacred rubrics and boundaries. Celebrating the Spirit could lead from the pulpit to the street, the radio, and the recording studio as religious expression nurtured by the southern experiences of African Americans flowed into mass culture to outrage purists, delight audiences, and perplex students who want expressiveness of the soul to be either sacred or profane, but not both at the same time.

The tendency of religious expression and sensibility to flow over boundaries —and at the same time to be fastidiously insistent upon them—accounts for the "Others" in the subtitle. We are reminded of other religious moods than evangelical Protestantism before revival. A Jewish woman reevaluating her life represents an Other becoming "the same." Whites emphasized difference, while blacks ambivalently denied it and embraced a wholly Other in a way that revealed the pretensions of white people's Christianity. Ashamed at distinctions that enforced a perception of African Americans as Others, some whites (often women) attempted to reach across the boundaries they themselves had made. And African Americans could find in religion a mystique and expressiveness that allowed them to push the other race to the margins of consciousness, raise their own suffering to the center of sacred drama, and in the process realize salvation through divine sacrifice and what it created: their own disciplined solidarity. The word "Others" is thus meant to connote difference (both addressed and ignored), possibility, and God.

If the shout of "Glory" could erupt from revivals, charismatic celebration, gospel music, nightclubs, prayer meetings, and lynchings, as we know it could, it is clear that the language of faith and celebration was pervasive in southern culture. We have tried to plumb its power and depth while also conceding its blindness and narcissistic superficiality. One did not have to be a Jew to appreciate the overwhelming and sometimes suffocating power of evangelical religion, but that power was extensive and intrusive for those who became subjects of special interest. Episcopalians who valued the Eucharist above the unleashed subjectivity of southern popular religion could be noticeably chagrined at evangelical pretensions to holiness, authenticity, and piety, as when a swaggering youth announced that he had never known "a religious Episcopalian" while he sat next to one.[2] The self-satisfied evangelical mood lay on the land like the inescapable and intense humidity of the Carolina low country in late July; it seemed to touch everyone, especially frightening the young Eli Evans, who quailed before the terrifying thought that Jesus was about to take hold of him just as the elders of his synagogue had warned.[3] Evangelical revivalism was one of the cultural engines of the South; its democratic drama and emotional expressiveness could move believers to self-awareness, tears, expectancy, and ecstasy even though "a religious Episcopalian" thought them "poor, blind dupes of a bewildered fantasy."[4] That the self-satisfaction of being fascinated with one's own salvation and purity could lead to segregation and permit brutal punishment does not mean that the religious mood of the South failed to offer succor, dignity, hope, courage, personal power, and authentic salvation. Southern stories of faith are ambiguous. Evangelical importunity—which some may well read as unwarranted intrusion—could be welcomed for its healing promises, its embracing, soothing, and loving invitation personally to surrender all before the "Throne of Grace," even by a woman whose father was a Jewish scholar. In order to relieve her anguish and pain, she had to inflict pain upon some members of her family. Indeed, anguish and pain have long been associated with southern religion, yielding varied interpretations. The crucified God was understood to symbolize not cosmic justification of cruel punishment by means of penal atonement, but subjective emancipation through suffering by African Americans, who drew strength from this image during the nadir of interracial relations even before Countee Cullen imagined the Black Christ in the 1920s.[5]

If our intentions were changed in the process of writing and editing, postmodernism tells us that no matter what our intentions finally became, they are essentially irrelevant to what happens to the texts when they are scattered to the four winds of reading, reviewing, reluctance, and selective perception. We hope that our many projects will stimulate questions and that they will be useful in thinking anew about eighteenth-century religious history, conversion narratives, theory and religious history, the cultural power of prayer, the importance of women in transforming and exploiting religious contexts in innovative ways, the interracialism of southern religious history, and the importance of building upon our work to incorporate "the South" into the study of American religious history. We have obviously not exhausted possible themes, but we hope that the implications of our work shed some light on nooks and crannies that religious historians have missed. For example, there is now a bias among many religious historians who have redressed the ignorance of evangelicalism that once afflicted American religious historiography. There is a triumphalism about this shift that has credited evangelicalism with much good and no evil in American history, and some of the essayists in this book have previously contributed to that bias. Scholars have also argued that evangelical movements of the early nineteenth century brought Americans reform, women's rights, and abolition, even though we know that the South was as evangelical as the North and yet was simultaneously suspicious of women's rights and abolition. This suggests that something other than evangelical Protestantism was needed to spur reform and change in the North, just as it was later needed in a South coming to an appreciation of its interracialism. The proslavery argument of southerners was just as evangelical as immediatism—perhaps more so. Seceding "rebs" were just as evangelical as Yankee abolitionists—possibly more so. The evangelical mood waxed in the American South as whites lynched with arrogant abandon in the 1890s; it embraced a voracious and exploitative capitalism as the savior of the New South; and it lent its sense of purity and danger to racial segregation. Thus readers will see both positive and negative aspects of southern Protestantism, but we hope they will see something else, too, namely, the ways in which different people wrestled with pain, suffering, isolation, innovation, difference, and possibility in religious moods and motivations that fulfilled them short of millennial satisfaction, leaving open hope and allowing celebration in sometimes surprising places and ways.

Notes

1. Samuel S. Hill Jr., ed., *Varieties of Southern Religious Experience* (Baton Rouge: Louisiana State University Press, 1988).

2. William Hooper Haigh Diary, August 14, 18, 1844, Southern Historical Collection, University of North Carolina, Chapel Hill, N.C.

3. "Be especially careful of the goyim," Evans had been warned; "Converting a Jew is a special blessing for them." See Eli N. Evans, *The Provincials: A Personal History of Jews in the South* (New York: Atheneum, 1976), esp. 120–39, 211–26, quote on 124; Howard N. Rabinowitz, "Nativism, Bigotry, and Anti-Semitism in the South," *American Jewish History* 77 (March 1988); and the negative reference to Jews in Erskine Caldwell, *Deep South: Memory and Observation* (Athens: University of Georgia Press, 1980), 148–49.

4. Haigh Diary, September 11, 1844. See also August 12, 1844.

5. Countee Cullen, *The Black Christ and Other Poems* (New York: Harper & Brothers Publishers, 1929), 69–110.

JON F. SENSBACH

1

Before the Bible Belt

Indians, Africans, and the New Synthesis of Eighteenth-Century Southern Religious History

Poor Charles Woodmason. For three years, from 1766 through 1768, this Anglican man of the cloth tramped tirelessly through the Carolina backcountry, taking the Word to the unconverted. No matter how many miles he walked or how earnestly he preached, he found himself losing the battle to his hated rivals, the Baptists, who were "stir[ring] up the minds of the people against the Established Church." His famous journal of those years, into which he poured his frustrations, remains a vivid chronicle of the time and place, wonderfully entertaining in its undisguised contempt for the backcountry settlers, whom he called "the lowest Pack of Wretches my eyes ever saw, or that I have met with in these Woods—As wild as the very Deer," and the itinerant Baptists, to whom the unchurched flocked. These "New Lights" were no better, Woodmason thought, than a "sett of Rhapsodists—Enthusiasts—Bigots—Pedantic, illiterate, impudent Hypocrites—Straining at Gnats, and swallowing Camels, and making Religion a Cloak for Covetuousness[,] Detraction, Guile, Impostures and their par ticular Fabric of Things." Presbyterians, too, were "vile unaccountable wretches," Quakers he called a "vile licentious Pack," and "in the Shape of New Light Preachers," Woodmason said, he had "met with many Jesuits." Little wonder, then, that the "sects [were] eternally jarring among themselves," and that among "this medley of Religions—True Genuine Christianity [was] not to be found." By turns self-pitying and boastful, Woodmason vowed to "disperse these Wretches," which he thought would "not be a hard Task, as they [would] fly before Him as Chaff."[1]

The New Lights did not fly before him, and, we now know, they got the last laugh; the plain folks' rough-hewn, egalitarian religion triumphed over that of the snobbish cleric. It was then, in the middle decades of the eighteenth century, that the stamp of evangelicalism was imprinted on the South. It has since come to be identified as the characteristic mark of southern religion. Evangelicalism helps explain what historians have called the "distinctiveness" of southern religion and the continued vitality of religion in southern culture. Religion is said to be more important in the region than elsewhere; religion and the American South, Donald Mathews has written, "belong together"; they are "fused in our historical imagination in an indelible but amorphous way." The region has been called "Christ-haunted." Indeed, scholars have concluded that "the central theme of southern religious history is the search for conversion, for redemption from innate human depravity." In his landmark study of 1977, *Religion in the Old South*, Mathews explained that his purpose was not to give "a history of the churches, nor of the denominations, nor of the theology, nor of the religious culture of the Old South," but rather to explore "how and why Evangelical Protestantism became the predominant religious mood of the South." The central tenet of that purpose, wrote Martin Marty in the book's foreword, was "to speak of southern religion as a gestalt, a whole, a belief system that helped many sorts of men and women make sense of a world." And according to Samuel Hill, one of the pioneers of southern religious historiography, so ironclad has been the grip of evangelicalism that it has rendered the South historically a "limited-options culture." Writing in the *Encyclopedia of Southern Culture*, Hill suggested that in "hardly any other aspect has the limitation of choices been more pronounced than in religion." The influence of Catholicism and the few Protestant churches outside the evangelical fold has been scant, and as a result "the impact of a single coherent way of understanding Christianity is extensive and tenacious in the South."[2]

The writing of southern religious history has accordingly proceeded from shared assumptions. Knowing that evangelical Protestant modes of worship have dominated the region since the early nineteenth century, historians have naturally sought to explain why that should have been. Plumbing the eighteenth-century record for answers, they have found plausible ones. Rhys Isaac mapped out important terrain in several essays on eighteenth-century evangelicalism that became the core of his immensely influential *The Transformation of Virginia, 1740–1790*. Isaac and others pointed to the institutional weakness of the Anglican Church and to its austere formalism, which alienated many ordinary worshippers; to the inroads made by Separate Baptists and Methodists beginning in midcentury in the southern British colonies; to the disestablishment of religion after the Revolution and the egalitarian appeal of the evangelical churches to humble folk, both free and enslaved; and to the cyclonic effect of the Second Great Awakening at the end of the century, which drew thousands of people hungering for spiritual renewal into the emotional and experiential embrace of revivalist fellowship in camp meetings and new congregations. In the rise of a distinctive southern religion, historians agree, two essential ingredients were its biracial character and its creative fusion of European and African belief systems.[3]

Important considerations, all. The significance of evangelicalism in southern history is beyond dispute. But to invoke its influence as "a gestalt, a whole," or a "single coherent way" of explaining southern religious history is to force too unwieldy a subject into too narrow a paradigm. To equate evangelicalism with southern religion is to convey that there was an air of inevitability about the outcome of eighteenth-century religious change and turmoil. The need to explain the origins and durability of Protestant evangelicalism, especially its Baptist and Methodist forms, has inadvertently imposed what we might call "the burden of southern religious history" on the study of the region. In following the evangelical trail, we risk reducing the colonial and revolutionary periods to a kind of foreshortened prelude to the seminal Cane Ridge revival of 1801, and we slight important forms of religious expression that had nothing to do with, or were later overshadowed by, evangelicalism. Most broad discussions of early southern religious history have adopted an English, Protestant perspective, have underestimated the impact of Catholicism and Islam, and have overlooked the fact that Protestants—in fact, Christians in general— were in the minority in most of the region through the 1760s. Protestant denominations outside the framework of the Anglicans, Baptists, Methodists, and Presbyterians have typically fared little better. The weight of an apparent Protestant evangelical destiny simply overwhelms the narrative of southern religious history, suggesting that the South was overwhelmingly evangelical in periods long before that triumph was achieved.[4]

Christine Heyrman's acclaimed 1997 work, *Southern Cross: The Beginnings of the Bible Belt*, challenged the momentum of this narrative, urging us instead to look at the South through Charles Woodmason's eyes and to reconsider the period when the New Lights were the upstarts, contentious but still outnumbered, the objects of disdain and fear for a majority of southerners. Evangelicalism, Heyrman writes, "came late to the American South, as an exotic import rather than an indigenous development," and hence was not at all assured of dominating the region's religious landscape. Rather, only after a protracted struggle against—and by making numerous compromises with—strong opposition did the evangelicals win any kind of mass support and a firm foothold, and they did not accomplish even that before the second and third decades of the nineteenth century.[5]

Heyrman's revisionism casts this crucial phase of southern religious history in welcome ways. Yet while her approach deepens our view of southern religion in the eighteenth century, the eighteenth-century South encompassed an even broader narrative of religious struggle, declension, and reinvention. We need to amend the traditional notion of the colonial South as the five southernmost of the thirteen British colonies and instead consider all the territory that would later gain the modern geopolitical appellation (however nebulously defined) "the South," "that wide and diverse region that stretches from the Baltimore suburbs to Irving, Texas," as Mathews describes it. Including the French and Spanish colonies and the Indian interior in this framework not only rearranges our mental map of the colonial South, but also forces us to reconsider the very idea of southern religion before the Bible Belt.[6]

From this perspective, the eighteenth century, far more than a mere enabler of the evangelical moment, was easily the most volatile and dynamic period in southern religious history. At no other time was the South so much a part of the transatlantic religious world and receptive to so many international influences from the British Isles, France, Spain, the German lands, and Africa. During the eighteenth century, the South contained more forms of spiritual expression and saw more cataclysmic changes in religious practice than perhaps any region at any point in American history. Not all faiths held equal stature or ability to influence the course of the region's spiritual outlook, to be sure. But the true measure of the South's religious complexion lay in its unprecedented mix and confrontation of Indian, African, and European beliefs, a process that long preceded, and later encompassed, the rise of the evangelicals. Whatever it became later, the South in the eighteenth century was hardly a limited-options religious culture.[7]

The story of the pre–Bible Belt South that emerges in recent scholarship describes the rise, adaptation, survival, or disintegration of religious communities up to now accorded little recognition. Venturing beyond evangelicalism's rise from the Anglican seedbed of Britain's southern colonies, much of the new work shows that religion was a key venue of both cross-cultural exchange and bitter antagonism in the struggle for power among many people across a huge swath of territory. Four prominent themes in the recent literature point the way to such an interpretation: the role of Indians, an inherent part of the southern religious landscape, as they struggled to survive the demographic and cultural losses wrought by European colonization; the incorporation of the colonial South into the transatlantic spiritual world (a theme that highlights the prevalence of several kinds of evangelicalism in the region); the role of religion as agent of cultural domination, resistance, and mediation among contending peoples from three continents; and the connections between religion and gender, especially the cross-cultural role of women's spirituality.

Southern colonial history, like American colonial history, was once written as though the human record of the region began with the arrival of Europeans. Indians, when they were mentioned at all, were generally portrayed as minor impediments to colonial settlement who, once subdued, vanished from sight. Though vestiges of those views remain in current writing about the South, excellent research during the last decade on Indians of the precontact and contact periods makes such approaches seem increasingly archaic. Indians, we are realizing with greater clarity, did not disappear, despite sustaining fierce population and cultural losses over the course of the eighteenth century. As late as the last quarter of the century, they still held a numerical majority and a political balance of power in some parts of the South. Yet scholars of southern religion have been slow to take account of the vast changes that accompanied the encounter between Europeans and Indians, and as a result Indians are still widely perceived as belonging in the realm of ethnohistory rather than as an integral part of a much more complex tapestry of southern religious history.[8]

Indian religious history is connected to the demographic revolution that changed the face of the eighteenth-century South. Historians still debate the size of precontact southeastern Indian populations and the effect of the European incursions that began in the sixteenth century on them. Nevertheless, it is clear that as late as 1685, Indians still comprised about 80 percent of the population in the vast southern region from Virginia to Florida to East Texas. Outside of Virginia, where they had been virtually wiped out, Indians outnumbered the tiny European and African population by nearly twenty to one. But, as Peter Wood's population survey of the region shows, in the early decades of the eighteenth century Indian numbers shrank drastically from disease, warfare and conquest, and slave raiding. Meanwhile, European and African populations grew sharply, particularly in Virginia and the Carolinas. By about 1710, Indians had become a minority in the Southeast, though in large subregions such as Florida, Louisiana, and the Creek, Choctaw, Chickasaw, and Shawnee interior (now Georgia, Alabama, Mississippi, and Kentucky) they still far outnumbered colonists, and they continued to do so in many places well into the 1770s. In the aftermath of the Revolution, the rapid spread of white and black populations into Indian lands doomed native inhabitants to cultural and territorial dispossession, making them a tiny fragment of the population in a region they had once dominated. And therein lay the most profound change in southern religious history: the virtual replacement of Indian religions by Christianity and its hybrid Afro-Christian offspring.[9]

This massive demographic and cultural shift had profound implications for the practice of religion at many levels. Indian decline and European ascendancy heralded a revolution in humans' relationship to the land, for example. Whereas Indians regarded the natural world as sacred and honored it with ceremonies and rituals before they hunted or used land, Europeans invoked Christianity to assert dominion over the landscape as an expression of private property rights grounded in a "natural" order supervised by man. Property ownership and husbandry were to provide the model of Christian civilization, which Englishmen expected Indians to emulate. As European tobacco and rice plantations and fence-enclosed farms replaced burial mounds and Indian worship sites of myth and memory across the southern coastal landscape, the alliance of religion with the world market incorporated the South ever more thoroughly in the eighteenth century. The conclusion of Tom Hatley's study of failed relations between Cherokees and white South Carolinians provides a haunting epitaph to Cherokee loss and the inverted religious symbolism inherent in it. Looking over an abandoned Cherokee village in the 1830s, a white visitor remarked: "This most delightful place is now owned by an enterprising gentleman of Macon County . . . by whom we may expect the site of the old Indian town to be converted into a paradise."[10]

Indians, of course, were never driven entirely away from the landscape they once inhabited, and their search for spiritual responses to demographic, cultural, and territorial loss forms a major chapter in the story of southern religious decline and renewal. Longstanding debates between proponents of acculturation and resistance intensified in Indian societies. Like the Guale and Apalachee converts to Catholicism in sixteenth- and seventeenth-century Florida, some southeastern Indians in the late eighteenth century gave over to the Baptist, Methodist, and Moravian missionaries entreating them and adopted Christianity. Most Indians, however, sought to strengthen themselves internally through revitalization movements aimed at reclaiming lost sacred power through dance, ritual, and ceremony. Whether they employed traditional forms or updated versions of ritual practices, Indians expressed what Joel Martin has called a "cultural 'underground,'" a "hidden set of beliefs and practices that reinforced their identity as Indians and strengthened their will to survive and resist." The Cherokee Booger Dance, for example, used scatological satire to lampoon white people—and the notion of whiteness—as a means of solidifying Indian identity and separateness. Muskogee prophecy produced an apocalyptic vision of an ancient spirit monster shaking the earth and unleashing powerful sacred forces that would purify and remake the world. Revitalization movements occasionally sparked armed resistance and warfare that was inevitably doomed, as with the Muskogees' Red Stick Rebellion of 1811. These spiritual struggles marked a revival movement that ran counter to the white evangelicalism steadily gathering momentum around them. Lying entirely within the mainstream of southern religious history, Indian revivalism has remained outside the mainstream of southern religious historiography.[11]

A second theme in recent literature is the increasingly transatlantic character and variety of religion in the eighteenth-century South. Like New England or the middle colonies, the colonial South was largely shaped by European immigrants, and their variety of religions imparted a polyglot quality to the region that has persisted ever since. The most visible of these immigrants included Anglicans, Presbyterians, and various dissenters in the southern British colonies; in Louisiana, Florida, and Maryland, there were also French Huguenots, Catholics, and German-speaking Lutherans, Reformed, Salzburgers, and Moravians. The presence of so many often discordant faiths gave the region a landscape of cacophonous spiritual competition. This diversity shows that the South was not an isolated religious backwater, but was incorporated into a larger transatlantic religious world. As recent studies are showing with ever greater precision, thousands of European immigrants, whatever their beliefs, considered themselves members of extended international church networks. They corresponded regularly with officials in Europe, sought to regenerate communities in America, received new infusions of ministers and parishioners from abroad, and often regarded their presence in America as part of a larger mission to non-Christians, all of which we might include as part of a broad understanding of evangelicalism.[12]

Yet several recent works on transatlantic Christianity do not mention the South. One study, for example, describes evangelicalism as a "fairly discrete network of Protestant Christian movements arising during the eighteenth century in Great Britain and its colonies," excluding any form of evangelicalism that was neither British nor Protestant and ruling out a great deal of religious activity in many parts of the South. As other work is beginning to show, the international intellectual and spiritual connections between Europe and the eighteenth-century South were in fact quite extensive.[13]

Recent research in German and American archives, for example, is beginning to reveal a great deal about immigration to the South—often through Pennsylvania—by German-speaking congregants, some of them more evangelical than others. We are learning that it is impossible to understand their migration without having a grasp of the religious and social turmoil in the German lands that drove them to asylum in America. A. G. Roeber and Aaron Fogleman have explored the high degree of coordination and planning with which Pietist church networks organized emigration, often by entire villages and congregations, to Maryland, Virginia, the Carolinas, and Georgia. Many of these German communities in the early South considered themselves diasporic members of a transatlantic spiritual web, maintaining constant contact with—and receiving detailed instructions from—church administrators in their homeland. Though historians have just begun to address such questions, a better picture is emerging of Germans' congregational life, their efforts to maintain communities of faith, their engagement with such issues as landownership, slavery, and family life, and their overall imprint on the region. For many parts of the eighteenth-century South, particularly the rural backcountry, to speak of religion is to speak of settlers whose language was not English and whose faith was not Anglican, Baptist, or Methodist.[14]

Likewise, historians are rediscovering Catholicism's powerful presence in the colonial Deep South. An older literature noted the church's role in Florida and Louisiana, occasionally sounding a celebratory tone for its mission outreach to Indians. That scholarship had little impact on the broader study of early America, partly because many historians of British America long perceived North America's Latin world to be on the exotic margins of colonial history. More recent work has begun to bring southern Catholicism into the mainstream of scholarship on both early America and southern religion by connecting the church to developments in France, Spain, and Rome, to the broader Spanish and Francophone Atlantic and Caribbean, and to the wider colonial South. Emily Clark's recent study of the Ursuline order in eighteenth-century New Orleans, for example, underscores the nuns' role in sustaining the church in Louisiana through education and mission work, and it effectively locates them in broad comparative perspective as an extension of European Catholic women's religious orders. The point is not that Catholicism was poised to take over the South in the way the Protestant evangelicals were; as the eighteenth century progressed, the Protestant population in the Upper South came to outnumber that of the Catholics in the French and Spanish Deep South by far. But even in the early nineteenth century, Catholicism still stood as the dominant religion across a huge swath of the Latin Gulf states, standing as an effective check against the Protestant evangelical ascendancy, which was years away from reaching there anyway. The Catholic Church must be reckoned with in any general accounting of early southern religious history.[15]

From a quite different perspective, to speak of the absorption of the early South in the broader transatlantic spiritual world is to confront the African slave trade. As the abundance of recent studies makes clear, the trade was the largest and most continuous source of new, albeit unwilling, immigrants to the region by the late seventeenth century. The religious worldviews that these forced migrants held, both in Africa and in America, have remained a source of controversy and speculation for years. What belief systems did Africans of many cultures, ethnicities, and nationalities bring with them to America, what was lost, and what survived? Jon Butler has suggested that the uprooting and brutal transfer of millions of Africans to America and the subsequent suppression of their beliefs disrupted religious systems in an "African spiritual holocaust." Others, such as Sylvia Frey and Betty Wood, have emphasized the creative adaptation of African beliefs to New World surroundings and the fusion of African cosmologies into a dynamic emergent Afro-Christianity. Such contrasting positions have no easy resolution. Butler's stance has a certain cruel logic to it. When half a million enslaved Africans in North America east of the Mississippi were violently prevented from worshipping as they did in Africa, when their children grew up completely severed from the social and kinship structures that nurtured spiritual belief systems in Africa and had to search for something new, then a religious calamity had indeed occurred. On the other hand, enough convincing evidence has accumulated over the past twenty-five years to demonstrate conclusively that Africans and their descendants showed enormous resilience in finding new ways to worship that expressed essential elements of African cosmologies. The tension between spiritual damage and regeneration defined the African religious experience in early America.[16]

Historians are also gaining a greater sense of how the ethnic composition and distribution of enslaved Africans in the early South shaped these peoples' religious lives. Work on the slave trade is helping to refine our ability to discern which beliefs Africans may have brought with them to America depending on their points of origin. It is now possible to isolate specific national, ethnic, or religious groups that left important cultural marks on certain southern regions. Historians have begun to recognize the importance of Islam in the early South, since unknown thousands of West African captives were Muslim. In American exile, many adhered to the faith, often regarding it as more important than their own ethnic affiliations. John Thornton and Mark Smith have shown that the Catholicism of enslaved Kongolese, converted to the faith in the seventeenth and early eighteenth centuries by Capuchin missionaries in Africa, played a crucial role in South Carolina's Stono Rebellion of 1739. Such connections drive home the importance of understanding the political and spiritual developments in Africa that influenced events thousands of miles away for historians of both African America and religion in the early South. As Annette Laing has demonstrated, familiarity with Christianity might have disposed some Kongolese captives in South Carolina to be more receptive to Anglican mission preaching in the early eighteenth century than historians have supposed. As with Catholic practice among the Kongo, some African worshippers even became lay catechists to fellow captives in the low country.[17]

Scholars still disagree, however, about the extent of religious differences and the process of religious collaboration and fusion among the many West African ethnic groups ensnared in the Atlantic trade. Some scholars have emphasized the change that resulted when Africans of disparate cultures—many of them traditional enemies—were thrown together on the slaving ship and the plantation and forced to remake themselves together. Others suggest that despite linguistic and cultural differences Africans shared many basic precepts and a religious vocabulary that made for relatively easy sharing and melding of beliefs in America. Scholars still have a relatively limited grasp of the degree to which various ethnic groups were clustered or scattered on plantations in many regions, what came of the resulting cultural fusions, and what specific beliefs were passed on to and reinterpreted by successive generations, particularly during their encounter with Christianity. The task is complicated by our growing awareness of the economic and demographic connections between the American South and the Caribbean, which fostered both the continual exchange of Africans among British, French, and Spanish colonies in those regions and the constant reshaping of African American cultures. As historians like Ira Berlin have emphasized, reaffirming traditional beliefs while rejecting Christianity became an important method of cultural resistance to the plantation regime for the great majority of enslaved Africans in the early South. In any case, the African slave trade, along with European immigration, gave early southern religious life an overwhelmingly international quality for most of the eighteenth century. Few regions in world history can claim a religious heritage molded from as heterogeneous a mix of peoples as the early American South.[18]

A third theme of recent literature is the importance of religion as a venue of cross-cultural exchange and mediation. Religion fortified early southerners' sense of national, ethnic, and racial identity, particularly as competition for land and resources intensified. But it also provided a crucial means for bridging differences and redefining power relations. Religious conversion was among the most pervasive forms of cultural fluidity and interpenetration in the region, especially as the geopolitical balance of power shifted toward Europeans.

Recent histories have focused on the search for such connections. Along with the violence and chaos that characterized so many colonial encounters, scholars have found cross-cultural cooperation, accommodation, assimilation, and hybridization. The study of early American frontiers has inspired much of this new interest a century after Frederick Jackson Turner famously took up the subject. "The essence of a frontier," according to one recent definition, "is the kinetic interactions among many peoples, which created new cultural matrices distinctively American in their eclecticism, fluidity, individual determination, and differentiation." From this perspective, the geographic and cultural frontiers among Indians, Europeans, and Africans in the eighteenth-century South represented real and symbolic zones of encounter in trade, diplomacy, language, sexual and gender relations, labor, and religion.[19]

Such meetings, far from being spiritually or socially neutral, were grounded in the geopolitical realities of European expansion. For many Indians and Africans, accommodating to European power pointed toward conversion to some form of Christianity. Religious change in the colonial southeast followed the spread of diseases among Indians, the enmeshment of Indians in European trade networks, the rise of the plantation system, and the flourishing of the European trade in African and Indian slaves. These forces produced an array of religious amalgamations that reflected the South's cultural diversity. Though their efforts have received less attention than those of their counterparts in Canada, Jesuit and Capuchin missionaries won converts among the Taensas, Houmas, Bayagoulas, and other Indians in Louisiana, and they were praised by Governor Bienville in 1726 as ideal support pillars for the colonial system.[20] Before its destruction by the English in 1704, the Spanish mission system in

Florida known as the "Republic of Indians" claimed thousands of Guale, Apalachee, and Timucua converts. Many more resisted Christianity, abandoned the missions, or rose in rebellion against them. As late as 1773, William Bartram observed that the "manners and customs" of Indians in Florida were "tinctured with Spanish civilization": "There are several Christians among them, many of whom wear little silver crucifixes, affixed to a wampum collar round their necks, or suspended by a small chain upon their breast. These are said to be baptized; and notwithstanding most of them speak and understand Spanish, yet they have been the most bitter and formidable Indian enemies the Spaniards ever had."[21] The complex interactions between Indians and Africans on a fluid southeastern frontier, for example, yielded mutual influences on often compatible belief systems, sometimes leading to the creation of unsanctioned forms of prophetic spirituality that proved threatening to white authorities. And we have, as yet, little knowledge of what influences Indian religions may have exerted on white Christians on the frontier, as in the Swiss mystic Gottlieb Priber's attempt to establish a multiracial utopia in Cherokee country in the 1740s.[22]

As the African presence swelled in the eighteenth-century South, the mix of African religions with various forms of Christianity produced even more spiritual hybrids. In the French and Spanish South, enslaved and free black people regularly sought baptism in the Catholic Church. Not only did the fusion of African and Catholic beliefs produce dynamic new forms of worship, people of African descent used the church to form families, gain protection against abuse, establish ties through baptismal sponsorship by white masters or free blacks of higher status, and gain freedom. Scholars are showing, in particular, how slaves and free blacks from Saint Augustine to Pensacola, Mobile, and New Orleans deployed Catholic godparenthood to create a web of fictive kin that provided an extended support group while echoing and adapting remembered African kinship practices.[23]

Likewise, African Americans' embrace of Christianity in the Protestant South not only aided their adjustment to a new life, but also served as a nexus between white and black in a surprising multiplicity of settings. During the second half of the eighteenth century, Baptist and Methodist revivals from Maryland to Georgia produced scores of interracial congregations that became experimental laboratories where black and white coreligionists tested the meanings of race, slavery, and spiritual inclusion. Africans and African Americans also gained their first exposure to Christianity in Anglican, Presbyterian, and Lutheran churches. In North Carolina's Moravian community, enslaved German-speaking Brethren worshipped and worked alongside white congregants, sharing bunk space in communal women's and men's dormitories, gaining literacy and training in classical music, and participating in intimate church rituals such as communion, foot washings, and love feasts. During the last three decades of the eighteenth century, fellowship often transcended racial identity among the Moravians, but white Brethren, gradually abandoning their German identity for a new American one, eventually banished African American members from their midst in the early nineteenth century. The exclusion would be repeated many times in biracial Protestant churches throughout the South.[24]

As these examples demonstrate, religion was an immensely important arena in the forging of the early South's many hybrid cultures, and the fusion of peoples and worldviews in turn shaped the South's religious complexion. Religion raised, but rarely provided decisive answers to, important questions about the social and symbolic lines of race and the boundaries between slavery and freedom, inclusion and exclusion, authority and subordination. The South's emerging religious cultures created entirely new categories of people who straddled these many lines and whose presence forced constant redefinition of normative religious experiences.

A fourth theme embraces all the previous categories: gender. Religion defined the social roles and inner lives of early Americans as men and women, giving varied and changing expression to worshippers' gender identities that can be mapped onto broader demographic and cultural shifts. A number of historians have suggested, for example, that whereas men and women in many pre-contact Indian societies held a rough balance of social and spiritual power, Indian retreat and the consolidation of European colonial power heralded the rise of Christian-derived patriarchal social relations that diminished Indian women's status. Kathleen Brown has wisely warned against a simplistic declension narrative "in which Indian women from 'good' egalitarian societies lose status when 'evil' colonial, Christian, or European commercial powers unhinge native gender roles from their moorings in kinship and economic systems." Still, as Theda Perdue's study of Cherokee women has shown, the collision of religious systems in the early Southeast wrought profound changes on Indian gender relations. The "civilizing" transition to Christianity, capitalism, and private property undermined matrilineal kinship and inheritance patterns from which Cherokee women traditionally derived status. Ostensibly seeking to elevate the status of women, whom they saw as degraded by traditional Cherokee culture, Protestant missionaries pressured converts to adopt roles within patriarchal family and social structures that left women in a "distinctly subservient, largely powerless position."[25]

The increasing dominance of Christianity in the early South may have entailed the expansion of patriarchy, but in the Christian congregational order male hegemony and female subordination were considerably qualified. Recent work has begun to explore the interior psychic and social spaces created by and for women within the Catholic and Protestant South. New Orleans' Ursuline order and its associated laywomen's confraternity created powerful means for women to organize, lead each other, hold property, conduct mission work, and worship. The Catholic Church gave enslaved women "legal protections and social opportunities significantly better than those of their counterparts in Anglo settlements," including charity, the shield of Christian paternalism, and the right to use the courts to file claims against their owners, petition for manumission, and manage their own property.[26]

Likewise, the rise of Protestant evangelicalism chiseled holes in the wall of patriarchy, creating new opportunities for female spiritual expression and leadership. Using critical approaches from feminist theory and cultural studies, historians of gender and Christianity in early America have shown how the language of evangelicalism exalted the purportedly female traits of emotion and sensuality above masculine reason. Worship was defined as an essentially feminine practice, and women gained a privileged place in a new congregational order that strove for "glorious Oneness" with Christ while de-emphasizing worldly differences among the regenerate.[27]

The implications of this quiet revolution of the spirit were profound. Late-eighteenth-century Methodist women, white and black, slave and free, "openly rebuked 'sinners' and were assertive and outspoken in their evangelism," according to Cynthia Lynn Lyerly. "Southern women found self-esteem, a need for their skills, and most important of all, agency in the church" by testifying to large audiences, exercising leadership, and even preaching. Methodist and Separate Baptist women gained moral authority as spiritual mentors to their husbands, undermining the logic of patriarchal honor. White and black Moravian women worshipped in separate "choir" groups that promoted female spiritual expression and leadership. In the 1770s, the dormitory-style Single Sisters' choir house and business complex in Salem, North Carolina, a Protestant equivalent to the Ursuline convent in New Orleans, was probably the largest, most powerful women's religious institution in the Upper South.[28]

In all of these cases, evangelicalism forced white men to respect the spirituality of enslaved women, who pressed the advantage by using church courts to levy charges of mistreatment, including sexual abuse, against masters. Black female exhorters were crucial instigators in creating and maintaining nascent Afro-Christian communities. Such aspects of evangelicalism posed a severe threat to white slaveholding patriarchy that provoked a backlash toward the end of the eighteenth century. To gain social respectability and converts, the evangelical churches redefined themselves as friends of masculine honor and slavery. They equated female volubility with disorderly conduct, punishable by excommunication. They silenced male and female African Americans' attempts to hold slaveowners to account in church courts. The eventual triumph of Protestant evangelicalism was thus achieved in no small measure by a counterrevolution in gender relations.[29]

The rise of the Methodist-Baptist evangelical axis continues to captivate historians of religion in the South. The recent burst of writing on the subject, particularly about the Methodists, reveals an enduring fascination with the origins of the evangelical grip on the region. Most of the work has centered on the late eighteenth and early nineteenth centuries. But there is much we have yet to learn about the earlier decades, when the leading radical edge of Protestant evangelicalism made its way into the South. Rhys Isaac's pathbreaking study of Virginia has just begun to generate comparative study of the Carolinas and Georgia, but we do not yet have a firm understanding of how revivals spread and how new congregations emerged there. Did the rise of the Baptists and Methodists constitute a popular revolt from below or, as Rachel Klein's work on South Carolina has countered, a conservative coup from above?[30]

The evidence, particularly concerning themes of gender and race, points in conflicting directions. Marjoleine Kars's study of the North Carolina Regulators has shown the links between popular evangelical Christianity and social radicalism in the South, but much remains to be learned about the decades when the evangelicals were an embattled minority mounting their assault against High Church resistance. In a study of eighteenth-century Baptist congregations in Virginia, Jewel Spangler found that they were essentially conservative social institutions: "Baptist spiritual egalitarianism was limited enough to leave basic household inequalities intact, while Baptist religious practice supported patriarchal relations and involuntary servitude, thereby shoring up rather than eroding the authority of planters and household heads." She argues, further, that it was not a sense of discontentment with their place in the social order that drew converts into the church, but rather the promise of fellowship to "provide social order through a heightened self-discipline and its ability to elicit intimate interpersonal contact and intense emotional release." Recruits were drawn to the church by preexisting social networks of kin, friends, and neighbors rather than by any overt attempts to challenge or accommodate social inequities.[31]

EVANGELICALISM EMBODIES and has shaped so much that seems quintessentially southern—the preoccupation with sin and guilt, the emotional search for redemption, the plainspoken directness of the faith of ordinary folk, the Laocoon-like twining of race and religion. The ironies brood over the southern religious landscape: the tension between an egalitarian religion of the heart and the undemocratic compromises it made on race, slavery, and gender to survive and flourish; the paradox that the same language of sin and freedom that inspired white evangelicals also fueled the radical moral vision of the black church. Evangelicalism helped shape the emergence of the modern South. Fittingly, in a region awash in tragedy, pathos, and squandered opportunities, the triumph of evangelicalism reaped its share of those harvests; it also brought a message of hope and redemption to the South.[32]

We can see all that only in hindsight. Before the early nineteenth century, the religious complexion of the South looked very different, and no one could know that the din of the camp meetings would come to dominate the region. While the rise of the evangelicals can be attributed to many causes, it should be understood as only one—albeit an increasingly aggressive one—among many competing forms of spirituality in the eighteenth-century South. To tell the religious histories of that earlier South as more than simply a preface to the great revivals is to consider a place that was more than a precursor to the Old South but was just as southern and every bit as marked by tragedy, loss, replenishment, and the search for spiritual resurrection. The eighteenth-century South saw a revolution in faith: the virtual replacement of native peoples and their religions with other people and different religions, including the reemergence of African belief systems in altered guises. In the eighteenth-century South, thousands of European migrants worshipped in different, and often competing, ways and considered themselves part of international fellowships at the same time that Catholicism and Protestantism collided in the southern theater. Religion helped people bridge these rapidly changing worlds, adjust to new and often cruel realities, and make sense of frightening change. The world the evangelicals made, and the gradual narrowing of other religious alternatives, can be understood only as part of a longer narrative of struggle stretching far back in southern religious history.

Notes

1. Richard J. Hooker, ed., *The Carolina Backcountry on the Eve of the Revolution: The Journal and Other Writings of Charles Woodmason, Anglican Itinerant* (Chapel Hill: University of North Carolina Press, 1953), 31, 42–43, 46, 78.

2. Donald G. Mathews has surveyed southern religious history and historiography in several recent essays: "'We Have Left Undone Those Things Which We Ought to Have Done': Southern Religious History in Retrospect and Prospect," *Church History* 67 (1998): 305–25; "'Christianizing the South'—Sketching a Synthesis," in *New Directions in American Religious History*, eds. Harry S. Stout and D. G. Hart (New York: Oxford University Press, 1997), 84–115; "Religion and the South: Authenticity and Purity—Pulling Us Together, Tearing Us Apart," in *Religious Diversity and American Religious History*, eds. Walter H. Conser Jr. and Sumner B. Twiss (Athens: University of Georgia Press, 1997), 72–101; and "Forum: Southern Religion," *Religion and American Culture* 8 (Summer 1998): 147–54. Quotations are from Mathews, "Forum," 147; Mathews, *Religion in the Old South* (Chicago: University of Chicago Press, 1977), xiii–xiv; Martin Marty, foreword to Mathews, *Religion in the Old South*, xi; Charles Reagan Wilson, *Judgment and Grace in Dixie: Southern Faiths from Faulkner to Elvis* (Athens: University of Georgia Press, 1995), 5–9; and Samuel S. Hill, "Religion," in *Encyclopedia of Southern Culture*, eds. Charles Reagan Wilson and William Ferris (Chapel Hill: University of North Carolina Press, 1989), 1269–70.

3. Rhys Isaac, *The Transformation of Virginia, 1740–1790* (Chapel Hill: University of North Carolina Press, 1982); Mathews, *Religion in the Old South*; Mathews, "Religion and the South"; John B. Boles, *The Irony of Southern Religion* (New York: Peter Lang, 1994).

4. Several scholars, including Mathews, Hill, and Beth Barton Schweiger, have begun to question the value of studying southern religion through the monolithic but bland and vague explanatory device of evangelicalism. Indeed, Schweiger questions whether the phrase "southern religion" has worn out its welcome. See the essays by all three authors in "Forum: Southern Religion," *Religion and American Culture* 8 (Summer 1998): 147–77.

5. Christine Leigh Heyrman, *Southern Cross: The Beginnings of the Bible Belt* (New York: Alfred A. Knopf, 1997), 9.

6. The view that the religious life of the colonial South was contained in, and defined by, the southern British colonies has had a long and durable tenure. See, for example, Hill, "Religion," 1271; Wilson, *Judgment and Grace in Dixie*, 4–5; Richard Beale Davis, *Intellectual Life in the Colonial South, 1585–1763* (Knoxville: University of Tennessee Press,

1973), 2:627–700; Mathews, "Religion and the South," 72–73; Mathews, "Christianizing the South"; and Boles, *Irony of Southern Religion*. Yet the non-English roots of the southern Gulf states are scarcely a secret. One state-by-state survey of southern religious history published in the 1980s pays due attention to non–Anglo-American colonies as well as to many non-Anglican, mostly Christian, religions within the British colonies. See Samuel S. Hill, ed., *Religion in the Southern States: A Historical Study* (Macon: Mercer University Press, 1983). Interpretations such as Hill's have generally remained outside the focus of the most significant synthetic works over the last twenty years, which have considered religion in the early South largely from the view of English-speaking settlers in the British colonies.

7. It might well be argued that in confining myself to the eighteenth century I am imposing another arbitrary narrowness upon a region whose colonial and precolonial origins obviously extend much further back. No doubt that is true, but my intention here is to focus on what I see as the period of greatest religious dynamism in southern history. For a recent overview of early American religious historiography that implicitly includes many themes pertinent to the South, see Charles L. Cohen, "The Post-Puritan Paradigm of Early American Religious History," *William and Mary Quarterly*, 3d ser., 54 (1997): 695–722.

8. For historiographical overviews, see Joel W. Martin, "Indians, Contact, and Colonialism in the Deep South: Themes for a Postcolonial History of American Religion," in *Retelling U.S. Religious History*, ed. Thomas A. Tweed (Berkeley: University of California Press, 1997), 149–80; James H. Merrell, "Some Thoughts on Colonial Historians and American Indians," *William and Mary Quarterly*, 3d ser., 46 (1989): 94–119; and M. Annette Jaimes, "The Scholarship of Cultural Contact: Decolonizing Native American History," *Historical Reflections/Reflexions Historiques* 21 (Spring 1995): 207–391. Though it is impossible to survey here all of the recent scholarship on southern Indians during the colonial period, some excellent examples include M. Thomas Hatley, *The Dividing Paths: Cherokees and South Carolinians through the Revolutionary Era* (New York: Oxford University Press, 1995); Peter H. Wood, Gregory A. Waselkov, and M. Thomas Hatley, eds., *Powhatan's Mantle: Indians in the Colonial Southeast* (Lincoln: University of Nebraska Press, 1989); James H. Merrell, *The Indians' New World: Catawbas and Their Neighbors from European Contact through the Era of Removal* (Chapel Hill: University of North Carolina Press, 1989); Daniel H. Usner Jr., *Indians, Settlers, and Slaves in a Frontier Exchange Economy: The Lower Mississippi Valley before 1783* (Chapel Hill: University of North Carolina Press, 1992); Patricia Galloway, *Choctaw Genesis, 1500–1700* (Lincoln: University of Nebraska Press, 1995); Charles Hudson and Carmen Tesser, eds., *The Forgotten Centuries: Indians and Europeans in the American South, 1521–1704* (Athens: University of Georgia Press, 1994); and Claudio Saunt, *A New Order of Things: Property, Power, and the Transformation of the Creek Indians, 1733–1816* (New York: Cambridge University Press, 1999). Scholars of New England and Canada have somewhat more frequently viewed the encounter between Indians and Europeans as a confrontation of religious worldviews. See,

for example, Neal Salisbury, *Manitou and Providence: Indians, Europeans, and the Making of New England, 1500–1643* (New York: Oxford University Press, 1982), and James Axtell, *The Invasion Within: The Contest of Cultures in Colonial North America* (New York: Oxford University Press, 1985). The Spanish missions in colonial Florida have provided scholars with the most fruitful southern counterpart. See Jerald T. Milanich, *Florida Indians and the Invasion from Europe* (Gainesville: University Press of Florida, 1995) and *Laboring in the Fields of the Lord: Spanish Missions and Southeastern Indians* (Washington, D.C.: Smithsonian Institution Press, 1999).

9. Peter H. Wood, "The Changing Population of the Colonial South: An Overview by Race and Region, 1685–1790," in Wood, Waselkov, and Hatley, *Powhatan's Mantle*, 35–103.

10. Virginia DeJohn Anderson, "Animals into the Wilderness: The Development of Livestock Husbandry in the Seventeenth-Century Chesapeake," *William and Mary Quarterly*, 3d. ser., 59 (2002): 377–78; Hatley, *Dividing Paths*, 241. The environmental approach to Indian-European relations pioneered by William Cronon in *Changes in the Land: Indians, Colonists, and the Ecology of New England* (New York: Hill & Wang, 1983) has been productively adapted by scholars of the colonial South. In addition to Hatley, *Dividing Paths*, 3–16, 204–15, see Timothy Silver, *A New Face on the Countryside: Indians, Colonists, and Slaves in South Atlantic Forests, 1500–1800* (New York: Cambridge University Press, 1990), 187–91, and Mart A. Stewart, *"What Nature Suffers to Groe": Life, Labor, and Landscape on the Georgia Coast, 1680–1920* (Athens: University of Georgia Press, 1996), 23–25. See also Michael Leroy Oberg, *Dominion and Civility: English Imperialism and Native America, 1585–1685* (Ithaca: Cornell University Press, 1999).

11. Joel W. Martin, "From 'Middle Ground' to 'Underground': Southeastern Indians and the Early Republic," in *Religion and American Culture: A Reader*, ed. David G. Hackett (New York: Routledge, 1995); Martin, *Sacred Revolt: The Muskogees' Struggle for a New World* (Boston: Beacon Press, 1991); Gregory Evans Dowd, *A Spirited Resistance: The North American Struggle for Unity, 1745–1815* (Baltimore: Johns Hopkins University Press, 1992); Hatley, *Dividing Paths*, 204–41. While recent scholarship has helped illuminate the ritual world of Indian societies under intense duress, much remains to be done to strip away the varnish of obscurity and modern oversight that has hidden this world from view.

12. In *Intellectual Life in the Colonial South* (2:662–700), Davis surveys some transatlantic connections among Anglicans and other colonial churches in the British colonies, but his study, still the only overview of religion in the British colonial South, made no claim to be comprehensive when it was published, and it now suggests a huge range of research questions. More recent examples of the international quality of religion in the early South include Leigh Eric Schmidt, *Holy Fairs: Scottish Communions and American Revivals in the Early Modern Period* (Princeton: Princeton University Press, 1989); Jon Butler, *The Huguenots in America: A Refugee People in New World Society* (Cambridge, Mass.: Harvard University Press, 1983); and A. G. Roeber, *Palatines, Liberty, and Property: German Lutherans in Colonial America* (Baltimore: Johns Hopkins University Press, 1993).

13. Mark A. Noll, David W. Bebbington, and George A. Rawlyk, eds., *Evangelicalism: Comparative Studies of Popular Protestantism in North America, the British Isles, and Beyond, 1700–1990* (New York: Oxford University Press, 1994), 6. The editors make several disclaimers, explaining that evangelicalism might have other useful definitions and that their volume makes no attempt to be comprehensive. Still, their otherwise useful collection is representative of one approach that does little to open up study of the early South. On transatlantic evangelical connections between Britain and the American colonies that leave much room for exploration of southern themes, see Susan O'Brien, "A Transatlantic Community of Saints: The Great Awakening and the First Evangelical Network, 1735–1755," *American Historical Review* 91 (1986): 811–32; Harry S. Stout, *The Divine Dramatist: George Whitefield and the Rise of Modern Evangelicalism* (Grand Rapids: Eerdmans, 1991); Rebecca Larson, *Daughters of Light: Quaker Women Preaching and Prophesying in the Colonies and Abroad, 1700–1775* (New York: Alfred A. Knopf, 1999); and Timothy D. Hall, *Contested Boundaries: Itinerancy and the Reshaping of the Colonial American Religious World* (Durham: Duke University Press, 1994).

14. English-language works on German-speaking religious immigrants in the early South include Roeber, *Palatines, Liberty, and Property* and "What the Law Requires Is Written on Their Hearts: Noachic and Natural Law among German-Speakers in Early Modern North America," *William and Mary Quarterly*, 3d ser., 58 (2001): 883–912; Aaron S. Fogleman, *Hopeful Journeys: German Immigration, Settlement, and Political Culture in Colonial America, 1717–1775* (Philadelphia: University of Pennsylvania Press, 1996); Daniel B. Thorp, *The Moravian Community in Colonial North Carolina: Pluralism on the Southern Frontier* (Knoxville: University of Tennessee Press, 1989); Jon F. Sensbach, *A Separate Canaan: The Making of an Afro-Moravian World in North Carolina, 1763–1840* (Chapel Hill: University of North Carolina Press, 1998); Elisabeth Sommer, *Serving Two Masters: Faith, Authority, and Community among the Moravian Brethren in Germany and North Carolina, 1727–1801* (Lexington: University Press of Kentucky, 2000); and Stephen Scott Rohrer, "Planting Pietism: Religion and Community in the Moravian Settlements of North Carolina, 1750–1830" (Ph.D. diss., University of Virginia, 1999) and "Evangelicalism and Acculturation in the Backcountry: The Case of Wachovia, North Carolina, 1753–1830," *Journal of the Early Republic* 21 (2001): 199–229. A study of relations between German Pietists and (mainly German) Jews in the early South can be found in Holly Snyder, "A Tree with Two Different Fruits: The Jewish Encounter with German Pietists in the Eighteenth-Century Atlantic World," *William and Mary Quarterly*, 3d ser., 58 (2001): 855–82. Among the many examples of scholarship on religious and political motivations for German emigration, see Mack Walker, *The Salzburg Transaction: Expulsion and Redemption in Eighteenth-Century Germany* (Ithaca: Cornell University Press, 1992).

15. For French and Spanish Louisiana, see Charles E. O'Neill, *Church and State in French Colonial Louisiana: Policy and Politics* (New Haven: Yale University Press, 1966); Jerah Johnson, "Colonial New Orleans: A Fragment of the Eighteenth-Century French

Ethos," in *Creole New Orleans: Race and Americanization*, eds. Arnold R. Hirsch and Joseph Logsdon (Baton Rouge: Louisiana State University Press, 1992), 12–57; Carl A. Brasseaux, "The Moral Climate of French Colonial Louisiana, 1699–1763," *Louisiana History* 27 (Winter 1986): 27–41; Emily Clark, "'By All the Conduct of Their Lives': A Laywomen's Confraternity in New Orleans, 1730–1744," *William and Mary Quarterly*, 3d ser., 54 (1997): 769–94; Clark, "A New World Community: The New Orleans Ursulines and Colonial Society, 1727–1803" (Ph.D. diss., Tulane University, 1998); Jean Delanglez, *The French Jesuits in Lower Louisiana, 1700–1763* (Washington, D.C.: Catholic University of America, 1935); and Kimberly S. Hanger, *Bounded Lives, Bounded Places: Free Black Society in Colonial New Orleans, 1769–1803* (Durham: Duke University Press, 1997). On Catholicism in Maryland, see Ronald Hoffman, *Princes of Ireland, Planters of Maryland: A Carroll Saga, 1500–1782* (Chapel Hill: University of North Carolina Press, 2000).

16. Opposing positions are found in Jon Butler, *Awash in a Sea of Faith: Christianizing the American People* (Cambridge, Mass.: Harvard University Press, 1990); Sylvia R. Frey and Betty Wood, *Come Shouting to Zion: African American Protestantism in the American South and British Caribbean to 1830* (Chapel Hill: University of North Carolina Press, 1998); and Philip D. Morgan, *Slave Counterpoint: Black Culture in the Eighteenth-Century Chesapeake and Lowcountry* (Chapel Hill: University of North Carolina Press, 1998), 610–58. For a review essay further explicating various sides of the debate, see Jon Butler, "Africans' Religions in British America, 1650–1840," *Church History* 68 (1999): 118–27.

17. Michael Gomez, "Muslims in Early America," *Journal of Southern History* 60 (1994): 671–710; Allan D. Austin, ed., *African Muslims in Antebellum America: Transatlantic Stories and Spiritual Struggles* (New York: Routledge, 1997); Sylviane A. Diouf, *Servants of Allah: African Muslims Enslaved in the Americas* (New York: New York University Press, 1998); John Thornton, "On the Trail of Voodoo: African Christianity in Africa and the Americas," *Americas* 44 (1988): 261–78; Thornton, "African Dimensions of the Stono Rebellion," *American Historical Review* 96 (1991): 1101–13; Mark M. Smith, "Remembering Mary, Shaping Revolt: Reconsidering the Stono Rebellion," *Journal of Southern History* 67 (2001): 513–34; Annette Laing, "'Heathens and Infidels'? African Christianization and Anglicanism in the South Carolina Low Country, 1700–1750," *Religion and American Culture* 12 (2002): 197–228. For other discussions of African ethnicity among slave societies in the early South, see Peter Caron, "'Of a Nation Which the Others Do Not Understand': Bambara Slaves and African Ethnicity in Colonial Louisiana, 1718–60," *Slavery and Abolition* 18 (1997): 98–121, and "Ethnicity in the Diaspora: The Slave Trade and the Creation of African 'Nations' in the Americas," *Slavery and Abolition* 22 (2000): 25–39.

18. Recent broad overviews of African acculturation in North America include Ira Berlin, *Many Thousands Gone: The First Two Centuries of Slavery in North America* (Cambridge, Mass.: Harvard University Press, 1998), esp. 171–73; Morgan, *Slave Counterpoint*; Michael Gomez, *Exchanging Our Country Marks: The Transformation of African*

Identities in the Colonial and Antebellum South (Chapel Hill: University of North Carolina Press, 1998); and Frey and Wood, *Come Shouting to Zion*.

19. Andrew R. L. Cayton and Fredrika J. Teute, eds., *Contact Points: American Frontiers from the Mohawk Valley to the Mississippi, 1750–1830* (Chapel Hill: University of North Carolina Press, 1998). A sample of other works representative of this approach with a variety of applications includes Richard White, *The Middle Ground: Indians, Empires, and Republics in the Great Lakes Region, 1650–1815* (New York: Cambridge University Press, 1991); James H. Merrell, "'The Customes of Our Countrey': Indians and Colonists in Early America," in *Strangers within the Realm: Cultural Margins of the First British Empire*, eds. Bernard Bailyn and Philip D. Morgan (Chapel Hill: University of North Carolina Press, 1991), 117–56; and Kathleen M. Brown, "Brave New Worlds: Women's and Gender History," *William and Mary Quarterly*, 3d ser., 50, no. 2 (1993): 311–28.

20. Mary Miceli, "The Christianization of French Colonial Louisiana: A General View of Church and State in the Context of Eighteenth-Century French Colonization and a Theory of Mission," in *The French Experience in Louisiana*, ed. Glenn R. Conrad (Lafayette: Center for Louisiana Studies, 1995), 494–505; Delanglez, *French Jesuits in Lower Louisiana*; James Axtell, *The Indians' New South: Cultural Change in the Colonial Southeast* (Baton Rouge: Louisiana State University Press, 1997), 53–54.

21. William Bartram, *Travels of William Bartram*, ed. Mark van Doren (New York: Dover, 1928), 164. The literature on the Spanish missions is extensive, but for examples see Michael V. Gannon, *The Cross in the Sand: The Early Catholic Church in Florida, 1513–1870* (Gainesville: University of Florida Press, 1967); Bonnie G. McEwen, "The Missions of Spanish Florida," special issue, *Florida Anthropologist* 44 (1991): 104–330; and Amy Turner Bushnell, "Ruling 'the Republic of Indians' in Seventeenth-Century Florida," in Wood, Waselkov, and Hatley, *Powahatan's Mantle*, 134–50. On Indian-European religious encounters generally, see Martin, "Indians, Contact, and Colonialism in the Deep South."

22. For a bibliography of works on Indian-black relations in the early South, see, for example, Martin, *Sacred Revolt*, 73–76; Saunt, *A New Order of Things*, 111–35; and Daniel H. Usner Jr., "Indian-Black Relations in Colonial and Antebellum Louisiana," in *Slave Cultures and the Cultures of Slavery*, ed. Stephan Palmie (Knoxville: University of Tennessee Press, 1995), 145–61.

23. Hanger, *Bounded Lives, Bounded Places*, 104–8; Clark, "A New World Community," 140–51; Emily Clark and Virginia Meacham Gould, "The Feminine Face of Afro-Catholicism in New Orleans, 1727–1852," *William and Mary Quarterly*, 3d ser., 59 (2002): 409–48; Caryn Cossé Bell, *Revolution, Romanticism, and the Afro-Creole Protest Tradition in Louisiana, 1718–1868* (Baton Rouge: Louisiana State University Press, 1997); Gwendolyn Midlo Hall, *Africans in Colonial Louisiana: The Development of Afro-Creole Culture in the Eighteenth Century* (Baton Rouge: Louisiana State University Press, 1992); Virginia Meacham Gould, "In Full Enjoyment of Their Liberty: The Free Women of Color of the Gulf Ports of New Orleans, Mobile, and Pensacola, 1769–1860" (Ph.D. diss., Emory

University, 1991); Jane Landers, "Gracia Real de Santa Teresa de Mose: A Free Black Town in Spanish Colonial Florida," *American Historical Review* 95 (1990): 9–30, and *Black Society in Spanish Florida* (Urbana: University of Illinois Press, 1999).

24. Recent writing on black Protestant Christianity and interracial worship in the late eighteenth and early nineteenth centuries includes Frey and Wood, *Come Shouting to Zion*; Morgan, *Slave Counterpoint*, 420–37; Cynthia Lynn Lyerly, "Religion, Gender and Identity: African American Methodist Women in a Slave Society, 1770–1809," in *Discovering the Women in Slavery: Emancipating Perspectives on the American Past*, ed. Patricia Morton (Athens: University of Georgia Press, 1996), 202–26; John B. Boles, ed., *Masters and Slaves in the House of the Lord: Race and Religion in the American South, 1740–1870* (Lexington: University Press of Kentucky, 1988); and Sensbach, *A Separate Canaan*. Earlier standard works include Albert Raboteau, *Slave Religion: The "Invisible Institution" in the Antebellum South* (New York: Oxford University Press, 1978); and Mechal Sobel, *The World They Made Together: Black and White Values in Eighteenth-Century Virginia* (Princeton: Princeton University Press, 1988) and *Trabelin' On: The Slave Journey to an Afro-Baptist Faith* (Westport, Conn.: Greenwood Press, 1979).

25. Brown, "Brave New Worlds," 321; Theda Perdue, *Cherokee Women: Gender and Culture Change, 1700–1835* (Lincoln: University of Nebraska Press, 1998), 135–84, quote on 159. On changing roles for Indian women, see also Hatley, *Dividing Paths*, and Merrell, *The Indians' New World*.

26. Clark, "A New World Community" and "By All the Conduct of Their Lives"; Jane Landers, "'In Consideration of Her Enormous Crime': Rape and Infanticide in Spanish St. Augustine," in *The Devil's Lane: Sex and Race in the Early South*, eds. Catherine Clinton and Michele Gillespie (New York: Oxford University Press, 1997), 207.

27. Susan Juster, *Disorderly Women: Sexual Politics and Evangelicalism in Revolutionary New England* (Ithaca: Cornell University Press, 1994), 4–6; Catherine A. Brekus, *Strangers and Pilgrims: Female Preaching in America, 1740–1845* (Chapel Hill: University of North Carolina Press, 1998), 27–44.

28. Cynthia Lynn Lyerly, *Methodism and the Southern Mind, 1770–1810* (New York: Oxford University Press, 1998), 95; Dee Andrews, *The Methodists and Revolutionary America, 1760–1800: The Shaping of an Evangelical Culture* (Princeton: Princeton University Press, 2000), 199–222; Jon Sensbach, "Interracial Sects: Religion, Race, and Gender among Early North Carolina Moravians," in Clinton and Gillespie, *The Devil's Lane*, 154–67.

29. Frey and Wood, *Come Shouting to Zion*; Brekus, *Strangers and Pilgrims*, 61–67; Heyrman, *Southern Cross*; Sensbach, "Interracial Sects." Other interpretations of the rising social conservatism of evangelicalism in the early nineteenth century include Andrews, *The Methodists and Revolutionary America*; A. Gregory Schneider, *The Way of the Cross Leads Home: The Domestication of American Methodism* (Bloomington: Indiana University Press, 1993); John H. Wigger, *Taking Heaven by Storm: Methodism and the Popularization of American Christianity, 1770–1820* (New York: Oxford University Press, 1998); and Gregory A. Wills, *Democratic Religion: Freedom, Authority, and Church Discipline in*

the Baptist South, 1785–1900 (New York: Oxford University Press, 1996). Two essays by Janet Moore Lindman explore the role of evangelical religion in regulating the bodies of worshippers as an expression of white masculinity. See "The Body Baptist: Embodied Spirituality, Ritualization, and Church Discipline in Eighteenth-Century America," in *A Centre of Wonders: The Body in Early America*, eds. Janet Moore Lindman and Michele Lise Tarter (Ithaca: Cornell University Press, 2001), 177–90, and "Acting the Manly Christian: White Evangelical Masculinity in Revolutionary Virginia," *William and Mary Quarterly*, 3d ser., 57 (2000): 393–416.

30. Rachel M. Klein, *Unification of a Slave State: The Rise of the Planter Class in the South Carolina Backcountry, 1760–1808* (Chapel Hill: University of North Carolina Press, 1990).

31. Jewel Spangler, "Salvation Was Not Liberty: Baptists and Slavery in Revolutionary Virginia," *American Baptist Quarterly* 13 (1994): 221–36.

32. These are the central themes of Mathews, *Religion in the Old South*, and Boles, *The Irony of Southern Religion*.

For Further Reading

Berlin, Ira. *Many Thousands Gone: The First Two Centuries of Slavery in North America.* Cambridge, Mass.: Harvard University Press, 1998.

Boles, John B. *The Irony of Southern Religion.* New York: Peter Lang, 1994.

Butler, Jon. *Awash in a Sea of Faith: Christianizing the American People.* Cambridge, Mass.: Harvard University Press, 1990.

Clark, Emily. "'By All the Conduct of Their Lives': A Laywomen's Confraternity in New Orleans, 1730–1744." *William and Mary Quarterly*, 3d ser., 54 (1997): 769–94.

Cohen, Charles L. "The Post-Puritan Paradigm of Early American Religious History." *William and Mary Quarterly*, 3d ser., 54 (1997): 695–722.

Davis, Richard Beale. *Intellectual Life in the Colonial South, 1585–1763.* 2 vols. Knoxville: University of Tennessee Press, 1973.

Frey, Sylvia R., and Betty Wood. *Come Shouting to Zion: African American Protestantism in the American South and British Caribbean to 1830.* Chapel Hill: University of North Carolina Press, 1998.

Heyrman, Christine Leigh. *Southern Cross: The Beginnings of the Bible Belt.* New York: Alfred A. Knopf, 1997.

Hill, Samuel S. "Religion." In *Encyclopedia of Southern Culture*, edited by Charles Reagan Wilson and William Ferris, 1269–74. Chapel Hill: University of North Carolina Press, 1989.

Isaac, Rhys. *The Transformation of Virginia, 1740–1790.* Chapel Hill: University of North Carolina Press, 1982.

Martin, Joel W. "Indians, Contact, and Colonialism in the Deep South: Themes for a

Postcolonial History of American Religion." In *Retelling U.S. Religious History*, edited by Thomas A. Tweed, 149–80. Berkeley: University of California Press, 1997.

———. "From 'Middle Ground' to 'Underground': Southeastern Indians and the Early Republic." In *Religion and American Culture: A Reader*, edited by David G. Hackett, 127–46. New York: Routledge, 1995.

Mathews, Donald G. "'We Have Left Undone Those Things Which We Ought to Have Done': Southern Religious History in Retrospect and Prospect." *Church History* 67 (1998): 305–25.

———. "Forum: Southern Religion." *Religion and American Culture* 8 (Summer 1998): 147–54.

———. "'Christianizing the South'—Sketching a Synthesis." In *New Directions in American Religious History*, edited by Harry S. Stout and D. G. Hart, 84–115. New York: Oxford University Press, 1997.

———. "Religion and the South: Authenticity and Purity—Pulling Us Together, Tearing Us Apart." In *Religious Diversity and American Religious History*, edited by Walter H. Conser Jr. and Sumner B. Twiss, 72–101. Athens: University of Georgia Press, 1997.

———. *Religion in the Old South*. Chicago: University of Chicago Press, 1977.

Raboteau, Albert. *Slave Religion: The "Invisible Institution" in the Antebellum South.* New York: Oxford University Press, 1978.

Schweiger, Beth Barton. "Forum: Southern Religion." *Religion and American Culture* 8 (Summer 1998): 161–66

Sensbach, Jon F. *A Separate Canaan: The Making of an Afro-Moravian World in North Carolina, 1763–1840*. Chapel Hill: University of North Carolina Press, 1998.

Thornton, John. *Africa and Africans in the Making of the Atlantic World, 1400–1800*. New York: Cambridge University Press, 1998.

BETH BARTON SCHWEIGER

2

Max Weber in Mount Airy,
Or, Revivals and Social Theory
in the Early South

On a Sunday afternoon in early October of 1904, a North Carolina Baptist preacher stood waist deep in a cold creek in his best black suit.[1] He waited to receive ten candidates for baptism. One at a time, the candidates vowed their faith before the pastor, who then quickly submerged them in the frigid water. They came up sputtering and shivering to clamber up the bank, where they were congratulated and wrapped in thick blankets.

Among the families massed along the bank to watch was a middle-aged German man. He observed the ceremony with bright and intelligent eyes, most likely pausing to scribble a few notes. Next to him stood a kinsman who spit disdainfully over his shoulder. "Look at him," he scoffed while one man was being baptized. "I told you so."

Turning to leave, the German struck up a conversation with the skeptic. "Why did you anticipate the baptism of that man?" he asked. "Because," the man replied, "he wants to open a bank." Puzzled, the German pressed him: "Are there so many Baptists around that he can make a living?" "Not at all," came the reply, "but once being baptized he will get the patronage of the whole region and he will out compete everybody."[2]

The German man was Max Weber, who was visiting relatives outside of Mount Airy, North Carolina. He probably relished the opportunity to observe a baptism in the rural South. But the image of him standing in a southern landscape is jarring. Although Weber's work has spawned mountains of scholarship, it has had little currency in the literature of southern history. It is odd to imagine one of the dons of European social theory standing on a creek bank near the mythical Mayberry, R.F.D.[3]

Weber stood witness to a ritual at the heart of southern culture. Beginning in the mid-eighteenth century, people in the South apparently needed saving, and revivals were their preferred venue. Baptism followed, the outward symbol of the inner mystery of conversion, the ritual rite of passage into a sacred community.[4] In the South, everyone knew what a dousing in a muddy creek meant. "I ran home to my mother," Eli Evans recalled of a childhood revival meeting, "thinking Jesus had gotten me at last and vowing never to go to one of those things again."[5] Young Evans understood the danger: new hearts demanded new communities.

For Weber, the danger was different. He saw the baptism of an aspiring banker as yet another sign of secularization, the process at the heart of his theory of religion. The visit to North Carolina affirmed the theme of his earlier book, *The Protestant Ethic and the Spirit of Capitalism*, that is, the long slide of the sacred vocation into a secular, bureaucratic cage. By his telling, the southerners who lined the banks near Mount Airy displayed the range of religious sensibilities and the predisposition toward the secular he had found elsewhere in the United States and Western Europe. If he perceived differences there from what he had observed in New York City, Buffalo, or Cincinnati, he did not say so. In Weber's eyes, the ancient ritual of baptism brought the "spirit of capitalism" to rural North Carolina.[6]

What Max Weber saw in Mount Airy is a problem for American religious history. He did not think the South was unique, and he ignored what historians long ago codified as "southern evangelicalism." This flies in the face of nearly everything that has been written since. Early interpreters of American religion such as Robert Baird and Leonard Woolsey Bacon cast the region as unique because of its *lack* of religiosity,[7] but twentieth-century writers of every persuasion assumed the South to be uniquely pious in a nation that itself remains raucously religious for the twenty-first-century West. From gaunt preachers pointing skyward in eighteenth-century Virginia to Confederate soldiers kneeling in prayer to the spectacular folly of the Scopes trial to the eccentric rituals of Appalachian snake handlers, religion has served as a shorthand for southern exceptionalism. Christianity, we have been told, was inextricably bound up with the region's premodern, rural, and agricultural—or, more pejoratively, backward—character. The South has appeared in scholarship as the sole American region that remains immune to secularization, which scholars tell us has swept the rest of the West.[8]

Revivals stand at the center of this conviction. Although revivals were ubiquitous in the United States, historians think they were different in the South. Whereas other American revivals spurred change, southern revivals furthered tradition. Whereas other American Protestants embraced innovation, southern Protestants shunned it. Whereas other Americans either welcomed or at least sought to reconcile with modernity, southern Protestants remained fiercely antimodern.[9]

A brief summary cannot do justice to the huge body of scholarship on American religion in the long century between the First Great Awakening and the Civil War, but the comparison holds. The literature presents southern evangelicalism as mainly backward, static, and even fundamentalist, and it draws northern evangelicalism as dynamic and open to change. Since both regions experienced revivals from the eighteenth century onward, these distinctions cannot come from any definition of what a revival is or of what it does. Instead, they reflect the debates over the political economy of slavery that have determined our vision of the South. Was American slavery premodern or modern, paternalistic or patriarchal, precapitalist or capitalist? With few exceptions, historians of slavery have argued the former, and they have apparently convinced most students of southern Protestantism. The premodern character of slavery has been so often linked to revival religion that it has become akin to a geological formation in the literature.[10] Political economy, not theology, has defined regional differences in the history of American Protestantism between 1730 and 1860.

Consequently, a theorist like Max Weber has been deemed of little use to understanding Christianity in the South. Weber's chief concerns — secularization, bureaucratization, and capitalism — do not resonate with the categories of analysis that historians have applied to this slave society. Even those who have insisted that slavery was implicated in the market economy have resisted the idea that Protestantism might have been an ally of modernity and the market.[11]

In the end, such simple oppositions as premodern to modern and traditional to progressive cannot characterize differences between northern and southern revivals between 1730 and 1860.[12] Regional differences between revivals in this century and a half have been asserted by scholars rather than demonstrated. Like Max Weber, I am concerned with the relationship of Protestantism to modernity. Unlike Weber, I do not believe that the encounter between religion and modernity resulted in secularization. Weber lived in a world in which modernization secularized, and as one sympathetic to religion and antipathetic to modernity, he wrote of the disenchantment of the world as a tragedy.

But social theory has changed since 1904. Secularization theory's credibility had plummeted by the early 1980s, when "traditional religion [began] to come threateningly alive," in Mary Douglas's apt phrase. Islamic and Protestant fundamentalism suddenly made old theories about the incompatibility of modernity and religion inadequate, and scholars scrambled to account for these changes. Secularization shrank from a universal rule to a Western European exception. Since then, scholars have argued that the encounter between religion and modernity has revitalized traditional religions.[13] In light of this new work, the position of the American South in scholarly literature has changed dramatically. It may now stand as Exhibit A in defense of an emerging understanding that stresses the compatibility of modernity with persistent, and even growing, religiosity. The history of Protestant revivals in the South indicts any understanding that pits religion against modernity.

Revivals were modern events in the nineteenth-century South, as they were throughout the United States.[14] They pressed converts forward, demanding the progress of the soul in a powerful affirmation of American material progress. More concretely, they created a set of institutions—Baptist associations, Methodist conferences, Presbyterian synods, the Christian Church of Alexander Campbell, missionary organizations, ladies' sewing circles, and Sunday schools—that endure. These institutions did not look remarkably different in Dixie than they did in the North. Arguably, Protestants in the slave states were better organizers than their northern peers. The Southern Baptist Convention, created in 1845, is the largest Protestant denomination in the United States. Southern Protestant bureaucrats have flourished.

Old-time southern revivals were never very old-time at all. Instead of looking back, southern revivals looked forward. To be sure, white evangelicals embraced nostalgia in their revivals very early in the nineteenth century—such a pure strain of nostalgia that historians have mistaken it for the real thing. Evangelicals deceived themselves with such talk in the manner that Pierre Bourdieu has described as "habitus," a set of deeply learned, even unspoken, dispositions. The southern evangelical disposition toward nostalgia has borne a peculiar power. It pervades the historical record, persuading scholars to ignore the vast record of southern Protestant innovation.[15]

Most grievously, the characterization of southern revivals as backward or traditional ignores the contributions of slave and free black converts.[16] The deep influence of Afro-Christianity on white evangelical style and practice in the revivals, and vice versa, is a commonplace of American religious history, and it thwarts any conclusion that revivals created a traditional religion in the nineteenth century. Slaves had little incentive to deflect change by clinging to an old-fashioned religion; their Afro-Christianity was a stunning innovation. The United States "bore within it no possibility of becoming God's new Israel" for African Americans. Instead, it loomed as "Egypt the enslaver."[17]

White southerners shared American Protestantism's uncertainty about whether the evangelization of this new country was creating something new at all. Alexander Campbell collapsed almost two millennia of history in his call to recreate the ancient church, a call that had been received enthusiastically by thousands across the Upper South by 1860. The Protestant Reformation was three hundred years old, and the wonders of Cotton Mather's Christian religion had been "flying from the depravations of Europe" for two full centuries. White and black Protestants were creating something new in this "American strand" of Protestantism. But white Protestants could not release their claim on the past. Baptist leaders in booming southern cities of the 1840s yearned for the "simpler" faith of their rural childhoods. Confederate chaplains trumpeted the army revivals as worthy of those stirring "old-fashioned" camp meetings that had taken place earlier in the century. The "intentional" historical record shows white Protestants who were eager to revive the piety of a former age, and it is these voices that have dominated the scholarship.[18] But equally important as what Protestant leaders said they were doing—restoring—is what they actually were doing: inventing.

Donald G. Mathews has recently called for more attention to be paid to theology in the study of Protestants in the South.[19] This essay calls for attention to be paid to theoretical analysis, and it is intended to suggest a direction of critical inquiry rather than to stand as a definitive statement. It examines revivals in the early South as modern in two senses: first, in the ways in which they nurtured the importance of the individual for both black and white converts; and second, in the aggressive organizing they sparked—what Mathews has called the revivals' "organizing process."[20]

Revivals and Region

Allen Guelzo's recent definition of revivals is a good place to begin to examine differences between northern and southern revivals. He emphasizes three characteristics: "The [First Great] Awakening crystallized a particular religious ideology shaped around the experience of direct conversion, disinterested benevolence, and a peculiar connection between individualistic assent to religious experience and the possibility of a new heightened shape of communal order."[21]

Historians of northern revivals have emphasized what Guelzo calls "disinterested benevolence." The impulse to benevolence created social networks, institutions, and a new role for Protestantism in the emerging market economy of the early nineteenth century. It also radicalized some women and free black people. Scholars have debated whether revivals were a means of social control or self-discipline, but the broad consequences of these events for social reform have never been in question.

Revivals in the Northeast are described as engines (or at least partners) of economic and social change. The First Great Awakening sparked a communications revolution, created a new itinerant model for ministry, spurred a popular consumer culture, challenged hierarchical social practices, and created a transatlantic community. The Second Great Awakening, meanwhile, was an agent of democratization, a spur to early industrialization and unionization, a creator of social reform of all kinds, and the reason behind new middle-class family relations.[22]

Revivals in the South look very different. There, we are told, they created a thoroughly traditional Protestant culture that was in thrall to slavery, reinforcing patriarchal control of women and slaves. By the 1830s and 1840s, not even the growing numbers of slave and free black converts could dent the conservative and static character of southern revivals.[23]

Scholars have focused on what Guelzo calls "individualistic assent to religious experience" in their analyses of the South. Historians have recognized the importance of the individual in southern evangelicalism with respect only to what they have termed "individual piety." This pious individual bears no resemblance to the emerging individual that American historians have traced in the context of the market economy. Instead, these pious southern individuals were obsessed only with the salvation of their own souls. According to this view, southern Protestants differed from their northern kin chiefly because of their preoccupation with personal salvation. Southern souls crafted a narrow Christianity that ignored social reform, and their obsession has been called the "central theme" of southern religious history.[24] In practical terms, it crippled benevolence in the South. It explains why women demanded the vote in Seneca Falls rather than in Savannah. Above all, this inward turn meant that slavery stood unchallenged by southern Christians who valued faith above works of benevolence.

Southern evangelical individualism denied the possibility of benevolence. Further, it unified the South. The emotional and personal experiences of southern revivals affirmed the individual conscience and insisted that religion should not change society. The distinctive culture that emerged from the revivals was built on individuals rather than institutions. The resulting "spirituality of the church" doctrine apparently explains why southern churches never criticized slavery. "In the North," William G. McLoughlin concludes, "the Second Great Awakening challenged the older way of life at every turn," while "in the South, after some initial denominational turmoil at the beginning of the century, this awakening confirmed the prevalent life style [and] increased religious homogeneity."[25]

This interpretation of southern Protestant individualism owes everything to the civil rights movement of the mid-twentieth century and very little to the Old South. Samuel S. Hill's brilliant critique of white Protestantism of the 1960s, *Southern Churches in Crisis*, has deeply influenced subsequent histories of Protestants in the region. The book drew on history and theology to make a point that was prophetic in 1966: evangelism was the prevailing historic social ethic of white churches. The necessity of personal salvation determined the work of these congregations, leaving them with neither the will nor the means to engage the racial crisis of the 1960s. Hill's stance against the complacent white churches of the civil rights era required his "pain, passion, and anger"; running just under the book's scholarly surface lay his agonized plea for white Protestants to take up Niebuhr's task of transforming culture.[26]

Hill's interpretation was a powerful and necessary call for reform in the mid-twentieth century. But there are alternative ways to read early southern revivals. The emphasis on personal spirituality obscures some deep contradictions in the sources. Ever since an angry monk nailed his complaints to a church door in 1517, Protestants have wavered between an individualistic ethic and a communitarian one. Revivals in the South created *both* pious individuals *and* gathered communities of believers. The latter have been the theme of only a few studies, most of them about slave religion. The importance of community among Christians in the slave quarter has been repeatedly demonstrated. Studies of frontier religion have also shown how Protestant converts built community in places like early Kentucky.[27] The story of Protestantism among slaves and on the frontier suggests that the individuals nurtured by southern revivals should be read in contexts beyond the narrow confines of individual salvation, including those of nineteenth-century modernity, the emergence of the market economy and the appearance of the consumer, the romantic self, and the expansion of democracy among white men. There is abundant evidence running through histories of the Old South to prove that the individuals shaped by revivals resonated with nineteenth-century individualism.

Nathan O. Hatch's *The Democratization of American Christianity*, for example, should be read as a book about the South. Hatch's argument that the Second Great Awakening democratized American Christianity need not be rehearsed here. But one strand stands out: "Rather than looking backward and clinging to an older moral economy, insurgent religious leaders espoused convictions that were essentially modern and individualistic."[28] Four of the five groups of "insurgent leaders" that Hatch examines in detail, which included white religious leaders such as Alexander Campbell, John Leland, and Francis Asbury and African American preachers such as Richard Allen and George Liele, worked in traditions that flourished in the South: they were Disciples of Christ, Baptists, Methodists, and Afro-Christians. Alexander Campbell and his colleague Barton Stone hailed from Virginia and Kentucky respectively; John Leland was an antislavery resident of Virginia; Francis Asbury spent the majority of his itinerancy in the South and the Old Southwest; and the South was the heart of Afro-Christianity and the source of many of its early leaders. Methodist camp meetings created nineteenth-century revival culture, and Russell Richey has argued persuasively that Methodism was a southern movement.[29]

In the end, the southern accent of Hatch's work challenges the view that southern and northern revivals were fundamentally different events. The book raises the intriguing possibility that the individualism the revivals promoted in the South should be read in contexts other than the one that has so long prevailed, that is, the context of obsession with individual salvation. Read as a book about the South, Hatch's work suggests that revivals in northern and southern states shared many characteristics.[30]

Creating Cultures

Historians have read southern revivals in yet another way: as creators of culture. Estimations of eighteenth-century revivals' agency have been revised since Alan Heimert and Perry Miller credited them with creating a uniquely American culture. The approach of William G. McLoughlin, who applied "revitalization movement" theory to American revivals, has been replaced by an emphasis on cultural anthropology and ethnography.[31] A version of the Miller-Heimert thesis has lingered in scholarship on the South, however. In that region, we are told, revivals created a distinctive "southern culture." White and black southerners, slave and free, claimed conversion to evangelical Protestantism in unprecedented numbers, developing a cultural style that was unique to the region. In 1730, there was not a "southern religion." In 1860, there may have been one.[32]

Or two. Historians have argued that Protestant revivals in the South in fact created two cultures, two religious communities, and two institutions: white evangelicalism and Afro-Christianity.[33] The encounter of black and white in Christianity is one of the central themes of American religious history, and the conversion of many African Americans that began in the late eighteenth century marked a turning point in American history.[34] The magnitude of those conversions sharply refutes any notion of the awakenings as an "interpretive fiction."[35]

The two southern cultures of white evangelicalism and Afro-Christianity were not entirely discrete, however. Scholars have paid particular attention to the influence of Afro-Christian styles and practices on white evangelicals.[36] Nevertheless, the ways in which enslaved and free Protestants practiced and thought about their religion differed profoundly; C. Eric Lincoln has identified the distinction as the difference between "American Christianity" and "black religion."[37] Historians have struggled to reconcile these differences within the dialectic of white and black Protestantism. Questions remain: How is it that two distinct Protestant cultures emerged from a single revival process? And what is distinctively "southern" about either of them?

Churches, Sects, and the South

The story of Afro-Christianity is a well-known counterpoint to that of white evangelicalism. Eighteenth-century evangelicalism appeared as a countercultural movement that appealed deeply to both white and black southerners; in the beginning, evangelicals opposed slavery. Slaves and free blacks appropriated the Gospel message and reshaped it into Afro-Christianity, but white evangelicals eventually abandoned their early antislavery position because they aspired to respectability among slaveholders.

The narrative of white evangelicalism thus follows Ernst Troeltsch's church-sect typology: what began as a radical sect eventually ossified into the socially aspiring proslavery church.[38] When the story of churches and sects in the South is told, the climax always comes when white evangelicals turn from their early antislavery stance, when the early sects mature into established churches. By the 1830s and 1840s, white evangelicals went beyond mere toleration of slavery to cast it as a positive good, creating what has been called "proslavery Christianity."[39] Even in the hands of those unconcerned with the truth claims of Christianity, this has been written as a tale of declension.[40]

Slaves, meanwhile, made the Protestant Gospel their own. As it has been written, the story of Afro-Christianity does not neatly follow the church-sect typology. Slave religion apparently retained a subversive ethos that, according to Troeltschian logic, left it more sectlike than churchlike. The question is an open one: How did black evangelical sects become institutionalized? Did the institutionalization of Afro-Christianity, which began before the Civil War and accelerated in the postwar period, represent a conservative shift for Afro-Christianity —a move toward the church side of the church-sect typology? If so, how did this institutionalization change Afro-Christianity?[41]

The difficulty in answering such questions underscores historians' struggles to come to terms with Afro-Christianity in the era of slavery, particularly the difficulty they have faced in trying to understand (and then to articulate in the language of history) how slaves used it for both accommodation and resistance. Accounts of early Afro-Christianity emphasize that it functioned as a means of resistance. Undeniably, however, the apparently radical political potential of Afro-Christianity was never realized.[42] It certainly did not radicalize all Christian slaves: few rose up against their masters, while many slaves never converted to Christianity at all.

Afro-Christianity and the Slave Self

What then do historians think that revivals did for slaves? Was evangelical Protestantism an ideology that inspired accommodation or resistance? While acknowledging that evangelical Protestantism did in fact lead to accommodation, scholars have tended to concentrate on the ways in which it fostered slaves' resistance to oppression. Slaves' appreciation for a "true Christianity," one that apparently affirmed individual freedom, empowered them. Albert Raboteau writes that "slaves distinguished the hypocritical religion of their masters from true Christianity and rejected the slaveholder's gospel of obedience to master and mistress." Some attributed spiritual significance to their decision to escape slavery. Like conversion, the decision to escape entailed an agonized vision of hell in pursuit and capture, and of heaven in freedom.[43]

In arguing that slaves found the true Christianity in the hypocritical ideology handed to them by their masters, Raboteau entwines theology around his history: he declares that the slaves' Christianity was true in their experience. He is not alone. It has been nearly impossible for contemporary academics to assert that the slaves were misguided, misled, or deranged in following Christianity, or that their conversions were purely a result of social control. The Afro-Christianity in our histories indicts the self-sacrifice of an Uncle Tom. The possibility that slaves who possessed a sense of self might have accommodated the slave power has not been considered. In their long reaction against the Elkins thesis, with its passive slave victims, historians have found in Afro-Christianity an important source of slave agency.[44]

But agency to what end? Slave testimony reveals the vital importance of Christianity to the slave self. However thin is the evidence that Christianity radicalized slaves politically, there is substantial evidence that conversion somehow radicalized slaves internally.[45] Historians have given the psychology of conversion a particularly important place in the story of Afro-Christianity. Raboteau writes:

> Slave religion had a this-worldly impact, not only in leading some slaves to acts of external rebellion, but also in helping slaves to assert and maintain a sense of personal value—even of ultimate worth. . . . In the role of preacher, exhorter, and minister, slaves experienced status, achieved respect, and exercised power, often circumscribed but nonetheless real. . . . the conversion experience equipped the slave with a sense of individual value and a personal vocation which contradicted the devaluing and dehumanizing forces of slavery. . . . That some slaves maintained their identity as persons, despite a system bent on reducing them to subhuman level, was certainly due in part to their religious life. In the midst of slavery, religion was for slaves a space of meaning, freedom, and transcendence.[46]

But this connection between Christianity and liberation, and the ability of historians to discern it, remains problematic. Spiritual freedom and empowerment by the Spirit seem to be concepts better suited to the language of theology than to that of history.[47] What was spiritual freedom, and how do historians find it? Which historical records can testify to the power of the Spirit? Like many scholars of their generation, sociologist Orlando Patterson and historians Eugene D. Genovese and David Brion Davis wanted to explain slave resistance. Patterson's early work *The Sociology of Slavery* and his later study *Slavery and*

Social Death deeply influenced the scholarship that followed them, particularly that of Eugene Genovese.[48] In a striking passage in the earlier work, Patterson found that in order to understand slave resistance, he had to leave sociology behind: "Whence arose the spirit of rebellion in the slave? . . . Sociological explanations can only partly explain the persistence of this spirit of rebellion. The ultimate answer . . . lies—strictly speaking—outside the framework of the sociologist." Patterson asked how slaves' need for freedom—a need for something that they had never experienced but for which they were willing to die, a need "which seem[ed] to survive under conditions which in every way conspire[d] to smother it"—could be accounted for. On the final page of his book, he turned to French existentialists Albert Camus and Gabriel Marcel to argue that slaves discovered a "universal value"; "As soon as a subject begins to reflect on himself," Patterson wrote, "he inevitably comes to the conclusion that 'I must become free.'"[49]

In his later book, Patterson turned to Georg Wilhelm Freidrich Hegel to address the problem of transcendence and the self. Hegel argued that it is the condition of slavery itself that creates the slave consciousness. "Through work and labor this consciousness of the bondsman come[s] to itself," Hegel wrote, for labor "is desire restrained and checked, evanescence delayed and postponed; in other words labor shapes and fashions the thing." Consciousness, Patterson concluded, "through work, creates object, becomes externalized, and passes into something that is permanent and remains." He continued: "The consciousness that toils and serves accordingly comes by this means to view that independent being as its self. . . . thus precisely in labor where there seemed to be merely some outsider's mind and ideas involved, the bondsman becomes aware, through this rediscovery of himself by himself, of having a being and a mind of his own." It is slavery itself that makes the slave "a person afire with the knowledge of and the need for dignity and honor," Patterson wrote. Slaves' own labor demonstrated their humanity to them.[50]

Like Patterson, David Brion Davis found Hegel critical to his understanding of slavery's effects on the human spirit. In an extended epilogue to *The Problem of Slavery in the Age of Revolution*, he argued that Hegel's "was the most profound analysis of slavery ever written": "The products [the slave] creates become an objective reality that validates the emerging consciousness of his subjective human reality. Through coerced labor, the slave alone acquires the qualities of fortitude, patience, and endurance. The slave alone has an interest in changing his condition, and thus looks to a future beyond himself. Only the slave, therefore, has the potentiality for escaping an imbalanced reciprocity and for becoming truly free." Davis focused on masters and abolitionists rather than slaves, but he held out the possibility that Christianity had a meaningful impact on slave consciousness. In a fleeting reference, he noted that although white preachers focused attention on obedience, "slaves were quick to catch every message of hope."[51] How they did so, and what happened when they did, are questions that remained beyond the bounds of Davis's story.

These questions were at the heart of Eugene D. Genovese's account of slave religion. *Roll, Jordan, Roll* demonstrates the difficulties of explaining the effects of slavery on the human spirit in the language of history. Genovese's characteristically eclectic approach led him to sources ranging from Hegel to Ambrogio Donini to George Santayana. His sympathy for religion was rooted in his reading of Santayana, who defined religion as the "poetic interpretation of experience" and cautioned that "the feeling of reverence should itself be treated with reverence."[52]

Like Patterson, Genovese was concerned with the relationship of Christianity to slave resistance and its political contribution to the "survival and mobilization" of black America. Although his first concern was with how "Christianity . . . based its strength upon the collective," he delved into the psychology of slave conversion. Christianity "drove deep into [the slave's] soul an awareness of the moral limits of submission," Genovese wrote, "for it placed a master above his own master and thereby dissolved the moral and ideological ground on which the very principle of absolute human lordship must rest." For Genovese, Christianity not only exposed the contradictions of slavery, but also caused them. In this assertion, he departed considerably from the Hegelian analysis of Patterson and Davis, which roots the slave's sense of self in the material conditions of slavery. In Genovese's unorthodox Marxist interpretation, Christianity spurred resistance to the dehumanization of slavery yet did not necessarily foster open rebellion.[53]

None of these studies, then, can solve the tension between accommodation and resistance in Afro-Christianity. The slaves embraced the faith of their masters, and, however creative and potentially subversive the result, most did not use their religion as an occasion to rise up against their oppressors. Christianity could function in the lives of Christian slaves as an incentive to political violence. But it could also offer something more difficult to discern with the naked eye, and all three of these scholars found a positive legacy in Christian conversion when it did not lead to rebellion. They all found the language of sociology and history better suited to express Christianity's coercive bent and that of philosophy and theology more apt to describe its positive effects.

In the end, it is the unresolved tensions that make these works most admirable, for they reflect a tension that cannot be resolved. The choice between accommodation and resistance is a false one. It assumes a dissatisfying functionalist approach to the question of what Christianity meant to the slaves. All of these studies, in the end, refused functionalist behaviorist explanations. In their searching analyses of slave life, these scholars all encountered something strangely irreducible in the experiences of Christian slaves, and they admitted the limitations of the language of history to comprehend it. Above all, they encountered the poverty of any analysis that would force a false choice between accommodation and resistance as the only two possibilities for understanding the meaning of Christianity for the slaves. Any implication that Afro-Christianity sustained only the resisting or rebellious slave, that the Christian self evaporated precisely at the point of apparent acquiescence to oppression, is a grievous misreading of the case.

White Evangelicalism and the Self

We know far more about the psychology of conversion for slaves than for white evangelicals. As Donald Mathews has observed, the remarkable studies of slave religion produced in the last generation "were diminished only by a tendency to stereotype white religion in contrasting black and white sacred worlds."[54] What we do know about the inner world of white converts focuses on the antislavery period of the early revivals. Individuals who challenged the slave power have attracted more interest from scholars than those who appear to have succumbed to it. For white southerners, as for slaves, the Christian self seems most apparent in acts of resistance, and scholars seem confident that they know resistance when they see it.

What do historians think that revivals did for white southerners? They believe that eighteenth-century revivals fostered an ideology of resistance among common white people. Rhys Isaac argued that white evangelicals crafted their identity in negative reference to social power. Evangelicals reacted sharply against a "style of life for which the gentry set the pattern." Isaac and many other scholars have emphasized the radical bent of the early revivals. For a time, the newly converted evangelicals threatened to turn the world upside down.[55] By the early nineteenth century, however, these impulses had faded. Conversion began to signal accommodation rather than resistance, chiefly because of the churches' new reluctance to condemn slavery. Within a few years, that reluctance had been transformed for some white evangelicals into a willingness to mount an unqualified defense of slavery.

This well-worn narrative leaves many questions unanswered, however. The protagonists in the second half of the story become people who aspired to social status rather than those who scorned it. Donald Mathews has shown that white evangelicals redefined their faith as that of "an enlightened and refined people" who restricted the liberties for which they had once preached so eloquently. Abruptly, revivalism becomes identified with the powerful rather than the powerless. This has not been adequately explained, as few historians have delved into census schedules and tax records to test the argument.[56] The history of white evangelicals comes to an abrupt turn at this proslavery moment. Revival religion for white southerners dissolves into the defense of slavery, and the white evangelical self is lost from the literature. As with slave converts, the self comes into view for historians only when it is engaged in resistance.

The narrative sketched above and its implications are particularly prominent in studies of evangelical women. Christine Heyrman finds the influence of churchwomen circumscribed by the mid-nineteenth century.[57] Pious women found the "evangelical boy-preachers" who stormed through the rural South to be lively companions who respected their theological views and affirmed their gifts by arguing that they should speak in public. But the "shared intensity" that bonded these preachers to their female coreligionists was ultimately broken. The maturing ministry aspired to ally itself with powerful planters. To please their social betters, pastors redrew their relationships with women in their congregations, emphasizing female deference rather than mutuality. The new standard for pious female behavior was "less assertive and more private than those exhibited by many women before 1800." The backlash against women included a stand against those who desired to preach, the redefinition of female piety strictly in terms of duty to household, and the "desexing of spiritually dynamic women." Heyrman grounds these changes in slavery and implies that they were peculiar to the South, but the claim is problematic. In separate studies, Catherine Brekus and Susan Juster have both found a similar pattern of declining female status in congregations across the United States. In the end, Heyrman's description echoes that of Jean Friedman, who in 1985 wrote of how women of the nineteenth-century evangelical South were dominated by men in churches that reinforced traditional gender roles.[58]

Heyrman's narrative moves from resistance to accommodation. Women who initially used evangelicalism to subvert gender conventions later succumbed to those same conventions. Few women tell their own story in this account of decline and fall, largely because the study is based on clerical biographies. Why a woman would have been drawn to such a constricting faith, or what she would have gained by adopting it, is never made clear.

Evangelical women are also embattled in Stephanie McCurry's South Carolina low country. But McCurry's tale is not the customary one of declension from an egalitarian ethic to a hierarchical one. From the beginning, evangelical congregations in South Carolina—particularly congregations that included slaveholders—took on a "conservative and nascent proslavery shape" that underscored male authority. Congregations "sacralized the social order," then, in both the eighteenth and nineteenth centuries. By the 1830s, the so-called Nullification Revivals fused religion and politics "into one system of meaning." As "households of faith," churches sacralized family relations and became "critical institutions in the region's political culture, providing both an unimpeachable logic and an unparalleled popular constituency for an increasingly aggressive defense of slavery and the social order it engendered."[59]

What, then, did antebellum revivals do for women in McCurry's South Carolina? As in Heyrman's account, few women's voices appear in the text. But in a world where wealth determined everything, the piety of women apparently counted far less than that of men with property. "The 'body' of the church might be black and female, but 'the mind of the church' was white and male," McCurry writes.[60] Nevertheless, the pews continued to fill with the powerless and disenfranchised. Women—slave and free—consistently made up two-thirds of all members in these churches in low-country South Carolina, as they did elsewhere in the country. Why?

Finding the answer requires historians to take the kind of nuanced approach taken by scholars of Christian slaves. As a framework for understanding women's piety, the dichotomy between resistance and accommodation is a false one, just as it is for understanding slaves' spirituality. How should the power that mattered in southern churches and in the lives of Protestant women be delineated? In a slave society full of dependents, power was not always apparent to the eye, as the slave's crafty "yes, Massa" proved again and again. Southern women did not use their piety to organize open resistance to male leadership in the antebellum period, but neither did they find in it only an imperative for destructive self-sacrifice.

Why women continued to fill southern pews becomes clear in a number of recent studies that demonstrate that "power and influence were no simple matter in the churches." Cynthia Lynn Lyerly's study of early national Methodists in the South emphasizes the power of religious conversion, which she calls a "revolution in consciousness," and the conflicting emotions it brought on. "Extatic raptures would creep through my heart, and Heaven slide through my crimson life," Sarah Jones wrote. "I set in the pomp of self-abasement, a-kin to nothing, a-kin to dust, and yet engulphed in the love of Christ." But the sense of power was unmistakable in women's descriptions of their lives. Jones was one day "called on to pray" in front of her "wicked relations." She recalled: "God stept in me; and they universally melted. . . . Thus, hell gave back, and devils were subject to me." Devils as well as slaves were subject to Sarah Jones. But she remained subject to her husband and was bound by his refusal to emancipate the slaves she desperately wanted to free. "Although the oppressed stare me through, I will try to be clear of their blood," she grieved. Power was painfully complicated in Sarah Jones's life.[61]

In an important study of antebellum Georgia, Frederick Bode has contended that evangelicalism created a "common sphere" for men and women in the South. While resisting any notion that evangelicalism leveled distinctions between men and women, Bode finds evidence that "religion became a common sphere in which men and women frequently acted together to save souls, nurture children, and perform works of benevolence." Bode discovered evidence of evangelical couples who worked together to nurture and to educate their children, such as the Presbyterians Adam and Sarah Alexander, who shared a common sense of responsibility to their ten children. Bode's findings in Georgia agree with what we know of the family of Benjamin Mosby Smith, who lived hundreds of miles to the north in the Shenandoah Valley of Virginia. Smith, a Presbyterian pastor in Staunton, kept detailed "memorandums" of his son's and daughter's childhoods that suggest he was an affectionate parent who engaged in the religious and physical nurture of his children. He read Mary and Josiah stories, nursed them when they were ill, and voiced constant concern about the state of their souls.[62]

This example suggests what Bode's work confirms: "On the subject of proper gender relations Georgia evangelicals did not differ very much, at least on the ideological level, from their northern counterparts." The implication is that the rural cast of life in the South, rather than slavery alone, determined the shape of evangelical practice. Evangelical families in the rural North and the rural South shared much more in common than historians have considered. This requires further study. But John Quist's detailed comparison of communities in Alabama and Michigan has already confirmed some similarities between the regions in the practice of benevolence.[63]

Finally, Bode makes the critical point that women's initiative "was obscured by a religious discourse that affirmed their deference and subordination to men and hid the reality of cooperation between women." Religious people, particularly new converts, were apt to confuse prescription with practice, and their writings require careful and critical reading. Bode's findings are confirmed and amplified in the work of Scott M. Stephan. In a sensitive and important study of evangelical families, Stephan compared a diary and family letters to find that whereas women lamented their own failures privately, they publicly applied high standards of conduct to their children and families. Stephan argues that "the clergy's 'official' sanction of [women's] superior piety and virtue in the home" gave them "an informal but wide-ranging power from within the home that ended up expanding their influence beyond it." It was this informal power —the "expansive definition of motherly duties"—that historians have missed in their focus on gender roles within formal institutions in this period.[64]

Dissident Social Space, Doctrine, and the Evangelical Self

Women's informal power was obscured, as Bode has argued, by a discourse that hid much of the reality of their religious lives under a facade of submission to human authority. Just as it did for slaves, Christianity offered women many resources that defy the categories of accommodation and resistance. Christianity has historically been the faith of the rulers *and* the ruled. It has justified power *and* empowered the oppressed. It has offered formal *and* informal power. As James C. Scott has observed, there is a "vast territory" between the two poles of accommodation and resistance. Most people neither overtly defied power nor completely accommodated it, and it is between these two poles that "most of the political life" of oppressed groups can be found.[65] The vast territory between accommodation and resistance is the space in which slave converts and women lived in the Old South. Neither evangelical women nor Christian slaves began a revolution, but this fact does not begin to tell the story of their lives. Social protest is far too blunt an instrument by which to measure liberation and change among Christians in the slave South.

Women and slaves found themselves in Christianity, and they carved out dissident spaces in their hierarchical society. They did so in a variety of ways that require further study. I want to suggest that one of the most important of these was through sectarian debate—disagreement over doctrine. Sometimes their dissent was formal, resulting in schism within congregations and traditions. At its most powerful, however, theological dissent was forced into informal channels. It took the form of the slaves' dissent over the very message of Christianity, what Scott has called their elaborate "hidden transcript." The slaves' interpretation of Christianity was a theological statement, and it rebuked the power of white preachers, sometimes in striking ways. Charles Colcock Jones reported that while he was preaching in 1833 on Paul's condemnation of runaway slaves in his Epistle to Philemon, "one half of [his] audience deliberately rose up and walked off with themselves." He recalled: "Some solemnly declared 'that there was no such Epistle in the Bible,' others 'that they did not care' if they ever heard me preach again."[66]

The practice of Protestantism in the Old South encouraged believers to follow the individual conscience, just as it had in Reformation Germany and eighteenth-century England.[67] In the Reformed tradition, this encouragement was rooted in the theology of the grace of election, which fosters a sense both of responsibility to Christ and of the importance of self-control. In the Wesleyan tradition, self-confidence grew from the belief that converts "could, should and indeed must take control of their hearts and minds and bend their wills into the shape that God desired."[68]

Across the early United States, this theological heritage was remade in the context of republican ideology. Although there is some indication of difference between northern and southern theology in this period, it is clear that the conversion experience opened new opportunities for individual agency in the South as well as in the North. "It is the inalienable right of all laymen to examine the sacred writings for themselves, and . . . not to believe what the church believes, because the church believes it; but to judge and act for, and from themselves," Alexander Campbell declared from western Virginia in 1826. The God of whom the slaves sang was intimate and personal. "Mass Jesus is my bosom friend," they sang, or "I'm goin' to walk with King Jesus, by myself, by myself." What John Dollard observed of black churches in the depression-era South was equally true of earlier congregations: humble people found in them an opportunity for self-expression and the development of their talents.[69]

In the antebellum South, their self-expression manifested itself most clearly in raucous sectarian conflict. Doctrine mattered, and it was personal. Accounts that stress the emotional nature of southern revivals need to be balanced by an understanding that emotion was brought on by the comprehension of doctrines, even for self-educated people. The long-held and sentimental view that the common people settled for an emotional religion because they could not or would not think about doctrine is not supported by the evidence.[70]

That evidence includes data about the religious practices of African American and female converts. Studies of African American religion have focused on differences in style and expression in worship between denominations and have paid little mind to disagreements about doctrinal issues between black Christians. C. Eric Lincoln, for example, has dismissed the importance of theology as the root of black sectarianism, arguing that the divisions were sociological in nature.[71] More research is needed, but evidence of the importance of doctrine to black Christians has already been found. Erskine Clark's study of low-country Presbyterians has reminded us that a "distinct African American Reformed community, with roots in the colonial period, had evolved in the Carolina low country during the antebellum period." He argues that Denmark Vesey was a Presbyterian in a region where African American Presbyterians outnumbered the white members of rural Presbyterian churches.[72] It is unlikely that Vesey chose Presbyterian over Methodist doctrine for purely social reasons.

Some time between 1826 and 1842, Betsy Payne wrote a letter to Great Crossings Baptist Church in Scott County, Kentucky. It read:

> I wish you to give me a letter or a dismission in any way you think proper. I am dissatisfied with the doctrin I under stand is preached there. I also understand that some of your favorite preachers considers all that believes the doctrine I do is Stumbling blocks in the way of making all the people Christians and I do not wish to be in the way of making Christians. . . . I am afflicted in body and mind not in body as much as in mind. Because this boddy will have an end I mourn on account of sin I ask the Lord to teach me the way in truth and Holyness. . . . I am Ready to be a witness against those who would not obey the gospel, I cannot believe the gospel that is so much preached.

In the end, Payne's decision was painful. "I am distressed to say fare well to the Great Crossings Church," she wrote. "I have a feeling for that church that will never leave me in this life. . . . I think of you in the night when I suppose you are all asleep."[73]

Betsy Payne thought hard about doctrine and endured the consequences of the actions she took because of it. She was not alone. Many common southerners

—white and black—thought long and hard about the distinctive doctrines of congregations before they joined them, and, like Payne's, their disagreements sometimes occasioned painful breaks with their communities of faith. They regularly listened to sermons that stretched to three hours only to subject them to severe criticism either in the pages of their diaries or in conversation. They read voraciously from the Bible and other books. Allen Turner, a Methodist pastor and colporteur who rode circuits near Augusta, Georgia, in 1826, sold more than seven hundred books that year. Turner sold titles by John Wesley, Richard Baxter, John Bunyan, Francis Asbury, William Law, and Richard Watson in addition to church histories, ancient histories, hymnals, and dictionaries.[74]

Southern converts read so that they might equip themselves to argue about religion.[75] The commonsense spirit of their age made them confident that they knew the mind of God, that their reading of the Bible was the correct (and only) one. It is difficult to overestimate the kind of self-confidence that such a stand could inspire. For common southerners, as for many Low Church Protestants, this "ability to handle abstract and consecutive argument was by no means inborn; it had to be discovered against almost overwhelming difficulties" such as the lack of leisure, the cost of candles, and the near absence of formal schooling.[76] Nevertheless, sectarian argument could not be contained in church. It spilled out into lanes and shops and post offices. It informed conversation around the family hearth and colored political speechmaking. Argument and debate were critical manners cultivated in and outside of southern churches, ones that informed social discourse well beyond the bounds of doctrine and theology.

Revivals as Organizing Process Redux

The unyielding doctrinal distinctions between Baptists and Methodists, Christians and Presbyterians did more than require converts to decide about doctrine. They also organized the South. "The Awakening in its social aspects was an organizing process . . . a general social movement that organized thousands of people into small groups," Donald G. Mathews argued more than thirty years ago.[77] Conversion and baptism nearly always ended with informal or formal affiliation with a church congregation. "The polarity of 'community' and 'individual' simply did not exist for Evangelicals," he wrote.[78] Christian conversion was, in short, both a deeply personal and a profoundly social event.

"Community" does evoke what antebellum people themselves meant by their gatherings. But in a twenty-first-century context, "community" is tinged with a romanticized gemeinschaft that does not reflect the raw determination of evangelicals to extend their Gospel by organizing the South. On the frontier, in the slave quarters, and in small towns, evangelicals came together in communities that took on a concrete form: church congregations.

Congregations were the heart of Protestant experience for both Afro-Christians and white evangelicals. Recent studies have rightly stressed that the number of formal church members was limited in the eighteenth and nineteenth centuries, but a congregation was not limited to church members. Instead, the community called a "congregation" embraced all of those who attended worship services, those with both formal and informal ties to the church.

And from early in the nineteenth century, congregations were not simply local bodies. Instead, they were part of a larger denominational network that stretched across the region and even beyond it. Recent work has established the importance of African American churches *as organizations* in creating slave community.[79] Revivals invited slave participation in both formal institutional churches and in an informal "invisible institution" identified by Albert Raboteau.[80] C. Eric Lincoln has pointed out that denominational distinctions prevented the unity of any "black church" in the early United States. "For the first hundred years of the black experience in America, religion was more an index of separation than of integration," he wrote.[81] And some of the most important evidence for slaves' commitment to the church as an institution appears in their devotion to supporting the church with their money. Sylvia Frey and Betty Wood have described in detail how "for most enslaved church members the expenditure of time and money on their churches became top priorities." Slaves and free black members paid to build meetinghouses, support foreign and domestic missions, and provide for their ministers. Nor were black members immune to the expenses entailed by growing denominational organizations. Money was needed to pay for denominational publications and to join regional organizations.[82]

White evangelicals, of course, had means of creating formal organizations that were not available to slaves. From the beginning, the spread of evangelicalism in the South was accomplished by networks of circuit riders, Baptist associations, Methodist class meetings and conferences, and all manner of local, regional, and national organizations. Methodist class meetings were the smallest and most local of these, but the Methodist mania for gathering people into groups spread quickly. And it worked. Every congregation in the country had an interest in a doctrinal stance that connected it to other congregations in the state, region, and nation. Membership and monies raised grew steadily throughout the century. The lure of organization triumphed even over the most antiorganizational of the southern sects. Alexander Campbell's Christians and the Antimission Baptists scoured the countryside for the like-minded, and when they found them, they signed them up. Antimissionists rallied around the Kehukee Declaration of 1827, in which they agreed to "discard all Missionary Societies, Bible Societies, and Theological Seminaries . . . and in begging money from the public." The result was "a stir among churches and Associations all over the land," many of which "followed the example of old Mother Kehukee" by banding together in associations that were against associations.[83] Campbell's folk, meanwhile, organized themselves across the Upper South, hoping to find in their sectarianism an elusive Protestant unity.[84]

Like slaves, white churchgoers demonstrated their loyalty to their churches with their money. Southern churches and their associated societies, like their counterparts in the North, carried significant economic weight in their communities. Churchwomen did some particularly brilliant fundraising with their sewing circles and church fairs and with their ability to wrangle donations out of the most tightfisted Christians. Their efficiency inspired bewildered jealousy among clerical and lay leaders, the most pragmatic of whom gave women an official role in finance. From very early on, the financial commitment evangelicals made to religion extended beyond the local congregation to denominational mission boards, Bible societies, and Sunday school unions. Their vision of what revival religion should do extended far beyond the neighborhood.[85]

The organizing of society accomplished by revivals worked against any notion of tradition in the Old South. Denominational bureaucracies were breathtakingly new. From the first trembling moment of decision at the church rail, the convert knew that the society of the saved extended into the wider world. To join that society was to become a member of an organization that literally stretched all the way to China. Even among the fiercest Baptist defenders of the independence of the local church and the antiorganizational groups such as Antimission Baptists and Campbell's Christians, individual congregations sought out other likeminded communities and banded together into associations or conferences, published proceedings and newspapers, and exchanged delegates. Larger numbers of southern evangelicals did more: they formed regional organizations with regular meetings, budgets, and publications that in turn sent delegates to state and national gatherings and missionaries to the other side of the world. Devotion to slavery did not lessen commitment to organized religion among white evangelicals: it encouraged and expanded it. The schisms of the 1840s between northern and southern Methodists and Baptists heightened the regional loyalty and fed the financial ambitions of southern denominations.[86]

Conclusion

In the end, Max Weber was right to ignore what scholars have called "southern evangelicalism" in Mount Airy. Southern and northern revivals were kindred expressions of an American revival culture that stitched Protestants together in communities across the United States. In the South and the North alike, American Protestants shared a taste for innovation, for using religion to change individuals and ultimately society itself. Evangelicalism did not inspire reform as much as it was reform for antebellum southerners. Doctrine, not geography, marked out the most important differences in the ways in which rural Americans practiced social reform.

The chief accomplishment of American evangelicals in this period was neither temperance nor antislavery nor any other of the causes they trumpeted. Instead, their triumph was to organize the country into a set of denominations that endures to this day. There is no evidence that slavery hampered this drive to organize along doctrinal lines, and there is some evidence that it spurred it.

Much of the organizing innovation of evangelicals was obscured in the South by a rhetoric that celebrated religion as nostalgia and focused on individual conversion. For a brief time in the eighteenth century, revivals were breathtakingly new. But the radical and ecumenical New Light quickly institutionalized, shattering as it did so into denominational interests, as Philip N. Mulder has demonstrated.[87] Church leaders hungry for influence saw no harm in putting their religion at the service of slavery. They began to write histories that accorded with the view that the church should not take a political stand on slavery. Old-time revivalism was thus born, and an apolitical nostalgia became the customary manner of expression for white evangelicalism early on in the nineteenth century. In Mount Airy, as in hamlets across the country, the ancient ritual of baptism made a man new in a town that was eager to have a banker who would cleave to the old-fashioned values of honesty and integrity. In their revivals, white southerners backed into the future, using their old-time religion for new-fangled ends. Revivals did not mark a yearning for an imagined past as much as they measured a struggle against it.

"Old Souths" have arisen again and again in the history of the region. As

C. Vann Woodward so powerfully demonstrated half a century ago, white southerners have been quick to justify their society on the basis of tradition. This impulse has ranged broadly, from segregation to the Lost Cause to the Southern Agrarians to southern white gospel music. Throughout their history, white southerners have had an uncanny ability to turn their innovation into nostalgia, and they have often learned to turn a profit from it.[88]

The triumphant progress of the denominational bureaucracies was not good news. Max Weber knew this in 1904. The repentant banker who was baptized that day would soon lend his financial and administrative expertise to a bureaucracy called a Protestant denomination. Although these organizations have been celebrated as agents of democratization in nineteenth-century America, they also foiled democracy. Denominations collected monies, purchased property, erected buildings, published books and newspapers, hired administrators, and filled countless filing cabinets with charts, graphs, statistics, reports, and minutes. They trained and educated a class of professionals who administered these little empires and who decreed many of the denominations' members unfit to lead them. They were above all what Weber despised, the chief agents of the bureaucracies that disenchanted the world and ushered in the loss of meaning that he mourned in his work.

In the nineteenth century, American Protestant denominations sanctioned the killing and maiming of a generation of American men on the battlefields of the Civil War. By characterizing religion in the American South as premodern or backward, historians have seriously underestimated the social power of the institutions that evangelicals created in the South. Southern evangelical Protestants did not merely put themselves at the service of the political economy of slavery. Slavery shaped the message of southern churches, but it could not dictate the organizational form that they took, one that was mirrored exactly by denominations in the free-labor North. Different systems of labor produced precisely the same kinds of organized religion.

But Weber missed something in Mount Airy as well. Revivals in the South did more than usher in modern bureaucracies and justify the impure motives of many of those who ran them. Revivals brought good news to many in the South. The disenfranchised—particularly slaves and women—found in them a hope that transcended the sharp limits of their lived experiences. The majority of those who filled the pews in southern churches—women and slaves—rejected the nostalgic elements of Southern religion. Because they were powerless, they were not constrained by Weber's "iron cage." What Weber called "the pure interest of the bureaucracy in power" ironically left the powerless to put Christianity to their own purposes in the antebellum South.[89]

This is what makes the South essential to the story of American Christianity. The practice of religion in a slave society embodied at once the worst and best impulses of the Christian tradition; the bodies of the slaves bore the scars of their masters' political ambitions, ambitions that were sacralized by white understandings of Christianity. Christian slaves became the body of their tortured Savior. As Charles Taylor has observed, "The highest spiritual ideals and aspirations also threaten to lay the most crushing burdens on mankind." The story of revivals in the slave South demonstrates how this happened in nineteenth-century America.[90]

Notes

1. This essay is much revised from an earlier piece, "The Captivity of Southern Religious History," which I read to the Southern Intellectual History Circle in Birmingham, Alabama, in February 1997. I am grateful to Emily Bingham, Lynda L. Coon, Paul Harvey, Samuel S. Hill, Randal M. Jelks, Briane K. Turley, Gregory Wills, and Betty Wood for their generous readings of this version. I am especially indebted to Kurt O. Berends, E. Brooks Holifield, and J. Gregg Taylor for their extensive comments.

2. Max Weber, "The Protestant Sects and the Spirit of Capitalism," in *From Max Weber: Essays in Sociology*, eds. H. H. Gerth and C. Wright Mills (New York: Oxford University Press, 1946), 302–22. For Weber's visit to North Carolina, see James L. Peacock and Ruel W. Tyson Jr., *Pilgrims of Paradox: Calvinism and Experience among the Primitive Baptists of the Blue Ridge* (Washington, D.C.: Smithsonian Institution Press, 1989), xix–xx, 59–60.

3. Max Weber, *The Protestant Ethic and the Spirit of Capitalism*, trans. Talcott Parsons (New York: Charles Scribner's Sons, 1958). For recent assessments, see John Patrick Diggins, *Max Weber: Politics and the Spirit of Tragedy* (New York: Basic Books, 1996), and Hartmut Lehmann and Guenther Roth, eds., *Weber's Protestant Ethic: Origins, Evidence, Contexts* (New York: Cambridge University Press, 1993).

4. Pierre Bourdieu presents this kind of ritual as the legitimation of an arbitrary boundary, separating a before and an after, hence as a "rite of passage" (*Language and Symbolic Power* [Cambridge, Mass.: Harvard University Press, 1991], 117–26).

5. Eli N. Evans, *The Provincials: A Personal History of Jews in the South* (New York: Atheneum, 1973), 123.

6. William H. Swatos Jr. has suggested that Weber's interpretation of this event was in error. This would not compromise the larger point, however. See "Sects and Success: *Missverstehen* in Mt. Airy," *Sociological Analysis* 43 (1982): 375–80.

7. I am grateful to J. Gregg Taylor for this insight.

8. "Secularization," in *The Encyclopedia of Religion*, ed. Mircea Eliade (New York: Macmillan, 1987); Peter L. Berger, *The Sacred Canopy: Elements of a Sociological Theory of Religion* (New York: Doubleday, 1967; Anchor Books, 1969); Bryan R. Wilson, *Religion in Sociological Perspective* (New York: Oxford University Press, 1982); Eileen Barker, James A. Beckford, and Karel Dobbelaere, eds., *Secularization, Rationalism, Sectarianism: Essays in Honour of Bryan R. Wilson* (New York: Oxford University Press, 1993).

9. The work of Samuel S. Hill and John B. Boles has been most influential on this point. See Hill, *The South and the North in American Religion* (Athens: University of Georgia Press, 1980); and Boles, *The Great Revival: Beginnings of the Bible Belt* (Lexington: University Press of Kentucky, 1972; reprint, 1996) and *The Irony of Southern Religion* (New York: Peter Lang, 1994).

10. Protestant revivals have been deemed of little direct relevance to the political economy of slavery (except to rationalize it) or even to the wrenching transition from slave to free labor later in the nineteenth century. This contrasts sharply to studies of nineteenth-century Britain and the American Northeast in which historians have argued that revivals were critical to economic change in these areas. On Britain, see E. P. Thompson, *The Making of the English Working Class* (New York: Vintage Books, 1966), and Thomas W. Laqueur, *Religion and Respectability: Sunday Schools and Working Class Culture, 1780–1850* (New Haven: Yale University Press, 1976). On the United States, see Mary P. Ryan, *Cradle of the Middle Class: The Family in Oneida County, New York, 1790–1865* (New York: Cambridge University Press, 1981); Paul E. Johnson, *A Shopkeeper's Millennium: Society and Revivals in Rochester, New York, 1813–1837* (New York: Hill & Wang, 1978); Richard L. Bushman, *The Refinement of America: Persons, Houses, Cities* (New York: Alfred A. Knopf, 1992; Vintage Books, 1993); and Carroll Smith-Rosenberg, *Religion and the Rise of the American City: The New York City Mission Movement, 1812–1870* (Ithaca: Cornell University Press, 1978).

11. James Oakes, *Slavery and Freedom: An Interpretation of the Old South* (New York: Vintage Books, 1990).

12. I take the view of James D. Bratt, who has urged that this century should be considered a single era of revivals. See "The Reorientation of American Protestantism, 1835–1845," *Church History* 67 (March 1998): 52–82.

13. There is a huge body of work on this subject. For a learned refutation of secularization theory, see Mary Douglas, "The Effects of Modernization on Religious Change," *Daedalus* 111 (Winter 1982): 1–19, quote on 18. See also Patrick Collinson, "Religion, Society, and the Historian," *Journal of Religious History* 23 (June 1999): 149–67; William H. Swatos Jr. and Kevin J. Christiano, "Secularization Theory: The Course of a Concept," *Sociology of Religion* 60 (1999): 209–28; and R. Stephen Warner, "Work in Progress toward a New Paradigm for the Sociological Study of Religion in the United States," *American Journal of Sociology* 98 (1993): 1044–93. Richard Wightman Fox grapples with the meaning of secularization in twentieth-century liberal Protestantism in "Experience and Explanation in Twentieth-Century American Religious History," in *New Directions in*

American Religious History, eds. Harry S. Stout and D. G. Hart (New York: Oxford University Press, 1997), 394–413.

14. The modern character of revivals in the northern states has been demonstrated by a number of scholars. See Nathan O. Hatch, *The Democratization of American Christianity* (New Haven: Yale University Press, 1989).

15. Bourdieu, *Language and Symbolic Power*; Beth Barton Schweiger, *The Gospel Working Up: Progress and the Pulpit in Nineteenth-Century Virginia* (New York: Oxford University Press, 2000), 196.

16. "There is no historical reason to argue that the blacks' religion was any less an extension of Evangelical Protestantism than that of whites" (Donald G. Mathews, *Religion in the Old South* [Chicago: University of Chicago Press, 1977], xvi).

17. Quote is from Judith Weisenfeld, "On Jordan's Stormy Banks: Margins, Centers, and Bridges in African American Religious History," in Stout and Hart, *New Directions in American Religious History*, 417–44. See also Mathews, *Religion in the Old South*; Sylvia R. Frey and Betty Wood, *Come Shouting to Zion: African American Protestantism in the American South and British Caribbean to 1830* (Chapel Hill: North Carolina University Press, 1998); and Mechal Sobel, *Trabelin' On: The Slave Journey to an Afro-Baptist Faith* (Princeton: Princeton University Press, 1988).

18. Marc Bloch distinguishes between intentional and unintentional sources. See *The Historian's Craft* (New York: Vintage Books, 1953), 60–69.

19. Donald G. Mathews, "'We Have Left Undone Those Things Which We Ought to Have Done': Southern Religious History in Retrospect and Prospect," *Church History* 67 (June 1998): 305–25.

20. Donald G. Mathews, "The Second Great Awakening as an Organizing Process, 1780–1830: An Hypothesis," *American Quarterly* 21 (Spring 1969): 23–43.

21. Allen C. Guelzo, "God's Designs: The Literature of the Colonial Revivals of Religion, 1735–1760," in Stout and Hart, *New Directions in American Religious History*, 160.

22. Harry S. Stout, *The Divine Dramatist: George Whitefield and the Rise of Modern Evangelicalism* (Grand Rapids: Eerdmans, 1991); Timothy D. Hall, *Contested Boundaries: Itinerancy and the Reshaping of the Colonial American Religious World* (Durham: Duke University Press, 1994); Frank Lambert, *Inventing the Great Awakening* (Princeton: Princeton University Press, 1999); Rhys Isaac, *The Transformation of Virginia, 1740–1790* (Chapel Hill: University of North Carolina Press, 1982); Leigh Eric Schmidt, *Holy Fairs: Scottish Communions and American Revivals in the Early Modern Period* (Princeton: Princeton University Press, 1989); Hatch, *Democratization of American Christianity*; Deborah Vansau McCauley, *Appalachian Mountain Religion: A History* (Urbana: University of Illinois Press, 1995); Johnson, *A Shopkeeper's Millennium*; Jama Lazerow, *Religion and the Working Class in Antebellum America* (Washington, D.C.: Smithsonian Institution Press, 1995); William R. Sutton, *Journeymen for Jesus: Evangelical Artisans Confront Capitalism in Jacksonian Baltimore* (State College: Penn State University Press, 1998); Ryan, *Cradle of the Middle Class*.

23. Boles, *The Great Revival*; Rachel M. Klein, *Unification of a Slave State: The Rise of the Planter Class in the South Carolina Backcountry, 1760–1808* (Chapel Hill: University of North Carolina Press, 1990); Stephanie McCurry, *Masters of Small Worlds: Yeoman Households, Gender Relations, and the Political Culture of the Antebellum South Carolina Low Country* (New York: Oxford University Press, 1995); Christine Leigh Heyrman, *Southern Cross: The Beginnings of the Bible Belt* (New York: Alfred A. Knopf, 1997).

24. Samuel S. Hill, *Southern Churches in Crisis Revisited* (Tuscaloosa: University of Alabama Press, 1999), 73–88.

25. William G. McLoughlin, *Revivals, Awakenings, and Reform: An Essay on Religion and Social Change in America, 1607–1977* (Chicago: University of Chicago Press, 1978), 137, quoted in Hill, *South and the North in American Religion*, 30. "Spirituality of the church" is discussed in Hill, *Southern Churches in Crisis Revisited*; Hill, "The South's Two Cultures," in *Religion and the Solid South*, ed. Samuel S. Hill (Nashville: Abingdon Press, 1972), 24–56; and Charles Reagan Wilson, *Baptized in Blood: The Religion of the Lost Cause, 1865–1920* (Athens: University of Georgia Press, 1980), 8–9. A few studies have suggested that the revivals disrupted traditional society in the South. See Mathews, "Second Great Awakening as an Organizing Process"; McCauley, *Appalachian Mountain Religion*; and Heyrman, *Southern Cross*.

26. Hill, *Southern Churches in Crisis Revisited*, quote on xiii.

27. Ellen Eslinger, *Citizens of Zion: The Social Origins of Camp Meeting Revivalism* (Knoxville: University of Tennessee Press, 1999); Stephen Aron, *How the West Was Lost: The Transformation of Kentucky from Daniel Boone to Henry Clay* (Baltimore: Johns Hopkins University Press, 1996).

28. Hatch, *Democratization of American Christianity*, 14.

29. Ibid., 67–113; Russell Richey, "The Southern Accent of American Methodism," in *Early American Methodism* (Bloomington: Indiana University Press, 1991), 47–64.

30. The only dissenters from the argument I make here that I have found are Donald G. Mathews, "Religion in the Old South: Speculation on Methodology," *South Atlantic Quarterly* 73 (Winter 1974): 34–52, and Daniel Walker Howe, "The Evangelical Movement and Political Culture in the North during the Second Party System," *Journal of American History* 77 (March 1991): 1216–39.

31. Alan Heimert, *Religion and the American Mind from the Great Awakening to the Revolution* (Cambridge, Mass.: Harvard University Press, 1966); Alan Heimert and Perry Miller, eds., *The Great Awakening* (Indianapolis: Bobbs-Merrill, 1967); McLoughlin, *Revivals, Awakenings, and Reform*.

32. Boles and Heyrman have argued explicitly (and others have implied) that the Bible Belt was created in this period (*Great Revival*, *Southern Cross*). For dissenting views, see Kurt O. Berends' essay in this volume and Gaines M. Foster, *Moral Reconstruction: Christian Lobbyists and the Federal Legislation of Morality, 1865–1920* (Chapel Hill: University of North Carolina Press, 2002).

33. Mathews has argued this point most forcefully in *Religion in the Old South*. Debo-

rah Vansau McCauley has argued that Appalachian religion counts as a third distinctive Protestant culture (*Appalachian Mountain Religion*, esp. 168–237).

34. David W. Wills, "The Central Themes of American Religious History: Pluralism, Puritanism, and the Encounter of Black and White," in *African-American Religion: Interpretive Essays in History and Culture*, eds. Timothy E. Fulop and Albert J. Raboteau (New York: Routledge, 1997), 9–20; Frey and Wood, *Come Shouting to Zion*; Sobel, *Trabelin' On*.

35. Jon Butler, "Enthusiasm Described and Decried: The Great Awakening as Interpretive Fiction," *Journal of American History* 69 (September 1982): 305–25; Butler, *Awash in a Sea of Faith: Christianizing the American People* (Cambridge, Mass.: Harvard University Press, 1990), 164–93.

36. Mathews, *Religion in the Old South*; Frey and Wood, *Come Shouting to Zion*; Sobel, *Trabelin' On*.

37. C. Eric Lincoln, *Race, Religion, and the Continuing American Dilemma* (New York: Hill & Wang, 1984; reprint, 1999), 59.

38. Ernst Troeltsch, *The Social Teaching of the Christian Churches*, 2 vols. (New York: Macmillan, 1931), 2:461–67.

39. This was, in fact, an argument for a "Christian slavery" instead of a "proslavery Christianity." The distinction is important. Schweiger, *The Gospel Working Up*, 78–80.

40. Donald G. Mathews has argued that a proslavery stance was entirely compatible with evangelicalism, contradicting a literature that, he maintains, has reflected the "moral sensibility of liberal historians and their alter-egos, the radical abolitionists." See *Religion in the Old South*, xv–xvi.

41. Work has recently begun to reinvigorate the history of black churches as institutions. See Albert J. Raboteau and David W. Wills, "Retelling Carter Woodson's Story: Archival Sources for Afro-American Church History," in *Religious Diversity and American Religious History: Studies in Traditions and Cultures*, eds. Walter H. Conser Jr. and Sumner B. Twiss (Athens: University of Georgia Press, 1997). C. Eric Lincoln has also emphasized the import of the early—if, in his view, conventional—black denominations and of African Methodist Episcopal churches in particular. See *Race, Religion, and the Continuing American Dilemma*, 60–86.

42. "There is no record that conversion brought liberty to a single slave throughout the long history of slavery in America," C. Eric Lincoln observed (ibid., 52).

43. Albert Raboteau, *Slave Religion: The "Invisible Institution" in the Antebellum South* (New York: Oxford University Press, 1978), 294.

44. This is not only true of black Christians. Scholars across disciplines have "[written] into the definition of the subject the notion that religion is good for the human psyche" (Mary Douglas, "The Effects of Modernization on Religious Change," 2). Tragically, the radical doctrine of Christian submission was distorted by the power relations of slavery. Wilson Moses has noted that Uncle Tom was not intended to be pejorative, but that the character instead embodied the qualities that would redeem the world—kindliness, patience, humility, and altruism—and thus represented a messianic ideal in the nineteenth

century. Jane Tompkins has argued that "[in] the system of belief that undergirds Stowe's enterprise, dying is the supreme form of heroism." See Moses, *Black Messiahs and Uncle Toms: Social and Literary Manipulations of a Religious Myth*, rev. ed. (State College: Penn State University Press, 1993), 49, and Tompkins, *Sensational Designs: The Cultural Work of American Fiction, 1790–1860* (New York: Oxford University Press, 1985), 127.

45. This categorization is itself a product of nineteenth-century thought that stressed separation of the public from the private. See Charles Taylor, *Sources of the Self: The Making of Modern Identity* (Cambridge, Mass.: Harvard University Press, 1989).

46. Raboteau, *Slave Religion*, 318.

47. Glenn Hinson has written eloquently of this problem in his ethnographic account of black Pentecostal worship. See Hinson, *Fire in My Bones: Transcendence and the Holy Spirit in African American Gospel* (Philadelphia: University of Pennsylvania Press, 2000), 5, and especially the appendix, "Stepping Around Experience and the Supernatural."

48. Orlando Patterson, *The Sociology of Slavery: An Analysis of the Origins, Development, and Structure of Negro Slave Society in Jamaica* (London: MacGibbon & Kee, 1967) and *Slavery and Social Death: A Comparative Study* (Cambridge, Mass.: Harvard University Press, 1982).

49. Patterson, *Sociology of Slavery*, 260, 283.

50. Patterson, *Slavery and Social Death*, 98–100.

51. David Brion Davis, *The Problem of Slavery in the Age of Revolution, 1770–1823* (Ithaca: Cornell University Press, 1975; New York: Oxford University Press, 1999), 562, 556.

52. George Santayana, *Reason in Religion* (New York: Scribner, 1930; Dover, 1982), 13.

53. Eugene D. Genovese, *Roll, Jordan, Roll: The World the Slaves Made* (New York: Random House, 1974; Vintage Books, 1976), 163, 166, 165, 183. On "the inner reality of slaveholding," see Genovese, *The Political Economy of Slavery: Studies in the Economy and Society of the Slave South* (New York: Vintage Books, 1967), 32–33.

54. Mathews, "We Have Left Undone."

55. Isaac, *Transformation of Virginia*, 172; Heyrman, *Southern Cross*. Jewel Spangler and Rachel Klein have dissented from this view.

56. An exception can be found in Catherine Greer O'Brion, "'A Mighty Fortress Is Our God': Building a Community of Faith in the Virginia Tidewater, 1772–1845" (Ph.D. diss., University of Virginia, 1997).

57. Heyrman, *Southern Cross*, 161–205.

58. Ibid., 197, 203; Catherine A. Brekus, *Strangers and Pilgrims: Female Preaching in North America, 1740–1845* (Chapel Hill: University of North Carolina Press, 1998); Susan Juster, *Disorderly Women: Sexual Politics and Evangelicalism in Revolutionary New England* (Ithaca: Cornell University Press, 1994); Jean E. Friedman, *The Enclosed Garden: Women and Community in the Evangelical South, 1830–1900* (Chapel Hill: University of North Carolina Press, 1985).

59. McCurry, *Masters of Small Worlds*, esp. chapters 4–6. Quotes appear on 154, 207.

60. Ibid., 142.

61. Frederick A. Bode, "A Common Sphere: White Evangelicals and Gender in Antebellum Georgia," *Georgia Historical Quarterly* 79 (Winter 1995): 775–809, quote on 801; Cynthia Lynn Lyerly, *Methodism and the Southern Mind, 1770–1810* (New York: Oxford University Press, 1998), 27, 39, 185–86.

62. Bode, "A Common Sphere"; Benjamin Mosby Smith, "Memorandum of the Infancy and Childhood of My Daughter Mary Moore Smith," and "Memoranda of the Infancy and Childhood of My Son Josiah Morrison Smith, Prepared for His Use, Should God Spare His Life," microfilmed copies, Records of the Lexington (Va.) Presbytery, William Smith Morton Library, Union Theological Seminary, Richmond, Va.; Francis R. Flournoy, *Benjamin Mosby Smith, 1811–1893* (Richmond: Richmond Press, 1947).

63. Bode, "A Common Sphere," quote on 780; John W. Quist, *Restless Visionaries: The Social Roots of Antebellum Reform in Alabama and Michigan* (Baton Rouge: Louisiana State University Press, 1998).

64. Bode, "A Common Sphere," quote on 785; Scott M. Stephan, "Re-creating Conversion: An Examination of Domestic Devotion in the Old South" (paper presented at the meeting of the Southern Historical Association, November 2000); Stephan, "Faith and Family in the Old South" (Ph.D. diss., Indiana University, 2001).

65. James C. Scott, *Domination and the Arts of Resistance: Hidden Transcripts* (New Haven: Yale University Press, 1990), 136.

66. Quoted in Raboteau, *Slave Religion*, 294.

67. Troeltsch, *Social Teachings of the Christian Churches*; Weber, *Protestant Ethic and the Spirit of Capitalism*.

68. Troeltsch, *Social Teachings of the Christian Churches*, 2:589–90; Weber, *Protestant Ethic and the Spirit of Capitalism*; Lyerly, *Methodism and the Southern Mind*, 33.

69. Mark A. Noll, *America's God: From Jonathan Edwards to Abraham Lincoln* (New York: Oxford University Press, 2002); Hatch, *Democratization of American Christianity*; Alexander Campbell, "On the Rights of a Layman," *Christian Baptist*, January 2, 1826; songs quoted in Lawrence W. Levine, "Slave Songs and Slave Consciousness: An Exploration in Neglected Sources," in Fulop and Raboteau, *African-American Religion*, 73–74; John Dollard, *Caste and Class in a Southern Town*, 3d ed. (Garden City, N.Y.: Doubleday Anchor, 1957), 223–24.

70. This assumption from Troeltsch's church-sect typology echoes throughout H. Richard Niebuhr: "What had the Westminster Confession . . . to do with the piety of craftsman and yeoman?" See *The Social Sources of Denominationalism* (Hamden, Conn.: Shoe String Press, 1954), 31, quote on 42–43.

71. Lincoln, *Race, Religion, and the Continuing American Dilemma*, 80–81.

72. Erskine Clark, *Our Southern Zion: A History of Calvinism in the South Carolina Low Country, 1690–1990* (Tuscaloosa: University of Alabama Press, 1996), 229.

73. Quoted in Blair A. Pogue, "'I Cannot Believe the Gospel That Is So Much Preached': Gender, Belief, and Discipline in Baptist Religious Culture," in *The Buzzel about Ken-*

tuck: Settling the Promised Land, ed. Craig Thompson Friend (Lexington: University Press of Kentucky, 1999), 217, 236.

74. Allen Turner Account Book, 1826, Manuscript Department, Perkins Library, Duke University.

75. On the importance of doctrinal debate as public entertainment, see E. Brooks Holifield, "Theology as Entertainment: Oral Debate in American Religion," *Church History* 67 (September 1998): 499–520.

76. Thompson, *Making of the English Working Class*, 713.

77. Mathews, "Second Great Awakening as an Organizing Process," 27. See also Hatch, *Democratization of American Christianity*; Christopher H. Owen, *The Sacred Flame of Love: Methodism and Society in Nineteenth-Century Georgia* (Athens: University of Georgia Press, 1998), 28–56; and McCauley, *Appalachian Mountain Religion*, esp. 228–33.

78. Mathews, *Religion in the Old South*, 39.

79. Raboteau and Wills, "Retelling Carter Woodson's Story"; Frey and Wood, *Come Shouting to Zion*; John B. Boles, ed., *Masters and Slaves in the House of the Lord: Race and Religion in the American South, 1740–1870* (Lexington: University Press of Kentucky, 1988).

80. Raboteau, *Slave Religion*.

81. Lincoln, *Race, Religion, and the Continuing American Dilemma*, 78.

82. Frey and Wood, *Come Shouting to Zion*, 190–203, quote on 191. See also Betty Wood, *Women's Work, Men's Work: The Informal Slave Economies of Lowcountry Georgia* (Athens: University of Georgia Press, 1995).

83. Cushing Biggs Hassell and Sylvester Hassell, *History of the Church of God . . . Including the History of the Kehukee Primitive Baptist Association* (n.p.: 1886), quoted in McCauley, *Appalachian Mountain Religion*, 120.

84. Alexander Campbell, "Preface," in *A Connected View of the Principles and Rules by Which the Living Oracles May Be Intelligently and Certainly Interpreted* (Bethany, Va.: M'vay & Ewing, 1835).

85. Schweiger, *Gospel Working Up*, 77–89; Mark A. Noll, ed., *God and Mammon: Protestants, Money, and the Market, 1790–1860* (New York: Oxford University Press, 2002).

86. Schweiger, *Gospel Working Up*, 149–70.

87. Philip N. Mulder, *A Controversial Spirit: Evangelical Awakenings in the South* (New York: Oxford University Press, 2002).

88. C. Vann Woodward, *The Strange Career of Jim Crow* (New York: Oxford University Press, 1955); Gaines M. Foster, *Ghosts of the Confederacy: Defeat, the Lost Cause, and the Emergence of the New South, 1865–1913* (New York: Oxford University Press, 1987); Michael O'Brien, *The Idea of the American South, 1920–1941* (Baltimore: Johns Hopkins University Press, 1979); Tony Horwitz, *Confederates in the Attic: Dispatches from the Unfinished Civil War* (New York: Pantheon, 1998); James R. Goff Jr., *Close Harmony: A History of Southern Gospel* (Chapel Hill: University of North Carolina Press, 2002).

89. Weber, "Bureaucracy," in Gerth and Mills, *From Max Weber*, 196–244. It should be

noted that both women and African Americans excelled at institution building when they had the opportunity later in the century.

90. Taylor, *Sources of the Self*, 519. See also William T. Cavanaugh, *Torture and Eucharist* (Malden, Mass.: Blackwell Publishers, 1998).

For Further Reading

Berger, Peter L. *The Sacred Canopy: Elements of a Sociological Theory of Religion*. New York: Doubleday, 1967; Anchor Books, 1969.

Bode, Frederick A. "A Common Sphere: White Evangelicals and Gender in Antebellum Georgia." *Georgia Historical Quarterly* 79 (Winter 1995): 775–809.

Boles, John B. *The Great Revival: Beginnings of the Bible Belt*. Lexington: University Press of Kentucky, 1972; reprint, 1996.

————, ed. *Masters and Slaves in the House of the Lord: Race and Religion in the American South, 1740–1870*. Lexington: University Press of Kentucky, 1988.

Bourdieu, Pierre. *Language and Symbolic Power*. Cambridge, Mass.: Harvard University Press, 1991.

Bratt, James D. "The Reorientation of American Protestantism, 1835–1845." *Church History* 67 (March 1998): 52–82.

Collinson, Patrick. "Religion, Society, and the Historian." *Journal of Religious History* 23 (June 1999): 149–67.

Davis, David Brion. *The Problem of Slavery in the Age of Revolution, 1770–1823*. Ithaca: Cornell University Press, 1975; New York: Oxford University Press, 1999.

Douglas, Mary. "The Effects of Modernization on Religious Change." *Daedalus* 111 (Winter 1982): 1–19.

Frey, Sylvia R., and Betty Wood. *Come Shouting to Zion: African American Protestantism in the American South and British Caribbean to 1830*. Chapel Hill: University of North Carolina Press, 1998.

Genovese, Eugene D. *Roll, Jordan, Roll: The World the Slaves Made*. New York: Random House, 1974; Vintage Books, 1976.

————. *The Political Economy of Slavery: Studies in the Economy and Society of the Slave South*. New York: Vintage Books, 1967.

Guelzo, Allen C. "God's Designs: The Literature of the Colonial Revivals of Religion, 1735–1760." In *New Directions in American Religious History*, edited by Harry S. Stout and D. G. Hart, 141–72. New York: Oxford University Press, 1997.

Hall, Timothy D. *Contested Boundaries: Itinerancy and the Reshaping of the Colonial American Religious World*. Durham: Duke University Press, 1994.

Hatch, Nathan O. *The Democratization of American Christianity*. New Haven: Yale University Press, 1989.

Heyrman, Christine Leigh. *Southern Cross: The Beginnings of the Bible Belt*. New York: Alfred A. Knopf, 1997.

Hill, Samuel S. *Southern Churches in Crisis Revisited*. Tuscaloosa: University of Alabama Press, 1999.

Howe, Daniel Walker. "The Evangelical Movement and Political Culture in the North during the Second Party System." *Journal of American History* 77 (March 1991): 1216–39.

Lambert, Frank. *Inventing the Great Awakening*. Princeton: Princeton University Press, 1999.

Lyerly, Cynthia Lynn. *Methodism and the Southern Mind, 1770–1810*. New York: Oxford University Press, 1998.

Mathews, Donald G. "'We Have Left Undone Those Things Which We Ought to Have Done': Southern Religious History in Retrospect and Prospect." *Church History* 67 (June 1998): 305–25.

———. *Religion in the Old South*. Chicago: University of Chicago Press, 1977.

———. "Religion in the Old South: Speculation on Methodology." *South Atlantic Quarterly* 73 (Winter 1974): 34–52.

———. "The Second Great Awakening as an Organizing Process, 1780–1830: An Hypothesis." *American Quarterly* 21 (Spring 1969): 23–43.

McCauley, Deborah Vansau. *Appalachian Mountain Religion: A History*. Urbana: University of Illinois Press, 1995.

McCurry, Stephanie. *Masters of Small Worlds: Yeoman Households, Gender Relations, and the Political Culture of the Antebellum South Carolina Low Country*. New York: Oxford University Press, 1995.

McLoughlin, William G. *Revivals, Awakenings, and Reform: An Essay on Religion and Social Change in America, 1607–1977*. Chicago: University of Chicago Press, 1978.

Mulder, Philip N. *A Controversial Spirit: Evangelical Awakenings in the South*. New York: Oxford University Press, 2002.

O'Brion, Catherine Greer. "'A Mighty Fortress Is Our God': Building a Community of Faith in the Virginia Tidewater, 1772–1845." Ph.D. diss., University of Virginia, 1997.

Owen, Christopher H. *The Sacred Flame of Love: Methodism and Society in Nineteenth-Century Georgia*. Athens: University of Georgia Press, 1998.

Patterson, Orlando. *Slavery and Social Death: A Comparative Study*. Cambridge, Mass.: Harvard University Press, 1982.

———. *The Sociology of Slavery: An Analysis of the Origins, Development, and Structure of Negro Slave Society in Jamaica*. London: MacGibbon & Kee, 1967.

Peacock, James L., and Ruel W. Tyson Jr. *Pilgrims of Paradox: Calvinism and Experience among the Primitive Baptists of the Blue Ridge*. Washington, D.C.: Smithsonian Institution Press, 1989.

Pogue, Blair A. "'I Cannot Believe the Gospel That Is So Much Preached': Gender, Belief, and Discipline in Baptist Religious Culture." In *The Buzzel about Kentuck: Settling the Promised Land*, edited by Craig Thompson Friend, 217–41. Lexington: University Press of Kentucky, 1999.

Quist, John W. *Restless Visionaries: The Social Roots of Antebellum Reform in Alabama and Michigan*. Baton Rouge: Louisiana State University Press, 1998.

Raboteau, Albert. *Slave Religion: The "Invisible Institution" in the Antebellum South*. New York: Oxford University Press, 1978.

Raboteau, Albert, and David W. Wills. "Retelling Carter Woodson's Story: Archival Sources for Afro-American Church History." In *Religious Diversity and American Religious History: Studies in Traditions and Cultures*, edited by Walter H. Conser Jr. and Sumner B. Twiss, 52–71. Athens: University of Georgia Press, 1997.

Richey, Russell. "The Southern Accent of American Methodism." In *Early American Methodism*, 47–64. Bloomington: Indiana University Press, 1991.

Schweiger, Beth Barton. *The Gospel Working Up: Progress and the Pulpit in Nineteenth-Century Virginia*. New York: Oxford University Press, 2000.

Scott, James C. *Domination and the Arts of Resistance: Hidden Transcripts*. New Haven: Yale University Press, 1990.

Stephan, Scott M. "Faith and Family in the Old South." Ph.D. diss., Indiana University, 2001.

Swatos, William H., Jr., and Kevin J. Christiano. "Secularization Theory: The Course of a Concept." *Sociology of Religion* 60 (1999): 209–28.

Taylor, Charles. *Sources of the Self: The Making of Modern Identity*. Cambridge, Mass.: Harvard University Press, 1989.

Troeltsch, Ernst. *The Social Teaching of the Christian Churches*. 2 vols. New York: Macmillan, 1931.

Warner, R. Stephen. "Work in Progress toward a New Paradigm for the Sociological Study of Religion in the United States." *American Journal of Sociology* 98 (1993): 1044–93.

Weber, Max. *The Protestant Ethic and the Spirit of Capitalism*. Translated by Talcott Parsons. New York: Charles Scribner's Sons, 1958.

———. "The Protestant Sects and the Spirit of Capitalism." In *From Max Weber: Essays in Sociology*, edited by H. H. Gerth and C. Wright Mills, 302–22. New York: Oxford University Press, 1946.

Weisenfeld, Judith. "On Jordan's Stormy Banks: Margins, Centers, and Bridges in African American Religious History." In *New Directions in American Religious History*, edited by Harry S. Stout and D. G. Hart, 417–44. New York: Oxford University Press, 1997.

Wills, David W. "The Central Themes of American Religious History: Pluralism, Puritanism, and the Encounter of Black and White." In *African-American Religion: Interpretive Essays in History and Culture*, edited by Timothy E. Fulop and Albert J. Raboteau, 9–20. New York: Routledge, 1997.

Wood, Betty. *Women's Work, Men's Work: The Informal Slave Economies of Lowcountry Georgia*. Athens: University of Georgia Press, 1995.

3

EMILY BINGHAM

Thou Knowest Not What a Day May Bring Forth

Intellect, Power, Conversion, and Apostasy in the Life of Rachel Mordecai Lazarus (1788–1838)

In Raleigh, North Carolina, during the summer of 1835, a forty-seven-year-old wife and mother of four decided that the time had come for her to enter the full fellowship of Jesus Christ. Having undergone a protracted searching of her soul, she had reached the commitment stage in her conversion. "Verily it appears to me," she wrote to a friend, "as if a little more time were graciously lent me, that I might improve it to the glory of God and say 'I will take the cup of salvation and call upon the name of the Lord, now in the presence of all his people.'"[1]

When it comes to the historiography of religion in the South, or for that matter of American religion more broadly, such a portrait could not be more familiar. Countless men and women—rich, poor, middling, enslaved, and free—have participated in the evangelical experience of personal spiritual transformation driven by a new conviction of the role of God in the universe and in their own lives.

However, on closer examination, Rachel Mordecai Lazarus's religious awakening suggests that there may be new angles from which to read the history of conversion and southern religious expression. Rachel Mordecai Lazarus was a Jew, a self-educated and intellectually engaged resident of the urban South whose family had, during her lifetime, accomplished its own transformation from economic and social marginality to middle-class respectability. Her pedigree is anomalous in light of the plantation-dominated, intellectually benighted, entirely Protestant image of the Old South that persists in many textbooks. Indeed, Rachel's apparent exceptionalism speaks to opportunities within the scholarly literature surrounding conversion, antebellum religion, and Jewish assimilation. It suggests what might be gained were historians to focus on a broader definition of conversion, one that included shifts from no faith system to a faith commitment, from affiliation with one system to affiliation with another, from one orientation to another within a single faith system, and from lackadaisical to intense commitment within a single faith tradition.[2]

With the advantage of rich documentation, this essay takes a narrative, case study approach to Rachel's experiences, something many scholars cannot do in studies of Jewish communities, evangelical awakenings, and the religious institutions connected with them.[3] Reading Rachel's letters, it is possible (indeed impossible not) to see beyond the conversion to her wider life and to the effects of her religious experiences on her family. The case study approach to Rachel's conversion may afford at least a glimpse of what historian Allen Guelzo has called the complex "devotional, spiritual and familial meanings [of conversion] which we ignore only at the price of misunderstanding the entire enterprise." Whereas scholars rarely pursue the complex meanings of conversion beyond the period immediately before and through an individual's decision to join a body of believers, this story looks at a much larger time frame that spans the end of the early republic and the beginning of the antebellum era. It is not enough to simply investigate the moment in which Rachel committed to convert. Time scarcely began or halted there, nor did her story have the happy ending that conversion implies in many accounts of the history of religion. In our fascination with explaining the social forces that inform religious awakenings—or the social consequences we seek to attach to such events—historians too easily lose track of the contentious nature of religious experiences, the contingency of spirituality or religiosity over the course of a life, and how such fluidity can be experienced in various historical settings.[4]

Jewish assimilation, and especially its most extreme expression, apostasy, remains a sensitive, potentially divisive topic. For Jews, conversion to Christianity has typically represented tragedy, betrayal, weakness, and sin. Because Jews have been subject throughout the ages to violent persecutions, expulsions, rigid political and economic repression, and, in the wake of emancipation in Germany, genocide, the figure of the convert carries great symbolic weight for anyone concerned with the survival of Judaism. Christian proselytizing—whether in its modern "persuasive" form or its often brutal earlier expressions—has always elicited Jewish defenses and is often viewed as fundamentally anti-Semitic. Frequently absent from polemical or historical consideration of such issues as assimilation, proselytism, and apostasy have been the individuals lodged at the nexus of these challenges to Jewish identity: the converts themselves and their families.[5]

Recent years, however, have yielded a flowering of work on Jews in the American South.[6] The Mordecai papers, concentrated in half a dozen archival collections, are the richest of any pre–Civil War southern Jewish family, and their content relating to women is especially strong.[7] When Jews came to the South in greater numbers after the war, they applied immense social and material resources to establishing congregations in cities and small towns throughout the region.[8] Their reception and the choices they made were conditioned in part by the experiences of earlier Jewish southerners like the Mordecais who reared a generation of children without the benefit of a fully viable religious community.

The challenge of maintaining Jewish identity in the South has been complicated by geographical isolation and the culture's evangelical character. For Rachel and her family, who lived while the Second Great Awakening was rolling across the region, the problem grew increasingly weighty after 1810. Rachel's narrative is a single story about that encounter, and as such it reflects only one resolution of it. Members of her family each confronted the task of determining what it meant to be Jewish, southern, and American. From within Rachel's extended clan, responses ranged from energetic orthodoxy to nonpracticing but fully identified Jewishness to the decision to marry a Gentile and have children who would meld into the majority to outright apostasy.[9]

Thousands upon thousands of southerners embraced Jesus as their savior; not many of them began as Jews. Nevertheless, it is possible that an exploration of Rachel's shift from one major religious tradition to another can help reveal the drama underlying the kind of spiritual shifts that even a nominal Christian who is born again in Jesus Christ may undergo. Perhaps Rachel's awakening, with its particularity and complexity stemming from her Jewish identity and from the process of assimilation, can help make visible internal and external conflicts that are glossed over when conversion is expressed as an individual's progression from darkness to light, from sin and unbelief to redemption. What meanings could a conversion carry for marriages, families, children, parents, and friends?[10]

IN 1787, THE YEAR BEFORE Rachel was born, Jacob Mordecai and his wife, Judy, came to Virginia from New York in search of a better living. Both came from the tiny colonial Jewish community—population about two thousand—

that was concentrated mainly in Charleston, New York, and Philadelphia. Although plagued by a string of poor jobs in the postrevolutionary depression, Jacob was ambitious and imbued with the promise of freedom and equality that was the spirit of the age. His father was dead, and his mother, a convert to Judaism, had remarried to one of the earliest Jews to live and trade in Richmond, Virginia. This connection showed Jacob that there was money to be made in the South.[11]

Jacob and Judy's daughter Rachel was born outside Richmond, but Virginia proved unprofitable, and the Mordecais resettled in Warrenton, a county seat in North Carolina that was without other Jewish residents. Jacob opened a store. The family had high hopes for their own advancement within the new republic. The Bill of Rights protected religious freedom, as did numerous state constitutions written during the revolutionary era, but the right to hold elective office remained restricted in many parts of the nation, including North Carolina.[12]

Like other Americans of this time, the Mordecais drew on aspects of the Enlightenment worldview emerging both from revolutionary ideology and from the newly articulate and culturally authoritative transatlantic middle class.[13] Virtue and progress were to be advanced by reason in matters of state and of the household. Family members pursued education, economic advancement, and self-improvement in the context of companionate marriage, privacy, and domesticity. Jacob and Judy's liberal bent also shaped the family's approach to religion. Members of a historically persecuted minority, Jews had good reason to preach pluralism, tolerance, and "true religion." The Mordecai children were taught, as their father once wrote, to love "virtue in whatever garb it appeared."[14]

When Judy died in childbirth, this set of convictions was burned into the heart of seven-year-old Rachel, her eldest daughter. On her deathbed, Judy spoke the traditional Jewish prayer for forgiveness: "May my present sufferings be atonement for all my transgressions." According to family records, she then asked that her funeral "omit" elements that, "from their novelty," would make Jacob "appear ridiculous." It is not clear what mourning rituals (which can include turning mirrors to the wall, ceasing to shave or cut hair, rending garments, and serving special foods) Judy referred to, but, as Jacob told his children in the wake of her death, the Mordecais lived "among people unaccustomed to [their] religious rites."[15] The loss of Judy awakened in Jacob and their six children a determination to fulfill the covenant she had shaped; Jacob soon married Judy's younger sister, and the family forged ahead, its members committing themselves to diligent labor, affectionate domesticity, intellectual cultivation, and religious liberalism. Such values fit relatively comfortably with the interests and manners of Warrenton's genteel whites, a population largely unmoved by organized religion, and this was the population—not the slaves and farmers who had responded most strongly to early Baptist and Methodist revivals—with which the Mordecais mingled.[16]

As eldest daughter, Rachel kept the family flame burning brightly. She diligently copied over her father's description of Judy's life and death, the covenant setting forth the precepts that would keep her mother's influence alive among them and that mapped their route to virtue, recognition, and acceptance. Judy would have wanted them to give glory and thanks to God in some way every day, although it was emphasized that this need not interfere with their work or play. While the Jewish people were burdened by a history of prejudice, anti-Semitic persecution did not determine the shape of the Mordecais' lives. Rachel maintained that in the United States, unlike other places in other times, "religious distinctions [were] scarcely known" and "character and talents [were] all sufficient to attain advancement." While historians have generally confirmed this assessment of Rachel's, such a sweeping statement suggests, perhaps, the presence in Rachel of the quintessentially American wishfulness that anyone plagued with a sense of difference can employ to ease discomfort. Rachel stuck by her heritage, declaring: "Our faith is assuredly a good one." And in her early twenties, she earned a degree of celebrity for criticizing a popular British author's anti-Semitic portrayal of a Jewish character. The author's apology—in the form of another novel—examined the irrational psychological roots of anti-Semitism.[17]

It was not so much religion but the need for economic security and emotional support that preoccupied the Mordecais, Rachel in particular. With something like religious conviction, they embraced in their covenant principles that, while not peculiar to them, have yet to be framed in historical terms. These principles united men and women in a project of domestic enlightenment in ways that were highly attractive to a woman of Rachel's intellectual ambitions. Enlightenment philosophy posited that reason produced virtue and that virtue yielded both individual happiness and social harmony. Having absorbed Lockean concepts of cognitive development—that experience, perhaps especially early experience, shapes an adult's character—republican ideology held that success in the American experiment depended upon a rational and enlightened citizenry. Thus education, which began in the household and, in Rachel's view, needed to take place continually within it, became a primary means of achieving national as well as familial success. In applying these concepts to the home and family, Rachel and other believers in the goal of domestic enlightenment claimed for women the same capacity for reason and virtue accorded to men and argued that both sexes should work closely together to construct a cultivated and loving family capable of worldly accomplishments. The home could form a productive, cooperative, and emotionally and intellectually fulfilling world unto itself—a microcosm of the ideal nation.[18]

This domestic scaffolding helped support the Mordecais through the death of Judy, the expansion of the family with Jacob's remarriage (there were eventually thirteen children), the failure of Jacob's store, and the ups and downs of running a boarding school for girls, which engaged them from 1809 to 1818. As her father's star instructor at the academy, Rachel was at the center of an educating and educated family. School teaching was not the ideal occupation for a respectable young woman in North Carolina, but she enjoyed the challenge, applied innovative pedagogical methods, and won respect both within her family and from outsiders for her talents.[19] Rachel had often "wish[ed] that [she] had been a son, that like [her] brothers [she] might at least" do "something for [her] own support." Her wish had come true, and the academy did a fair business; for several years, it enrolled over one hundred scholars. "Your dear Mother told me you would be a blessing to me," Jacob once said, "and so you are."[20] So content did Rachel seem to one brother that he teasingly asked whether she could "recollect the dissatisfaction [she] used to express at occupying uselessly a space on this planet."[21]

But in 1810, one year after the Mordecais opened the academy, religious activity in and around Warrenton opened new strains in their relations with the community, and these strains spilled over to their extended family, many members of whom were by this time settled in Richmond. A "party of Methodists" came to town and held nightly gatherings. Rachel's sister reported that Warrentonians, a largely unchurched lot, were "turning religious as fast as they [could] conveniently fall, without hurting, one another." In response, Rachel's brother Sam, apprenticed as a clerk in his uncle's Richmond countinghouse, announced his determination to make "a speculation in Bibles, broad-brimmed hats, psalters and psalm books" and simultaneously to "[obtain] whisky and apple brandy very low." It would not have been a bad venture. A revival was taking hold.[22]

Three weeks later, Warrenton's less holy citizens were laying bets: Had Jacob Mordecai embraced Jesus Christ as his savior, or had he not? Rachel laughed off the idea, though her father had attended several evening gatherings. Then, her brother Sam encountered Warrenton's pious innkeeper in Richmond and received "the plain unequivocal assertion" that "papa [had] become one of the elect." It had become common for genteel southerners to attend revivals to gawk at the assembly and ridicule the preachers, but Jacob's case appeared to be something more. Jacob's religious loyalties had become, most unpleasantly for Sam, the subject of public speculation. Sam worked and lived largely among Jews; even speculation about such matters besmirched the Mordecai name.[23]

Insolvency, geographic isolation, and rumors of religious irregularity set Jacob and his family on the margins of the Jewish community. But in practicing Judaism somewhat haphazardly, the Mordecais had plenty of company in Richmond. Nor were they unobservant. References to "matzohs," "commemorative crackers," and "the bread of affliction" appeared in springtime correspondence, marking Passover. Other Jewish holidays—Rosh Hashanah, Yom Kippur, Sukkoth—also appeared in their letters, and their travel plans sometimes changed to conform to their observance. Sometimes they did not. As for the Sabbath, many school duties went on without interruption on that holy day.[24]

This flexible, undogmatic approach to religion—the approach Judy outlined on her deathbed and folded into the family's covenant—eased daily life, which the Mordecais passed almost exclusively among Gentiles. It in no way signaled a rejection of Judaism itself. Apostasy, as the Mordecais well knew, was something else entirely. Spotty religious observance might provoke criticism among Jews, but converts were shunned.[25]

What, then, did Jacob's presence at the 1810 revival meetings mean? Later in life, he wrote that he had for a time grown "estranged from his brethren in faith" and had met the earnest invitations of friendly Christians "with a mind little trammeled by the Religion in which he was born." Approached by evangelicals who sought to spread the joy of their conversions, Jacob said that he had "avoided . . . every kind of opposition to their sentiments."[26] The question remained: How much of his avoidance stemmed from politeness, the desire not to offend, and how much from some spiritual uncertainty of his own? The suspense continued for more than two months. Finally, in a letter to Sam that amounted to an open statement to Richmond's Jews, Jacob "spoke in a way too plain to be misunderstood." He wrote that he no longer attended Christian gatherings and that he had adopted "a serious deportment" that, he said, "had been noticed by many."[27]

In 1818, the Mordecais sold the school, and Jacob purchased a 400-acre plantation outside Richmond, Virginia. While an overseer and slaves would work the farm, Jacob would apply his time to his growing passion: reading and research that would enable him to defend Judaism against Christian attacks and, as his wife Becky said, to "make his own children and grand children well acquainted with the religion they profess[ed]." In effect, Jacob had undergone his own conversion to the religion of his birth and organized his life accordingly.[28]

Rachel, having long passed the typical marriage age, planned a life of self-cultivation and family-based teaching. (Rachel had assumed the responsibility of educating her half sister Eliza.) The comfortable conditions did not last long, however. Two brothers departed for professional training, the Panic of 1819 swallowed up the family's investments, and domestic life was marred by one sister's mental illness and the intermarriage (over Jacob's protests) of another. Rachel's younger sister Ellen wailed into her diary: "We all sunk at once powerless when we thought our life of comfort . . . just about to commence." Approached in 1820 by a well-to-do widower, a merchant shipper from Wilmington, North Carolina, Rachel accepted his offer of marriage and set out to establish her ideal of domestic enlightenment in a household of her own.[29]

Rachel's husband, Aaron Lazarus, had spent his youth in Charleston, home to the early nineteenth century's largest Jewish community. He was, paradoxically, a believing Jew and a pewholder at Wilmington's Saint James Episcopal Church. No synagogue would be erected in Wilmington until the 1850s, and Aaron, expressing the Enlightenment respect for an overarching God, claimed to be able to "worship Jehovah in any temple."[30]

So it was that a Sunday afternoon in 1823 found Rachel seated in her parlor, preparing to write a letter, hearing the church bells calling congregants to the day's second service and "congratulating" herself that she was "not in duty bound" to follow their call. The "unpleasantness" of doing so, she told Ellen, had been "sufficiently impressed by . . . having attended [church that] morning, the sun very warm, the streets very sandy, and moreover the sermon very dry." More gratifying tasks lay before Rachel. With her "dear husband" reading beside her, she surveyed family news and sketched her hopes for their toddler son.[31]

In Wilmington, Rachel continued her mission of domestic enlightenment as best she could. Her correspondence with Maria Edgeworth, the author whose anti-Semitic novel she had criticized in 1815, became more frequent, a performance that added luster to Rachel's endeavors. Her commitment to learning and her ever vigorous "taste for domestic happiness" stood front and center in her life there, as it had in Warrenton and at the Mordecais' farm outside Richmond. Almost since she could remember, Rachel had guided and instructed young people, whether siblings, paying students, or, as in Wilmington, stepdaughters. Always, she sought to improve herself by broadening her knowledge of the world through literature and natural science. By embedding intellect so wholly within the private sphere, Rachel imagined a life that disdained limits on women's minds even as it honored taboos against female public or professional roles. The world of knowledge and her participation in it was central to her vision of the rearing and educating of children. She was responsible for educating nine children—five of Aaron's from his first marriage and four the couple had together—while managing a large city household with half a dozen slaves.[32] Following the birth of her son Marx, she prayed for the strength "to form his infancy, to guide his childhood, and advise his youth, that in opening manhood he [might] love and revere his parents as his best of friends." It required constant monitoring; unlike most of her peers, whose children were watched over by slaves, Rachel generally kept her children within sight and seized opportunities to instruct them throughout the day. In all her roles—daughter, head teacher, beloved sister, family leader, wife, and parent—Rachel folded into domesticity her intense longing for intellectual life. One sister exclaimed that with such a mother Marx would surely "be one of the best managed children of the age."[33]

And yet Rachel confided to her sister: "[If] I never have another [child] I shall account myself most happy."[34] The strain of forcing her aspirations though the keyhole of domestic life and measuring their success by her pupils' progress was already obvious one year into her marriage. Fourteen years later, when Rachel announced her intention to "'take the cup of salvation,'" she felt that she had fallen short in implementing the domestic enlightenment that gave her life meaning.

Because her mother had died in childbirth, each pregnancy was for Rachel an exercise in dread. Moreover, she was acutely conscious of the moral and educational guidance each child would demand.[35] The household management, sewing, nursing, and daily instruction of children made Rachel yearn to "call some part of [her] time [her] own." She tried to reconcile herself to the idea that it was "*right* to give [her] whole time to the care of [her] family" rather than use it to improve or refresh her own mind, but Rachel never could convince herself that something so vital to her happiness (as well as to her model of domestic enlightenment) ought really to be relinquished.[36]

During the early years of her marriage, while Rachel learned to manage a complicated household, she was also drawn to examine what it meant to be a Jew. The circumstances were personal, specific, and multiple. Her father's once casual but now engrossing interest in the topic, her husband's orthodox upbringing, her fearful pregnancies, the responsibility of enlightened parenthood, and the friendship of several women who had experienced spiritual conversions all prompted Rachel to consider the place of what her husband once called the "Almighty God of [his] Fathers" in her world.[37]

Ashamed of her ignorance, Rachel resolved to read a chapter of the Pentateuch each day. Once a week, she gathered with her stepdaughters to discuss a religious topic. But two months of such inquiry did more to sharpen her critique of Judaism than to deepen her commitment to it. Rachel wrote home to her father, now a recognized authority on Jewish matters, and suggested that he turn his attention to American Jews' "religious exercises" and "present form of prayer," both of which she considered to be in dire need of improvement. The transcendence and "devotion" she sought seemed to her to be prevented by "so many epithets strung together." "As the hart panteth after the water brooks," she informed her father, quoting the psalmist, "so panteth my soul after thee, O God."[38]

But when a group of Charleston Jews proposed ritual reforms along the lines Rachel had suggested to Jacob, she learned to her dismay that he considered their leader to be an apostate and atheist.[39] Jacob's studies and his alarm over American Jews' lack of observance and their assimilation had taken him into new territory—to a kind of orthodoxy his daughter found foreign and unappealing. This rift signified the beginning of a period in which Rachel contemplated religious possibilities that had the power to bring her into conflict with the men she loved and upon whose approval she thrived. Lacking a reformist Jewish community of her own, Rachel contemplated her religious beliefs, experiences, and aspirations in a new, far riskier, light.

Rachel's inquiries and dissatisfactions eventually led her to form deeper relationships with several women in Wilmington. In a pattern described by historian Richard Rankin, many of Rachel's upper-class friends had undergone evangelical new births in the second and third decades of the nineteenth century. Methodists most likely initiated this largely female religious energy, but a young priest in Wilmington also adopted an evangelical style, introduced liturgical modifications into his services, and channeled converts into an Episcopal revival. The same Low Church style was ascendant in Virginia, where the church was under the leadership of Bishop Richard Channing Moore and Assistant Bishop William Meade.[40] For most of her life, Rachel had found little use for these enthusiasms, as her letter about the church bells indicated. But she had received a warm welcome from the town's ladies, and she found them kind and good. The more the pity, as she thought soon after her arrival in Wilmington, "that they [had] so little information and [took] so little pains to increase their store."[41] Few, if any, read with Rachel's breadth or approached the rearing and education of their children with Rachel's solicitude.

Nevertheless, she established a pleasant camaraderie with Jane Dickinson, a favorite pupil from her Warrenton days who was a newlywed in Wilmington when Rachel arrived there in 1821. Almost in tandem, the two women entered motherhood. Their children became playmates. But after the birth of a second child, Jane's health faltered. Rachel herself was in the early stages of her third pregnancy when Jane's tuberculosis reached its latter stage, drawing Rachel to her bedside.

Emaciated by disease, Jane counted her blessings—"oh how far beyond my poor deserts"—in her mother, sister, husband, children, servants, and friends. A few wishes yet remained. She asked that her slave Flora be freed. She wanted mourning rings made for her dearest friends, Rachel being one. She asked her sister to write to the priest who had brought her into communion with Christ to say how "she loved him and wished for him" at her death. Saint James's rector administered the last sacrament. Jane implored her husband to seek the comfort of the Lord for himself. Then she addressed to Rachel "a few solemn and affecting words" on the subject of Christ's saving grace. Two days later, she died. Rachel told her sister Ellen that Jane's death was "not simply distressing but soothing, edifying." She recalled: "It seemed to me I could bear all previous suffering to die the death of the righteous—as she did."[42]

Linguistic alterations often characterize the conversion process, reflecting the influence of newly relevant ideas, communities, or relationships. Rachel's description of Jane's deathbed scene, with its pious language and awe at the workings of faith so typical of evangelicals of this period, signaled a shift in her voice.[43] One of the friends who sought to reinforce that change was Lucy Ann Lippitt. A native of Rhode Island, Lucy Ann arrived in Wilmington in 1826 to visit her brother, a fellow merchant of Rachel's husband, Aaron. Educated, well-read, and serious, Lucy Ann was the kind of companion Rachel had sought since arriving in Wilmington five years earlier. Rachel felt awakened, her mind stretched and improved by her visits with Lucy Ann. "I do not know," Rachel wrote Ellen, "when I have felt so much attached to one but yesterday a stranger."[44]

But Lucy Ann was also religious. And Wilmington appealed to her not only because of her brother and Mrs. Lazarus, but also because of the genteel women who, like her, had been born again in Christ and had structured their lives around their faith. Beginning in 1820, the Ladies Working Society of Saint James raised funds independently both for bricks and mortar and for a "charity school." These activities were accomplished by a female community in which Christian faith gave everyday life transcendent purpose. Members of this circle shared what one woman called "the sweet but *powerful* tie of Christian affection." They nursed and nurtured one another through sickness, loss, death, and spiritual doubt. Another convert recalled the time "when *afflicted, bruised, and broken*, [she] lay under the rod of the Almighty" and a Wilmington friend gently "bound up [her] wounds—and taught [her] to feel the value of Christian friendship," which she described as "a love" that would "be eternal."[45]

Enthusiastic believers, buoyed by mutual support and anxious for friends and family members to join them in life in Christ, these women knew and respected Rachel. But respect meant that longtime acquaintances could press one another only so far on religious matters. Lucy Ann had no such compunctions. She spoke of the role of Jesus in her life—in all life. She questioned Rachel closely. What did God mean to her? People had quoted Scripture to Rachel before, had recommended books or tracts for her spiritual improvement, and it had always seemed wise to handle such situations calmly and politely. And so one day Rachel accepted from her new friend *The Restoration of Israel*, one of numerous volumes of the time that advocated the conversion of Jews.[46]

The effort to convert Jews to Christianity has a long and ignoble history pocked by torture, expulsion, and repression.[47] In the early nineteenth century, such efforts became more organized, and direct persuasion and indirect public pressure were the chosen methods. The success of the London Society for Promoting Christianity among the Jews inspired Americans to found the American Society for Evangelizing the Jews in 1816, spawning numerous local auxiliaries, traveling missionaries, and eventually a periodical, the dubiously titled *Israel's Advocate*. Support was warm and came from high places. Money flowed in based on the belief of many evangelicals that Christ's return required the Jews first to be gathered into the Christian fold.[48]

The Restoration of Israel, firmly planted within the missionary efforts of the period, was a starting point for a religious conversation between Rachel and Lucy Ann that stretched into the following year, through the time of Jane Dickinson's death and into the chamber where Rachel delivered her third child. There, in the fall of 1828, unfolded a crisis that brought Rachel face to face with her mortality—a liminal space where new spiritual understanding often crystallizes.[49] A few days after giving birth, Rachel took a turn for the worse. Her fever rose, and such violent chills and sweats coursed through her that Dr. Armand DeRosset was summoned. He confirmed that Rachel was stricken with malaria, the same disease that had taken her brother Moses' life and probably her mother's, as well. Having prescribed quinine, the doctor went home and told his wife, Catherine, a towering figure among the devout women of Wilmington who was known for her "deep, clear, and pervading" understanding of divine truths, that her friend was badly off.[50]

When she arrived at the Lazarus house, Catherine found Rachel already tended by Jane Dickinson's mourning sister, Mary Orme. The two women sat with Rachel as the fever crested and, as she later wrote, "a single thread" held her to this world. On the second day, Mary, exhausted and desperate at the thought of another death, left Rachel in Catherine's hands.[51]

Catherine saw in Rachel an excellent woman but a suffering and untethered spirit, and, like Jane Dickinson and Lucy Ann Lippitt, Catherine felt she had the answer. "Religion," she believed, was "the one thing needful," and she may have said as much. In any case, that night, with Catherine at her side, Rachel seemed to sense the spirit that only a few months earlier had blessed Jane's deathbed. Despite delirium, convulsions, and dire signs, she felt "perfectly collected" and, she told Ellen, "perfectly resigned to God's will." The following morning, the doctor took her pulse. It beat more evenly.[52]

In the several documents surviving from those days, Rachel did not explain exactly what had transpired during her illness. Yet the confrontation with death, coming as it did on the heels of her unsatisfying explorations of Jewish scripture, her critique of Jewish ritual, and her witnessing of Jane Dickinson's passing, was a watershed moment for Rachel and for her relationships with the Christian women around her. While Rachel still lay dangerously ill, a letter from Lucy Ann in Rhode Island arrived that implored her to think of her soul. Too weak to read it herself, Rachel asked Mary Orme to read it to her—over and over again. Clearly, Lucy Ann desired her friend's conversion to Christianity. Rachel understood this. Mary took down Rachel's reply. Rachel had, she told Lucy, "walked 'through the valley of the shadow of death,' confiding in [God's] mercy for pardon of [her] sins." Rachel explained: "You, my beloved friend, wish I could say more, but of this we will not speak." She wrote that her life, so "graciously preserved," would be "daily more devoted to [her] God." And she named her infant daughter Mary Catherine Lazarus in honor of the women who had nursed her through the dark valley of 1828.[53]

Mary Kate, as the baby was called, was two and her mother forty-two when Rachel's fourth and last child was born. Rachel's despair over her inability to rear another child to her standards returned, worsened by the jealousies and rebellions of her stepchildren, who may have resented Rachel's troubling religious preoccupations. Rachel leaned for support on Catherine DeRosset and on God: "There do I put my trust."[54]

Not that worldly wisdom ceased to matter to her. Self-cultivation and home education continued to be important. For years, Rachel had approached religion as she had all major ideas. She studied patiently and expected to apply her understanding to her own and to her family's improvement. But in midlife, she remained uncertain about the place of religion in her existence. Her enlightened approach to education, marriage, motherhood, and domesticity might have formed a modern expression of emancipated Jewish identity in another time or place—perhaps in late-eighteenth-century Germany or turn-of-the-century New York.[55] In Wilmington, it had not yielded up the happy community (even within her household) she had hoped for. Rachel began to delve more deeply into Christian devotional literature.[56]

In the spring of 1833, some members of Rachel's extended family had to confront the religious sentiments of the sister they considered their generation's leader, the family's female jewel in the crown. Aaron and Rachel planned an extensive tour and invited Rachel's former pupil and half sister Eliza to join them. One day in Washington, D.C., as Rachel, Eliza, and their brother Alfred (an army officer fast advancing in his profession) were riding in a carriage, Rachel questioned them about their "want of religion." Rachel announced that she had found new birth through Jesus' mercy and urged them to seek it, too. Alfred was stunned. He had had no idea of the extent of his sister's spiritual investigations and had never imagined her a Christian and a proselytizer. Alfred could not reconcile Rachel's appeal on the carriage ride with what he had always admired, her "sensible and reflecting mind." It was a common stereotype to view evangelicalism and rational thought as warring representatives of "heart" and "head," and Alfred was tempted to regard his sister's new outlook as an "abandonment of reason."[57]

Eliza found such pressing inquiries from the sister and teacher she revered even more difficult to digest. In Washington, where the women shared a hotel room, Eliza watched Rachel kneel in prayer each morning and night. She learned that Rachel felt prepared to convert but that Aaron strenuously objected. Less than two weeks into the journey, Eliza announced that she missed her husband and three-year-old son too much, and she abruptly returned to Richmond.[58]

An uneasy stalemate between Rachel and Aaron on religious issues continued for the remainder of Rachel's life. Rachel's threat of apostasy violated the deepest current of Jewish identity, for the survival of Judaism depended in some degree on Jews' ability to make conversion represent a crossing into another world. While Rachel might have viewed her awakening as a spiritual and intellectual evolution, Aaron could not see it that way. His wife was a Jew, and he vowed to remove their children from her care if she converted.[59] Rachel's dedication to family, home education, and domestic enlightenment—not to mention the fears and hopes she now harbored for her children's souls—made separation from them unthinkable. In 1834, the couple disagreed about what boarding school their eldest child, Marx, should attend. When Aaron overruled her choice (an Episcopal academy in Raleigh), he conveyed how little he trusted the woman whose expertise in educational matters he had never before questioned. That Aaron selected for Marx the Jesuit-run Georgetown College (where he believed his son's Jewishness would be less threatened) suggests the complexity of this family's conflict and of interfaith relations in antebellum America.[60]

Throughout this period, Rachel continued to attend church services at Saint James. She raised funds for the Ladies Working Society. She read the newly published letters of Hannah More, whose piety she admired and aspired to emulate. In private, Rachel prayed—Aaron would not tolerate seeing her in that posture—for her husband's conversion and for the chance to bring her children into the knowledge of Jesus. Rachel's condition mirrored that of many who have wrestled with their faith; however, the chasm that apostasy symbolized for Jews intensified her experience. Convinced of her sinfulness, certain of the way out, yet unable to take action, Rachel became severely anxious and depressed. She wrote: "It seems my mind would never again be what it has been—its cheerfulness is not innate—still no one sees, except those from whom I desire no concealment."[61]

Lucy Ann Lippitt knew. Catherine DeRosset knew. Aaron, their children, and several of Rachel's siblings all knew about her troubled state. Then, early in the summer of 1835, Rachel suffered yet another bout of malaria. Her doctor recommended recuperation on higher ground, and Rachel departed for a brother's house in Raleigh. She was bled, blistered, and purged. For weeks, her recovery was in doubt. When the danger finally passed, Rachel determined to claim the "freedom of conscience," as she said, to practice her faith.[62]

She told Ellen and Aaron as well as Catherine DeRosset that she would appeal to her father and entreat "his forgiveness, his indulgence, and his sanction to pursue the course which [her] feelings and convictions dictated." Did not the Mordecai covenant mandate respect and tolerance for believers of other persuasions than one's own? Jacob himself had once said it was "the right of every man to decide for himself on a subject so important as his religious faith." Her father's "sanction[,] once obtained," Rachel reasoned, would allow "hope for that of [her] husband." Aaron would almost certainly defer to her father as a Jewish scholar, congregational leader, and defender of the faith.[63]

Rachel's action is a dramatic testament both to her power and to its limits. She grew up in a household where her intellect was encouraged, her judgment respected, and her abilities rewarded by men and women alike. In the Mordecais' academy, she worked side by side with her father and brothers and gained a sense of real accomplishment. Her ideal of enlightened domesticity wove together family and intellectual life in ways that depended on mutual respect and cooperation between the sexes. It was a fortunate history for any woman of that time. And yet Rachel exercised her authority within a system of affectionate patriarchy by the grace and goodwill of the most important men in her life. Now she hoped to draw on her father's rich store of loving respect to enhance her position vis-à-vis her husband, whose response to her Christian faith seemed to threaten the very notion of enlightened partnership.[64]

Instead, Rachel's entreaty outraged her father. By the 1830s, he had become acutely conscious of the dangers of assimilation. Of his thirteen children, three had married non-Jews, one had converted, and many appeared likely to remain single. Only two had married within the faith. Now, the daughter of his heart stood ready, as he thought, to betray her God. In a manner typical of converts and well calculated to insult Jacob, Rachel starkly contrasted her beliefs to those she was leaving behind. In her letter to him, she underscored "the wretched state in which most of the nation calling themselves Israelites . . . lived, without religion of any kind and without God in the world."[65] Within days, seventy-three-year-old Jacob, himself in ill health, set off from Richmond to confront Rachel.

It was, she later said, a "soul-harrowing" scene. From his waistcoat, he pulled her letter asking his blessing on her apostasy. Then, "uttering a malediction on its contents . . . and almost on the writer," he "tore it . . . frantically into a thousand pieces." Never had Rachel seen him this way, "almost a maniac, feeling himself bound by the [Jewish] law to utter curses against his apostate child, while yet his heart yearned toward her." Rachel was willing to do anything to bring the interview to a close. Falling to her knees, she swore: "[I will never] adopt any faith but that of my fathers. . . . I will lay aside the writings of men and adhere to my Bible alone."[66]

Jacob wanted Rachel explicitly to renounce Christ, but here her brothers, George and Augustus Mordecai, stepped forward and begged him to be still. Rachel's pledge was all he could require, they said, and finally Jacob relented. Writing to her stepmother, Rachel castigated herself. "Blind, wicked, presumptuous, how can I hope for forgiveness?" she asked. But the self-recrimination mixed with anger and betrayal. Pressed to revoke her "inmost thoughts," the product of a decade of "study and mature reflection," she had been "denied the power" to act on her convictions by the men she most loved.[67]

Between the agonizing events of 1835 and her death three years later, Rachel battled "darkness" and despair. She prayed secretly in her room over the twenty-seventh chapter of the Book of Proverbs: "Boast not thyself of tomorrow; for thou knowest not what a day may bring forth." Even more dangerously, she sometimes spoke to her children about Jesus, provoking Aaron. When her sister Ellen announced that she, too, looked for salvation in Jesus Christ, Rachel's alarm almost overshadowed her joy. "My mind has been torn, my spirit broken," Rachel told Ellen, and she said that she could not bear the thought of Ellen's suffering the same "miseries." Yet Ellen proved a comfort as the toll on Rachel's marriage grew. Rachel could no longer speak openly with Aaron about her beliefs; "It occasions him," she said, "to use such sinful expressions in his opposition to and disavowal of my sentiments." Rachel wrote to Ellen of Jacob: "[He is in] every other respect . . . as kind to me as formerly, but this discordance forms a sad barrier to our happiness. You say truly that even our thoughts would not be free were it in the power of man to control them, and yet the want of toleration is condemned as an evil and an absurdity, but do we not feel it my sister in as full force as ever it was exercised short of torture?" Thenceforth, the sisters wrote secretly.[68]

Two years later, Rachel received word that Jacob Mordecai was dying. Business detained Aaron, but Rachel and two of their daughters left Wilmington in hopes of reaching Jacob's bedside before he breathed his last. During the journey, Rachel herself fell ill. Having traveled two days, she reached Petersburg, Virginia, home of her brother Samuel and her sister Ellen. Rachel could scarcely whisper. When the doctor confirmed that nothing remained to be done, she recognized that death stood near.

Referring to her religious "impressions" and "wishes," Rachel asked to be buried in the nearby Petersburg churchyard. Would she now like to see a minister? Ellen asked. Fearful of offending Aaron, Rachel hesitated. Ellen became earnest. "My dear Rachel," she cried, "you have done your duty to your husband[,] do not now deny yourself the comfort you desire." Rachel assented, but when the priest arrived and asked whether she wished to receive baptism, Rachel again demurred. According to Ellen, she said she could not leave "such a thorn" in Aaron's "bosom." But, after prayers, she said in deliberate tones: "Let me die a Christian." So ended the attenuated conversion of Rachel Mordecai Lazarus. Jacob, who lingered for ten weeks more, never learned of his daughter's death, but her children, siblings, nieces, and nephews would feel its impact and struggle over its implications for decades. One sibling wrote: "This must I say . . . that our family has never been the same in point of union, happiness, and I will even add, respectability, since the spirit of proselytism entered it."[69]

MUCH HAS BEEN WRITTEN on the history of evangelical awakening in America and the South. Scholars have debated its conservative and liberal aspects, weighed its individualistic and communal character, counted its achievements in terms of church membership rolls, and parsed its impact on the household, slavery, race, and gender relations. Writing from the perspective of Jewish studies, Amos Funkenstein has urged scholars to avoid the "dialectical pitfalls" in which the "essential" is opposed to the "acquired" (or the authentic to the assimilated, the loyal to the traitorous) in Jewish history. Rather, he suggested examining the outcomes of Jews' engagement with their times. From either perspective, to be understood historically, conversion must be studied not merely as a matter of individual choice or mass movement, but as a process inseparable from families, communities, and the intellectual and emotional lives of men and women.[70]

Rachel Mordecai Lazarus's story is a reminder of how much more complex lived religion could be than the dichotomized narratives historians have tended to offer suggest. This urban, slaveholding, southern, Jewish, and Christian woman's life, which spanned the end of the early republic and the beginning of the antebellum era, unfolds on a stage littered with historiographical props. Assimilation and resistance, individual choice and heritage (or consent and descent, in Werner Sollors's terms), personal quest and communal longings, intellect and feeling, independence and submission to earthly and heavenly male figures, and insider and outsider status all vie for the spotlight. And yet what emerges is a sense of the contradictory pieces from which real lives were constructed and religious lives experienced. Obviously, religious identity was fluid. But it was not the easy matter such a word connotes. In the life of Rachel Mordecai Lazarus, we see spiritual life inseparable from family tradition, filial duty, romantic love, friendship, emotional need, intellectual understanding, and social status. At times, historians tend to count and label converts (whether Jewish apostates, Methodists, Baptists, or Episcopalians), putting them on a shelf to then examine, with the implication that there they shall ever remain. Within such a framework, Rachel's story becomes absurd, as would the experiences of many others. How, for instance, should the intellectual, evangelical Rachel be "counted"? As a Jew? An Episcopalian?

That would depend on when one did the counting. Although conversion narratives and the literature of missiology implicitly rank converts' destinations over their religious origins, it would be a mistake to privilege her deathbed identity over that of the proud "Jewess" so admired by fellow Jews a decade earlier.[71] Historians, whether they celebrated the spreading of the Word or saw in its spread something else—a democratic impulse, an independent American identity—have sometimes followed the missionaries.[72] Over the past generation, scholars more interested in subordinate groups have often swung in the opposite direction, critiquing the missionary effort and sometimes calling converts to task for what they may have left behind.[73] Yet so much of spiritual life is not "But now I see," but rather "Now I see differently" or "How do I see now what I could not see then?" Captive to our own notions of self-improvement and the accretion of wisdom, the latest model may seem better than the last. But telling Rachel's and her family's story has meant watching those who changed their religious affiliation and granting the same respect to them as to those who sustained or adapted the one they grew up with, and to those who never figured out what they felt about God.

Rachel's biography, entwined with that of her family, raises questions for religious historians about people who resisted conversion or who wavered in and out of expressions of faith. Were all such individual shifts taken into account, how would the church membership numbers look? Rachel's narrative is suggestive of what might be found—fluctuating identities, family conflict, empowerment and repression, and plain wonder at faith working through lives—if official religious records were more yielding.[74]

What, if anything, about this story is southern? Rachel spent almost her entire life in small towns and cities in the Upper South. Her family belonged to an ethnic and religious minority that was just as much a minority in the North until the 1840s, when greater numbers of Jews emigrated from Germany. Her male relatives were shopkeepers, merchants, educators, lawyers, doctors, and military officers. Nearly all owned slaves, but only one of her brothers, an attorney who married into North Carolina's planter aristocracy in 1817, was a large-scale planter during Rachel's lifetime. A handful of Jews, some kin to the Mordecais, had settled in Richmond, but Rachel's friends were chiefly Gentiles, well-off urban slaveholders. One of her most important relationships was with an evangelical Rhode Island woman. Rachel's greatest intellectual influence was a popular Anglo-Irish novelist, children's author, and pedagogical theorist with whom she corresponded for more than twenty years. And Rachel—before, during, and after her spiritual time of trial—looked to the family and cultivated household as her own field of achievement and as the cultural center of an empowered American nation.

Though they go somewhat against the themes of regional exceptionalism, none of these aspects of Rachel's existence are wholly unfamiliar to scholars of southern history, southern religious history, or southern women's history in the period of the 1780s to the 1830s.[75] Taken together, Rachel's ethnicity, intellect, and cultivation—side by side with her conversion—suggest the absurdity of reducing the southern landscape to one of plantation slavery and poor white evangelical Protestants uninterested in intellectual life. However significant those elements were, at least up to the period of Rachel's death in 1838, the Mordecais and those with whom they associated had yet to conceive of the region as separate from the nation to which it belonged.

Rachel Mordecai Lazarus's remains lie beneath a gentle slope above the old Blandford Episcopal Church in Petersburg, Virginia. That she was buried there spoke volumes about the religious experiences that set her against husband and father and created such a rift in her family. But in 1838, these matters were too overwhelming or contested to be engraved into stone. Rachel's epitaph harkens to her lifelong passion for a home where she could express her intellect, share it with a wider world through education and friendships, and thereby take part in the larger liberal project of individual self-formation, always filtered through family and community.

> Endowed with superior talents
> and the most estimable virtues
> She was an ornament to Society
> and a blessing to her domestic circle.[76]

Of course there was more. For the last years of her life, Rachel inhabited a space of prayer and seeking, reaching for God, knowing "not what a day may bring forth."

Notes

Abbreviations

AJA	Jacob Rader Marcus Center, American Jewish Archives, Hebrew Union College, Cincinnati, Ohio
AM	Alfred Mordecai
AMP	Alfred Mordecai Papers, Manuscript Division, Library of Congress, Washington, D.C.
CMP	Caroline Mordecai Plunkett
DRFP	DeRosset Family Papers, Southern Historical Collection, University of North Carolina, Chapel Hill, N.C.
EM	Ellen Mordecai
JM	Jacob Mordecai
JMP	Jacob Mordecai Papers, Rare Books, Manuscripts, and Special Collections Library, Duke University, Durham, N.C.
LMFP	Little Mordecai Family Papers, North Carolina Division of Archives and History, Raleigh, N.C.
MFP	Mordecai Family Papers, Southern Historical Collection, University of North Carolina, Chapel Hill, N.C.
MM	Moses Mordecai
MYFP	Myers Family Papers, Virginia Historical Society, Richmond, Va.
PMP	Pattie Mordecai Papers, North Carolina Division of Archives and History, Raleigh, N.C.
RM	Rachel Mordecai
RML	Rachel Mordecai Lazarus
SM	Samuel Mordecai
Sol	Sol Mordecai

1. Ps. 116:13–14, quoted in RML to Catherine DeRosset, August 1, 1835, DRFP. On the stages of the conversion process, see Lewis R. Rambo, *Understanding Religious Conversion* (New Haven: Yale University Press, 1993). For a full treatment of Rachel's life within her broader family's history, see Emily Bingham, *Mordecai: An Early American Family* (New York: Hill & Wang, 2003).

2. Rambo, *Understanding Religious Conversion*, 2. Some historians and literary scholars have used "conversion" in other ways, in relation to racial attitudes (Fred C. Hobson, *But Now I See: The White Southern Racial Conversion Narrative* [Baton Rouge: Louisiana State University Press, 1999]). Of course, the seminal early study is William James, *Varieties of Religious Experience: A Study in Human Behavior* (1902; reprint, New York: Routledge, 2002).

3. Significant archival collections about the Mordecai family, which together include thousands of documents, are located at the University of North Carolina, Duke University, the North Carolina Department of Archives and History, the Virginia Historical Society, the Library of Congress, and the Jacob Rader Marcus Center of the American Jewish Archives.

4. Allen C. Guelzo, "God's Designs: The Literature of the Colonial Revivals of Religion, 1735–1760," in *New Directions in American Religious History*, eds. Harry S. Stout and D. G. Hart (New York: Oxford University Press, 1997), 147–48. Other works that call for an exercise like this conversion study include an essay by Martin Marty that is cited by Guelzo ("Explaining the Rise of Fundamentalism," *Chronicle of Higher Education*, October 28, 1992, A56) and Lewis R. Rambo's "The Phenomenology of Conversion" (*Handbook of Religious Conversion*, eds. H. Newton Malony and Samuel Southard [Birmingham: Religious Education Press, 1992], 256–57).

5. An important addition to the literature is Elisheva Carlebach, *Divided Souls: Converts from Judaism in Germany, 1500–1750* (New Haven: Yale University Press, 2001). For treatments of assimilation, see Todd Endelman, *Radical Assimilation in English Jewish History, 1656–1945* (Bloomington: Indiana University Press, 1990); Endelman, ed., *Jewish Apostasy in the Modern World* (New York: Holmes & Meier, 1987); Michael Ragussis, *Figures of Conversion: "The Jewish Question" and English National Identity* (Durham: Duke University Press, 1995); Paula E. Hyman, *Gender and Assimilation in Modern Jewish History: The Roles and Representations of Women* (Seattle: University of Washington Press, 1995); Deborah Hertz, "Women at the Edge of Judaism: Female Converts in Germany, 1600–1750," in *Jewish Assimilation, Acculturation, and Accommodation: Past Traditions, Current Issues, and Future Prospects*, ed. Menachem Mor (Lanham, Md.: University Press of America, 1992), 87–109; and Steven M. Lowenstein, *The Berlin Jewish Community: Enlightenment, Family, and Crisis, 1770–1830* (New York: Oxford University Press, 1994). Two helpful formulations of the problem of assimilation can be found in Werner Sollors, *Beyond Ethnicity: Consent and Descent in American Culture* (New York: Oxford University Press, 1986), and Amos Funkenstein, "The Dialectics of Assimilation," *Jewish Social Studies* 1 (1995): 1–14.

6. The Museum of the Southern Jewish Experience in Utica, Mississippi, was dedicated in 1989 (⟨http://www.msje.org/⟩). The Southern Jewish Historical Society has published an annual journal, *Southern Jewish History*, since 1998. For a survey of the field of southern Jewish studies, see Stephen Whitfield, "In the High Cotton," *Southern Jewish History* 4 (2001): 123–44. See also Leah Elizabeth Hagedorn, "Jews and the American South, 1858–1905" (Ph.D. diss., University of North Carolina at Chapel Hill, 1999); Abraham J. Peck, "That Other 'Peculiar Institution': Jews and Judaism in the Nineteenth-Century South," *Modern Judaism* 7 (1987): 99–114; Stephen Whitfield, "Jews and Other Southerners," in *Voices of Jacob, Hands of Esau: Jews in American Life and Thought* (Hamden, Conn.: Archon Books, 1984), 211–29; and Leonard Rogoff, "Is the Jew White? The Racial Place of the Southern Jew," *American Jewish History* 85 (1997): 195–230. Several fine community studies have also been conducted, among them Myron Berman, *Richmond's Jewry, 1769–1976: Shabbat in Shockoe* (Charlottesville: Published for the Richmond Jewish Community Council by the University Press of Virginia, 1979), and Leonard Rogoff, *Homelands: Southern Jewish Identity in Durham and Chapel Hill, North Carolina* (Tuscaloosa: University of Alabama Press, 2001). In the popular realm, see also Alfred Uhry, *Driving Miss Daisy* (New York: Theater Communications Group, 1988); Uhry, *Last Night of Ballyhoo* (New York: Theater Communications Group, 1997); and Mike Dewitt's documentary, "Delta Jews," which aired on PBS in 1999. A number of memoirs and family histories have attracted attention: Eli N. Evans, *The Lonely Days Were Sundays: Reflections of a Jewish Southerner* (Jackson: University Press of Mississippi, 1994) and *The Provincials: A Personal History of Jews in the South*, rev. ed. (New York: Free Press, 1994); Stella Suberman, *The Jew Store* (Chapel Hill: Algonquin Books, 1998); Leta Weiss Marks, *Time's Tapestry: Four Generations of a New Orleans Family* (Baton Rouge: Louisiana State University Press, 1997); and Louis D. Rubin, *My Father's People: A Family of Southern Jews* (Baton Rouge: Louisiana State University Press, 2002). Eli N. Evans's *Judah P. Benjamin: The Jewish Confederate* (New York: Free Press, 1988) is an important exception to the emphasis on post–Civil War southern Jewry.

7. A prominent Philadelphia Jewish family, the Gratzes, have left large archival collections, as well. The most helpful biography to date of an antebellum Jewish woman is Dianne Ashton's *Rebecca Gratz: Women and Judaism in Antebellum America* (Detroit: Wayne State University Press, 1997).

8. See, especially, Evans, *The Provincials*; Hagedorn, "Jews and the American South"; Gerald Sorin, *A Time for Building: The Third Migration, 1880–1920* (Baltimore: Johns Hopkins University Press, 1992), 137–38, 152–61; and the "Alsace to America" exhibit at the Museum of the Southern Jewish Experience in Utica, Mississippi.

9. The Mordecais figure prominently in Anne C. Rose, *Beloved Strangers: Interfaith Families in Nineteenth-Century America* (Cambridge, Mass.: Harvard University Press, 2001). Myron Berman contemplates the family's range of Jewish identification in *The Last of the Jews?* (Lanham, Md.: University Press of America, 1998).

10. The family tensions evangelical conversion sometimes sparked are discussed in

Christine Leigh Heyrman, *Southern Cross: The Beginnings of the Bible Belt* (New York: Alfred A. Knopf, 1997), 117–29, 140–41. On interfaith marriages and family conflict in the early antebellum period, see Rose, *Beloved Strangers*, 14–47.

11. Esther Mordecai Cohen married Jacob I. Cohen. See Berman, *Richmond's Jewry*, 1–2, 6–11.

12. In 1809, after an open debate, the North Carolina legislature seated Jacob Henry, who had been elected as a representative. For restrictions in the 1780s and the Henry case, see Eli Faber, *A Time for Planting: The First Migration, 1654–1820* (Baltimore: Johns Hopkins University Press, 1992), 129–30, 139.

13. See Henry F. May's *The Enlightenment in America* (New York: Oxford University Press, 1976) and Dorinda Outram, *The Enlightenment* (New York: Cambridge University Press, 1995). On the consolidation of bourgeois culture in the nineteenth century, see Richard L. Bushman, *The Refinement of America: Persons, Houses, Cities* (New York: Vintage Books, 1992); Jack Larkin, *The Reshaping of Everyday Life, 1790–1840* (New York: Harper Perennial, 1988); Mary P. Ryan, *Cradle of the Middle Class: The Family in Oneida County, New York, 1790–1860* (New York: Cambridge University Press, 1981); Burton Bledstein, *The Culture of Professionalism: The Middle Class and the Development of Higher Education in America* (New York: W. W. Norton, 1976); Jan Lewis, *Pursuits of Happiness: Family and Values in Jefferson's Virginia* (New York: Cambridge University Press, 1983); Stephen Mintz, *Prison of Expectations: The Family in Victorian Culture* (New York: New York University Press, 1983); and Leonore Davidoff and Catherine Hall, *Family Fortunes: Men and Women of the English Middle Class, 1780–1850* (Chicago: University of Chicago Press, 1987). The Mordecais were among the vanguard of Jews who embraced transatlantic bourgeois domesticity, and in this they closely resembled their German coreligionists. See Paula Hyman, "Introduction: Perspectives on the Evolving Jewish Family," in *The Jewish Family: Myths and Reality*, eds. Steven Martin Cohen and Paula Hyman, (New York: Holmes & Meier, 1986), 3, 8, 11, and Marion A. Kaplan, *The Making of the Jewish Middle Class: Women, Family, and Identity in Imperial Germany* (New York: Oxford University Press, 1991).

14. On true religion, see EM to Sol, September 19, 1821, JMP. She wrote: "All religions are equally good and that a strict adherence to what our consciences tells us is right, is the conduct most acceptable to our maker." See "Virtue," JM to MM et al., July 20, 1796, MYFP.

15. JM to MM et al., July 20, 1796, MYFP. The nature of religious observance in the Mordecai family and how it changed over time cannot be precisely determined, in spite of the existence of extensive family papers. The Mordecais did not keep kosher. The women had no access to a mikvah. It is not likely that their southern–born sons were circumcised, as there is no record that a mohel visited the region or that they traveled to obtain the service elsewhere. Religious holidays were observed, though not always in a fully orthodox manner. The Sabbath was not strictly observed, at least not during the years when Jacob

was a justice of the peace (court met on Saturdays) and when the family operated a school (Saturday classes were held and other duties performed).

16. For the tenor of well-off North Carolinians' religious views in the last decades of the eighteenth century, see Richard Rankin, *Ambivalent Churchmen and Evangelical Church-women: The Religion of the Episcopal Elite of North Carolina, 1800–1860* (Columbia: University of South Carolina Press, 1993), 11–22.

17. JM to MM et al., July 20, 1796, MYFP; RM to Maria Edgeworth, August 7, 1815, in *The Education of the Heart: The Correspondence of Rachel Mordecai Lazarus and Maria Edgeworth*, ed. Edgar E. MacDonald (Chapel Hill: University of North Carolina Press, 1977), 6; RM to SM, July 27, 1817, JMP. Relations between Rachel and the Anglo-Irish writer Maria Edgeworth stretched over three decades. The correspondence is collected in MacDonald, *Education of the Heart*. The novel Edgeworth penned in response is *Harrington* (1817). For more on that work, see Ragussis, *Figures of Conversion*. Historian Gerald Sorin, for instance, has judged Jews' position in early America in comparison to other places as "the freest in the world" (*Tradition Transformed: The Jewish Experience in America* [Baltimore: Johns Hopkins University Press, 1997], 16).

18. The term "enlightened domesticity" has much in common with other ideological models that have received attention from historians of American women. It also bears important similarities to the much debated concept of *bildung* (enlightened self-culture) that characterized German emancipationist thought during the same period. The literature on both is extensive. See, for instance, Linda K. Kerber, *Women of the Republic: Intellect and Ideology in Revolutionary America* (Chapel Hill: University of North Carolina Press, 1980); Rosemarie Zagarry, "Morals, Manners, and the Republican Mother," *American Quarterly* 44 (1992): 192–215; Ruth Bloch, "American Feminine Ideas in Transition: The Rise of the Moral Mother, 1785–1815," *Feminist Studies* 4 (1978): 102–26; Mary Kelley, "Reading Women/Women Reading: The Making of Learned Women in Antebellum America," *Journal of American History* 183 (1996): 401–24; David Sorkin, *The Transformation of German Jewry, 1780–1840* (New York: Oxford University Press, 1987); Hyman, *Gender and Assimilation in Modern Jewish History*; and Jonathan M. Hess, *German Jews and the Claims of Modernity* (New Haven: Yale University Press, 2002).

19. On Rachel's teaching, see Emily Bingham and Penny Richards, "The Female Academy and Beyond: Three Mordecai Sisters at Work in the Old South," in *Neither Lady nor Slave: Working Women in the Old South*, eds. Susanna Delfino and Michele Gillespie (Chapel Hill: University of North Carolina Press, 2002), 174–97.

20. RM, "Memories," MYFP; [EM], "Past Days: A Simple Story for Children," 52, MYFP. For enrollment, see Penny Leigh Richards, "'A Thousand Images, Painfully Pleasing': Complicating Histories of the Mordecai School, Warrenton, North Carolina, 1809–1818" (Ph.D. diss., University of North Carolina at Chapel Hill, 1996), 43 and fig. 3.4.

21. SM to RM, May 4, 1808, MFP.

22. EM to SM, September 7, 1810, MFP; SM to RM, October 3, 1810, JMP. For the growing influence of evangelicalism on genteel southern culture, see Lewis, *The Pursuit of Happiness*; May, *Enlightenment in America*, 327–34; and Rankin, *Ambivalent Churchmen*.

23. RM to SM, September 24, 1810, PMP; SM to RM, October 3, 1810, JMP; RM to SM, July 28, 1807, JMP. For another example of better-off southerners ridiculing evangelicals, see Heyrman, *Southern Cross*, 35.

24. On Richmond Jews and religious practice, see Berman, *Richmond's Jewry*, 38–40. At the national level, orthodoxy may have been on the decline among American Jews (Faber, *A Time for Planting*, 123). For mentions of Passover, see, for instance, EM to SM, March 21, 1808, MFP; RM to SM, April 29, 1807, MFP; and RM to SM, April 21, 1807, JMP. For references to other holidays, see SM to MM, September 19, 1817, MFP, and note from JM in Julia Mordecai to Sol, August 10, 1817, MFP. For school activities and the Sabbath, see Richards, "A Thousand Images, Painfully Pleasing," 71, and RM to SM, May 8, 1814, MFP.

25. In a study based on late medieval Germany, one scholar has pointed out that "the repeated bitter experience of violent compulsion to baptism contributed to the absolute rejection of conversion by Jews of Ashkenaz and turned willing converts into renegade figures regarded with the greatest loathing and derision." He explains that "these Jews regarded baptism as a betrayal of communal values, a rejection of Jewish destiny," and in referring to converts, Jews employed "the term *meshummad*, from the root *shmad*, meaning utter destruction" (Carlebach, *Divided Souls*, 12).

26. JM, "Introduction to the New Testament," n.d., AJA; JM to SM, November 29, 1810, MFP.

27. JM to SM, November 29, 1810, MFP; SM to Sol, December 17, 1810, JMP.

28. JM to SM, November 28, 1817, JMP; Rebecca Myers Mordecai to RML, February 2, 1824, MFP. The selling price was $10,000 (Bingham and Richards, "The Female Academy and Beyond," 174). A number of Jacob's religious writings have survived. See, for example, JM, "Discourse Delivered at the Consecration of the Synagogue of the [Richmond, Va.] Hebrew Congregation Beth Shalome," September 15, 1822, Mordecai Family Papers, American Jewish Historical Society, Center for Jewish History, New York, N.Y. For the concept of converting (or radically awakening) to one's own faith, see Rambo, *Understanding Religious Conversion*, 2; Michael Graubart Levin, *Journey to Tradition: The Odyssey of a Born-Again Jew* (Hoboken: Ktav Publishing House, 1986); and Lynn Davidman and Arthur L. Greil, "Gender and the Experience of Conversion: The Case of 'Returnees' to Modern Orthodox Judaism," *Sociology of Religion* 54 (1993): 87.

29. EM Journal, June 28, 1820, MFP.

30. Ida Brooks Kellam and Elizabeth Frances McKoy, *St. James Church Historical Records* (Wilmington, N.C.: n.p., 1965), 1:35–36; Tony Wrenn, *Wilmington, North Carolina: An Annotated Architectural and Historical Portrait* (Charlottesville: Published for the Junior League of Wilmington, N.C., by the University Press of Virginia, 1984), 171.

31. Rankin, *Ambivalent Churchmen*, 57–59; and RM to EM, January 30, 1814; RML to

EM, June 22, 1823; RM to SM, January 30, 1814; and RML to EM, April 26, 1823, all in MFP.

32. Rachel reestablished contact with Edgeworth following her marriage, and the letters between the two women picked up in number and length. See MacDonald, *Education of the Heart*. Just how little sympathy existed between the mistress and her slaves is suggested by the story of the cook, whom Rachel called "Saint Sophia." After a year of difficulty, Aaron finally sold the slave, who had announced, Rachel said, that "the great difference in our religions made it impossible for her to be contented with me." Rachel apparently interpreted Sophia's piety as an excuse for insubordination—and perhaps it was. Or perhaps Sophia wanted time to attend church or prayer meetings and had been denied permission. RML to EM, June 23, 1822, MFP.

33. On Rachel and domesticity, see Sara Ann Hays to RML, September 12, 1833, AMP; RML to CMP, November 11, 1822, MFP; RML to EM, September 14, 1823, MFP; RML to EM, April 26, 1823, MFP; and Julia Mordecai to George Washington Mordecai, August 4, 1823, LMFP.

34. RML to CMP, November 11, 1822, MFP.

35. RML to Lucy Ann Lippitt, October 28, 1828, MFP.

36. RML to EM, October 5, 1823, MFP.

37. Aaron Lazarus to Richard C. Moore (Episcopal bishop of Virginia), July 1, 1823, JMP.

38. RML to EM, September 14, 1823, MFP; RML to EM, November 8, 1823, JMP; RML to JM, October 10, 1824, MFP; Ps. 42:1, KJV.

39. Gary Phillip Zola, *Isaac Harby of Charleston, 1788–1828: Jewish Reformer and Intellectual* (Tuscaloosa: University of Alabama Press, 1994); A Congregationalist of Richmond, Virginia [JM], "Remarks on Harby's Discourse Delivered in Charleston, [South Carolina,] on the 21st of November 1825 Before the Reformed Society of Israelites on Their First Anniversary," [January 1826], AJA.

40. Rankin, *Ambivalent Churchmen*, 27–60; and EM to Sol, February 12, 1818; EM to SM, February 25, 1818; and RML to CMP, March 24, 1822, all in JMP.

41. RML to EM, May 4, 1823, MFP.

42. RML to Sol, June 28, 1821, PMP; RML to EM, May 7, 1828, MFP.

43. Donald G. Mathews, *Religion in the Old South* (Chicago: University of Chicago Press, 1977), xvi–xvii, 19–20, 42; Rankin, *Ambivalent Churchmen*, 31, 46–48; Heyrman, *Southern Cross*, 3–5. Susan Juster examined the gender implications of evangelical language in "'In a Different Voice': Male and Female Narratives of Religious Conversion in Post-revolutionary America," *American Quarterly* 41 (1989): 34–62.

44. RML to EM, April 16, 1827, MFP.

45. "St. James Church History," 2–3, DRFP; Leora Hiatt McEachern, *History of St. James Parish* (Wilmington, N.C.: n.p., 1983), 41; Ann Hill to Catherine "Kitty" DeRosset, August 6, 1817, DRFP; Eliza Hassell to Catherine DeRosset (Kitty's mother), August 26, 1826, DRFP. Many women in this period found an outlet for social and political action

through church networks. See, for instance, the activities outlined in Suzanne Lebsock, *The Free Women of Petersburg: Status and Culture in a Southern Town, 1784–1860* (New York: W. W. Norton, 1984), and in Ryan, *Cradle of the Middle Class*. A critical interpretation of the effect of evangelical religion on women's lives in a slightly later period is found in Jean E. Friedman, *The Enclosed Garden: Women and Community in the Evangelical South, 1830–1900* (Chapel Hill: University of North Carolina Press, 1985).

46. Joseph Crool, *The Restoration of Israel* (London: B. R. Goakman, 1814); RML to EM, April 16, 1827, MFP.

47. The literature on anti-Semitism is massive. For a taste of recent work, see Carlebach, *Divided Souls*; James Carroll, *Constantine's Sword: The Church and the Jews, A History* (Boston: Houghton Mifflin, 2001); and Anna Sapir Abulafia, *Religious Violence between Christians and Jews: Medieval Roots, Modern Perspectives* (New York: Palgrave, 2002).

48. See Jonathan D. Sarna, "The American Jewish Response to Nineteenth-Century Christian Missions," *Journal of American History* 68 (1981): 35–51; Lee M. Friedman, "The American Society for Meliorating the Condition of the Jews and Joseph S. C. F. Frey," in *Early American Jews*, ed. Lee M. Friedman (Cambridge, Mass.: Harvard University Press, 1934), 96–112; and Lorman Ratner, "Conversion of the Jews and Pre–Civil War Reform," *American Quarterly* 13 (1961): 43–54. While there were formal missionary efforts to Jews from 1816 onward, they expanded dramatically later in the century when premillennialist eschatology spread and Protestant missionary organizations viewed the restoration of Israel as a priority. See Faber, *A Time for Planting*, 132, and Yaakov Ariel, *Evangelizing the Chosen People: Missions to the Jews in America, 1880–2000* (Chapel Hill: University of North Carolina Press, 2000).

49. Rambo, *Understanding Religious Conversion*, 51–52.

50. RML to EM, April 16, 1827, MFP; Rankin, *Ambivalent Churchmen*, 38, 42–43, 45–46; Obituary for Catherine DeRosset, *Wilmington Advertiser*, March 17, 1837, 4. Women in the second half of pregnancy were especially susceptible to malaria, and its effect on their health could be devastating (Sally McMillen, *Motherhood in the Old South: Pregnancy, Childbirth, and Infant Rearing* [Baton Rouge: Louisiana State University Press, 1990], 48–50, 119–20, 125–26).

51. RML to EM, October 13, 1828, JMP; Mary Orme (for RML) to EM, September 26, 1828, MFP.

52. RML to EM, October 13, 1828, JMP; Mary Orme (for RML) to EM, September 26, 1828, MFP; Catherine DeRosset Daybook, May 31, 1817, Moses Ashley Curtis Papers, Southern Historical Collection, University of North Carolina, Chapel Hill, N.C.

53. RML to Lucy Ann Lippitt, October 26, 1828, MFP. On the bonds formed between women during childbirth in this time, see Judith Walker Leavitt, *Brought to Bed: Childbearing in America, 1750–1950* (New York: Oxford University Press, 1986), 95–98.

54. RML to EM, February 15, October 4, 1830, MFP.

55. For Berlin's late-eighteenth-century *salonnieres*, see Deborah Hertz, "Seductive Conversion in Berlin, 1770–1809," in Endelman, *Jewish Apostasy in the Modern World*,

48–82; Hannah Arendt, *Rahel Varnhagen: The Life of a Jewish Woman*, trans. Richard Winston and Clara Winston (New York: Harcourt Brace Jovanovich, 1974); and Amos Elon, *The Pity of It All: A History of Jews in Germany, 1743–1933* (New York: Metropolitan Books, 2002), 65–100. For the interweaving of Enlightenment and Jewish culture within Germany's Jewish middle classes, see Kaplan, *The Making of the Jewish Middle Class*, and Sorkin, *The Transformation of German Jewry*. For American Jewish women's activities in the late nineteenth and early twentieth centuries, see, for instance, Faith Rogow, *Gone to Another Meeting: The National Council of Jewish Women, 1893–1993* (Tuscaloosa: University of Alabama Press, 1993), and Joyce Antler, "Zion in Our Hearts: Henrietta Szold and the American Jewish Women's Movement, 1912–1945," in *American Jewish Women's History: A Reader*, ed. Pamela S. Nadell (New York: New York University Press, 2003), 129–52.

56. Rachel's religious bibliography included Thomas Chalmers (1780–1847), a Scottish theologian who embraced Evangelicalism; Alexander Keith (1791–1880), who later visited Palestine as part of an effort to evangelize the Jews; and Thomas Hartwell Horne (1780–1862), author of *Introduction to the Critical Study and Knowledge of the Holy Scriptures* (1818). See RML to EM, October 23, 1836, MFP. Jacob Mordecai attacked Keith's arguments in his "Remarks to Miss [Harriet] Martineau's Tract entitled Providence as Manifested through Israel and on the Writings of the Reverend Alexander Keith Entitled Evidence of the Truth of the Christian Religion," n.d., AJA.

57. AM to EM, May 24, 1833, AMP.

58. AM to EM, June 7, 1833, AMP; RML to EM, June 5, 1833, JMP.

59. EM to Sol and CMP, July 3, 1838, MFP.

60. RML to EM, May 18, 1834, MFP; RML to CMP, September 14, 1834, MFP. Rose touches on the patience exhibited by the American Catholic Church toward interfaith unions; such an attitude may have also characterized the church's educational institutions (*Beloved Strangers*, 100–109).

61. RML to EM, May 18, 1834, MFP; Emma Mordecai to RML, December 21, 1835, JMP; RML to EM, April 9, 1835, MFP; RML to EM, September 6, 1834, MFP. For a description of the kind of mutually empowering, spiritually empowered marriage that Rachel and other women of her circle might have prayed for, see Frederick A. Bode, "A Common Sphere: White Evangelicals and Gender in Antebellum Georgia," *Georgia Historical Quarterly* 79 (1995): 775–809.

62. Aaron Lazarus to SM, May 3, 1835, JMP; George Washington Mordecai to SM, June 14, 1835, MFP; Henry Mordecai and RML to EM, July 29, 1835, MFP.

63. JM to Sol, March 29, 1829, JMP; Henry Mordecai and RML to EM, July 29, 1835, MFP.

64. The term "affectionate patriarchy" is derived from Elizabeth Kowaleski-Wallace, *Their Fathers' Daughters: Hannah More, Maria Edgeworth, and Patriarchal Complicity* (New York: Oxford University Press, 1991).

65. Jacob Mordecai, in his response to the reformers in Charleston, defended orthodox

practices as the means of preventing Jews from disappearing into the "common mass" and thereby ceasing to be Jews (JM, "Remarks on Harby's Discourse," 3, AJA). See also RML to EM, September 18, 1836, MFP. Carlebach noted the tendency among Jewish converts to denigrate either their earlier beliefs or Jews in general (*Divided Souls*, 88).

66. RML to Rebecca Myers Mordecai, August 26, 1835, JMP.

67. Ibid.; RML to EM, June 26, 1836, MFP.

68. Prov. 27:1, KJV; RML to EM, December 28, 1835, June 26, August 21, 28, 1836, MFP; RML to Catherine DeRosset, August 1, 1835, DRFP.

69. SM to CMP and Sol, June 24, 1838, JMP; EM to CMP and Sol, July 3, 1838, JMP; Eliza K. Mordecai Myers to CMP, August 3, 1845, PMP. The legacy is discussed in part 4 of Bingham's *Mordecai*.

70. Funkenstein, "Dialectics of Assimilation," 4, 10.

71. Carlebach, *Divided Souls*, 88–123; Hugh T. Kerr and John M. Mulder, eds., *Famous Conversions* (Grand Rapids: Eerdmans, 1983), ix–xviii; Arthur F. Glasser, "Conversion in Judaism," in Malony and Southard, *Handbook of Religious Conversion*, 55–77; Gordon T. Smith, *Beginning Well: Christian Conversion and Authentic Transformation* (Downer's Grove, Ill.: InterVarsity Press).

72. Guelzo, "God's Designs," 142–47; Nathan O. Hatch, *The Democratization of American Christianity* (New Haven: Yale University Press, 1989).

73. Larry W. Hutaldo, "Convert, Apostate, or Apostle to the Nations: The 'Conversion' of Paul in Recent Scholarship," *Studies in Religion* 22 (1993): 273–84; Marc Galanter, *Cults: Faith, Healing, and Coercion* (New York: Oxford University Press, 1989); Larry D. Shinn, "Who Gets to Define Religion? The Conversion/Brainwashing Controversy," *Religious Studies Review* 19 (1993): 195–207.

74. In telling Rachel's story, I have sought to return to what Guelzo called "the affectional, the personal, and the mystical" that is integral to any conversion story and is "most compelling" to those undergoing it ("God's Designs," 147–48).

75. In 1954, Charles G. Sellers wrote that "the size and importance of the urban middle class in the Old South has yet to be fully appreciated" ("Who Were the Southern Whigs?" *American Historical Review* 59 [1953–54]: 341), but with most scholars focusing on the difference between the sections (and with middle-class values being viewed as northern), progress in that field has been slight. See, however, Keith C. Barton, "'Good Cooks and Washers': Slave Hiring, Domestic Labor, and the Market in Bourbon County, Kentucky," *Journal of American History* 84 (1997): 435–60. On women's lives, some historians have commented on the shared bourgeois values of early antebellum culture, North and South. See, for instance, Lebsock, *Free Women of Petersburg*; Victoria Bynum, *Unruly Women: The Politics of Sexual and Social Control in the Old South* (Chapel Hill: University of North Carolina Press, 1992); Jane Turner Censer, *North Carolina Planters and Their Children* (Baton Rouge: Louisiana State University Press, 1984); and Anya Jabour, *Marriage in the Early Republic: Elizabeth and William Wirt and the Companionate Ideal* (Balti-

more: Johns Hopkins University Press, 1998). In the realm of religious life, see Beth Barton Schweiger's *The Gospel Working Up: Progress and the Pulpit in Nineteenth-Century Virginia* (New York: Oxford University Press, 2000).

76. See Aaron Lazarus to EM, September 4, 7, 1838, JMP. Also see Rachel's obituary, *Wilmington Advertiser*, June 29, 1838.

For Further Reading

Ariel, Yaakov. *Evangelizing the Chosen People: Missions to the Jews in America, 1880–2000*. Chapel Hill: University of North Carolina Press, 2000.

Ashton, Dianne. *Rebecca Gratz: Women and Judaism in Antebellum America*. Detroit: Wayne State University Press, 1997.

Berman, Myron. *Richmond's Jewry, 1769–1976: Shabbat in Shockoe*. Charlottesville: Published for the Richmond Jewish Community Council by the University Press of Virginia, 1979.

Bingham, Emily. *Mordecai: An Early American Family*. New York: Hill & Wang, 2003.

Bingham, Emily, and Penny Richards. "The Female Academy and Beyond: Three Mordecai Sisters at Work in the Old South." In *Neither Lady nor Slave: Working Women in the Old South*, edited by Susanna Delfino and Michele Gillespie, 174–97. Chapel Hill: University of North Carolina Press, 2002.

Evans, Eli N. *The Lonely Days Were Sundays: Reflections of a Jewish Southerner*. Jackson: University Press of Mississippi, 1994.

———. *The Provincials: A Personal History of Jews in the South*. Rev. ed. New York: Free Press, 1994.

———. *Judah P. Benjamin: The Jewish Confederate*. New York: Free Press, 1988.

Faber, Eli. *A Time for Planting: The First Migration, 1654–1820*. Baltimore: Johns Hopkins University Press, 1992.

Guelzo, Allen C. "God's Designs: The Literature of the Colonial Revivals of Religion, 1735–1760." In *New Directions in American Religious History*, edited by Harry S. Stout and D. G. Hart, 141–72. New York: Oxford University Press, 1997.

Hagedorn, Leah Elizabeth. "Jews and the American South, 1858–1905." Ph.D. diss., University of North Carolina at Chapel Hill, 1999.

Hyman, Paula E. *Gender and Assimilation in Modern Jewish History: The Roles and Representations of Women*. Seattle: University of Washington Press, 1995.

James, William. *Varieties of Religious Experience: A Study in Human Behavior*. 1902. Reprint, New York: Routledge, 2002.

MacDonald, Edgar E., ed. *The Education of the Heart: The Correspondence of Rachel Mordecai Lazarus and Maria Edgeworth*. Chapel Hill: University of North Carolina Press, 1977.

Marks, Leta Weiss. *Time's Tapestry: Four Generations of a New Orleans Family*. Baton Rouge: Louisiana State University Press, 1997.

Peck, Abraham J. "That Other 'Peculiar Institution': Jews and Judaism in the Nineteenth-Century South." *Modern Judaism* 7 (1987): 99–114.

Rambo, Lewis R. *Understanding Religious Conversion*. New Haven: Yale University Press, 1993.

Richards, Penny Leigh. "'A Thousand Images, Painfully Pleasing': Complicating Histories of the Mordecai School, Warrenton, North Carolina, 1809–1818." Ph.D. diss., University of North Carolina at Chapel Hill, 1996.

Rogoff, Leonard. *Homelands: Southern Jewish Identity in Durham and Chapel Hill, North Carolina*. Tuscaloosa: University of Alabama Press, 2001.

———. "Is the Jew White? The Racial Place of the Southern Jew." *American Jewish History* 85 (1997): 195–230.

Rose, Anne C. *Beloved Strangers: Interfaith Families in Nineteenth-Century America*. Cambridge, Mass.: Harvard University Press, 2001.

Rubin, Louis D. *My Father's People: A Family of Southern Jews*. Baton Rouge: Louisiana State University Press, 2002.

Sarna, Jonathan D. "The American Jewish Response to Nineteenth-Century Christian Missions." *Journal of American History* 68 (1981): 35–51.

Sorin, Gerald. *Tradition Transformed: The Jewish Experience in America*. Baltimore: Johns Hopkins University Press, 1997.

Suberman, Stella. *The Jew Store*. Chapel Hill: Algonquin Books, 1998.

Whitfield, Stephen. "In the High Cotton." *Southern Jewish History* 4 (2001): 123–44.

———. "Jews and Other Southerners." In *Voices of Jacob, Hands of Esau: Jews in American Life and Thought*, 211–29. Hamden, Conn.: Archon Books, 1984.

Zola, Gary Phillip. *Isaac Harby of Charleston, 1788–1828: Jewish Reformer and Intellectual*. Tuscaloosa: University of Alabama Press, 1994.

4

KURT O. BERENDS

Confederate Sacrifice and the "Redemption" of the South

How did the Civil War shape Christianity in the Confederacy? Countless Confederates claimed divine favor for their cause, and many used the Christian message for political purposes. But it is equally clear that the politics of war changed southern Protestantism. During the Civil War, ministers transformed the Christian message in an effort to convert the army and to sanctify the cause. In the process, they recast doctrines, especially those related to salvation. More significantly, the fusion of Confederate identity with salvation made faith in the cause, and especially in death on behalf of the cause, into a talisman, or theological good-luck charm. No longer was Jesus' death the only efficacious death. Many southerners became convinced that death on behalf of the Confederacy was also salvific. In other words, both deaths offered a path to heaven. This refashioned faith provided Confederate armies with an endless supply of grist for the Confederate cause. Blaming Christianity for Confederate defeat, as some historians have done, requires a misunderstanding of how that faith changed and functioned in the war.

Three Views of Confederate Christianity

A number of historians have examined the ways in which religion determined the outcome of the war. Thus far, they have made three somewhat contradictory arguments. Some describe Christianity as central to the creation and sustenance of Confederate nationalism and morale. Others have maintained that basic Christian doctrines or features of the faith undermined any possibility of Confederate victory. A third group of scholars, finally, combines these two positions to argue that Christianity both supported and undermined the Confederacy.

James W. Silver's *Confederate Morale and Church Propaganda*, published in 1957, was one of the first books to argue that religious rhetoric both defined and supported the Confederate cause.[1] W. Harrison Daniel, Drew Gilpin Faust,

James McPherson, Kurt Berends, and, most recently, Steven Woodworth have all examined the contributions Christianity made to the Confederacy, especially to the men in the rank and file.[2] Collectively, these studies argue that the Christian faith fostered morale and increased discipline in the ranks; that it helped to forge a sense of nationalism; that the promise of eternal life encouraged bravery in the face of the enemy; and that revivals created a sense of camaraderie and unity among the soldiers. They reflect the nineteenth-century view of E. B. Lane, who, after hearing several sermons in camp, wrote home to his sister-in-law that he believed men who found religion "would . . . be better qualified to perform the duties and bear the hardships of a soldier's life."[3]

Other historians have suggested that Christian beliefs undermined Confederate success. These arguments fit broadly into two groups. One group of scholars focuses on slavery and argues that a large number of Confederates shared an underlying guilt over slavery—prompted by their faith—that sapped their conviction of the justness of their cause. Gaines M. Foster's "Guilt over Slavery: A Historigraphical Analysis" provides a superb overview of the evolution of this thesis.[4] In various fashions, Kenneth Stampp, Bell I. Wiley, C. Vann Woodward, Charles G. Sellers, William W. Freehling, and Drew Gilpin Faust have all made this argument. Southerners, they insist, questioned the morality of their peculiar institution. One finds few expressions of guilt over slavery, however, in the letters, diaries, or theological journals of the day.[5]

A second group of historians finds the seeds for Christianity's subversion of the Confederacy in the very nature of southern evangelicalism. C. C. Goen's *Broken Churches, Broken Nation*, something of a modern-day jeremiad, castigates churches both North and South for their failure to develop a constructive social ethic that critically addressed the issues of the day, particularly the problem of slavery. Because they understood sin and salvation as primarily personal issues, he argues, neither northern nor southern evangelicals could adequately address systemic evil. Slavery, according to southern ministers, was a civil institution under the domain of secular legislation, and their adoption of a "world-rejecting ecclesiology," or what Presbyterians called the "spirituality of the church," simply compounded the problem. Likewise, Goen maintains that northern Protestants failed to solve the problem of slavery as they engaged in simplistic moral reasoning that bred naive strategies for coping with society's moral woes.[6] Ultimately, for Goen, the moral failures of both the northern and southern churches—their inability and unwillingness to address systemic evil—made political failure all but inevitable.

Likewise, Gardiner Shattuck, in his study of religion in the Civil War armies, argues that the concept of personal salvation emphasized in army revivals "failed to serve a proper social function." He writes: "Rather than strengthening the resolve of the southern people to support the struggle for political independence, religion in the South actually undermined the Confederate war effort."[7] Shattuck's critique leaves the impression that if the southern churches had proclaimed a Gospel message that served an adequate social function (seemingly a good thing), the Confederacy might have won the war (presumably a bad thing).

The authors of *Why the South Lost the Civil War*, Richard E. Beringer, Herman Hattaway, Archer Jones, and William N. Still Jr., combine these two views. They note both that churches promoted the Confederate cause and that religious language was prominent in the conflict, but they insist that as the war progressed and defeats mounted, the basic Christian belief that God controlled all events forced Confederates to consider the possibility that "God willed they should not win."[8] Whether Confederates expressed guilt over slavery or questioned the morality of the cause, these scholars insist, Christianity ultimately sapped Confederate morale. "Religion not only sustained morale," they write, but "it also had the effect, eventually, of undermining it."[9]

The analysis of southern Christianity as a privatized faith made by Goen, Shattuck, Beringer, and others is accurate in many ways, but its proponents have drawn the wrong conclusions. It is precisely because the Christian religion had long been principally reduced to a personal decision and a set of private experiences that it proved so useful to the creation and sustenance of Confederate nationalism.

The evolution of Christianity from the practices of a community engaged in the worship of God to a set of private convictions first began at the close of the fifteenth century. Gradually, the term "religion" began to describe an internal sense or feeling in a person (or common to all people) rather than those liturgical and ritual practices and behaviors particular to the church. As religion came to represent private beliefs or internal emotions, its meaning was divorced from any specific outward manifestations. William Cavanaugh describes how the rise of the modern state, and in particular the so-called Wars of Religion and the ideas advocated by the Protestant Reformers, transformed religion.[10] Early modern political theorists like Jean Bodin, Thomas Hobbes, and John Locke adopted the new vision of religion, since it let them construct a role for religion that existed in a deferential relationship to the state. It mattered not if there was only one established religion (Hobbes) or a plurality of religions (Locke). These theorists shared the belief that religion should be subservient to the state. Locke, in *A Letter Concerning Toleration*, called religion "the inward and full persuasion of the mind." Locke excluded English Catholics while making his case for religious toleration precisely because their religion was more than an inward set of convictions; it demanded allegiance to the Catholic Church, which still offered a potential challenge to the state. The state was open to religion insofar as religion remained an inward matter and did not usurp its authority. Those who understood or practiced religion differently, such as English Catholics, were not tolerated.[11]

A similar understanding of and attitude toward religion has shaped the American experience. Governing authorities have historically shown little tolerance for religious groups whose practices seemed to threaten their authority. In the colonial period, authorities persecuted Roger Williams, his fellow Baptists in Massachusetts and Virginia, and Quakers at various times and in various places. After achieving independence, the primary goal of the Founding Fathers was not to enshrine religious freedom, but to "frame a government that was adequate to make the infant nation of recently liberated states viable."[12] Nevertheless, religion was one of the most divisive issues they faced, and their "overriding concern was to neutralize religion as a factor that might jeopardize the achievement of the federal government."[13] Even if some founders believed religion was necessary to establish the common good, they also assumed that the state should ultimately define that good for its citizens. The government tolerated a wide range of religious practices so long as they did not threaten the state's goals. The experience of Catholics, Mormons, and even Mennonites testifies to this understanding of religion.[14]

With few exceptions, ministers and laity alike wholeheartedly pledged their allegiance to the newly created Confederacy because religion had long since been reduced to "a set of beliefs that [was] defined as personal conviction and which [could] exist separately from one's public loyalty to the State."[15] It was precisely this private Christianity that warring politicians and clergy used to drum up enthusiasm for the cause, but not without implications for the Christian faith. As the political scientist Michael Budde notes, the distinctions that "emerge between the 'essence' of religion (interior experiences, private beliefs) and their 'manifestations' (in specific and contingent human constructs including ritual, practices and habits)," have become a basic feature of liberalism.[16] Of course, the possibilities for molding a religion thus defined are virtually endless. Budde writes: "If the manifestations of 'religion' are simply one among many possible derivatives of a more fundamental religious essence, then the truth claims of any specific manifestation may be set aside, bracketed, or marginalized in favor of establishing a favorable equilibrium among preferences (a presumably desired end in much of liberal economic and political theory). Further, the decline or erosion of any specific religious manifestation is a matter of indifference: religious manifestations may wither and die, but religion lives on."[17]

Not only does religion live on when particular religious manifestations die, new symbols, rituals, practices, and habits are created to take their places. Wars offer rich opportunities for the creation of new (as well as the refashioning of old) religious manifestations toward ends determined by the state.[18] While in many respects the Confederacy did not meet the definition of a modern liberal nation-state, Confederate authorities readily conscripted the privatized religion of the antebellum South into the service of the new nation's goals. In other words, religious convictions proved to be malleable in the newly formed Confederate nation. The challenge for historians is both to chart Christianity's transformation and to understand how this refashioned faith contributed to the Confederacy.

Holding to a private, interior understanding of faith did not prevent antebellum Christians from expressing strong opinions about social issues. The numerous reform and benevolent movements of the period attest to the vitality of religion's public role. As Mark Noll has observed, the Founding Fathers who argued against the creation of a national established church still looked to Christianity to "provide the morality without which a republic would collapse."[19] Still, the rapid expansion of Christianity in the first half of the nineteenth century failed to produce a uniform—or even unified—Christian politics.[20] Rather, the reduction of religion to the private sphere made it possible for the government to lay claim to citizens' ultimate allegiance and to demand the paramount sacrifice: their lives. While newly formed governments often find their claims on the lives of those living within their borders tenuous, they do offer their citizens protection from an assortment of enemies. Moreover, the civil authority insists its primary interest is in the peace, or common good, of its citizens. To this end, it propagates myths to culturally unify its inhabitants. These myths, whether they focus on ethnicity, religion, language, or some combination of these and other cultural attributes, allow governments to preempt their citizens' loyalties from competing allegiances. As the Confederacy took shape, leaders turned to the language of honor, to the institution of slavery, and to the region's self-proclaimed Cavalier heritage in order to highlight regional distinctions between North and South. In the process, the Confederate government, with the support of ministers, did not ask southern Christians to abandon their faith during the conflict; rather, it encouraged them to baptize the conflict and sanctify the myths it had created with their faith.[21]

Like most good myths, the myths created by the Confederacy fused historical experience with an uprooted theology and used them to demand fidelity from the nation's citizens. Myths that are told in times of violence, baptized by the blood of citizens, have tremendous endurance. It is precisely because so many southerners suffered loss that elements of certain southern myths as they were constructed during the war—the myth of the Lost Cause, the belief that southern evangelicalism survived as the stalwart of Christian orthodoxy, the perception that the term "Bible Belt" accurately describes the antebellum South —have endured so long.

The Bible Belt was created during the American Civil War. Too often, historians take the widespread use of a Christian vocabulary and cultural ethos as evidence of the triumph of Christianity. These things do testify to Christianity's presence, but they are also evidence of the cultural heritage of most white Americans, who came from countries where rituals, holidays, ceremonies, and law all had ties to the church and its calendar, but who mixed these Christian practices with folk customs and superstitions. The Bible was the book most people owned, learned to read from, and could readily quote. Yet to call the antebellum South "the Bible Belt" is a misnomer.[22] When historians look at the antebellum South, they should no more expect to find a culture void of Christianity's presence than to find explicit statements by individuals who denied the existence of God. As James Turner reminds us, at the dawn of the nineteenth century "disbelief in God remained scarcely more plausible than disbelief in gravity."[23] So although Christians made significant gains in terms of church memberships, and although their influence spread before the Civil War, southern churches were not the preeminent formulators of a southern identity. That remained the prerogative of the white male, who in the context of a slave-based economy remained convinced that honor stood as the underlying principle of any proper society. True, antebellum ministers did fashion themselves as honorable men, but they were only marginally successful in convincing southern men that Christianity was an honorable faith.[24] Christianity, as it was refashioned and proclaimed during the war, was a key component of these myths.

During the war, southern identity, with its emphasis on honor, became fused with Christian identity. For many southerners, saving the Confederacy became tantamount to saving Christianity. At first, ministers wrote that the war was a means to preserve civil liberties and constitutional heritage. This civic vocabulary never completely disappeared, but ministers and even soldiers merged it with a second rhetoric, one of Christian conviction.[25] Ministers often proclaimed in the religious press that the fight was about preserving the true Christian religion. W. B. Wellon, the newly installed editor of the *Army and Navy Messenger*, celebrated the paper's efforts to "cheer [the soldiers] on in the struggle for civil and religious liberty—for the right of self-government, and the privilege of worshipping God according to the dictates of the conscience and the teachings of His word."[26] William Norris offered an even more forceful statement concerning the divine nature of the war: "This war is on our part, a war for our Religion. . . . The import of these instructive sentences has not been enough studied by our people for them to see how much this war has put our religious interests in peril."[27] In similar fashion, Methodist J. W. Tucker told his audience: "Your cause is the cause of God, the cause of Christ, of humanity. It is a conflict of truth with error—of Bible with Northern infidelity —of pure Christianity with Northern fanaticism."[28] Clergy who waffled on secession up to the onset of the war made similar statements throughout the war. With secession settled, most Christians vigorously channeled their energies into supporting the new nation, and they subsumed their loyalty to the church into their loyalty to their nation.

Salvation Southern Style

Whether explaining how religion supported the Confederacy or describing it as detrimental to the odds of Confederate victory, those historians who have focused on the subject of religion and the Confederate experience have done so from a single vantage point, one that considers religion's contributions, both positive and negative, to political and military events.[29] Such one-dimensional thinking ignores the ways in which the Civil War changed religion in America.

During the Civil War, ministers fashioned a message to suit the conflict. In doing so, they called their listeners to rethink their understanding of salvation. Evidence from the diaries and letters penned by clergy, soldiers, and family back home indicates that the clergy's message resonated widely. Most chaplains and missionaries to the army believed that the message of personal salvation they proclaimed was consonant with their antebellum preaching, and they failed both to acknowledge how they changed their message over the course of the war and to see how the war changed how that message was heard. In the end, they accelerated a turning away from Reformed theology that had begun before the war. Presbyterians and Baptists who had formerly emphasized God's sovereignty in conversion began to stress the individual's role in choosing salvation. Their message was twofold: Confederate soldiers could choose salvation, and death in the ranks offered redemption to both the soldier and the country. The Civil War was a holy war.

Antebellum revival preaching had focused on the need for individual conversion. At the heart of the conversion message stood the language of surrender and submission.[30] In conversion, individuals surrendered control of their lives to God. Such surrender was demanding, for it frequently entailed the formation of new friendships, practices, and values, and, at least in theory, it privileged a mutual submission among believers.

Many southern men had a problem with this Gospel message. Christian virtues sounded remarkably similar to female virtues. In the sentimental religious literature of the late antebellum period, ministers joined with other writers in portraying females as gentle, pure, virtuous, sensitive, and submissive. Public discourse, especially in the South, described women as reticent, restrained, and accepting of circumstance. The Christian faith was steeped in practices and attitudes that, in the minds of many men, best suited women. Those descriptions combined with a female-dominated church population to make the Christian faith suitable for wives and sisters but not for many men.[31]

Thomas Miles Garrett faithfully attended church and chapel services while a student at University of North Carolina in the 1850s. In his view, religion was important for the health of both the individual and the republic. But Garrett disdained elements of the Christian message. After listening to a sermon on Jesus' teachings that insisted one needed to forgive others in order to be forgiven, Garrett noted: "However much it may serve to make up a fine theory of human conduct[, it] is neither consistent with notions of man, nor with the formation of society. For on the one hand a man who does not resent an injury done him will sink beneath the standard of honour. . . . I hold that there must always be a show of resentment sufficient to keep men from transgressing the rights of others."[32] Garrett did not summarily dismiss Christianity, but neither did he wholeheartedly embrace its message. Before the war, ministers struggled to bring southern men into the fold, and when their revivals produced significant numbers of male converts, especially wealthy male converts, they celebrated.[33]

Many Confederate soldiers entered the war convinced that Christian virtues like love, patience, gentleness, and forgiveness could not be reconciled with their understanding of honor, with its emphasis on the public presentation of the self and the establishment of reputation.[34] Ministers struggled to combat this notion. During the war, the normal rhythms of Sunday preaching and annual revivals gave way to sporadic preaching and subdued revivals. No longer did chaplains and army missionaries preach to predominantly female congregations. Instead, war offered clergy the opportunity to address the southern male and reshape his attitude toward the Christian religion. They spoke to battle-hardened soldiers who had faced tremendous physical hardships, long periods of separation from kin and neighbors, and death. In this environment, ministers actively promoted an honorable brand of Christianity. Through tracts, religious newspapers, and even sermons, chaplains illustrated how the conversion experience changed a person both inside and out. One of the most popular tracts, more than a quarter million copies of which were distributed in its first year of publication, was Jeremiah Bell Jeter's "A Mother's Parting Words to Her Soldier Boy." It vividly illustrates how honorable Christianity was pitched to Confederate soldiers: "I am sure, my child, you will not be a worse soldier for being a good Christian. Piety will not make you effeminate or cowardly. Some of the bravest soldiers of the world have been humble Christians. Cromwell, Gardiner and Havelock, thunderbolts of war, were as devout as they were heroic. . . . Why should not the Christian be courageous? He has less cause to love life or dread death than other men. In the path of duty he has nothing to fear. Life and death may be equally pleasing to him."[35] As the Baptist newspaper the *Soldier's Friend* explained, the Christian soldier was a virtuous killing machine: "We may *love* them—their souls—and at the same time *kill* their bodies. Hence, there was not only no inconsistency, but also evidence of high sense of religious obligation, in that officer who in the early history of this war, said, 'Lord have mercy on their souls! *Fire!*'"[36]

Preachers, with this valiant Gospel in hand, confronted soldiers with their manly obligation to choose God, and to choose God now. A writer for the *Army and Navy Herald* reminded his readers: "Years or months of penitence are not necessary to salvation; but whenever and wherever the soul is truly penitent, and looks to God in faith, *then* and *there* the seal of pardon is given."[37] Each soldier was duty bound to respond to the Gospel.

Prior to the war, Presbyterians and many Baptists disagreed with Methodists on the question of human agency.[38] This tension is apparent in a letter Susan Webb wrote to her younger brother in which she pondered the question of human agency in redemption: "Mr. Penick preached at Bethlehem last Sab-[bath] at 11 o'clock & at night—& then again Monday night. His sermons are well prepared but they are *lined* & *bound* with Calvinism. At one moment I listened with delight—to the story of the Cross, salvation *free* & full, & then again, I was an Eagle chained, taunted with fly, fly escape for your life; when there was no escape, no life offered. I was not one of the *Elect*."[39] Webb, like most Methodists, remained suspicious of Reformed theology that seemed to limit the individual's ability to respond to the Gospel.

Ministers had always exhorted their listeners to make a decision about salvation, but as the war progressed they spoke less of God's role in salvation and more of the individual's role. This shift is most apparent in conversion narratives. Antebellum conversion accounts most often narrated a conversion experience that occurred over an extended period of time. Converts described weeks, months, and even years spent living with acute guilt over their sin. At some point, through the work of the Holy Spirit, the guilt disappeared and gave way to a feeling of intense joy. Though stories of this type never completely disappeared, for many soldiers the time of conversion became condensed. The realization that they might die in the next day's battle contributed to this change. So, too, did the sermons and conversion stories in the religious press that emphasized men responding to God and taught that conversion was an individual man's decision and one that demanded an immediate response. Being a penitent seeker did little good for a soldier. Men had to respond to God's call quickly. If, as the war persisted, chaplains and missionaries failed to gain conversions, they failed, according to one cleric, because of their "lack of knowledge of human nature, and the best means of gaining access to the hearts of the men in the ranks."[40] Of course, not all soldiers chose God, but many who did not came to believe that they would find their salvation in death—their own death—through submission to and participation in a sacred cause.

The biblical story as it has been interpreted in Western Christianity, and especially the drama of salvation, centers on violence: the sacrificial death of Christ on the cross. Christian theology posits that sin is a barrier between people and

God. Unless humanity's sinfulness is atoned for, humans cannot enter the presence of a holy, just God. Although the authors of the New Testament did not develop a uniform theory of atonement as it related to their account of the cross, resurrection, and humanity's sinfulness, they did portray sin as the obstacle and Christ as the solution. In the eleventh century, Anselm of Canterbury wrote about what theologians call "the doctrine of atonement." The Western church has argued that Anselm taught that God demanded death to satisfy his honor. Only if humankind *satisfied* God's honor could punishment be avoided.[41] But humanity's sinfulness prevented humankind from offering a satisfactory sacrifice to God. Christ's "voluntary acceptance of death and of the punishment that men had deserved was the means by which salvation was accomplished."[42] Western Christians adopted Anselm's "satisfaction theory of atonement," although often with modifications and at times with "other ideas that contrasted with it or even contradicted it."[43] Nineteenth-century southern Protestants differed on the question of whom Christ had saved by his sacrifice: Reformed Christians insisted Christ had died only for the elect, while Methodists believed Christ had died for all humankind. But whether Regular Baptist, Primitive Baptist, Lutheran, Methodist, Presbyterian, or Episcopalian, all southern Christians agreed that Christ's death on the cross had been necessary to satisfy God's honor.

Over the course of the war, Confederate clergy proclaimed their message of death and redemption in a manner that encouraged men and women to closely align God and country so that professing faith in the country became tantamount to professing faith in God. Preachers portrayed the Confederate cause as God's cause, described Confederate leaders as God's anointed, and interpreted both victories and defeats as signs of God's favor.[44] In doing so, they invited soldiers and civilians to use the Gospel message to meet their emotional and physical needs during the war. As the war progressed, many soldiers and civilians saw death on the battlefield as an atoning sacrifice, one that ensured their entrance into heaven. To put it another way, ministers had so convincingly described the Confederate cause in religious language that many soldiers found their salvation in the cause. Death was still essential for redemption, but for some, a soldier's death on the field of battle became salvifically equivalent to Christ's death on the cross.[45]

That Christianity and Confederate nationalism fused together so well should surprise no one. Confederate nationalism, like most forms of nationalism, had a deeply religious character.[46] Furthermore, both Christianity and nationalism posit a role for violence in salvation. Good citizens are willing to die for their nation, and with few exceptions the denominations that make up Western Christianity claim that God demanded death to satisfy his honor. When Christianity is proclaimed as a set of personal convictions and experiences, the gap between the honorable patriotic death for the salvation of a nation and the death required for personal salvation can appear quite small. It is no accident that few Americans have died for their faith (despite the high percentage of Americans who claim to be Christian), while hundreds of thousands have willingly died for their country.[47] In the Confederacy, it became easy to equate death in the interest of one cause—the Confederate nation—as a sufficient sacrifice for both the nation and God. In other words, not only was there a religious intensity to Confederate patriotism, but this nationalist fervor was itself deeply religious, so much so that it offered redemption. Calling men to support the Confederate cause sounded remarkably like calling men to follow Christ. The violence of war was a sacred violence laden with honor. Ministers blurred distinctions between Christianity and civic liberty until at times the two became interchangeable.[48]

Mary Bethell, a devout Methodist, sent her two sons off to war. Before the conflict, she had regularly expressed concern for their salvation. After their departure, she prayed for "God to cover their heads in the day of battle." Yet she knew God might will their deaths, and if such was the case, Bethell believed that "if either of them died from wounds received in the battle, God for Christ's sake [would] forgive their sins and take them home to Heaven."[49]

Bethell was not alone. William R. J. Pegram served as captain of an artillery battalion in the Army of Northern Virginia. An Episcopalian, Pegram frequently translated the events transpiring around him into religious categories. Like all Confederates, Pegram was deeply saddened by Stonewall Jackson's untimely death. Yet he was convinced this was part of God's larger plan, and he commented: "Some of our troops made too much of an Idol of him, and lost sight of God's mercies."[50] Pegram knew how to interpret the soldiers' misplaced faith in their military leadership. That was idolatry. But faith in the cause was different from faith in a man, and Pegram remained convinced that all southerners who died in defense of their holy cause would enter heaven.[51]

Some ministers warned of colleagues who, by proclaiming salvation through death on the battlefield, had misconstrued the Gospel message. In the fall of 1864, Methodist minister George Butler wrote home to his sister. He described the power of religion among the soldiers: "The men appear to be much interested in religious worship. I never saw men pay better attention at preaching, and that too when there is no 'great preacher' present." But a note of caution tempered Butler's joy. He continued: "I dare not preach as some talk, that their sufferings in their country's behalf, will atone for their sins, and that their souls will be saved in Heaven because they are killed in battle. I know of but one atonement, one sacrifice for sin; and that our blessed Saviour made."[52]

Other ministers joined Butler in challenging the message that death on the battlefield ensured a soldier's entrance into heaven. The frequency of such warnings indicates that the belief was widespread. Religious newspapers published for the military echoed Butler's warning. The *Soldier's Friend* counseled against the belief that proclaimed, "If a soldier falls fighting bravely for his country, he will go direct to Heaven!"[53] The *Army and Navy Messenger* warned the men that death on the battlefield did not guarantee entrance into heaven: "It is not the blood of man but *'the blood of Jesus Christ that cleanseth from all sin.'*"[54] Yet these same papers had in many an earlier article sanctioned the Confederate cause as holy, righteous, and honorable.

Confederate Christianity emphasized salvation through sacrifice. The sacrifice of Christ on the cross offered the soldier entrance into heaven, but so, too, did the sacrifice of the soldier's life on the field of battle. In their efforts to Christianize the cause and pay tribute to martyred heroes, many ministers and rank and file fused the Christian message with the Confederate political message. While some ministers, civilians, and soldiers drew a distinction between a Christian martyr and a noble patriot, many did not. The belief that a soldier's death on the battlefield gained him entrance into heaven meshed with the widespread revivals that swept through the Confederate armies. The conversion they advertised was not the personal conversion demanded in antebellum religious revivals, but conversion to an ideology that offered salvation through death for a nation. Southerners often fused these two messages during the war, demonstrating that the politics of war transformed the Gospel.

Onward Christian Soldiers

With knowledge of Union victory in hand, historians have had difficulty explaining why Confederates fought so long when abundant evidence suggests that the war was all but over by the spring of 1864. A partial answer to this question can be found in the refashioned Gospel message that both underscored a sense of nationalism and imbued the Army of Northern Virginia with hope. The message of salvation, including the message that death on the battlefield offered redemption, was embodied in the army revivals, and it boosted Confederate morale, especially for soldiers. Drew Gilpin Faust has shown how southerners' faith contributed to the formation and sustenance of nationalism in the region by casting Confederates as God's chosen people.[55] The religious underpinnings of Confederate nationalism were made manifest in the revivals, and as word of the revivals spread throughout the armies it furthered soldiers' sense that their task was divinely ordained.

By all accounts, large-scale revivals swept through the Confederate army during the Civil War. Participants and historians alike have measured the revivals' success by the number of soldiers who converted. Estimates of the number converted have ranged as high as 150,000.[56] Historians attribute the success of the revivals to a number of factors. The message of salvation—the promise of entrance into heaven—clearly appealed to many in the context of war. Others found hope in the promise that Christianity would make them better, braver soldiers. The revivals also had the potential of creating strong bonds of comradeship. Conversion bound soldiers together.[57] One even finds a competitive spirit lurking in these religious gatherings. Johnny Green recalled that as revivals swept through the army, his commander warned his soldiers. "If we did not send in as many recruits to the church as any other regiment in the army he thought he would be compelled to have details made to join the church," Green recounted, "for our regiment must not be outdone in any way."[58]

The various explanations for the revivals' success do not undermine the sincerity of the soldiers' decision to convert. Rather, they suggest that a privatized, personalized Gospel was compatible with the call to go to war, with the call to slaughter an enemy, and with the message that God favored the Confederacy. Yet to simply calculate the number of conversions misses the point and understates the revivals' prominence; it is far more significant to recognize that the revivals became huge events, widely publicized in both the religious and secular papers of the day. Army revivals, like their predecessors in civilian circles several decades before, were major cultural events, and clergy used the print media to interpret and define the significance of the revivals for their readers.

The revival cycle—with its pattern of blessings conferred, blessings abused, declension, and repentance followed by restoration—created optimism among Confederates. Revivals provided ministers with the categories through which they filtered battle news and assessed the prospects of the nation. Clergy had entered the war worried about the debilitating influence of camp life on soldiers' morality, and throughout the war they penned numerous tracts and articles testifying to their continuing concern with the sins of drunkenness, swearing, Sabbath breaking, and gambling. But these men also believed that revivals had a positive impact on camp life. Revivals offered "a stand point amid the smoke and blood and disruption of the times from which the earnest minded Christian [might] look toward the future with hope."[59] The Presbyterian *Soldier's Visitor* expressed gratitude that "it . . . pleased God, to arrest in a large measure this desolating tide." The army, the paper reported, had "become to a large extent pervaded by a wholesome and powerful religious influence," and "the circumstances, at first deemed so unfavorable to [soldiers'] moral and spiritual welfare, [had] been turned to be a source of the richest blessings."[60] Reverend Stiles, writing for the *Soldier's Visitor*, declared: "*The simplest way to convert a nation is to convert its army.*" With the revivals spreading through the armies, he asked: "What . . . could prevent that whole nation from being carried over bodily to the Lord's side?"[61]

The logic of the revival cycle and the revivals' widespread occurrence in southern armies led many to view military defeat as temporary. Soldiers' repentance ensured divine restoration. Ministers, confident the Confederacy would eventually achieve victory in the cause, explained each defeat on its own terms. It appears to have occurred to few writers that a succession of defeats could lead to total defeat. Even in the wake of seemingly catastrophic losses such as the surrender of Vicksburg, the fall of Atlanta, and the retreat from Gettysburg, clergy found signs of hope. No matter how strategically significant the loss of Vicksburg, Atlanta, or Richmond might have been, writers understood them as singular rather than symptomatic events. Implicit in their accounts of the battles was the conviction that a special relationship existed between the Confederacy and God. In the minds of Confederate clergy, even a defeat ensured ultimate victory.

Gary Gallagher has argued that beginning in 1862 Confederates increasingly found hope not in their government and their political leaders, but on the battlefield, and that "Robert E. Lee and his Army of Northern Virginia eventually became the most important national institution."[62] He continues: "The written record . . . affirms incontrovertibly that Lee and his soldiers influenced Confederate hearts and minds."[63] As long as Lee was in the field, southerners believed that the Confederacy would survive. But while adroitly drawing attention back to Lee's army as the central source of hope for eventual Confederate victory, Gallagher misses the way in which religion infused the Confederacy with hope for Lee's army and for the cause for which the army fought. The enduring optimism that the Confederacy would ultimately triumph was not based on Lee's military exploits alone. Rather, the Army of Northern Virginia gained its place on a pedestal for both its military and its religious exploits. It is not coincidental that the largest and most publicized revivals occurred in the Army of Northern Virginia.[64] Christianity, institutionalized in army revivals, created the aura of divine blessing even in the last days of the war. In revivals, clergy faithfully preached the message that death—both Christ's and the soldier's—led to both personal and national salvation, and in doing so they created confidence in both Lee and his men.

Of course, Christianity was neither the only source of nationalism nor the only builder of Confederate morale. Christianity did not fight the battles, nor were all soldiers and civilians interested in the churches' message. Alone, it can neither claim the triumph of victory nor bear the burden of defeat. Nevertheless, many contemporaries interpreted the war in religious terms and found hope in the redemptive messages they heard preached. In particular, they drew hope from the revival message as it was proclaimed to and embedded in the experience of the army, especially in Robert E. Lee's Army of Northern Virginia.

The refashioned Christian message did more than provide hope during a period when, hindsight suggests, any hope of victory had long since passed. It became the foundation of a civil religion *during* the war, not simply after it, as some have argued. The Confederacy subsumed basic features of antebellum evangelical Protestantism and redirected them toward its own ends. The Confederacy sanctioned Christianity because private religion did not threaten to usurp its goals. Ministers proclaimed the Gospel message to both soldiers and civilians, and southern churches finally gained the male converts they had long sought in the antebellum era. The message preached during the war demanded a sacrifice for salvation. It sanctioned violence against the enemy as honorable and Christian. The tremendous amount of blood shed during the war by Christian soldiers on behalf of a Christian cause sealed the relationship between Confederate ideology and Christianity. The Confederate cause took on an efficacious quality for many southerners and, in particular, for many in the army. Ministers had effectively described the southern cause and its heroes in language laden with religion. The army revivals gave their words potency. Soldiers and civilians took their cue from preachers and fused together the secular and religious, making their cause and many of its leaders symbols of divine favor.

Historians have focused much attention on the civil religion that filtered through the Lost Cause rhetoric. Clearly, Confederate nationalism, even as it endured after the war, contained a religious component.[65] Carolyn Marvin and David W. Ingle have observed that, often, the amount of bloodshed is far more important in defining ritual success than is the outcome of the war.[66] A people's identity, its sense of loyalty to a nation, is directly tied to the cost of the sacrifice required to create or maintain that nation. Though the South lost the war, the suffering of southerners preserved a sense of identity among them.

Yet to describe the Lost Cause as civil religion has limitations.[67] Where does the civil end and the religious begin? It is difficult to reduce the religiously inspired events and rhetoric of the war and the period after to a "civil religion." Historians need to explore how the faith that emerged during the war lived on after it. René Girard suggests that sacrificial theology does not bring an end to violence, but ultimately perpetuates it.[68] Furthermore, violence, when tied to religion, often finds expression in language about purity.[69] Professions of purity become a way to control those who either disagree or do not fit with the established ideal. During the war, the southern church made violence a sacred, honorable activity that furthered a Christian cause. There are alternative questions that should be asked about the place of religion in the New South. In addition to exploring the civil meanings of religion, historians should ask how the religious sanctioning of violence during the war shaped life after Appomattox. In other words, how did the Christian faith, as molded during the conflict, contribute to "the rhetoric of white religious and cultural separatism" that continued throughout the rest of the nineteenth century?[70] If the religious sanctioning of killing for the cause of the Confederacy fostered ritualized violence in the New South, how did the patterns of violence crystallized in lynching keep white southern honor pure?

The Civil War transformed southern evangelical Protestantism, moving theology away from its Calvinist heritage toward an Arminian understanding of conversion. Along the way, it sacralized the idea of sacrifice on behalf of the cause. The legacy of this transformation for southern Christianity and society has yet to be fully understood.

Notes

Abbreviations

ANM   *Army and Navy Messenger*
SF   *Soldier's Friend*
SHC   Southern Historical Collection, University of North Carolina, Chapel Hill, N.C.

1. James W. Silver, *Confederate Morale and Church Propaganda* (Tuscaloosa: Confederate Publishing, 1957).

2. W. Harrison Daniel, "The Southern Baptists in the Confederacy," *Civil War History* 6 (1960): 393; James McPherson, *For Cause and Comrade: Why Men Fought in the Civil War* (New York: Oxford University Press, 1997), 62–76; Drew Gilpin Faust, "Christian Soldiers: The Meaning of Revivalism in the Confederate Army," *Journal of Southern History* 53 (February 1987): 63–90; Kurt O. Berends, "Wholesome Reading Purifies and Elevates the Man: The Religious Military Press in the Confederate States of America," in *Religion and the American Civil War*, eds. Randall M. Miller, Harry S. Stout, and Charles Reagan Wilson (New York: Oxford University Press, 1998), 131–66; Steven E. Woodworth, *While God Is Marching On: The Religious World of the Civil War Soldiers* (Lawrence: University Press of Kansas, 2001), 117–44.

3. E. B. Lane to his sister-in-law, August 14, 1864, SHC.

4. Gaines M. Foster, "Guilt over Slavery: A Historiographical Analysis," *Journal of Southern History* 56 (November 1990): 665–94.

5. Kenneth Stampp, *The Imperiled Union: Essays on the Background of the Civil War* (New York: Oxford University Press, 1980), 246–69; Bell I. Wiley, *The Road to Appomattox* (Memphis: Memphis State College Press, 1956), 102–5; C. Vann Woodward, *The Burden of Southern History* (Baton Rouge: Louisiana State University Press, 1960), 3–25; Charles G. Sellers, "The Travail of Slavery," in *The Southerner as American* (Chapel Hill: University of North Carolina Press, 1960), 40–71; Drew Gilpin Faust, *The Creation of Confederate Nationalism: Ideology and Identity in the Civil War South* (Baton Rouge: Louisiana State University Press, 1988), 41–42; Richard E. Beringer, Herman Hattaway, Archer Jones, and William N. Still Jr., *Why the South Lost the Civil War* (Athens: University of Georgia Press, 1986), 336–67. August Wenzel found virtually no expressions of guilt over slavery in the theological quarterly journals published either during or immediately following the war. See "Theological Implications of the Civil War," unpublished manuscript, n.d., Buswell Library, Wheaton College, Wheaton, Ill., 9–10. Christians did not feel guilty, because their worldview sanctioned slavery. See Elizabeth Fox-Genovese and Eugene D. Genovese, "The Divine Sanction of Social Order: Religious Foundations of the Southern Slaveholders' World View," *Journal of the American Academy of Religion* 55 (Summer 1987): 211–33.

6. C. C. Goen, *Broken Churches, Broken Nation: Denominational Schisms and the Coming of the Civil War* (Macon: Mercer University Press, 1985), 146–69.

7. Gardiner Shattuck, *A Shield and Hiding Place: The Religious Life of the Civil War Armies* (Macon: Mercer University Press, 1987), 9.

8. Beringer, Hattaway, Jones, and Still, *Why the South Lost the Civil War*, 336–67, quote on 102.

9. Ibid., 83.

10. William T. Cavanaugh, "'A Fire Strong Enough to Consume the House': The Wars of Religion and the Rise of the State," *Modern Theology* 11 (October 1995): 397–420.

11. I am indebted in the above paragraph to the insights of Bill Cavanaugh. See "A Fire Strong Enough To Consume the House," 404–8. See also Wilfred Cantwell Smith, *The Meaning and End of Religion* (New York: Macmillan, 1962), 30–49; John Locke, *A Letter Concerning Toleration*, quoted in Cavanaugh, "A Fire Strong Enough to Consume the House," 407; and John Neville Figgis, *From Gerson to Grotius, 1414–1625* (New York: Harper Torchbooks, 1960).

12. John F. Wilson, "Religion, Government, and Power in the New American Nation," in *Religion and American Politics: From the Colonial Period to the 1980s*, ed. Mark A. Noll (New York: Oxford University Press, 1990), 81.

13. Ibid., 82, quote on 84.

14. See Edwin S. Gaustad, *Liberty of Conscience: Roger Williams in America* (Grand Rapids: Eerdmans, 1991); Samuel Horst, *Mennonites in the Confederacy: A Study in Civil War Pacifism* (Scottdale, Pa.: Herald Press, 1967); and Rhys Isaac, *The Transformation of Virginia, 1740–1790*, 2d ed. (New York: W. W. Norton, 1988), 161–63.

15. Cavanaugh, "A Fire Strong Enough to Consume the House," 403.

16. Michael L. Budde, "The Origins and Inadequacy of the Contemporary Understanding of Religion as 'Mere Preference,'" unpublished paper, in author's possession, 3.

17. Ibid., 10–11.

18. One need look no further than how Christianity has been incorporated into the public's reaction in the aftermath of the tragic events of September 11. The slogans "In God We Trust" and "United We Stand" have been blended together and have become something of a national motto. Likewise, no one should be shocked at the public outcry after San Francisco's Ninth Circuit U.S. Court of Appeals ruled in a 2–1 vote that the phrase "one nation under God" was unconstitutional. Within hours, the U.S. Senate passed a unanimous resolution denouncing the court's decision, and the members of both the House and the Senate stood and said the pledge in protest of the ruling. Of course, to believe that such a ruling would have evoked a similarly unanimous response had it happened prior to the events of September 11 is naive. The court's ruling on June 26, 2002, received a phenomenal amount of negative publicity and was quickly set aside.

19. Mark A. Noll, "Evangelicals in the American Founding and Evangelical Political Mobilization Today," in *Religion and the New Republic: Faith in the Founding of America*, ed. James H. Hutson (Lanham, Md.: Rowman & Littlefield, 2000), 151.

20. Ibid.

21. William T. Cavanaugh, unpublished paper, in author's possession, 4. Of course, this

same process can be found in the Union. However, each side told different myths and sanctified different elements in the war.

22. Christine Leigh Heyrman, *Southern Cross: The Beginnings of the Bible Belt* (New York: Alfred A. Knopf, 1997).

23. James Turner, *Without God, without Creed: The Origin of Unbelief in America* (Baltimore: Johns Hopkins University Press, 1985), 44.

24. This is the core argument of Christine Heyrman's *Southern Cross.*

25. Kurt O. Berends, "'Thus Saith the Lord': The Use of the Bible by Southern Evangelicals in the Era of the American Civil War" (D.Phil. thesis, Oxford University, 1997). Woodworth also finds evidence that soldiers understood this as a war for religion, but he finds such assertions "puzzling." See *While God Is Marching On,* 129–30.

26. W. B. Wellon, "Our Paper," *ANM,* December 15, 1864, 1.

27. William Norris, "Massachusetts, and a War for Religion," *Army and Navy Messenger for the Trans-Mississippi Army,* September 29, 1864, 2.

28. J. W. Tucker, "God's Presence in War," May 16, 1862, quoted in Ronald Glenn Lee, "Exploded Graces: Providence and the Confederate Israel in Evangelical Southern Sermons, 1861–1865" (master's thesis, Rice University, 1990), 63.

29. Several scholars, including Steven Woodworth, make casual mention of the impact of war on religion but see it as either something of a quaint oddity or a development of minor significance. See, for example, Woodworth, *While God is Marching On,* 141–42.

30. Lewis O. Saum, *The Popular Mood of Pre–Civil War America* (Westport, Conn.: Greenwood Press, 1980), 68.

31. Bertram Wyatt-Brown, *Southern Honor: Ethics and Behavior in the Old South* (New York: Oxford University Press, 1982), 226–53. On southern notions of feminine Christianity, see Timothy A. Long, "Divine Confederacy: Southern Evangelicals and the Civil War" (master's thesis, University of North Carolina at Chapel Hill, 1990), 4–6, 22. On the almost two to one ratio of women to men, see Donald G. Mathews, *Religion in the Old South* (Chicago: University of Chicago Press, 1977), 47–8, 101–24.

32. Thomas Miles Garrett Diary, July 1, 1849, SHC. The offending text was Matthew 6:12. Garrett's use of the Bible differed little from Thomas Jefferson's, though Garrett was not a Deist. In the same way that Jefferson put together his own New Testament that emphasized moral instruction but omitted miracles, Garrett looked for those elements of Christianity that, in his mind, contributed to a better society.

33. Daniel Baker's revivals in 1831 and 1832 were especially celebrated for the number of men they brought into the fold. See William M. Baker, *The Life and Labours of the Rev. Daniel Baker, D.D.* (Philadelphia: n.p., 1859). On ministers valuing certain converts more highly than others, see Stephanie McCurry, *Masters of Small Worlds: Yeoman Households, Gender Relations, and the Political Culture of the Antebellum South Carolina Low Country* (New York: Oxford University Press, 1995), 153–54. It is worth asking how the quest to evangelize white men, especially wealthy white patriarchs, shaped the Gospel message. Heyrman suggests that southern evangelical ministers began constructing a message of

honor in the very first decades of the nineteenth century. Biographies portrayed early preachers as especially masculine, selectively confrontational, and able to defend their honor. While her description of that change is accurate, that message for the most part failed to convince a majority of southern men, who remained prized converts for preachers. See *Southern Cross*, 306–32.

34. Wyatt-Brown, *Southern Honor*.

35. [Jeremiah Bell Jeter], "A Mother's Parting Words to Her Soldier Boy," no. 13 (n.p., n.d.). Publication figures are from Bell I. Wiley, *The Life of Johnny Reb* (1943; reprint, Baton Rouge: Louisiana State University Press, 1978), 178. "A Mother's Parting Words" has also been attributed to Frances Brokenbrough. The question of authorship does not alter the main point of my argument.

36. [Adolphus Worrell], "How Should We Regard Our Enemies?" *SF*, May 2, 1863, 2.

37. W. A. P., "Sketches and Incidents—No. II," *Army and Navy Herald*, March 23, 1865, 6.

38. Historians continue to slight the role of doctrine in southern evangelicalism. In an otherwise good book on Christianity and the causes of the war, John Daly writes, "This popular ecumenical spirit necessitated a de-emphasis of doctrine" (*When Slavery Was Called Freedom: Evangelicalism, Proslavery, and the Causes of the Civil War* [Lexington: University Press of Kentucky, 2002], 7–8). The religious newspapers of the day, as well as the diaries and letters of ordinary people, are filled with musings and debates on doctrinal differences among the three largest denominations, the Baptists, Methodists, and Presbyterians. That they all agreed on the priority of a conversion experience did not diminish their passion about their differences.

39. Susan A. Webb to her brother, February 3, 1860, SHC (emphasis in original). For a more detailed description of the theological differences related to soteriology in the antebellum South, see Berends, "Thus Saith the Lord," 144–61.

40. "Go Among Them," *ANM*, January 2, 1865, 2; "There Is a Saviour," and "Come, for He Lives for Sinners," *ANM*, February 1, 1864, 2–3. The interdenominational papers were composed by a board of editors representing each major denomination, whose responsibility it was to ensure that no article offensive to any single denomination would be published.

41. Anselm is commonly misread as placing the burden of satisfaction on humans. For Anselm, the judge condemns but then comes down from the bench to take the place of the condemned.

42. Jaroslav Pelikan, *The Growth of Medieval Theology (600–1300)*, vol. 3 of *The Christian Tradition: A History of the Development of Doctrine* (Chicago: University of Chicago Press, 1978), 113–14, 140–42, quote on 142; John Van Engen, "Anselm of Canterbury," in *Evangelical Dictionary of Theology*, ed. Walter A. Elwell (Grand Rapids: Baker Book House, 1984).

43. Jaroslav Pelikan, *Reformation of Church and Dogma (1300–1700)*, vol. 4 of *The Christian Tradition: A History of the Development of Doctrine* (Chicago: The University of Chi-

cago Press, 1984), 22–38, 160–64, quote on 25. Pelikan points out that Anselm did not set out to write a systematic doctrine of the atonement and that it is possible that later theologians have misunderstood his basic arguments. Nevertheless, the various governmental, penal, and substitutionary theories of atonement that came to prominence in the West claim to draw upon Anselm. The Eastern church did not adopt the satisfaction theory of atonement, but proclaimed Christ's victory over death as the central motif. See Gustaf Aulen, *Christus Victor: An Historical Study of the Three Main Types of the Idea of Atonement* (New York: Macmillan, 1969).

44. For numerous examples, see Berends, "Wholesome Reading Purifies and Elevates the Man," 131–66.

45. Several historians have noted this message in passing, but they fail to understand both its genesis and its impact on the Confederacy. See, for example, Woodworth, *While God Is Marching On*, 142.

46. Faust, *Creation of Confederate Nationalism*, 1–41. On the religious character of American patriotism, see Carolyn Marvin and David W. Ingle, *Blood Sacrifice and the Nation: Totem Rituals and the American Flag* (New York: Cambridge University Press, 1999), 9–10.

47. Marvin and Ingle, *Blood Sacrifice*, 9–28.

48. I am not arguing that this fusion of religion and cause is unique to the Confederacy. I simply show how it influenced both Confederate nationalism and the postwar South.

49. Mary M. Bethell Diary, March 10, 1862, SHC.

50. Quoted in Peter S. Carmichael, *Lee's Young Artillerist: William R. J. Pegram* (Charlottesville: University Press of Virginia, 1995), 93.

51. Ibid., 3. Steven Woodworth observes this tendency to interpret death as redemptive, citing examples from civilians, soldiers, and the religious press in *While God Is Marching On*, 141–42.

52. George Butler to Emma Butler, August 16, 1864, in *Tulip Evermore: Emma Butler and William Paisley, Their Lives in Letters, 1857–1887*, eds. Elizabeth Paisley Huckaby and Ethel C. Simpson (Fayetteville: University of Arkansas Press, 1985).

53. "A Dangerous Fallacy Exposed," *SF*, January 10, 1863, 3.

54. "Patriotism Not Piety," *ANM*, April 1, 1864, 1 (emphasis in original).

55. Faust, *Creation of Confederate Nationalism*, 22–40.

56. Faust, "Christian Soldiers," 63. Confederate chaplain Rev. W. B. Wellon estimated that more than 140,000 had converted by December of 1864. See "The Confederate Army as a Field for Religious Labor," *ANM*, December 15, 1864, 1.

57. Faust, "Christian Soldiers," 75, 82; McPherson, *For Cause and Comrade*, 62–76.

58. A. D. Kirwan, ed., *Johnny Green of the Orphan Brigade: The Journal of a Confederate Soldier* (Lexington: University of Kentucky Press, 1956), 121.

59. E. M. M., "Revivals in the Trans-Miss. Department," *Army and Navy Messenger for the Trans-Mississippi Department*, October 27, 1864, 1.

60. "The War and the Church," *Soldier's Visitor*, November 1863, 12.

61. Rev. Stiles, "Fruits of the Revival in the Army," *Soldier's Visitor*, September 1863, 3 (emphasis in original).

62. Gary Gallagher, *The Confederate War* (Cambridge, Mass.: Harvard University Press, 1997), 8.

63. Ibid., 86.

64. Faust, "Christian Soldiers."

65. Charles Reagan Wilson, *Baptized in Blood: The Religion of the Lost Cause, 1865– 1920* (Athens: University of Georgia Press, 1980); Carolyn Marvin and David W. Ingle, "Blood Sacrifice and the Nation: Revisiting Civil Religion," *Journal of the American Academy of Religion* 64 (Winter 1996): 767–68.

66. Marvin and Ingle, *Blood Sacrifice*, 89.

67. Gaines Foster rightly points out the problems with ascribing the term "civil religion" to the Lost Cause. See *Ghosts of the Confederacy: Defeat, the Lost Cause, and the Emergence of the New South* (New York: Oxford University Press, 1987), 7–8.

68. René Girard, *Violence and the Sacred*, trans. Patrick Gregory (Baltimore: Johns Hopkins University Press, 1977). See also Willard M. Swartley, ed., *Violence Renounced: René Girard, Biblical Studies, and Peacemaking* (Telford, Pa.: Pandora Press, 2000).

69. Swartley, *Violence Renounced*, 64.

70. Paul Harvey, *Redeeming the South: Religious Cultures and Racial Identities among Southern Baptists, 1865–1925* (Chapel Hill: University of North Carolina Press, 1997), 17

For Further Reading

Aulen, Gustaf. *Christus Victor: An Historical Study of the Three Main Types of the Idea of Atonement*. New York: Macmillan, 1969.

Berends, Kurt O. "Wholesome Reading Purifies and Elevates the Man: The Religious Military Press in the Confederate States of America." In *Religion and the American Civil War*, edited by Randall M. Miller, Harry S. Stout, and Charles Reagan Wilson, 131–66. New York: Oxford University Press, 1998.

———. "'Thus Saith the Lord': The Use of the Bible by Southern Evangelicals in the Era of the American Civil War." D.Phil. thesis, Oxford University, 1997.

Beringer, Richard E., Herman Hattaway, Archer Jones, and William N. Still Jr. *Why the South Lost the Civil War*. Athens: University of Georgia Press, 1986.

Cavanaugh, William T. "'A Fire Strong Enough to Consume the House': The Wars of Religion and the Rise of the State." *Modern Theology* 11 (October 1995): 397–420.

Daly, John. *When Slavery Was Called Freedom: Evangelicalism, Proslavery, and the Causes of the Civil War*. Lexington: University Press of Kentucky, 2002.

Daniel, W. Harrison. "The Southern Baptists in the Confederacy." *Civil War History* 6 (1960): 389–401.

Faust, Drew Gilpin. *The Creation of Confederate Nationalism: Ideology and Identity in the Civil War South*. Baton Rouge: Louisiana State University Press, 1988.

———. "Christian Soldiers: The Meaning of Revivalism in the Confederate Army." *Journal of Southern History* 53 (February 1987): 63–90.

Foster, Gaines M. "Guilt over Slavery: A Historiographical Analysis." *Journal of Southern History* 56 (November 1990): 665–94.

———. *Ghosts of the Confederacy: Defeat, the Lost Cause, and the Emergence of the New South.* New York: Oxford University Press, 1987.

Fox-Genovese, Elizabeth, and Eugene D. Genovese. "The Divine Sanction of Social Order: Religious Foundations of the Southern Slaveholders' World View." *Journal of the American Academy of Religion* 55 (Summer 1987): 211–33.

Gallagher, Gary. *The Confederate War.* Cambridge, Mass.: Harvard University Press, 1997.

Girard, René. *Violence and the Sacred.* Translated by Patrick Gregory. Baltimore: Johns Hopkins University Press, 1977.

Goen, C. C. *Broken Churches, Broken Nation: Denominational Schisms and the Coming of the Civil War.* Macon: Mercer University Press, 1985.

Horst, Samuel. *Mennonites in the Confederacy: A Study in Civil War Pacifism.* Scottdale, Pa.: Herald Press, 1967.

Isaac, Rhys. *The Transformation of Virginia, 1740–1790.* 2d ed. New York: W. W. Norton, 1988.

Lee, Ronald Glenn. "Exploded Graces: Providence and the Confederate Israel in Evangelical Southern Sermons, 1861–1865." Master's thesis, Rice University, 1990.

Long, Timothy A. "Divine Confederacy: Southern Evangelicals and the Civil War." Master's thesis, University of North Carolina at Chapel Hill, 1990.

Marvin, Carolyn, and David W. Ingle. *Blood Sacrifice and the Nation: Totem Rituals and the American Flag.* New York: Cambridge University Press, 1999.

———. "Blood Sacrifice and the Nation: Revisiting Civil Religion." *Journal of the American Academy of Religion* 64 (Winter 1996): 767–68.

McPherson, James. *For Cause and Comrade: Why Men Fought in the Civil War.* New York: Oxford University Press, 1997.

Noll, Mark A. "Evangelicals in the American Founding and Evangelical Political Mobilization Today." In *Religion and the New Republic: Faith in the Founding of America,* edited by James H. Hutson. Lanham, Md.: Rowman & Littlefield, 2000.

Saum, Lewis O. *The Popular Mood of Pre–Civil War America.* Westport, Conn.: Greenwood Press, 1980.

Sellers, Charles G. "The Travail of Slavery." In *The Southerner as American,* 40–71. Chapel Hill: University of North Carolina Press, 1960.

Shattuck, Gardiner. *A Shield and Hiding Place: The Religious Life of the Civil War Armies.* Macon: Mercer University Press, 1987.

Silver, James W. *Confederate Morale and Church Propaganda.* Tuscaloosa: Confederate Publishing, 1957.

Smith, Wilfred Cantwell. *The Meaning and End of Religion*. New York: Macmillan, 1962.

Stampp, Kenneth. *The Imperiled Union: Essays on the Background of the Civil War*. New York: Oxford University Press, 1980.

Swartley, Willard M., ed. *Violence Renounced: René Girard, Biblical Studies, and Peace-making*. Telford, Pa.: Pandora Press, 2000.

Wenzel, August. "Theological Implications of the Civil War." Unpublished manuscript, n.d. Buswell Library, Wheaton College, Wheaton, Ill.

Wiley, Bell I. *The Road to Appomattox*. Memphis: Memphis State College Press, 1956.

Wilson, Charles Reagan. *Baptized in Blood: The Religion of the Lost Cause, 1865–1920*. Athens: University of Georgia Press, 1980.

Wilson, John F. "Religion, Government, and Power in the New American Nation." In *Religion and American Politics: From the Colonial Period to the 1980s*, edited by Mark A. Noll, 77–91. New York: Oxford University Press, 1990.

Woodward, C. Vann. *The Burden of Southern History*. Baton Rouge: Louisiana State University Press, 1960.

Woodworth, Steven E. *While God Is Marching On: The Religious World of the Civil War Soldiers*. Lawrence: University Press of Kansas, 2001.

Wyatt-Brown, Bertram. *Southern Honor: Ethics and Behavior in the Old South*. New York: Oxford University Press, 1982.

5

The Royal Telephone

Early Pentecostalism in the South and the Enthusiastic Practice of Prayer

My sheep hear my voice, and I know them, and they follow me.
—John 10:27

Central's never busy,
Always on the line,
You may hear from heaven,
Almost any time,

'Tis a royal service,
Free for one and all,
When you get in trouble,
Give this royal line a call.

. . . .

If your line is "grounded,"
And connection true,
Has been lost with Jesus,
Tell you what to do,

Pray'r and faith and promise,
Mend the broken wire,
Till your soul is burning,
With the Pentecostal fire.

Telephone to glory,
O what joy divine!
I can feel the current,
Moving on the line,

Made by God the Father,
For His blessed own,
We may talk to Jesus,
O'er this royal telephone.

—F. M. Lehman, "The Royal Telephone" (1909)

Early Pentecostals in the South practiced prayer in ways that most of their evangelical Protestant neighbors would have recognized. First, regular prayer strengthened the practitioner. Such "exercise of the soul," Sam Perry insisted, "carries us forward to spiritual progress."[1] Second, prayer was supplication to God for a blessing such as physical healing, protection of a loved one, or financial assistance. Evangelist F. M. Britton boasted, "I always could pray a hole in heaven big enough to get a blessing out."[2] Pentecostal prayer, though, was far more than spiritual discipline or supplication. Above all else, Pentecostals desired the assurance and guidance that came from hearing the voice of God. Both individually and corporately, these enthusiasts prayed to live in the Lord's presence—that place in the spiritual landscape where monologue becomes dialogue. According to Edith Blumhofer, Pentecostals in the early twentieth century thought of themselves "as indwelt by Christ, and yielded to impressions and subjective 'leadings' as well as to prophetic utterances." Not only were public meetings expected to be "led by the Spirit," many individuals "alleged that the Spirit directly and perceptibly controlled the smallest details of their lives."[3] Exactly how pioneer southern Pentecostals experienced and interpreted the voice of God is the subject of this essay.

I began gathering and listening to the life stories of first-generation Pentecostals more than a decade ago, largely in response to Grant Wacker's plea for scholars to take time to uncover the "forgotten world" of the movement's "internal culture."[4] In 2001, Wacker answered his own challenge with the publication of *Heaven Below: Early Pentecostalism and American Culture*, an impressive mix of original research, lively writing, and nuanced interpretation. In this generally empathetic study, Wacker identifies the tension between an idealistic "primitivism" and a realistic "pragmatism" as the key to understanding the evolution of a Pentecostal ethos, and he gives credit for the movement's initial success in the first quarter of the twentieth century to the creative resolution of these equally urgent otherworldly and this-worldly impulses. He is most persuasive when using this "Mary and Martha" paradigm as a lens for viewing the negotiation by pioneer Pentecostals of such thorny issues as biblical interpretation and spiritual authority, proper dress and preaching women, interracial fellowship and just wars. Indeed, the very breadth of coverage in *Heaven Below* means that many of the discussions are only long enough to whet the reader's appetite. Certainly, students of the movement will spend many years testing, extending, and modifying Wacker's arguments.

The following discussion of the enthusiastic practice of prayer by early southern Pentecostals engages the arguments in *Heaven Below* at two important points. First, while Wacker shrewdly identifies the primitivist impulse as "believers' yearning to be guided solely by God's Spirit in every aspect of their lives," he does not have the space to work out the various ways in which first-generation Pentecostals actually heard God's voice. What Wacker does say, however, is that the newly popular practice of delivering and interpreting "messages in tongues" was the "most common means of direct Holy Spirit instruction"—an assertion that may seem obvious, but that needs testing. Second, although Wacker calls for students of the movement to recreate the lost world of "Mr. and Ms. Average Pentecostal," the preponderance of his sources for the movement in the South come from a limited number of leaders of the inchoate denominations, especially judicatory officials, missionaries, and educators. In fact, he downplays the value of the most important source for the emergence of Pentecostalism in the region during the decade following 1907: the hundreds of testimonial letters published in the Atlanta-based paper the *Bridegroom's Messenger*. Yet the very letters Wacker dismisses for their "mawkishness" and lack of serious theological reflection—and countless similar "syrupy" testimonies surviving in subsequent southern periodicals and book-length memoirs—actually provide scholars with a wonderful opportunity to reinhabit the emerging revival in the region by listening to the reflections of Spirit-baptized southerners as they worked out the competing demands of primitivism and pragmatism in their daily lives.[5]

Consequently, this case study of the predominately white and southern Pentecostal Holiness Church (PHC) employs a mix of familiar and rare sources to suggest that an enthusiastic understanding of prayer as dialogue formed the core of the emerging Pentecostal worldview. The PHC resulted from the 1911 and 1915 mergers of the Fire-Baptized Holiness Church, the Pentecostal Holiness Church of North Carolina, and Tabernacle Pentecostal Church, radical Holiness organizations that each formed in the closing years of the nineteenth century and had by 1908 embraced the Pentecostal message of speaking in tongues as the proper "initial evidence" of Holy Ghost baptism. In 1918, the new church located its central offices and publishing house in Franklin Springs, Georgia. By the 1920s, the primary area of PHC strength ran in a crescent from Baltimore to Birmingham, with a strong secondary concentration in Oklahoma and developing works in Ontario, China, India, and South Africa.[6]

In addition to the frequently cited writings of a few prominent leaders like George Floyd Taylor, Nickels John Holmes, and Joseph Hillary King, the PHC produced an impressive range of sources that offer the opportunity to reconstruct the "forgotten world" of the early Pentecostal movement in the South. These include published testimonial letters, sermons, prayer requests, and local revival reports; annual conference reports loaded with numerical data; congregational records, including membership rosters and summaries of business meeting debates; unpublished memoirs penned by out-of-favor preachers; privately printed life stories of lay women; and personal libraries, which include the revelations of marginalia. Rarely utilized by historians, these materials can bring to the forefront of the church's story the rhythms of Pentecostal living, including attitudes about time, space, work, and social change as well as patterns of family life, consumer decisions, worship, and prayer. As a step in this direction, the following pages draw primarily on published autobiographies and letters by Spirit-filled believers associated with the PHC before 1920 in order to explore the nature and importance of these individuals' practice of prayer.[7]

Taken together, these testimonies present a God who speaks through physical sensations, mental impressions, dreams and visions, audible instructions, religious books and periodicals, personal Bible study, and prophetic messages. Conversations on the "Royal Telephone" provided the narrative frame for the life stories of southern Pentecostals, empowering them to speak boldly for their faith in the face of customary class, gender, age, and family restrictions.[8] These stories reveal, moreover, that reliance on divine communication typically long preceded exposure to Pentecostalism. Although the Pentecostal revival added new forms of dialogue with God such as the delivery and interpretation of "messages in tongues," these only served to intensify a preexisting enthusiasm, and they rarely became the dominant form of divine guidance.

Mary Williams's Conversations with God

The autobiography of Mary Wilson Williams provides an excellent starting place from which to assess the role of divine dialogue among early Pentecostals. Born in the North Carolina mountains near Hendersonville, Mary Wilson grew up in a Baptist environment where conversations always seemed to turn into discussions of death, eternal life, and Jesus. "I was afraid that I would miss heaven," she recalled. In 1885, during a revival at Old Liberty Baptist Church, eight-year-old Mary prayed with her schoolteacher at a small bench in front of the pulpit and was "wonderfully saved." As a result of her conversion, people "were shouting and having a glorious time." Mary immediately began a lifelong commitment to pray for the salvation of others. While praying in her school desk for a classmate "who seemed unable to pray through" to God, Mary first experienced divine direction: "Then the Lord spoke to my heart and said she was trying to take her father with her and she could not do that. God told me to get her during the intermission and take her to the grove and tell her about it; tell her to get saved first and then she could get her father." Mary talked and prayed with the reluctant girl "until she screamed out and cried, 'I'll give him and everything up.'" At that point, Mary remembered, "all Heaven came down."[9]

After about five years of preaching to "small crowds" at school, Mary became dissatisfied with her Christian experience. She felt an increased "need of God's help to overcome things." Mary's mother was "in the same boat." Together, they "kept reading and praying and God kept leading." During the next revival, Eliva Wilson received her blessing. While taking some girls to a pasture to pray with them, she suddenly began to sing under a great anointing. "The power was so great," according to her daughter, "that the girls ran from the place . . . and said the very ground was holy where she stood." At the evening service, Mary experienced her first vision when her transformed mother led in prayer: "I was bowed in prayer, and the Lord let me see my mother with a spiritual eye. I saw a ladder come down from Heaven to her and when she would pray a word she would go up a round of the ladder. When she reached the top, the Lord poured something all over her." Mary grew despondent because she "had no ladder," but soon she found satisfaction in a rush of enthusiastic experiences: "Jesus came to me and said, 'If you will put your trust in me I will bring you through.' When I told the Lord that I trusted him, I found myself at the top of the same ladder my mother was on. Then I felt something being poured all over me." Years later, Mary Williams looked back at this combination of physical sensation, vision, and Christ's voice through the lens of Pentecostal Holiness doctrine and identified it as the "second blessing" of sanctification.[10]

The intensity of Mary's prayer life waned during adolescence. At seventeen, she married J. M. Williams, the clerk of her church but a man "who did not know God." The marriage provided her with her "greatest test of obedience." Her husband did not pray at night, and Mary followed his example because "he was the head of the house." The Lord, Mary recalled, used a series of calamities to get the young couple's attention: "God began dealing with us by taking our first baby at only two days of age. Then I was stricken with fever and lay seven weeks between life and death." Mary's healing and spiritual revitalization resulted from a conversation with Christ:

Jesus was there with a host of angels, and He spoke to me and said, "Mary, my child, I have come for you, do you want to go or stay here and work for me a little longer, and have more sheaves to lay at my feet?" I told Him that I wanted to go, because I had suffered so much, but the Lord explained how it would be, and then I told Him that He had done so much for me that I wanted to do something for Him. He asked me if I would work for Him, and I told Him I would try. Then a large congregation stood in front of me, and He asked me if I would witness for Him in front of them, and I said yes. Then my home church came up before me, and I saw a young man, who was our neighbor, laughing at me. The Lord asked me if I would witness here, and I told Him I would with His help. Now all of the heavenly host left me, and for the first time I turned myself over in bed. My! what a rejoicing time they had, those who were standing by my bed.

Despite Mary's dramatic recovery, her husband still refused to establish a family altar. Mary, too, "failed to obey God." She felt impressed to make many changes in her home but declined to stand up to her husband. As a result, she recalled, "God saw fit to take our second boy when he was four years and four months old." "This was a lesson to us," Mary reflected, "and we reared the remainder of our family . . . by praying two and three times a day with them."[11]

A letter Williams wrote more than two decades before her autobiography suggests that she recovered from her son Brackston's death very slowly—and then only with the help of divine communication. "It was two years before I gave him up," she remembered in 1927, a quarter of a century after the child died. She praised God for easing her pain by allowing the child to speak to her from heaven: "I heard his voice calling me twice since he died. At one time I was alone and afraid. He came over me and said, 'Mamma, I will stay with you.'" Equally comforting was Eliva Wilson's testimony that she saw the revenant of her deceased grandson in attendance at a prayer meeting.[12]

Through Brackston's death, in particular, Mary Williams learned that God was "the head" and it was her duty to "obey." Her narrative is replete with incidents in which the significant men in her life stand in awe at her direct connection with heaven. For example, one dark night she was carrying her baby home from church with only "star light to go by." Her husband kept warning her to walk carefully. Suddenly, she recalled, "the brightest light came down and I could see as good as day." Mary's account continued: "Neither my husband nor the preacher who was walking with us could see it, but it made me so happy that I started running and praising the Lord. My husband, not knowing what had taken place, started after me trying to make me stop, but I ran right on into the house and the light followed me. When my husband came in the house he stumbled over the chairs, and it was so funny to see him falling over the things when I could see so plainly." On another occasion, Mary Williams astonished her husband when he returned home during a snowstorm by rehearsing his entire route through the mountains, even naming the families with whom he had taken shelter. She told him that in the midst of her worry, she had asked God to let her see where he was. Sitting on the floor with a Bible in her lap, she had followed him each step of the way. A "most serious look" came over J. M.'s face, and he began to cry. "Later," Mary added, "I heard him telling the boys never to do anything that they would not want her to find out, because I would find out anyway."[13]

From her special prayer citadel amid the rocks atop Bearwallow Mountain, Mary Williams sought God's direction for the evangelization of her community. Her sons and their friends told Mary that they had heard her call their names while they were hunting on the mountainside. She claimed that one man supernaturally heard her call his name in prayer when he was miles away. While on the mountain, Mary also received specific ministry instructions: "I would pray and whatever He said to do I would do it." God spoke to her "through nature as well as His spirit," often directing her to visit particular homes, where she would pray and read the Bible.[14]

Mary Williams's enthusiasm sometimes repelled neighbors and family. She was estranged from her uncle, for example, because they "didn't believe alike." Yet, in Mary's interpretation, God used this tension as an opportunity to pour out a third blessing on her: the baptism of the Holy Spirit. She attended, at her husband's insistence, a prayer meeting at her uncle's home, but she hid behind a door to avoid any confrontation. God spotted her there, however, and said, "Mary, my child, what are you doing? I cannot use cowards." After she repented, the Lord instructed Mary to bow at her uncle's feet. "He told me to pray for him and to wash his feet with my tears and dry them with my hair," she recalled. In humble obedience, she prayed until she "punctured the sky and the blessed Holy Ghost" came into her soul. She spoke in tongues for two hours that evening in 1906, even though news of the inchoate Pentecostal revival in the western United States—in which tongues speech played a prominent part—had not yet reached her community. In the days that followed, some mocked her; others claimed she was faking. Her father came by to see if her jaws were sore. People who were not at the prayer meeting visited in hope of a repeat performance. Some even claimed she had lost her mind.[15]

Williams defended her Spirit baptism by claiming that nothing bad happened to her "by having the Holy Ghost." The experience did, however, lead her into an even deeper enthusiasm. Dreams warned her more frequently, and voices led her more specifically than before. One night as she lay in her bed, for example, Mary saw through the window "a star as large as a wagon wheel." When the star came through the window, she could neither move nor speak. She soon found herself "in a large hall with a crowd of children running up and down . . . shouting 'Glory to God.'" After two hours, Williams came out of the vision and questioned God about its meaning. Instantly, she said, "the Lord brought one of my cousins and her husband to my bedside, and said, 'If they don't draw nigh to me I am going to visit their home.'" The next day, Mary told her cousin what she had seen. The woman "broke down and cried," but her husband, Joe, rejected the warning. That evening, Mary had a premonition that Joe would come to her house during the night. She awoke to the light of Joe's lantern shining through the window. He begged Mary and her mother to come and pray for his sick daughter. The sad result validated Williams's vision: "When we got there she was very ill and only lived one hour after we arrived. After she died I heard the sweetest music, and my mother did too. It was coming from one of the windows, and it was the most beautiful music I have ever heard, but it was so sad when the parents of the child would try to hear the music but could not." Shortly after, Joe left his wife. The next year, he committed suicide on the path to his daughter's grave.[16]

Perhaps Mary Williams did not always enjoy going where the Spirit led her, but her autobiography makes clear the value she placed on hearing God's voice. Whether from a dream or a vision, an impression or a burden, a voice or a verse of the Bible, supernatural direction was involved in every pivotal episode in Williams's construction of her life story. Her prayer life was an ongoing dialogue with God. Sometimes she started the conversation; at other times, initiation came from above. Hearing the voice of God gave Mary her voice—first with her classmates, then in her family and church, and ultimately in the pages of a book. The other early Pentecostals who chose to publish some of their experiences shared with Mary Williams an enthusiastic understanding of prayer. While God spoke to each in a unique combination of ways, divine communication invariably formed the scaffolding on which they built their life stories. Like Mary Williams, most reported hearing God's voice at important points in their lives before they received the "Pentecostal blessing" and spoke in ecstatic tongues; and while the intensity and frequency of their enthusiastic encounters generally increased after this experience, surprisingly few gave interpreted tongues messages a prominent role in their narratives.

Convictions and Burdens

Like Mary Williams, most Pentecostal pioneers first experienced God's voice as a "conviction" to repent. George Stanley did not "get saved" until after he married, but he remembered that the "Lord began to deal with [his] heart at the early age of five."[17] Laura Hylton's earliest memories included the hymns that her mother sang: "My heart was touched and made light, while tears of joy flowed." Although Hylton did not attend church until she was a teenager, she asserted firmly, "God deals with children, and I know that for a truth."[18] Watson Sorrow stressed that he and his brother were not converted from their rowdy way of living until they "got under old time conviction" at a Holiness camp meeting in Abbeville, South Carolina. Sorrow vividly described the experience of his brother-in-law, Henry Finley, who "thought he was sick and had the doctor come to see him"; the problem, it turned out, "was just old time conviction for his sins." Sorrow continued: "When the doctor had done he sent for some of us to come and pray for him, and as we were praying he began confessing and begging for mercy, and the Lord saved him and he was well."[19]

God also spoke conviction through nature. In 1886, when Florence Goff was five years old, an earthquake shook her North Carolina community. Since her parents were "praying people," neighbors soon filled her home: "Two of the most wicked men in the neighborhood woke me up praying. They were kneeling at the head of my bed praying for God to save them."[20] Sometimes, nature spoke conviction to a particular individual. At a Georgia tent meeting conducted in 1897 by fire-baptized evangelist Richard Baxter Hayes, a man fell under "deep conviction" and began to confess. Suddenly, "he heard a rooster crowing and asked the Lord what that meant." He testified that the Lord reminded him of a rooster he had stolen several years before and "asked him if he would make it right." The following night, after he had confessed his crime to the rooster's owner, he thought he heard a swarm of bees near the altar. Hayes recalled: "He asked the Lord about this and the Lord said, 'Don't you remember that gun of bees you took several years ago from so-and-so?' He said, 'Yes, Lord, I'll go see him tomorrow.'"[21]

Pentecostals distinguished between convictions and burdens. A conviction called a sinner to repentance; a burden caused a consecrated Christian to yearn for the salvation of others. As Joseph King left the Chinese city of Canton in 1911, a "mighty burden of prayer" overwhelmed him. After more than an hour spent in spiritual groaning for the success of the missions in Canton, King "prayed through," and the burden left him.[22] George Stanley developed a burden for an affluent bootlegger and his wife while staying in their Danville, Virginia, home. The husband had invited Stanley to conduct a tent meeting on his property. Stanley's burden grew when he discovered that the couple no longer talked to one another. In fact, the last time they had eaten together, she broke a bowl over his head, and he sent her to the hospital with two broken ribs. The bootlegger attended the tent meetings for a few days, but after falling under a "conviction" he suddenly demanded that Stanley leave. Stanley recounted the incident: "He said, 'Just tell the people to go to hell; they don't want any religion anyway.' I said, 'No, I'm going to stay here until this burden for you leaves me, and I'm going to eat your meat and bread.'" Stanley's burden birthed a boldness that produced results. Two days later, after Stanley exorcised the wife of a demon, the couple repented and helped to establish a Pentecostal Holiness congregation.[23]

Women especially witnessed to having burdens for their family members. Lucy Simpson Holmes, like many other Pentecostal women, suffered these burdens long before her Spirit baptism. During the anxious summer of 1876, as Wade Hampton struggled to redeem South Carolina from "foreign rule," Lucy's two sisters and her "dear mother" found their way to the cross. Her father, John W. Simpson, could not attend the Presbyterian revival because he was canvassing the state as Hampton's candidate for lieutenant governor. Lucy was "burdened and praying all the time" when her father returned home unexpectedly and agreed to attend the final revival service. As he stood to make a profession of faith, Lucy's "heart almost burst with gratitude to God for what He had done."[24] The burden for her father's spiritual progress did not stop with his salvation. After Lucy and her husband became acquainted with the Holiness movement, she mailed her father books on the "higher life" that she hoped he and her brother would "find interesting."[25]

Bodily Sensations

Like Lucy Holmes, most believers felt the weight of a burden emotionally. Early Pentecostal writers frequently recorded other occasions, however, when God dramatically communicated through the body. Soon after Laura Hylton's Spirit baptism, the future missionary interpreted a persistent toothache as God's displeasure at her reluctance to enter the ministry.[26] In 1899, railroad foreman

M. D. Sellers encountered the restraining hand of the Holy Ghost. Tired of hearing his irreligious comments and unpaid debts announced at a Holiness revival, he bolted from the meeting with the intent to commit "a crime that was really bad." He walked about a mile down a dark road. Sellers recalled: "Something seized me and turned me clear around in the road. It frightened me awful bad, and I hastened back to the tent."[27]

Sensations of physical ecstasy, though, far outnumbered incidents of heaven-sent pain or restraint. In 1910, when the newly Pentecostal Watson Sorrow was conducting a winter meeting near Ocklocknee, Florida, "a man named 'Joshua Red' prayed through, and got happy and climbed to the top of this old barn, and then hit the ground, turning hand springs."[28] Three years earlier, Florence Goff had received her Spirit baptism in an equally dramatic fashion: "Four or five saints came, laid hands on me, the Holy Ghost struck me; my hands began to draw; my jaws became stiff; the power went all over me. The saliva flew four feet from me; my tongue became first stiff; they said, 'Praise God.' I tried to; my tongue just flew."[29] Dan Muse experienced his Pentecost in 1913 at an Oklahoma City street mission: "There was never anything sweeter in my life than to feel myself completely in the power of God—I felt so good when the Spirit commenced to use my tongue that I guess I shouted . . . and the folks said I woke up the neighborhood." For more than three days, Muse wrote messages to coworkers on scraps of paper because nearly every time he opened his mouth he spoke in tongues.[30]

The Pentecostal Holiness Church grew out of the late-nineteenth-century Holiness movement, especially the Wesleyan variant that taught that sanctification was an instantaneous and transcendent experience of purification.[31] Surprisingly, autobiographers associated with the denomination often described their "second blessing" as more physically sensational than the baptism of the Holy Spirit. Lucy Holmes, for example, experienced sanctification while attending D. L. Moody's Christian Workers Convention in 1891: "Wave after wave of something like electric shocks would go over me from my head to my feet, and for days my weak body seemed unable to stand it any longer. I could only lie on the bed between services and weep and praise God." God communicated a "wonderful revelation" of true love to Lucy. Afterward, she found herself in possession of a new voice: "When from habit I would think to speak words of censure or fault finding, to my surprise, words of patience and love would be spoken as by another spirit within me."[32] Four years later, Lucy's husband experienced sanctification. Nickels J. Holmes remembered a "sudden flash of power that went through [his] body as an electric current." Next, he recalled, "God caused my heart to burn within me . . . as if a piece of hot cloth had been put right over my heart." Afterward, he "lay on the floor and shouted, and praised God for hours all alone."[33] Florence Goff witnessed Holiness meetings in the late 1890s where as many as a dozen men, women, and children were "slain in the Spirit." While some lay prostrate for hours, their "pulse and heart" the only indications of life, others reacted to the experience of sanctification by laughing "for an hour without stopping."[34] After the turn of the century, the Holiness language of physical ecstasy facilitated the description of the new Pentecostal outpouring. For instance, a North Carolinian wrote in 1909 of a meeting where "the power fell" and gave one man "such a shock from heaven's battery that he could not stop talking in an unknown tongue all the way home from service."[35]

Impressions

God communicated through both physical sensations and mental "leadings." Joseph H. King's lengthy memoir, *Yet Speaketh*, illustrates the importance of nonverbal impressions to an enthusiastic understanding of prayer. Before being born again, King felt an "inward leading to pray." Once he entered the ministry, the Holy Spirit often "pressed" him to deliver certain sermons. As an evangelist, he endeavored "to follow the leadings of the Lord from place to place." In the spring of 1900, King "was suddenly and unexpectedly impressed" that the Lord was going to give him a new type of ministry. Thus, King was "not altogether surprised" three months later when the leader of the Fire-Baptized Holiness Association fell "into great sin" and King was selected to replace him. In 1907, not long after receiving his Spirit baptism, King shared the platform at an Indianapolis church with a prominent Pentecostal pioneer. The Fire-Baptized leader was "suddenly and powerfully impressed" that his colleague was "not right before God." Although King "found nothing objectionable" in the minister's sermons, the "impression continued to abide." A few days later, the preacher's shocking "defense of an open saloon" proved to King that God had indeed planted the reservations in his mind.[36]

Although divine impressions drove King's narrative, he often experienced prolonged periods of difficulty in discerning God's intent—even after embracing the Pentecostal movement. For example, confusion and mistakes plagued his 1910–1912 tour of world missions. King embarked for Japan intent to follow no itinerary other than the promptings of God. After moderately success-ful stops in China and India, he "felt confident that God was leading" him to Australia. When he ran out of money in Ceylon, King confronted some dis-turbing questions: "Had God led me to go to Australia? Had he brought me to Ceylon on the way? Was I led of God, or was I being made sport of by the great seducer?" Thanks to the unexpected arrival of a five-dollar check from Richard Hayes, King left Ceylon "with God's permission, but not according to His highest will." He bought passage to England but ended up visiting Israel, where he "was tossed to and fro between two propositions" concerning the next leg of his journey, "both of which seemed to be from the Lord."[37]

The practical theologians among early Pentecostal writers fretted consider-ably about impulsive or deluded leadings. Sam Perry, for example, advised his readers to avoid any hasty decisions when they felt "impressed in spirit," be-cause he believed that any true leading from the Lord would linger until it be-came "so plain" that they would "feel safe in going ahead." W. W. Avant, who car-ried the Pentecostal message throughout the coastal plain of the Carolinas, created the striking image of Satan fishing for souls with misleading impressions and "old fake notions": "He sticks his pole in the bank of life and puts a false bait on his hook and plays his bait around the mouth of the human family."[38] This was not a new concern. Most Pentecostal preachers had learned to be wary of impressions during their years in the Holiness movement. In one of Joseph H. King's earliest published sermons, for instance, he admitted that God often leads believers to do things that may "seem utterly ridiculous to the world"; never-theless, King appealed for the exercise of "true Christian intelligence and judg-ment" in discerning whether an impression was of divine, satanic, or human ori-gin. As proof, he wrote of hearing "one dear brother announce publicly that he had an impression that he would be shot by a pistol in his left side, and that it would result in his death"; in fact, the man "died a few months later from fever."[39] Writing only months before the Pentecostal revival exploded in the South, George F. Taylor similarly lamented, "Oh that people would learn to go slow with God!" They were, he thought, "too prone to follow impressions" suggested by their own desires or even by "some spirit of evil." He gave the familiar illus-tration of a testimonial service where someone jumps up about the time every-body is ready to go home and announces, "The Lord sent me here today with a special message, and I must deliver my soul." "It is best not to act at once," Taylor warned. "Take time to think, take time to pray."[40]

Visions and Dreams

Clear and forceful visions, although rarer than divine impressions, proved easier to interpret. For Holiness and Pentecostal folks alike, visions primarily spoke either an offer of assurance or a call to evangelism. In Florence Goff's 1924 autobiography, she repeatedly testified to the power of visions to bring assurance of eternal life. When her Holiness father lay on his deathbed, he suddenly cried out with joy, "There has been a wave of salvation over me all day, and I have seen Jesus on the cross." In 1896, Goff attended a Holiness revival near the Cape Fear River where people "lay in trances, some on the floor until nearly daybreak." She recalled: "Some had visions of heaven and saw their loved ones there. And it was all classes—well-bred, high toned college boys and hard-working people all got blessed." Later in her autobiography, Goff demonstrated the powerful effect a vision could have on a Pentecostal camp meeting. "The wife of Pierce Brooks" died during the meeting, and "Sister Ed Jolley" fell gravely ill. While a teenage girl named Mary Butler lay in a trance at the young people's prayer meeting, she cried out: "I see Sister Jolley. She's in heaven, skipping on the Golden Streets with Pierce's wife." Within ten minutes, news spread through the camp that Jolley had indeed died. As a result of Mary Butler's divine vision, Goff could write: "We had two very triumphant deaths while this meeting was in progress."[41]

Not all deaths were so triumphant. Nearly every extended Pentecostal memoir recounts the passing of at least one child. Mothers, in particular, reported difficulty accepting the loss of a child without some supernatural comfort. Mary Williams heard her dead son's voice several times; others saw their departed children in visions. One winter night in 1914, for example, Sarah Mitchel "was in a vision" for nearly four hours. She testified: "I went in at the pearly gates and saw my little one and she shook hands with me and said, Hallelujah! I said, Bless your little heart." Conversing with the revenant of her daughter not only allowed Mitchel to ease her suffering, it also unleashed a rush of enthusiastic encounters over the next twelve hours that transformed her life. In the midst of praying for a gravely ill boy, concern for the child—heightened by the visit with her deceased daughter—fused with Mitchel's desire to experience the Pentecostal baptism. "The preacher anointed the little boy and he fell close to me and looked like he was dying," she explained. "I had never seen anything like it. I looked around and saw the power falling. I looked back at the little boy and said, Oh Lord, if that is the power of the Holy Ghost, what is the reason

I can't have it after I have suffered everything that I have?" Then Mitchel "went away" in another vision: "The savior appeared on the cross, and I was at his feet, and I fell in the fountain rolling and saying, Glory, oh glory, every time I went from one side to the other." When Mitchel emerged from her vision, she was speaking in tongues. Upon entering the church later that evening, Mitchel suddenly "went running up the aisle, and tossed about the house three hours or more." Temporarily blinded while in this ecstatic state, she "saw four different visions": a red cloud, a lamp, the prodigal son, and the healing garment of Christ. Mitchel's spate of visions may have lasted only a day, yet they reconciled her to the loss of her child and filled her with the Holy Ghost. No longer afraid, the formerly bashful Mitchel began to pray and witness in public. She also gave up the "doctors and remedies" she had been so dependent on. Most of all, she achieved inner peace. Sarah Mitchel's one visionary day began with assurance but ended with empowerment.[42]

Visions did not have to occur frequently to be important. Ethel Smith recently described a vision that after eighty years remains as fresh in her mind "as if it just happened last night." When Smith was eight years old, her family was quarantined with smallpox. One sister in particular seemed near death. "The house was hot," Smith remembered, "and I got up at the window to get a breath of fresh air." It was "a moon-shining night," and Smith caught a glimpse "of what looked like a woman" gliding down the path to the spring. Smith recalled: "Then she appeared exactly straight across from where I was, and I felt like she looked me right in the eye. Whatever this was it looked like a woman—and it scared me. I got into the bed quick, but I never forgot how she moved along. It looked like she was floating, and yet I could see her feet." When Smith described at breakfast what she had seen through the window, her brother quickly dismissed it as a meaningless dream. Her mother, however, validated and interpreted the vision: "What did we pray last night before we went to bed? Lord, let your guardian angel encamp around this household." Then, chastening Ethel's brother, she explained: "Don't you ever say a thing like that again. That was God's angel taking care of us." Smith's vision renewed her parent's confidence that God would bring their family through its plague. More importantly, it provided a foundation for Ethel Smith's future faith. "It never, never, never left me," she reflected. "Whenever it seemed like I was afraid or things were not going right, that experience would come back to me."[43]

Whether of loved ones in heaven or of ministering angels on earth, visions of assurance brought solace and strength. Evangelistic visions, on the other hand, often demanded immediate action. F. M. Britton first experienced the sure, urgent direction of a vision while still a Baptist evangelist. Staying at the South Carolina home of a Sister Cook, Britton awoke one morning to the image of "a white horse coming down the road with some one driving at a rapid rate." "I had an assurance," he wrote, "that they were coming after me to go and pray for some one that was very sick." Britton remembered that after he meditated on the vision for a few moments, "the Lord said, Get ready as quick as you can, for they are coming after you to pray for a sick person." Reacting to the combination of vision and voice, he dressed quickly and headed outside to wait for his divine appointment. He continued: "Then I walked out on the front porch of the house, and looked up the road in the direction I saw the horse coming in the vision, and lo, the white horse was in sight. I said, Sister Cook, look yonder, that is the one that is coming for me now." Before the rider spoke, the emboldened Britton said, "Turn around, I am ready to go." Upon entering the home of Welse Huggins, Britton found the bedridden newlywed "very sick with bilious colic and a very high fever." As Britton read from the Epistle of James in preparation to pray for Huggins's healing, he sensed that the young man had a more important need. "I can't ask God to heal you for you to live in sin," Britton told him, "but if you will give God your heart, He will heal you and save you at the same time." After hearing Britton's prayer, Huggins "shouted aloud, 'I am healed and saved.'" On this memorable day in Britton's early ministry, prayer as dialogue facilitated a successful prayer as petition.[44]

Britton's white horse vision was short and specific. Before noon, its purpose had been accomplished. Other evangelistic visions spoke more broadly of the need to take the Gospel to every creature. Holiness believers frequently testified to seeing images of heaven or hell that called them to evangelize "a lost and dying world." These visions became more intense in the early years of the Pentecostal revival. Early on the first day of 1914, for example, Pearl Loftin, a student at Nickels J. Holmes's Altamont Bible and Missionary Institute, "awoke about one o'clock and immediately began singing in tongues a very sweet, inspiring song." As she sang, God showed her "the condition of this lost world." Suddenly, the scene switched. Loftin wrote: "I then saw a precipice and millions of souls just rushing into hell. Then I seemed to be let down into this place and O, the woe and misery, the degradation of that awful place. I screamed at the top of my voice. The Spirit said there was no place on earth so filthy as hell." The emotion of the experience was still strong nine months later when Loftin penned her testimony: "Oh! the weeping and wailing. The sad regret of opportunities lost forever. In hell, hell, hell, forever." After challenging her readers with John 4:35—"Lift up your eyes and look to the fields for they are white unto harvest"—Loftin concluded with the statement, "It is high time we were about our Father's business."[45]

The testimonies and autobiographies of early Pentecostals recorded fewer dreams than visions. The line between dream and vision, however, was often thin. Sarah Mitchel experienced her first vision in bed from about "three until day," and F. M. Britton saw the vision of a white horse riding toward him as he awoke.[46] One Georgia woman even distinguished between her "day visions" and her "night visions."[47] First-generation Pentecostals clearly preferred visions to dreams as a means of divine communication, even to the point of calling what was likely a dream a vision. Yet dreams—when identified as dreams—spoke of the same themes as visions: death, rebirth, family, and harvest. For example, William Hayes dreamed of standing in a railroad station and seeing his father, Richard, on an approaching train crowded with "mad, fussing" people. When the train stopped, William recalled, "I saw the old devil push my father off down the steps and they all cheered as the train rolled off." The dream troubled William for several years. After his father's death, he received the interpretation: "The train was this ungodly world and my father had fought the old devil so hard that he was glad when father stepped off the stage of action." His father's death also triggered the recurrence of a dream William had had over thirty years earlier of a smiling, gray-headed man cutting "golden ripe wheat." William explained: "This dream, which had faded for a number of years, came before me as a flash. God gave me the interpretation. The wheat field was the world. The old man was my father and he had finished and I must now take his place."[48]

An Audible Voice

While visions tended to carry clearer messages than the more symbol-laden dreams, neither could compete with hearing God speak audibly. The assurance of such direct communication could generate great boldness. For example, during a Pentecostal revival George Stanley attended in North Carolina, a young man disrupted the meetings with loud mockery. According to Stanley, "The second night the Lord told me to kneel down in between the seats in front of him and pray for him." He prayed: "Lord, if this man can be saved, save him; or if he has blasphemed and will never be saved, let him die and go to hell. It is better for him to go to hell than to cause others to by disturbing the services." The next night, a friend warned Stanley to get police protection because the mocker had recruited five other ruffians to help kill him. Confident that God had spoken, Stanley decided to "trust Jesus to protect [him]." He described what happened when he left the church: "Six men were lined up to kill me. There were three on each side with knives. I had about three feet of space to walk between them. I asked God to protect me, and if He was not through with me, not to let them harm me. They stood there as though they were paralyzed. Not one spoke; not one moved." A few days after Stanley's miraculous escape, the young mocker burned to death after spilling gasoline on his clothes.

Stanley also prayed for specific people to be healed at specific times. Thirty minutes before his brother's son-in-law was to have surgery, "God told [Stanley to] go and pray for him." "When I did," Stanley recalled, "he was healed." Immediately, "the Lord said" for Stanley to go to the home of a blind Baptist girl who had attended his revival in Star, North Carolina. He recounted: "I spoke to her and said, 'Sister Lizzie, if you will believe, the Lord will baptize you.' Before I got to her she was speaking in other tongues. Then the Lord said, 'I will heal her if you will pray.' I reached down and took her hand saying, 'In the name of Jesus, I demand your eyes be opened.'" As soon as Lizzie stopped speaking in tongues, "[she began] telling me how I looked," Stanley wrote.[49]

Like other first-generation Pentecostals in the South, Stanley experienced the clear direction of God's voice even before he received the Holy Spirit baptism. After Stanley obtained the "second blessing" of sanctification in 1899, he faced disciplinary proceedings at his Baptist church. As he sat before the congregational court, "the Lord then spoke to [him] and told [him] what to say." Stanley remembered: "I told them that it was a shame for them to have me up when I had done nothing wrong. I told them, also, that no one in that church had ever asked me about my soul before I was saved, that I use[d] to have dances in my home and that members of that church came, drank whiskey, and danced."[50] Nickels J. Holmes also heard God's voice prior to embracing Pentecostalism. In 1863, his oldest sister encouraged him from her deathbed to enter the ministry. Twenty-five years passed before Holmes accepted the call. His life changed dramatically in the spring of 1888. After fourteen years spent as a lawyer, "the call to preach seemed to have gone away"; yet the unexpected deaths of his father and his only child, as well as the pressure of running for political office, provided the context for his supernatural encounter with God. Holmes remembered that on the day after he officially entered the race to be circuit court solicitor, "these words came to [him] as if they had been sounded in [his] ears": "'You are seeking an office to prosecute men for crime. Had you better seek to save them from the commission of crime?'"[51]

Although Holmes "recognized immediately that it was God speaking to [him] and renewing the call to preach," he softened his autobiographical account of God's speech with the words "as if."[52] Like Holmes, most Pentecostals hesitated to claim that they had heard an audible voice. When Laura Hylton described her call to minister, she carefully used such qualifying expressions as "seemed to say" and "as if audible." Typically, she avoided the emphatic construction "God did say to me" in favor of the conditional "God would say to me."[53] When pioneer Virginia minister Delaware Whitenack gave his testimony, he, too, chose the words carefully. He remembered struggling to accept the call to preach until God spoke a message of encouragement to him "almost like he did to Moses."[54] Kenneth Spooner's description of his missionary call to Africa illustrates this tentative language: "It was in the year 1906, while engaged in my early morning devotions in a small room in New York City, that God spoke to me as it were in audible tones: 'I want you to go to Africa.' I was still on my knees and was very much afraid at the sound of the voice." Even though Spooner clearly remembered the "sound of the voice," he employed the tentative phase "as it were in audible tones."[55]

Perhaps this hesitancy sprang from the awareness that Satan, as well as God, had a voice. According to Nickels J. Holmes, Satan was "always hanging around" to confuse prayerful conversation. For example, after Holmes felt divinely urged to give up medical care and trust Christ as his healer, "Satan got specially busy after [him] and suggested all manner of consequences."[56] When Richard Hayes attended his first Holiness meeting, the Holy Spirit told him to go to the altar, "but the Devil was present" and reminded him of his community status as "a big merchant and a Deacon in the First Baptist Church."[57] "I know there is a personal devil," George F. Taylor assured his readers in 1906; "Sometimes he jumps upon me and I have to fight for my life." Taylor felt particularly susceptible to attack while in prayer: "Often when I go to pray Satan presents himself, and sometimes I battle with him for hours. I have met him time and again while at prayer in the woods, and fought him with all my might. I have known him to come and tell me, if God was all He claimed to be, He knew my wants and there was no need to be on my face telling Him about it. He has had the audacity a few times to tell me there is no God. He has puzzled me with perplexing questions that were of no good." Taylor recalled that even when he was in the midst of worship, "Satan would say, You have no experience of salvation." The Devil would ask him, "Do you not see how bright that person's face is?" and he would taunt Taylor by saying, "Your face does not shine that way." On another occasion, as Taylor prayed for divine guidance on what to preach, the Lord suggested one text and the Devil another. Discerning which subject was from God could be difficult, Taylor admitted.[58]

Reading

Even though George F. Taylor struggled to preach divinely inspired messages, Pentecostal autobiographers rarely reported hearing God speak through a sermon. In fact, they sometimes recalled that the Lord distracted their attention during a sermon in order to communicate with them.[59] They more often heard God during private Bible reading. When Richard Hayes began to preach, for instance, God "revealed" many sermons to him as he systematically studied the Bible.[60] Florence Goff described a young schoolteacher "diseased with egotism" who "became intrigued by holiness ideas": "He found his Bible after a long search, took an ax, and went off as if to cut wood. He took the Bible in his hand, and thus began to pray: 'Lord, if there is such an experience as sanctification, let my Bible open to a chapter that will make it plain to me.' The Bible opened at Hebrews, 10th chapter, which is full of sanctification. He shut the Bible after reading that chapter, and said, 'Lord, I believe it, and right now I want it.' He wrestled with God until the blessing came, and then went shouting, jumping and clapping his hands to the house."[61] The testimonies of Spirit-filled believers frequently identified persistent and anointed Bible reading as the main habit that differentiated those who entered deeper revelation from those who remained in "nominal" churches. William Blackburn, for example, remembered growing up in Presbyterian and Methodist congregations in which people "did not know about the Bible well enough to do what it taught."[62] And Sarah Mitchel, reflecting on her years as a Methodist, lamented: "I only read the Bible in Sunday School, and it was like reading an ordinary piece of paper. I soon forgot it."[63] Indeed, the spiritual arrogance that some scholars have detected among Pentecostals grew as much from their familiarity with Scripture as it did from their acquaintance with the Spirit.[64]

In addition to reading the Bible, some Pentecostals found dialogue with God through religious books and periodicals. Joseph H. King remembered his "all-consuming" desire to read after he was saved. Time with J. A. Seiss's *Lectures on the Apocalypse*, for example, completely changed the way King understood Bible prophecy, giving him a "new Bible." In 1906, an account of the Los Angeles Pentecostal revival in a religious paper stirred within King "a hunger" to receive the Spirit baptism. When attempting to reconcile his Methodist doctrinal heritage with the new Pentecostal teachings, King sought an answer through prayer and fasting, but the "way was closed and God would not hear." In desperation, he turned to his bookshelf: "I laid upon the table all the books I had that would give me any information on the subject. I began reading Dean Alford's Critical Notes on the New Testament in Greek, the volume that included the Book of Acts. The Spirit suggested the eighth chapter as the first portion to read." Through Alford's analysis of Greek grammar, God removed from King's mind "the stronghold of opposing the theory of tongues."[65]

Reading D. L. Moody's *The Secret of Power* first sparked in Nickels and Lucy Holmes an interest in Holiness.[66] An entry in Nickels's Bible reveals the importance of reading "anointed" materials: "Bamburg. May 28th, '96. Prostrated on the floor of my room, counting myself dead with Christ, after reading 'Christ Our Life,' by Andrew Murray."[67] A decade later, reports in the religious press of the Pentecostal outpouring in Los Angeles reached the campus of the Altamont Bible and Missionary Institute, which Nickels Holmes had founded in 1898 after losing his Presbyterian pastorate over the Holiness issue. Faculty and students alike began zealously praying to see the "gift of the Holy Ghost" manifested in South Carolina as well. By the fall of 1907, the former mountaintop resort was ablaze in Pentecostal power. Believers spoke, sang, and wrote in tongues; some danced and played musical instruments "as the Spirit led."[68] In some ways, these experiences hearkened back to the divine communication by physical ecstasy that characterized nineteenth-century revivalism, especially the Holiness version of the 1880s and 1890s. When the "gift of tongues" and "interpretation of tongues" operated in tandem, however, the Pentecostal revival introduced something new to the enthusiastic practice of prayer.

Tongues and Prophetic Speech

An interpreted tongues message became an actual prophecy from God. For example, when an Altamont teacher wrote a long message "in an unknown tongue," Nickels J. Holmes mailed all seventeen pages "to Mrs. Frank Bramblett, a lady in Laurens County, who had the gift of interpretation." She responded with an exhortation to evangelize the world: "You have no idle time to spare. Every breath you draw perishing souls are dropping into hell. The fields are white unto harvest, but where are laborers? Woe! be unto them that are at ease in Zion. Make haste to carry my Gospel to famishing souls. What is done must be done quickly." The prophecy continued with commands and biblical references that stressed the urgency of mission work and the nearness of Christ's return. Shortly after Bramblett's translation arrived, two students wrote shorter glossolalic messages. Bramblett translated them both as personal messages from God to Holmes in which God encouraged Holmes: "Urge My saints to carry My glad tidings of salvation to this dark benighted land."[69]

Writing from the coastal plain of eastern North Carolina, Florence Goff described the similar consequences of her 1907 Pentecostal baptism: "God has given me twelve different languages, enabling me to write in several, and play beautiful heavenly anthems with the words on the piano. . . . Often he interprets through me."[70] Within a decade, however, reports of both messages written in tongues and outbursts in actual languages unfamiliar to the speaker virtually disappeared from PHC literature. More typically, prophetic communication began to occur when one gifted believer delivered a message in a "heavenly tongue" and another interpreted. The setting could be a large church service or a small "cottage prayer meeting." In 1914, it even happened in the home of two North Carolina sisters, M. A. Bulbin and M. E. Whitt, who claimed that the Pentecostal revival had yet to arrive in their "dark country." Having apparently read of deeper Christian experiences, they sought sanctification and the baptism of the Holy Ghost. Early one morning as they were together in prayer, the "Holy Spirit fell." When one sister started speaking in tongues, the other "began to prophesy through the Royal Telephone to the mysteries of God's eternal kingdom." In particular, the message identified predestination as a false doctrine. All could choose salvation in these last days, the Spirit said, if only Christians would present the Gospel to them. Bulbin and Whitt drew enough inspiration and strength from the prophecy to enter the ministry against the wishes of family members who thought them both "crazy." Writing five years after their conversation on the "Royal Telephone," the sisters confidently explained that they may indeed have lost their minds that day, but that they "got the mind of Christ."[71]

Conclusion

Sisters Bulbin and Whitt appropriated the image of a "Royal Telephone" from F. M. Lehman's popular 1909 Holiness hymn by that title, but they expanded his understanding of the prayer dialogue to include the Pentecostal promise that Spirit-baptized believers could at times utter the very words of God. This possibility of regular prophetic communication clearly differentiated the Pentecostal movement from its nineteenth-century evangelical forebears. Testimonies and autobiographies from the formative years of the PHC, however, illustrate that long before many first-generation Pentecostals spoke in tongues, they had heard God speak through convictions, burdens, physical sensations, mental impressions, visions, dreams, voices, or inspired reading at nearly every critical juncture of their lives. And despite the obvious innovation of pervasive tongues speech, they stressed continuity with the past by consistently describing their services as old-fashioned and their faith as old-time.[72] Based on their accounts, it seems that the Pentecostal revival merely intensified and added new forms to their ongoing dialogues with God, which suggests that both the texture of Pentecostal faith and the secret of the movement's success lay in its revitalization of enthusiasm at the dawn of an insistently secular century.[73]

This conclusion must remain tentative, however, until historians listen carefully to the testimonies of the majority of pioneer Pentecostals who were not part of the predominately white and southern Pentecostal Holiness Church. Ethnicity, region, and organizational affiliation, for example, are just three of the factors that may have influenced the way Spirit-filled believers ordered their life stories. But as Grant Wacker demonstrates so forcefully in *Heaven Below*, the "forgotten world" of early Pentecostal culture is not beyond recovery, and students of the movement have barely scratched the surface of available firsthand sources.

Notes

Abbreviations

BM   *Bridegroom's Messenger*
PHC   Pentecostal Holiness Church
PHPHC   Publishing House of the Pentecostal Holiness Church

1. Sam C. Perry, "Continual Victory," *Church of God Evangel*, March 13, 1915, 3.
2. F. M. Britton, *Pentecostal Truth, Or Sermons on Regeneration, Sanctification, the Bap-*

tism of the Holy Spirit, Divine Healing, the Second Coming of Jesus, etc., together with a Chapter on the Life of the Author (Royston, Ga.: PHPHC, 1919), 238, 231.

3. Edith L. Blumhofer, "Restoration as Revival: Early American Pentecostalism," in *Modern Christian Revivals*, eds. Edith L. Blumhofer and Randall Balmer (Urbana: University of Illinois Press, 1993), 148–49.

4. Grant Wacker, "The Functions of Faith in Primitive Pentecostalism," *Harvard Theological Review* 77 (1984): 374.

5. Grant Wacker, *Heaven Below: Early Pentecostals and American Culture* (Cambridge, Mass.: Harvard University Press, 2001). On the first point, see the chapters titled "Introduction," "Tongues," and "Authority," esp. 12–13, 40–44, and 81–84. On the second point, see the chapters titled "Testimony" and "Society," especially 68 and 208.

6. On PHC history, see A. D. Beacham Jr., *A Brief History of the Pentecostal Holiness Church*, rev. ed. (Franklin Springs, Ga.: Advocate Press, 1990); Joseph E. Campbell, *The Pentecostal Holiness Church, 1898–1948: Its Background and History* (Franklin Springs, Ga.: PHPHC, 1951); and Vinson Synan, *The Old-Time Power: A Centennial History of the International Pentecostal Holiness Church* (Franklin Springs, Ga.: LifeSprings Resources, 1998). In the 1970s, the PHC added "International" to the front of its name and moved its headquarters from Georgia to Oklahoma City.

7. More than two dozen people associated with the early history of the PHC eventually published their life stories as books or as part of a collection of sermons or other doctrinal writings. Only Kenneth Spooner, a native of Barbados, was born outside the South; he was also the only nonwhite. Two of every three autobiographers were male, compared with only one of three in the general membership of the PHC, and all but one were ministers. (Several of the preachers included in this study never officially affiliated with the PHC, but they maintained close relations with the developing organization.) Examining testimonial letters sent to religious papers helps to redress the imbalance in the autobiographies by including more women and laity (although the distinction between clergy and laity, especially for women, was not always clear). The church's official organ, the *Pentecostal Holiness Advocate*, did not begin publication until 1917, but it regularly published letters in which writers recalled their spiritual histories. Before 1917, PHC members wrote to several independent Pentecostal periodicals. One such paper, the *Apostolic Evangel*, was published by several PHC leaders in Falcon, North Carolina, but few copies survive. The Atlanta-based *Bridegroom's Messenger*, founded in 1907 by G. B. Cashwell, is more helpful. Nearly a complete run of this paper exists, and the majority of the members of the editorial board during *BM*'s first decade were PHC ministers. In addition, Nickels J. Holmes began publication in 1911 of the *Altamont Witness*, which featured testimonies from faculty and students at his Greenville, South Carolina, school. Unlike the more reflective autobiographical writings, these early periodicals provide more immediate presentation of divine revelation and guidance. This study also includes a smattering of other sources, including a few interviews by the author with members of the PHC whose memories stretch back before 1920.

8. In *Heaven Below*, Grant Wacker shrewdly observes that the act of testifying—orally or in writing—"clothed individual lives with timeless significance" (69), but he does not highlight the centrality of enthusiastic prayer to the structure of these narratives. See especially his chapter on "Testimony," 58–69.

9. Mary Williams, *Memories of Childhood* (Hendersonville, N.C.: privately printed, [1950?]), 6–7.

10. Ibid., 8–9.

11. Ibid., 10–13.

12. Mrs. J. M. Williams, "Obituary," *Apostolic Evangel*, May 15, 1927, 2.

13. Ibid.; Williams, *Memories*, 13–14, 20.

14. Williams, *Memories*, 11, 13.

15. Ibid., 15–16.

16. Ibid., 17–18.

17. George W. Stanley, *My Life Experiences with God* (Franklin Springs, Ga.: PHPHC, n.d.), 10.

18. Laura Mae Hylton, *An Orphan as a Missionary* (Franklin Springs, Ga.: PHPHC, 1952), 3.

19. Watson Sorrow, *Some of My Experiences* (Franklin Springs, Ga.: PHPHC, 1954), 6, 47.

20. Florence Goff, *Tests and Triumphs* (Falcon, N.C.: privately printed, 1924), 13.

21. William M. Hayes, *Memories of Richard Baxter Hayes* (Greer, S.C.: privately printed, 1945), 24–25. This volume includes autobiographical statements by father Richard (b. 1859) and son William (b. 1885).

22. Joseph H. King and Blanche L. King, *Yet Speaketh: Memoirs of the Late Bishop Joseph H. King* (Franklin Springs, Ga.: PHPHC, 1949), 166–67.

23. Stanley, *My Life*, 34–35.

24. Nickels J. Holmes and Wife [Lucy Simpson Holmes], *Life Sketches and Sermons* (Royston, Ga.: PHPHC, 1920), 135. This volume includes autobiographies by both husband and wife.

25. Lucy Simpson Holmes to William Dunlap Simpson, November 12, 1890, William D. Simpson Papers, Southern Historical Collection, University of North Carolina, Chapel Hill, N.C.

26. Hylton, *An Orphan*, 39–40.

27. M. D. Sellers Memoir, W. Eddie Morris Collection, International Pentecostal Holiness Church Archives, Bethany, Okla.

28. Sorrow, *My Experiences*, 38.

29. Goff, *Tests and Triumphs*, 52.

30. Harold Paul, *Dan T. Muse: From Printer's Devil to Bishop* (Franklin Springs, Ga.: Advocate Press, 1976), 23.

31. For discussions of the relationship between the Holiness and Pentecostal movements in the South, see Vinson Synan, *The Holiness-Pentecostal Tradition: Charismatic*

Movements in the Twentieth Century, 2d ed. (Grand Rapids: Eerdmans, 1997), 44–67, 107–28, and Edward L. Ayers, *The Promise of the New South: Life after Reconstruction* (New York: Oxford University Press, 1992), 398–408.

32. Holmes and Holmes, *Life Sketches*, 306.

33. Ibid., 85–89.

34. Goff, *Tests and Triumphs*, 25–26.

35. Macon Cavenaugh, ["Testimony,"] *BM*, April 15, 1909, 3.

36. King and King, *Yet Speaketh*, 32, 90–91, 102, 106, 126–27.

37. Ibid., 225, 229, 282, 295–96.

38. Perry, "God's Servants Led by the Spirit," *Church of God Evangel*, February 12, 1916, 3; Waitus Woodson Avant, *Salvation and Principle* (Wilmington, N.C.: Free Will Baptist Publishing House, [1919?]), 16–17.

39. J[oseph] H[illary] K[ing], "Impressions," *Live Coals of Fire*, June 15, 1900, 1. Interestingly, King wrote this piece about the same time that he later remembered being "suddenly and unexpectedly impressed" that God was about to open a new field of ministry to him (King and King, *Yet Speaketh*, 102).

40. George Floyd Taylor, *The Devil: A Vivid Account of His Origin, His Malignity and His Works, Portraying His Maneuverings in This World and Depicting His Final Doom* (Goldsboro, N.C.: Nash Brothers, 1907), 34–35. (A date of August 4, 1906, at the bottom of the preface indicates that Taylor wrote this book before he received his Pentecostal baptism in January 1907.)

41. Goff, *Tests and Triumphs*, 32, 26–27, 83.

42. Sarah Mitchel, "Testimony," *Pentecostal Holiness Advocate*, September 12, 1918, 12–13.

43. Ethel Smith, interview by the author, Shenandoah, Va., April 16, 1996.

44. Britton, *Pentecostal Truth*, 228–30.

45. Pearl Loftin, "What Is Your Theme?" *Altamont Witness*, September 22, 1914, 3–4.

46. Mitchel, "Testimony," 12; Britton, *Pentecostal Truth*, 228.

47. Sarah D. Wooten, "Testimony of Sister S. D. Wooten," *BM*, September 15, 1909, 3.

48. Hayes, *Memories*, 107–11.

49. Stanley, *My Life*, 50, 54–55.

50. Ibid., 14–15.

51. Holmes and Holmes, *Life Sketches*, 61–62.

52. Ibid.

53. Hylton, *An Orphan*, 38.

54. W. W. Carter, "Reverend D. M. Whitenack," *Virginia Conference Messenger*, October 1944, 1, 3.

55. Mrs. K. E. M. [Geraldine] Spooner, ed., *Sketches of the Life of K. E. M. Spooner: Missionary, South Africa* (Franklin Springs, Ga.: PHPHC, [1938?]), 96.

56. Holmes and Holmes, *Life Sketches*, 75, 124.

57. Hayes, *Memories*, 12.

58. Taylor, *The Devil*, 44–45.

59. For example, see King and King, *Yet Speaketh*, 144, and Hylton, *An Orphan*, 68.

60. Hayes, *Memories*, 7.

61. Goff, *Tests and Triumphs*, 28.

62. William Henry Blackburn, interview by the author, Natural Bridge Station, Va., February 9, 1996.

63. Mitchel, "Testimony," 12.

64. James R. Goff Jr., in particular, has written frankly of this elitism in "Closing Out the Church Age: Pentecostals Face the Twenty-First Century," *Pneuma* 14 (Spring 1992): 15.

65. J. H. King, *From Passover to Pentecost* (Senath, Mo.: F. E. Short, 1914), 174–75.

66. Holmes and Holmes, *Life Sketches*, 301.

67. Ibid., 88. After finishing E. M. Bounds's *Power through Prayer* in 1913, one Virginia pastor scribbled a similar reaction on the front leaf: "The Lord is my witness. He used [this book] to bring me well into the Holiest of Holies." Bane T. Underwood Collection, Edward D. Reeves Library, International Pentecostal Holiness Church Archives, Bethany, Okla.

68. Ibid., 135.

69. Ibid., 180–81, 183.

70. "Mrs. H. H. Goff's Letter," *BM*, October 1, 1907, 4.

71. M. A. Bulbin and M. E. Whitt, "Testimony," *Pentecostal Holiness Advocate*, October 30, 1919, 12–13.

72. For example, see the following references to old-fashionedness: Avant, *Salvation and Principle*, 6–7, 33, 44–45, 49–50; A. E. Robinson, ed., *Memoirs of Thurman Augustus Cary* (Royston, Ga.: [Live Coals Press, 1907?]), 34; and W. D. York, *Life Events of Dan and Dollie York* (n.p., n.d.), 11. Late-nineteenth-century Holiness adherents had employed identical ritual language to describe their spirituality, which suggests the shrewdness of Robert Mapes Anderson's 1979 observation that the Pentecostal movement represented "the most recent expression" of a "revivalistic-pietistic tradition" that antedated even the Holiness movement (*Vision of the Disinherited: The Making of American Pentecostalism* [New York: Oxford University Press, 1979], 133). Increasingly, scholars have called attention to the enthusiastic aspect of eighteenth- and nineteenth-century evangelicalism. In *The Democratization of American Christianity* (New Haven: Yale University Press, 1989), Nathan O. Hatch persuasively argues that a variety of innovative preachers in the generation after the American Revolution "openly fanned the flames of religious ecstasy" by advocating enthusiasm "as an essential part of Christianity," even displaying an unprecedented willingness to treat dreams and visions as "normal manifestations of divine guidance and instruction" (10).

73. The remarkable growth of Pentecostalism should not obscure its equally remarkable schismatic tendency. Recently, theologian Harvey Cox contrasted the movement's "lightning spread" with its "runaway divisiveness," observing that the "more the pentecostals fought, the more they multiplied." Cox continued: "One of the most astonishing

features of the movement is that it seems to thrive not only on opposition (which many re-ligious movements have), but also on division" (*Fire from Heaven: The Rise of Pentecostal Spirituality and the Reshaping of Religion in the Twenty-First Century* [Reading, Mass.: Addison-Wesley, 1995], 71, 77). Though beyond the scope of this study, the enthusiastic practice of prayer has a double-edged quality that suggests a solution to this puzzle. Pentecostal spirituality attracts so many adherents because it provides a rationale and context for hearing the voice of God. While divine communication empowers Pentecostals with a satisfying sense of certainty, it also encourages them to confront other so-called Christians who believe differently — including their fellow Spirit-baptized believers. See Edith Waldvogel Blumhofer, Russell P. Spittler, and Grant Wacker, eds., *Pentecostal Currents in American Protestantism* (Urbana: University of Illinois Press, 1999), for several case studies which suggest that the link between dynamism and divisiveness continued throughout the twentieth century.

For Further Reading

Anderson, Robert Mapes. *Vision of the Disinherited: The Making of American Pente-costalism*. New York: Oxford University Press, 1979.

Ayers, Edward L. *The Promise of the New South: Life after Reconstruction*. New York: Oxford University Press, 1992.

Beacham, A. D., Jr. *A Brief History of the Pentecostal Holiness Church*. Rev. ed. Franklin Springs, Ga.: Advocate Press, 1990.

Blumhofer, Edith Waldvogel, Russell P. Spittler, and Grant Wacker, eds. *Pentecostal Currents in American Protestantism*. Urbana: University of Illinois Press, 1999.

Campbell, Joseph E. *The Pentecostal Holiness Church, 1898–1948: Its Background and History*. Franklin Springs, Ga.: PHPHC, 1951.

Cerillo, Augusto, and Grant Wacker. "Bibliography and Historiography of Pentecostalism in the United States." In *The New Dictionary of Pentecostal and Charismatic Movements*, edited by Stanley M. Burgess and Eduard M. Van Der Maas, 382–405. Grand Rapids: Zondervan, 2002.

Cox, Harvey. *Fire from Heaven: The Rise of Pentecostal Spirituality and the Reshaping of Religion in the Twenty-First Century*. Reading, Mass.: Addison-Wesley, 1995.

Paul, Harold. *Dan T. Muse: From Printer's Devil to Bishop*. Franklin Springs, Ga.: Advocate Press, 1976.

Synan, Vinson. *The Old-Time Power: A Centennial History of the International Pentecostal Holiness Church*. Franklin Springs, Ga.: LifeSprings Resources, 1998.

———. *The Holiness-Pentecostal Tradition: Charismatic Movements in the Twentieth Century*. Grand Rapids: Eerdmans, 1997.

Wacker, Grant. *Heaven Below: Early Pentecostals and American Culture*. Cambridge, Mass.: Harvard University Press, 2001.

DONALD G. MATHEWS

6

Lynching Is Part of the Religion of Our People

Faith in the Christian South

Religion in the American South has arrested historians' attention for over thirty years. Before 1970, Catharine Cleveland, Wesley Gewehr, Hunter Farish, Walter Brownlow Posey, and a few others had made impressive forays into reclaiming the religious life of southerners.[1] But in the past generation, Samuel Smyth Hill Jr., John Boles, Robert Calhoon, Wayne Flynt, Eugene Genovese, David Edwin Harrell, Ralph Luker, Albert Raboteau, and their colleagues and students have written about the many ways in which southerners have expressed themselves in religious language, society, and imagination. In the past few years, the craft of historical analysis has benefited, too, from the work of Emily Bingham, Ellen Eslinger, Sylvia Frey and Betty Wood, Paul Harvey, Christine Heyrman, Beth Schweiger, and Jon Sensbach, to name just a few of those who have written compellingly about the religious life of southerners.[2] These studies have in common brilliant insight, hard work, innovative research, and excellent writing. Some have focused on the ways in which religion wafted through and expressed the lives of people who were religious virtuosi, or defiantly independent, or resistant to the hegemonic, or dramatically innovative in creating religious institutions. Some have touched on the interaction of politics and religion,[3] and many have increasingly been sensitive to gendered and cultural issues;[4] generally, historians of southern religious culture have been—as some of their subjects would have said—"blessed" with the increased participation of talented and innovative colleagues. We have learned much from each other, and surely many students will continue to add to the growing corpus of work about the religious history of the American South. We will no doubt continue to benefit from studying the ways in which religion expresses culture, situates individuals, and grounds resistance to elites. That is, we will continue to study the functions of religion in memory, self-discipline, social solidarity, familial connections, gendered identity, and collective action.

Discussing function is safer (and easier) than imagining the meaning of meaning expressed in religious tones and based on some ground within the human experience that permits, sustains, and guides human religious action and mythmaking as ultimately significant in and of themselves. Thinking of religion within institutions that are dedicated to the spawning, nurturing, and justifying of identifiably religious feelings, ideas, relationships, and expectations is a perfectly respectable and even admirable enterprise. One would be foolish indeed to repudiate such exercises, especially after having engaged in them himself. But scholars sometimes need to move beyond the familiar into the ranges of thought and action in which ordinary people—including themselves—engage that know no boundaries such as religious/secular, ecclesiastical/lay, or theology/ideology, but within which the sacred and secular fuse into each other. We experience this fusion all the time: it is visible in the reverence with which some Americans greet martial achievements, the anger at those who burn the flag in protest, the dismay felt when the federal government acts to destroy the moral grounding of the republic, the fury at abortion rights activists, the celebration of America as if it were the Church Militant, and the ease with which political critics are transformed into religious heretics. In the southern past, the sacralization of memory, cause, duty, valor, and death among whites with regard to the Civil War was counterbalanced by the reverence for the Judgment and Promise of Emancipation among blacks. In a later day, the cadences, biblical references, sacred images, and eschatological expectations that expressed confidence in "overcoming" combined to transform civil rights demonstrations into movable camp meetings. There was no strictly defined secular realm; there was no holy of holies separable from the common life of the movement. Only a very dull observer would deny the power of the transcendent to suffuse meaning throughout the collective action of the inspired.

To be sure, students can quarrel with the attempt to pursue religion beyond institutions usually conceded to be religious, but that is probably the function of their believing that religion is about supernatural beings, a view best left in the nineteenth century. Since that time, generations of students have studied —with a variety of methods and theories—the presence of the religious quite apart from specifically religious institutions and ideas relating to deity.[5] As anthropologist Mary Douglas said long ago, "We shall not expect to understand religion if we confine ourselves to considering belief in spiritual beings however the formula may be refined."[6] Clifford Geertz's classic formulation of religion as a cultural system is an example of this fact. Inviting scholars to think of religion as a cultural system, he defined a religion as "a system of symbols which acts to (2) establish powerful, pervasive, and long-lasting moods and motivations in [humans] by (3) formulating conceptions of a general order of existence and (4) clothing these conceptions with such an aura of facticity that (5) the moods and motivations seem uniquely realistic."[7] If symbols are representations of reality, they also help create the reality we are prepared to imagine.[8] Thus, when a stark Southern Baptist, Methodist, and Presbyterian Christianity over the years employed symbols to represent a Christian drama of salvation, believers restricted as well as expanded their understandings of the reality they sought to represent. Peculiarly Christian symbols, however, were not the only representations through which southern whites hoped to convey the sacred and repudiate the profane. At the end of the nineteenth century, they also imagined the dramas of conflict between good and evil in terms of black skin, white skin, the New Negro, the black beast rapist, pure white women, "whites only" placards, and "colored" signs. All these symbols of segregation established "powerful, pervasive, and long lasting moods and motivations by formulating conceptions of a general order of existence and clothing those conceptions with such an aura of facticity that the moods and motivations seem[ed] uniquely realistic." These "moods and motivations" that conceived, projected, and authenticated "religious feeling" flowed from "an awareness of the group"[9] or community establishing its integrity, solidarity, and meaning so that every white person understood what was sacred without opening a Bible, raising a prayer, or singing a hymn. The point is that the things that a culture values most highly and places beyond conflicted discourse, that is, the things that a culture agrees are most sacred, are elevated to a status reserved for the reverence and awe traditionally conceded the divine. The natural inference, therefore, would lead one generally not to study cultural forms *and* religion, or specifically segregation *and* religion, but segregation *as* religion.

This way of thinking about religion is not new; all historians who have studied the religious history of the South will recognize it, even if they have not been guided by its insights when trying to understand the pervasiveness of religion in the South. We have tended to discuss religion and society, or religion and gender, or religious people in society, or the functions of religion with regard to power and powerlessness. All these issues are important, but beyond them we need to wrestle with the ways in which religion—not just Christianity or evangelical Protestantism—beyond traditional creeds and approved norms defined and expressed the ways in which southerners of all ethnic experiences lived. This rather mundane comment comes from my confronting the violent reality of southern lynching while researching religion in the New South, and thereafter being forced to think about religion and lynching, which then became religion as lynching. The process of moving from connections to comprehension was puzzling until it became clear that such dramatic and ultimate acts as execution and lynching are elemental acts in which life and death, community and individual, and good and evil—all basic and irreducible concepts —are involved simultaneously. These are the basic concepts of life and religion. To understand lynching merely as a pro or con issue upon which religious people had opinions would have been to belittle the profoundly existential issues and actions of people caught up in a culture in which piety, racial purity, and lynching—both independent of one another and taken together—could become stereotypical representations of the region. The connections among piety, purity, and lynching became troubling as I reclaimed Arthur Raper's discovery of 1931 (published in 1933) that lynching occurred in counties where church membership was high for both races.[10] The rediscovery of Raper led me to confront Walter White's sobering argument that the religion of southern whites was the fundamental basis for their emotion-driven compulsion to lynch blacks.[11] Those connections led me in turn to *The Lynching of Jesus*[12] and to René Girard's understanding of violence and the sacred.[13] In the latter work, White's theory of runaway emotions received a grounding in mimetic desire, through which Girard understood the crisis of community violence to occur.

Here were issues that religious historians of the South had not engaged. They—I—did not seem to care that a white terror had ravaged the American South between 1865 and 1940. They—I—did not seem to believe that the most elemental values of humanity were involved as Americans of African descent were raped, assaulted, tortured, and killed by the thousands during that time. Statistics for lynching alone suggest that about thirty-two hundred blacks and fourteen hundred whites were murdered by white mobs. Such spare figures do not, of course, tell the whole story of racial carnage in America; they are merely the most dramatic representation of what scholars have called a "festival of violence."[14] For every victim of lynching, there were probably thousands of people who suffered from both legal and illegal action that ranged from rigged financial transactions to draconian punishment. As is demonstrated by responses to recent exhibits of lynching photographs in New York and Atlanta, however, it is the stark fact of lynching that makes us gasp at our history. The book derived from those ghastly displays—*Without Sanctuary*—presents in obscene detail a perspective counter to professions of national innocence and demands that students of religious history engage the meanings of such formidable contempt for humanity.[15] As Americans currently contemplate with protestations of guiltlessness the violence that might possibly afflict them from abroad, it is important to face the violence that has already shamed us from within. Such violence did not just happen to the nation, as if satanic forces had somehow plunged Americans into a cauldron of hatred; some historians believe that our culture has found regeneration through violence.[16] Certainly, there is reason to believe that the culture that spawned lynching was sustained by the belief that violence would be regenerative; it was not a diffuse and vague ambience that erupted somehow into sporadic brutality. There was a source, and there were targets. The source was white, and the targets were black, but the colors, white and black, represent much more than color, prejudice, or the specious concept of race: they represent power and self-inflicted anxieties on the one hand versus hope and valiant self-determination on the other. Black and white do not represent polar opposites, such as victimizer and victim, but asymmetrical conditions. White people became obsessed with blacks, and black people became determined to transcend the violent logic of a people who they believed were crazed by a fascination with purity and profanation that cloaked political designs and made sacred whites' aspirations to supremacy.[17]

The ease with which acts of violence and ideas of purity, profanation, and the sacred can be fused in one sentence is not mere stylistic license. White southerners defended their violence against blacks as punishment for violating the purity of the white race by assaulting white women. At one level, this statement is about punishment and the exercise of power; at another, it is an expression of what a culture valued most, that is, what it held sacred. This overlay of violence, purity, and the sacred reflects an anomaly in what Mark Twain called "the United States of Lyncherdom." The anomaly lay partially in the fact that Americans—many of them southerners—were, at the time Twain wrote, diligently heeding the religious impulse to dispatch Christian missionaries to convert the Chinese, who Twain believed were already "excellent people, honest, honorable, industrious, trustworthy, [and] kind-hearted." Such people were "good enough just as they [were]," he wrote, but Twain had doubts about white Americans, whose capacity for illegal violence against black people was an international scandal. Missionaries could be better employed in the United States,

Twain suggested, for they had a "martyr spirit," and "nothing but the martyr spirit [could] brave a lynching mob."[18] What Twain meant by "martyr spirit" is not entirely clear, but he may have meant that white people would have to have braved death in order to both defend black people and, through this selfless defense, bear witness to the truth of human solidarity—an expectation almost inconceivable at the time. Twain hinted at other anomalies as well. For example, American culture nurtured both lynch mobs and missionaries, people capable of martyrdom invited death for the wrong cause in the wrong place, and a presumably republican nation would not protect its own citizens from terror. Beyond noting these contradictions, Twain could have been more explicit in pointing out that the South had become more likely to lynch as its people were becoming more likely to pray.[19] This conjunction of piety and vengeance, especially vengeance so obviously illegal, appears to be especially contradictory. A people coming increasingly under the rule of the Christian churches, and one so earnestly dedicated to the salvation of alien peoples heedless of race, should not have been the same people among whom were recruited the mobs that murdered black people. African Americans appealed to white ministers, who had turned their eloquence so brilliantly to missions, to lead a crusade against lynching. Surely the power of religion should have been able to quash the reign of rope, blood, and fire.[20]

Their hope was based in part on the fact that during the 1880s white religious activists had begun to mobilize communicants in crusades against the sale of alcoholic beverages; they had even briefly cooperated with African Americans in Prohibition campaigns.[21] Hope, too, may have been encouraged by memories of abolitionism, which had attracted religious activists prior to emancipation, and by recollection of the religious denominations that formed freedmen's commissions in the 1860s. Perhaps they were encouraged by the infrequent statements of white southern religious such as Methodist bishop Atticus G. Haygood and Baptist layman and former governor William Northen on behalf of African Americans.[22] Whatever had encouraged African Americans to find succor from religious whites, hope yielded to despair, for it had in fact been misplaced, as Walter F. White (1893–1955) accused. An official of the National Association for the Advancement of Colored People and the author of *Rope and Faggot: A Biography of Judge Lynch*, White reflected on more than forty years of lynching in 1929. He concluded that the Christianity of southern whites had originally nurtured the "invidious distinctions" that had birthed racism, sustained slavery, and created what he called the "fanaticism, which finds an outlet in lynching."[23] Simply and starkly put, White believed that white southern evangelical Christianity had nurtured lynching.[24] The predominant religious mood of the South, he wrote, through "acrobatic, fanatical preachers of hell-fire" and "the orgies of emotion created by them," had released "dangerous passions" that found "release through lynching." White himself had felt these passions directly when he conducted investigations throughout the South into illegal violence against blacks. He concluded that the carnage there resulted from whites' literally losing their reason. White's evidence lay in his understanding of the arguments whites made when confronted by African Americans' pressure for full citizenship rights. These demands, white southerners argued, were actually for complete "social equality," which White knew was a euphemism for sexual intercourse between white women and black men.[25] The emotions that accompanied white men's denunciations of something that White believed black men did not want seemed completely irrational to him; he did not understand—or at least he did not concede the relevance of—the connections white men made between their sexual prerogatives and their lust for political power. He selected the hysteria he inferred from white male pronouncements as the subject of his contempt, and he inferred further that the emotional intensity associated with the image of sexual intercourse between black men and white women was similar to the rage against sin that erupted in condemning fury from hell-obsessed preaching. Thus, for White, lynching became the natural issue of a religion that was characterized more by passionate expressiveness and emotional fury than by reflection.

The revival of the second Ku Klux Klan, going on as White wrote, was being led, he pointed out, by a former Methodist minister who—following the images in Thomas Dixon's novel *The Clansman*—had ignited a flaming cross to proclaim white Protestant supremacy. White wrote that the Reverend William Simmons's crusade to purify the nation rested on the South's power to hold "aloft the torch of Anglo-Saxon ideals [of] racial integrity, and religious purity."[26] Simmons's vision was as clear and uncompromising as White's indictment. To be sure, White knew that religion alone could not cause lynching, and he knew that southern religion was part of a complex cultural matrix of obsessions, moods, and situations. Within that matrix, White included a cultural affinity for violence, the allure of stereotypical simplicity, the ideology of white supremacy, and southern white men's tendency to justify anything they did as a defense of southern white women. The formidable challenge of combining all those things together in a credible explanation notwithstanding, we are still confronted with the simple problem of a section of the United States that reeked of illegal violence and shamelessly boasted of its piety. We are confronted by the conviction of a seasoned African American investigator such as White, who understood the South, white people, and lynching very well indeed, that hovering over them all were the passions associated with religion—"orgies of emotion," as he called them.

Most historians, however, have settled on passions distinctly not religious to explain lynching, namely those associated with gender, sex, difference, and power. Because power dominates this list, and because the accumulation and exercise of power is thought to be rational and calculating, the passion to which Walter White responded in *Rope and Faggot* is largely discounted. This response to the emotional garbage with which white southern male apologists littered the imaginative world of late-nineteenth-century discourse in what amounted to a white southern canon of immaculate protection is appropriate. Even though no more than a quarter of lynched black men were even suspected, much less guilty, of sex crimes against white females, southern apologists learned that they could justify—to their own satisfaction, at least—all mob action by claiming that it was the appropriate punishment for rape. Alarmist rumors of the late 1890s suggested that white women in the southern countryside were living in a state of extreme sexual danger. The resulting alert among white men meant that any illegal collective action punishing black men could be purged of guilt—made immaculate—by representing it as an act performed for the protection of white women. This posturing made white men feel guiltless not only because they were defending their families, but also because by doing so they were doing something essentially sacred. A nimbus of holiness radiated from the white southern patriarchs as the celebrated purity of white women refracted onto their own bodies the cleansing expectations of religion, honor, racial segregation, and collective violence. The righteousness derived from protecting white women's bodies, however, did not lead to a reasoned position defended by compelling logic, as one might have expected in the Victorian age of masculine self-control.[27] Rather, apologists confessed that the very thought of black men's desecration of their world pushed white men to the edge of sanity. From there, they fell into a holy madness that reinforced the innocence of their rage. Such madness was akin to that of men who, in time-honored cliché, discovered their wives in the embrace of rapists or lovers and reacted immediately and violently with consequences that every true man could understand.[28] Thus an essential element of immaculate protection was the loss of rational thought by white men when confronted with the possibility that black men had had the temerity to act like white men. To reinforce further the belief that this loss absolved white men of guilt, enthusiastic publicists wrote and talked about the compulsion of righteous provocation.[29]

Provocation could prompt a shriek of self-justifying fury throughout the region when a lynching became as widely anticipated and publicly discussed as the April 1899 lynching of Thomas Wilkes. Already hiding from the law under the pseudonym of "Sam Hose," Wilkes felt compelled to defend himself from his employer when the latter became enraged at what seems to have been Wilkes's request for back wages and time off to visit his sick mother. Fearing for his life when Alfred Cranford threatened him with a gun, Wilkes killed the white man with an ax. He was eventually captured after a manhunt that was driven by increasingly vivid and ghastly (if unsubstantiated) stories that Wilkes had raped Mrs. Cranford as she lay quivering in her husband's oozing brains and blood. This violation—so perfectly fitted to the sexualized imaginations of maddened white males—created sufficient provocation, observed one editor, that white men, "placed in view of the guilty wretch, [became] crazed and unaccountable for the particular form their vengeance [took]."[30] The provocation was too great to expect men to obey the rubrics of civilized behavior and dispassionate justice. Provocation justified yielding to an aboriginal fury of preternatural violence. Provocation endowed a crowd of five hundred men and boys in Newnan, Georgia, with an "intense feeling of right and justice" as they led Wilkes to the outskirts of town and burned him alive.[31] Reports never effectively captured the emotions of the moment, but public rumor and news accounts sustained the elements of provocation in the collective white mind long enough to combine carnival, brutality, and pain into an act of what the perpetrators believed was primal justice. Whether or not the burning of Thomas Wilkes qualified as what Walter White called an "orgy of emotion," it was based upon provocation that apologists believed justified the surrendering of reason to emotion in a way that validated anything the crowd did. And the crowd fully participated in the burning by shouting at Wilkes, mutilating his body, and observing with glazed fascination. Finally, one white-haired man could contain himself no longer. "Glory be to God!" he screamed while jumping up and down as if to imitate the writhing of the tortured black man. He shouted: "God bless every man who had a hand in this. Thank God for vengeance."[32] "Thank God for vengeance" and "Glory be to God!"—in such shouts, a reasonable person can well see the orgiastic character of which White would write thirty years later. That the pervasive white religious mood of the South rejected reason and self-control through an emotional experience that validated the self before God was the cultural fact that enabled Walter White to see a connection between lynching and religion. In shouting "Glory!" the old white man had echoed the shouts that revived Christians had uttered since the Great Awakening and in every camp meeting that the members of the crowd had ever attended. The white-haired man's celebration of what he saw knew no clear distinctions of honor, religion, and politics; in the excitement of pain, agony, and nauseating smell, he cried out from the seat of his selfhood: "Glory be to God!"

Glory and vengeance—the sense of wonder and the spontaneous religious celebration were clear! If the popular alibi of provocation suggested that passions associated with sex and gender ignited condign punishment by white men, the sense of awe at an act simultaneously wonderful and horrendous combined in a sacred oath and exhilaration to fuse the celebration of God and of pain. Such experiences are beyond gender, difference, sex, and power. To be sure, gendered responsibilities defined the assumption of immaculate protection. This was, after all, justified by the supposition southern white men had held since before the Civil War that dutiful private and public actions were to demonstrate that men possessed the stature, mastery, and will to protect dependents.[33] The rituals of personal and public relations in the antebellum South, which historians have subsumed under the word that southerners themselves used, "honor," were possibly more "high church" than those of the highest Catholic mass, and they were frequently performed in a language of etiquette and allusion that in some cases could be even more demanding than liturgical Latin.[34] The predisposition of southern white men eventually to justify anything they did relative to African Americans as a defense of southern white women was not, therefore, a mere mystification of their drive for mastery; it was a natural expression of the way in which they had learned to think about their personal responsibilities as men and of the public enactment of them, which was grounded in something far more substantial than socialization and shaming rituals.[35] If white men were as unnerved by African American assertiveness as the theory of provocation implies,[36] if they were as driven to distraction by the thought of "social equality" as Walter White observed, and if they could, in burning a black man, shout "Glory be to God!" then the emotional intensity came not simply from the culture of honor. To shout "Glory!" was to express oneself in a way familiar to and evocative of the religious mood of a white South that encouraged such animated eruptions from the existential sources of one's very selfhood.

IF THE "LYNCHING OF SAM HOSE" came out of the culture of honor that claimed almost religious devotion from its males, it also came out of a culture that had been accustomed to crowds being called together by the recurring need to renew life. In revival, one could reclaim one's life from Satan, cleanse the soul by renewing ancient vows, find some way to renew lives that had somehow gotten off track, or renew connections with family and friends within the circle of religious song, chant, sermon, and prayer. The religious mood was not restricted to Christian identity or theological reference. All the experiences of those enticed to camp meeting or revival expecting renewal, when considered in their variety, made it impossible to distinguish between sacred and secular. Revival meant rejection of whatever was past and renewal for whatever lay ahead. By 1900, southern culture was patently revivalistic in its drive for both purity and the self-conscious renunciation of the profane. Those who were associated with formal religious institutions persistently and angrily contested the claims and ways of the world, and they also stormed the citadels of vice and corruption by gradually and energetically imposing Prohibition upon the South by 1908.[37] The movement had corresponded with a generation-long drive for segregation of the races and for the disenfranchisement of African Americans in the name of both controlling the black workforce and purifying the culture, its people, and their politics.[38] In all these campaigns, African Americans came to represent a threatening presence; it was said that they endangered the innocence of white women, the purity of public life, and the spotlessness—read "pliability" —of the electorate. Whites claimed to fear "moral contamination" as they marginalized African Americans.[39] In their own minds, they made African Americans even more dangerous, since people at the cultural margins are always dangerous.[40] The religion that had made sexual intercourse outside marriage immoral fused with whites' fear of social equality and combined with aversive custom and political will to fabricate a broad, all-inclusive system of purity and danger. An evangelicalism ever alert to contamination could nurture segregation, because the holiness of one supported the holiness of the other; both established boundaries and distances that demanded individuals "conform to the class to which they belong[ed]." "Holiness," writes anthropologist Mary Douglas, "means keeping distinct the categories of creation."[41]

White Christian children, recalled writer Lillian Smith, had been taught "to love God, to love [their] white skin, and to believe in the sanctity of both."[42] She had learned sin and guilt from segregation as well as in Sunday school; the differences stipulated by segregation were indistinguishable from those of a religion that was "too narcissistic to be concerned with anything but a man's [own] body and a man's [own] soul." Such a religion encouraged the mental, moral, and emotional process of pushing "everything dark, dangerous, and evil" to "the rim of one's life." Segregation and whites' evangelicalism seemed to be identical or, perhaps, complementary halves of a pervasive sensibility that gushed from the human springs of religious devotion.[43] That devotion, however, was not to the crucified Christ so much as to the worshipping subject's own consciousness of himself or herself in the posture of worshipping. A self-conscious, narcissistic purity had shriven evangelical white Christians of the capacity for understanding religion as either judgment upon themselves or service to the kingdom through the salvation of the other. (Though they could, perhaps, understand the service of missionaries chosen to make other people like themselves.) Satisfaction with their own individual salvation and confidence in their own purity of intention and race allowed white evangelicals little perspective into the situation of African Americans, even those who were fellow Christians. If it is possible to argue that white males, afflicted by hard times and guilt, reacted in rage to an imagined threat from black men,[44] perhaps it would be worthwhile to look at the broader surge in white society that transcended the rage while making it authentic. The white body, which evangelicals had elevated to sacred status—its boundaries secured, its orifices purified, and its distancing perfected—reflected a society whose elites had demonstrated their willingness to control through violence. The fusion of southern evangelical Protestantism with Prohibition, repressed sexuality, and the canonization of white women blurred distinctions between sacred and secular where race was concerned. Far from being able to lend perspective to segregation, traditional southern evangelicalism affirmed it.

Prohibition, segregation, disenfranchisement, and the demonization of anomalous blacks did not remove danger. Like sin and Satan, threat was ever present; the more one contemplated it, the greater it became, and the threat became a contagion that criminalized African Americans in the minds of southern whites during the last decade of the nineteenth century. The emotion that fed the process —fear—nurtured the emotions of anger, racial contempt, and arrogance as white people began to believe that African Americans were changing for the worse. A new generation of black men, undisciplined, it was said, because they had not been reared in slavery, and educated with misleading Yankee propaganda about social equality, was becoming unruly. Since they insisted on breaking the rules of racial deference born of enslavement, these young men were, in effect, criminal. The perception seemed to have been transformed into reality by the increased tempo at which newspapers reported crimes attributed to African Americans throughout the United States. By the mid-1890s, even a casual reader of the *Atlanta Constitution* could become aware that black men were committing crimes from Seattle to Boston, Miami, Los Angeles, and Atlanta. Even a small-town newspaper such as the *Newnan (Ga.) Herald and Advertiser* marveled at how easy it was now to find news of African Americans' misdeeds from across the entire country.[45] One could glean stories of African American criminality from Indiana, Ohio, Tennessee, North Carolina, Louisiana, South Carolina, and Florida simply by selecting at random five issues of a provincial Georgia daily.[46] Almost any rumor of crimes committed by blacks could be believed. Even men who had reputations for defending African Americans repeated as fact in 1893 the lie that three hundred white women had been raped in three months by black men.[47] Authorities such as Virginia aristocrat Philip Alexander Bruce pontificated about the deterioration of the race, and Ivy League college professors supported such theses with social scientific data.[48] The confluence of cultural antipathy, punitive laws, and a religious mood that demonized every enemy who had been blackened by sin created a white moral sensibility prepared to make black men the personification of evil should something happen to ignite the tinder of racial contempt.

That is what Thomas Wilkes did when he killed Alfred Cranford in self-defense. As generally they had invented African American crime waves, now specifically white spokesmen and newsmen transformed the relatively slight farm hand into a monster. The trauma of her husband's murder that sent Mattie Cranford into silent seclusion in her mother's home was interpreted as the trauma of having been ravished in her husband's blood, and his killer became "fiend" as well as prey. From the beginning of the hunt for Wilkes, he was special: the governor, the *Atlanta Constitution*, and private citizens offered huge rewards for his capture. Newspapers followed every false lead and printed every brave statement made by pursuing whites, who were increasingly frustrated as their search was expanded and prolonged with each passing day. Wilkes became a will-o'-the-wisp;[49] he was here and there, in the swamps, in Alabama, in the next county, in La Grange, or in Savannah—everywhere and nowhere. Like the Second Coming among ancient Christians, his capture was ever imminent but never consummated. For eleven days, news reports evoked a frustrated, angry, vigilant countryside in arms, and from the very beginning, the sentiment existed that the "Negro [would] Probably Be Burned."[50] Whites trembled at the danger from lawless black men, white ministers bewailed pervasive black immorality, white mobs beat blacks who were insufficiently deferential, and leading white citizens wrote public statements about the all-encompassing danger from a degraded African American satanic presence.[51]

That presence, which had flowed from the minds of disturbed and troubled whites as a dangerous abstraction, was now projected onto the entire black community, as if it somehow had become an alternative reality such as that imagined by nativist white Americans elsewhere, or anticommunist neurotics in the 1920s and 1950s, or paranoid militia hate groups of the early twenty-first century. As an abstraction itself, the threatening African American presence justified the transformation of Wilkes—in a ghastly way that was thoroughly human —into something that represented the complete negation of humanity. One could sense it in what the crowd did to Wilkes in his last agonizing moments— torture unimaginable and agony beyond understanding. As long as he lived, Wilkes represented an alien presence, sentient, but as completely unlike white people as a fiend. His ascribed otherness permitted his tormentors to treat him not like an animal, but like the complete negation of humanity, a "counterhuman" who could be addressed by name and yet destroyed as one would destroy all the evil that white men had ever encountered. It was as if this one human/ counterhuman were anointed to bear the sin and guilt of the race. The drama of torture and death, in which observers became participants through inhaling the stench of burning flesh, could represent the cruelty of whites to blacks for hundreds of years, but it could also represent the fascination with which whites had contemplated blacks. This fascination seemed to transport white lynchers thousands of years into the primal past to the period before human sacrifice was supplanted by other forms of sacrifice in rituals that functioned to slough off both evil and conflict within a community and to purify and cleanse society by burning out the dross. In a ghastly reenactment of an unremembered past, whites seem to have used the negation of African American presence to make themselves good. It is not surprising, therefore, that a young scholar should have found among the public rhetoric of southerners in 1901 this statement: "The spirit which upholds lynch law as the only proper answer to the infamous outrage on female inviolability is the principle virtue which differentiates the civilization of the South from that of the North and West. It is part of the religion of our people."[52]

Ida B. Wells agreed, although she probably never read the comment from the *Sparta (Ga.) Ishmaelite*. Wells was a tough and feisty refugee from white violence in Memphis who had stumped the British Isles in the mid-1890s to denounce American violence and who had forthrightly challenged the canon of immaculate protection. Citing specific examples of consensual liaisons between black men and white women, Wells enraged champions of southern honor. She reflected on the sexual dynamics between the two races in a way consistent with community gossip, infrequent rumor, folktales, family lore, and cases that sometimes found their way into court records.[53] Blacks and whites of both sexes had coupled with members of the other race and had enjoyed doing so.[54] The accompanying emotion, authentic though it may have been, was insufferable according to the canon of immaculate protection, the obligations of southern honor, and, indeed, the entire emotional glossary of white southern convention. In seeking to state the truth about human relations and the emotions that shaped them, Wells, like every African American writer from David Walker to Frederick Douglass and from Charles Chestnutt to Walter White, wondered: Where were the white Christians? Citing what she called the *Red Record*, Wells confessed: "The heart almost loses faith in Christianity when one thinks of . . . the countless massacres of defenseless Negroes."[55]

Wells's comment on white Christianity was understandable, especially considering that the region was so proud of its religious temperament and its Christians so sure that their devotion to the faith was superior to that of most other Americans. Indeed, John Crowe Ransom, a young critic and poet who had been raised in the godliness of a Methodist minister's home, pitted what he considered to be the best of traditional southern religion against a religious liberalism that he believed had attempted to fuse modern science and faith in humanity into a grand and idealistic deity of principle. Ransom scorned this humanitarian god; from Hebraic roots, he conjured the furious god worshipped with sacrifice and burnt offerings whose holiness was so great that he could be sensed in awe as the author of both evil and good. He was the unuttered and unutterable Y-H-W-H, before whose mystery humans sank in groveling horror.[56] Let each true believer, Ransom entreated, "insist on a virile and concrete God, and accept no Principle as substitute." He asked: "Let him restore to God the thunder."[57] That Ransom had captured essential aspects of the southern God was confirmed ten years later when W. J. Cash (who was less chauvinistic than Ransom) picked up on the same themes in confessing, on the basis of his own experience in Baptist revival, that southerners demanded a faith of "primitive frenzy and the blood sacrifice."[58] Both authors captured the meaning implied in a southern theologian's insistence that "the orisons of faith and penitence must be accompanied with the streaming blood of a victim and the avenging fire of the altar,"[59] and every believer who had ever trembled before the furious denunciations of a southern evangelist knew what Robert Lewis Dabney was talking about. The images were not called to mind by reason, reflection, dogma, or creeds; the images came to life within the intense emotions of a faith in a punishing God whose honor was in part the projection of the honor-culture of which Bertram Wyatt-Brown writes so convincingly. Such a God's wrath easily evoked the metaphors of thunder, primitive frenzy, fiery altars, and what Walter White called "orgies of emotion." Southern culture, in which community tradition, popular notions of right conduct, and gendered definitions of obligation were so compelling, had been sustained in slavery by violence; it had been redeemed from Yankees and "Negro domination" by violence.[60] It is not surprising, therefore, that popular white male rule should have been sustained through the violence of charivari and lynching.[61] Both types of action were consistent with the religious history of the South. It was a history of collective celebration in camp meetings, rituals of evangelical purification, revivalistic denunciation of immorality, and the shaming rites of excommunication. In this history lay the firm conviction, born of personal experience, that collective action was legitimized by subjective solidarity, whether expressed in the aural power of familiar hymns or the terroristic excitement of an intensely focused lynch mob. In all these things, collective identity rested on the foundation of individuals' subjective experience, which humbled itself before community. Emotion ruled.

Wyatt-Brown points out how charivari and lynching were authentic ways of being religious. Reaching back through the history of community violence upon selected individuals, he notes that charivari included a range of collective action, from the wedding night "jollity" to shaming rituals that demeaned or damaged the body, from scapegoating rituals to threats of violence against authorities who had offended communal values. Throughout the whole range of possibility implicit in such community action, norms relating to sexuality, gender, obligation, and authority were imagined as having been in some way broken by those unfortunates chosen to become the focus of ritual acts. Hovering over all the rituals that enacted the communal will was the ambience of offended family values, male prerogative, and elemental justice, with young males serving as what one scholar has called the "raucous voice" of collective "conscience."[62] For to the people who participated in a deadly charivari, lynching could be a principled act that reset the balance of the moral universe. It sustained, writes

Wyatt-Brown, the "most sacred, ethical rules of the white populace," and it was justified as a form of defense of the purity of the white family—which was why the canon of immaculate protection was so important.[63] Wyatt-Brown finds, in the records of well over fifty years of lynching, abundant evidence of ritualized behavior in Klan punishments that paralleled legal public executions, which for centuries before the nineteenth had played out the evocative dramas of good punishing evil.[64] In analyzing such dramas, whether legal or illegal, scholars have frequently commented on the inherent scapegoating mechanism, by means of which the community acted as if it believed that the immolation of a victim could rid it of internal danger. Some students understand both capital punishment and lynching as human sacrifices in which communities elude intractable problems by deflecting the violence inherent within them onto the person being executed; by doing so, the communities falsely conclude that with specific punishment and the implications flowing from it, the conundrum of violence has been solved.[65] Thus, like the scapegoating rituals found in the Old Testament (upon which much Christian understanding of sacrifice was based), and like the crucifixion of Christ, community killing was a religious act.[66]

Was community killing thus a Christian act? The answer is not easy to find. The question itself is not easy: it is to be hoped that all religious people would be dismayed at the thought that killing should ever be seen as a religious act, even though it is possible for scholars to think of religion itself as flowing from primal violence.[67] Perhaps we could take refuge in the fact that the question is ambiguous as well as evocative; it appears to be simple, but in fact it is not, for we do not know what is meant by the concept "Christian act." At one level, Christian acts are performances within the broad range of Christian liturgies, from the simplest Quaker testimony to the most elaborate papal mass. Our immediate response here is that lynching does not qualify. At another level, Christian acts would be those acts approved by Christ in the Sermon on the Mount and in New Testament parables, such as making peace or selling one's possessions to feed the poor. Such acts would be characteristic of the ideal, perhaps, but not of the everyday life of most Christians, and certainly here lynching cannot be inferred to be a Christian act. At another level of consciousness, Christian acts would be those things that Christians actually do as self-conscious examples of their discipleship in extreme circumstances, and this definition would include bombing women's health clinics to prevent abortions as well as counseling pregnant women as to how best to exercise their powers of ethical choice in terminating pregnancy. Here we stumble, perhaps, into the realization that

Christian acts can sometimes represent irreconcilable differences and that they can frequently be violent in two different ways. Looking back into the southern past, Christian acts could conceivably include both the manumission of a slave for conscience's sake and the transfer of a servant from one person to another in order to sustain family solidarity. Some Christians might participate in servile rebellion (as Denmark Vesey did in Charleston, South Carolina, in 1822) or refuse to do so on Christian grounds. There are also acts that Christians do because they claim they "have to" in distinctly ambiguous circumstances in which their actions are indistinguishable from those that are non-Christian. In this instance, it is clear that some Christians sometimes did believe that they were absolutely justified in lynching, as did the man who believed lynching was "part of the religion of [his] people."[68] If one were to read such white southern Christian stalwarts as Bishop Atticus Haygood and Georgia's Governor William Northen when they justified the lynching of black men thought to be rapists, one could conclude that white Protestants believed that lynching was a Christian act.[69] Ida Wells certainly believed as much.[70]

Bishop Haygood and Governor Northen were well-known public men in their day. Both had spoken against lynching; each represented the intelligence, piety, and manners of the Christianized masculine South. Haygood had for years been an independent and aggressive publicist for the education of young Christian men as president of Emory College and on behalf of a new industrialized South that he hoped those young men would lead into a progressive future. Northen, like Haygood, believed that Yankee capital could help such young men recreate the South, and so, after his tenure as governor of Georgia expired, he accepted a position dedicated solely to attracting northern capital to the state. The former Confederate officer and the former Confederate chaplain both represented pious southern white manhood, and both also have a positive historical reputation for having been supportive of African Americans' aspirations. Northen stumped the state of Georgia on behalf of an antilynching law, and he could sometimes condemn white racism with more energy and passion than his fellow white men thought appropriate.[71] Haygood spent years doling out Yankee philanthropy to black southern colleges and wrote a book pleading for economic autonomy and support called *Our Brother in Black*. After he died, a distinguished black minister wrote to Mrs. Haygood, praising her husband for the many "sacrifices" he had borne on behalf of the minister's "struggling but hopeful race."[72] Both of these white men stood apart from many of their gender and race who supported the vicious rhetoric of racial vilification and contempt that swept racial demagogues such as James K. Vardaman, Ben Tillman, and Furnifold Simmons into power in Mississippi, South Carolina, and North Carolina. Haygood and Northen refused to scapegoat African Americans as responsible for all the ills of the South that could not otherwise be attributed to Yankees, and they attempted to change the attitudes of their white compatriots by encouraging them to be more understanding and supportive of African Americans. Yet at some critical, mysterious, and charged moment in which the canon of immaculate protection and the madness of righteous provocation short-circuited the meditation of these generous Christian men on issues of sexual identity, anomalous black men, and white masculine duty, their sense of honor and justice collapsed into the simple belief that lynching was just and, therefore, a Christian act.[73]

AFRICAN AMERICANS RESPONDED to white terror as one would expect, but their options and actions have to be understood within the historical context of slavery and the illegal white violence that followed emancipation for a generation. The social and cultural context of white racism deprived African Americans of ordinary concessions made to white persons acting in self-defense; it also denied black men the presumption of innocence theoretically conceded to all accused persons before trial. The hostility to which African Americans were subjected in the South after emancipation in state after state left scarred memories of rape, torture, depredation, and murder against blacks targeted by suspicious whites. African Americans fought back with appeals to the law, with appeals to the federal government, and with violence that occasionally caught white terrorists off guard. The history of white supremacy, in which African Americans were segregated in public, repudiated by Republicans, deprived of equal education, and all but cast out of electoral politics, demonstrated how whites could use the power of the state to stigmatize and punish people who wanted nothing more than to be productive citizens. And still African Americans in newspapers and journals, ad hoc meetings, regular public occasions, and the special proclamations of their leadership spoke in a voice that denounced the vicious crowds that murdered them and the public policies that demeaned them and stripped them of their citizenship rights.[74] Speaking in such a voice was not easy. In fact, it could be dangerous to life and limb, but silence could be dangerous to the soul. How black people could manage even in the most precarious of situations is suggested by the events that followed a lynching in Richmond County, Georgia, in May of 1900. Then, heated words between two young men on an Augusta streetcar led to the killing of a white man and the immediate arrest of a black youth. The latter was soon kidnapped from peace officers despite their best attempts to hide him; he was then mutilated and hanged by a mob of the dead man's comrades. The white Presbyterian minister and sheriff's deputies, among others, had attempted to stop the crowd, but it would not be denied its dramatic vengeance.

The black man's funeral became a major community event. Three African American ministers presided over an overflowing congregation that was still in a state of shock. Two "good" young men were dead. "Our sympathy," observed one preacher, "knows no color line." Remembering the deceased of each race, the speaker seemed to be trying to evoke, through carefully chosen words about a shared loss inflicted by a shared violence, hope for a shared resolution of tension within Richmond County. But the absence of any whites in the congregation meant that there was no physical basis for such a hope. If the fiction of a shared loss was embraced by a few of the mourners, most seem to have been profoundly saddened and silenced by the awful act of retribution exacted by the white mob, which had been made up in part of young men who had attended a YMCA meeting. Speaking in a climate thick with dismay, sorrow, and anger, one man attempted to calm his parishioners with an all-too-familiar cliché: "Vengeance belongs to God!" Once again there was silence. God had seemed to be silent, too. Another speaker hoped for "quietness and forbearance." He said: "Let us remember that under the strained conditions brought about by this sad tragedy, we must all take more and suffer more for the next two months than would have been necessary had this not occurred." The man contemplated the ways in which the community would be called upon to bear the burden of sacrificial living, surrendering the desire for revenge, repressing hostility against the dangerous self-righteousness of white Christians, and meeting the demands of selfless discipline. Laboring under the pall of the spectacular lynching of Thomas Wilkes, which had occurred over a year earlier on the other side of the state, he wished—as he knew his audience wished—that both black and white could return to the time before that testy confrontation on an Augusta streetcar. Only one in a thousand black men clashed with a white man, someone said, as if almost wistfully to lend a perspective to the event, but failing to do so because of its existential absurdity. If only the black man had not carried a gun, thought one man; if only the white man had kept his own counsel, others probably murmured to themselves; if only the white youth had been civil to the young black woman! Another person thought of retaliation but said instead: "We can't afford to fight." And then he added, "We do not *wish* to fight our brethren." (Few whites would have included blacks as "brethren.") But if white people insisted on "humiliating the whole race for the deed of one," said a man who recoiled in horror from what the mob of young churchgoing white men had done, he moved that African Americans should "stay off the [street]cars and walk." The congregation murmured its approval. In the solidarity of grief, sadness, and shock at the violence visited upon one of them, and thus upon themselves, by a crowd of "Christian" whites, they expressed their anger, dismay, and their need to do something. Vacating the streetcars was an act of self-denial that could reassure them of their collective support for one of their own who had been so hideously stripped of his humanity. Action affirmed their own humanity, even if it could not compensate for their loss.[75]

Compensation, however, was not a concept African Americans could afford if it implied vengeance, for whereas black leaders were counseling a disciplined and principled peace, white Augustans continued to hold court before Judge Lynch. Some of the white newspapers used the interracial tragedy to justify segregating the streetcars, and they conducted a campaign of vilification against black people instead of trying to lower the temperature of public discourse. These men, complained a black Baptist preacher, were intent on humiliating "the colored people to the last notch of endurance." The papers spoke of black people as if they were slaves, he pointed out, and he pleaded with responsible white people to "have this howl of Negro proscription stopped" and to "cultivate friendship and unity" among the people of the city even as he himself continued forcefully to oppose segregation.[76] William J. White was editor of the *Georgia Baptist*, and he had spoken clearly on behalf of African American interests for over a generation. He seemed to know every important white man in the city of Augusta, and if he complimented them when they did their public duty by all of Augusta's citizens, he also insisted that whites and blacks treat each other "with the deference that is due from equal citizens to one another" and that they "cultivate toward the other feelings of friendship."[77]

Three days after White published these words, a lynch mob came to his office to confront him. Somehow, someone on his staff had included as filler a brief comment from the *Washington (D.C.) Bee* to the effect that the black youth whom the mob had lynched had been defending the honor of a young black woman and was thus a "martyr." Between three and five hundred white men arrived at White's office while he was already busy disavowing the article to those members of Augusta's white elite (including two editors, the mayor, the chief of police, and the county solicitor) who had arrived to discuss the matter with him. In the end, he wrote an apologetic letter that was printed in one of the white dailies, thanked the police for protecting his family and property, and prepared the next day's sermon in a jail cell, where he spent the night for protection. Recalling what he called a "trying ordeal," he gingerly addressed the hypersensitivity that had allowed a white crowd to do what two people could have done in a simple visit to his office, that is, get the facts straight and secure an apology. The editor observed that he had been a public man for forty years and was very familiar with the etiquette of race relations, but that he was also familiar with the language required to tell the truth to his people in ways that would strengthen their resolve while avoiding white vengeance. In a "Word to Our Friends," he emphasized that African Americans lived in perilous times; he said that "the real trouble is not racial" and then proceeded to show that that was precisely what the trouble was. He could not believe that a white crowd would resort to violence "without reasonable pretext." (But it had.) He could not believe that a crowd of young white men would threaten violence to get him to do the right thing. (But it had.) Was he ready to quit the South—or America? The question seemed to imply that with one voice every American of African descent had to shout in fury "Yes!"—but he replied "No." White assured his readers: "God is still alive; and though he sometimes appears to take long naps, when he does move he straightens out the crooked places." White then listed excellent reasons for leaving the South and concluded by promising defiantly to remain.[78] The ambiguities of signifying, the imaginative twists of questions answered with both "yes" and "no" at the same time, and the shading of silences and promised action that belied easy solutions to intractable problems —all these things reflected the mental and spiritual virtuosity of people living under the shadow of white terror.

In this one episode that occurred during the late spring of 1900 in Augusta, Georgia, we can observe many of the ways in which African Americans responded to the threat of collective violence. Masters of public address, African American preachers could vent their anger and anguish at the helplessness black people felt rising up within them and find rhetorical ways to use that anger to strengthen resolve for whatever acts of resistance and affirmation they could muster. The solidarity of a community boycott of streetcars may not seem, to a culture painfully educated in the finer points of terrorism, to have been a real achievement, but it was. In the face of crowning white anger that could all too easily select targets for its own terror, the dignity and discipline of such collective purpose provided courage before the pervasive threat from those who possessed all the accoutrements of power but consent. When Editor White was challenged over two inches of filler hidden in a long unmarked column, he had already won a generation-tested reputation for asserting the rights of black people; he had fought the white primary, disenfranchisement, and segregation; he had urged southern blacks to work with northern whites to improve their institutions. In justifying himself to whites in language that was utterly gracious and carefully polite, he nonetheless wrote the truth about the oversensitive and scarcely-to-be-believed actions of thin-skinned whites who behaved in exaggerated, boorish, and dangerous ways to gain what politeness and courtesy could otherwise have accomplished. White's dignity and political acuity, displayed by sustaining personal contact with the white elite while at the same time asserting his independence, was quite remarkable. And even though White deferred to white authority when using it to protect himself and his family, he refused to compromise his opposition to white oppression, which had been evident the previous year in his reporting of the Darien Insurrection.

That event was, of course, misnamed. When citizens combine to protect themselves from harm and defer to the power of the state even when that power unjustly assails them, we have not an insurrection, but a complex dialectic of resistance and citizenship.[79] This event, too, demonstrates one aspect of African Americans' response to the overwhelming, hurricane-like depression of white racism. The incident began when Tilla Wallace, a white woman of questionable veracity, gave birth to a mixed-race infant and abruptly accused Henry Delegale of raping her. The widely respected black farmer immediately surrendered to the sheriff of McIntosh County. Rumors spread rapidly throughout the area, causing African Americans to congregate at the jail to prevent Delegale from being lynched. After a brief relaxation of tension, the alarm was sounded once again, and a crowd of African Americans rushed to defend the jail as they had before. Unnerved, the sheriff called in the state militia, half of which then escorted Delegale to Savannah while the other half remained in Darien to maintain order. Delegale's sons had been arrested for shooting two white men during a siege of their home by a white mob that had presumed to act as a posse comitatus. Colonel Alexander Lawton took charge of the brothers to protect them and worked with black leaders—ministers, public officials, and editors—who reassured the community that the militia would protect them. When the militia acted to reassure blacks that this was in fact true, tension lessened considerably, and further violence was averted. Black community spokesmen under-

stood their problematic position in a county where many whites wished to impose their will through violence and where the authorities refused to credit
claims of black innocence no matter how accurate they were. In their public an-
nouncements, black leaders warned their people to avoid contact with whites
and to remember their responsibility to act for the good of the race rather than
dwell on injustices to specific individuals. "The good for the entire people is
paramount to the interests of the individual," they said. "The courts must be
sustained; their officers at all hazards must be respected and obeyed. Law must
be upheld. Do not forget these things."[80]

This carefully phrased statement called for black people to sacrifice on behalf of the community no matter how unjustly they believed that their kins-
men, neighbors, and friends were being treated. In the tense days of late August
1899 in Darien, Georgia, the perception of injustice must have been palpable,
for even though Delegale was acquitted at trial in a change of venue, his sons
were sent to prison for life, and many other men who had prevented the elder
Delegale's lynching were sentenced as rioters. "The good for the entire people
is paramount to the interests of the individual": such words were thick with
meaning! Black leaders understood that within the context of white racism and
an almost hysterical white fear of African Americans defending themselves, their
only immediate protection was a disciplined deference to law that required in-
credible dignity and communal self-sacrifice. Such an appeal would not have
been answered with acquiescence had not black communities all over the South
—including Darien—already been prepared to act as their most articulate
spokesmen asked. Southern African Americans knew, as a thoughtful and reflective writer in the *Georgia Baptist* had already observed, that "inhumanities"
were capable of erupting from the white South at any time and that a "storm of
animal passion and arrogance" from whites had afflicted African Americans for
some time. The writer feared that "religion and intelligence must perish" in
such a tempest of human destructiveness. He also feared the silence that seemed
to have gripped African American communities throughout the region, for "silence," he insisted, "mothers tyranny." And white people were resoundingly silent when confronted with their own violence. Blacks could no longer trust the
"better class of white people," he pointed out, because there was no moral courage
in them. With the loss of federal commitment to black equality, the pervasive
white fear of blacks, and the failure of authorities to protect African Americans, he could find hope only in blacks' own ability to engage in conversations
among themselves about ways to strengthen their resolve to live responsible

and moral lives, to repress the community's capacity for violence and self-indulgence, and to raise a standard of self-discipline and achievement through which to create a strong, resilient, and moral people; this, he said, was "the imperative demand of the hour."[81] If action by the black Darien community demonstrated its capacity to use armed resistance to thwart lynching, its self-discipline was even more remarkable. It established credibility with white authorities, who knew they could trust the black elite to deliver peace in the face of provocation from the militia. Such action was not unique to coastal Georgia.[82]

THE ROLE OF BLACK MINISTERS in the Darien Insurrection was significant. Three Baptists, a Presbyterian, and an Episcopalian were active in negotiations. Their conversations with the white militia commander were important, to be sure—as was their willingness to use arms in self-defense—but, like other capable black ministers throughout the South, they had also prepared the community for the even greater task of achieving and sustaining solidarity in the face of white hostility and possible destruction. Before Tilla Wallace lied about Henry Delegale, Christian ministers had been preaching a gospel of solidarity and sacrifice since the days of slavery. McIntosh County, like contiguous Liberty County, had been under the care of an independent black ministry for many years. The area had been cited by apologists for slavery as the site of model missions to slaves, and after emancipation freedpeople had been landowners and aggressive political actors.[83] What black ministers could preach to their people can be inferred from the fact that one of the Baptists, E. M. Brawley, had been eloquent in asserting black autonomy and self-determination throughout the state.[84] He obviously believed that salvation for black people began in Georgia and not in heaven. This theme was obvious in the ubiquitous *Georgia Baptist* in the 1890s and was inherent in what preachers believed was the Christian message and the identification of black people with the person and work of Christ Jesus. The great achievement of Christ's work was to be understood not as gaining access to heaven, but "through the reign of love in the souls of men, constraining them to be grateful and self-sacrificing [in] labors on behalf of their fellowmen."

When a black preacher uttered these words, racial tension in east Georgia and western South Carolina was intense, widespread, and dangerous. In the face of impending threat from angry whites, he could emphasize that African Americans were "a race despised and rejected of men, a race of sorrows and acquainted with grief, a race that is shot down like rabbits, and denied in many ways the rights of life, liberty, and the pursuit of happiness." He said: "When I think of these things, I also remember that the God of Israel slumbers not nor sleeps, and that, if we trust him the God who brought us safely through the red sea of slavery will also deliver us from the hands of wicked and unjust men. And [if] we will not bless God for the night, we most certainly ought to thank Him that the night is no deeper, and that He has promised to deliver us, if we call on Him, in the time of trouble." This preacher's fusion of the language of the "suffering servant" in the book of Isaiah with the sacrificial life of Christ, the sacrificial life of the black community, and the promised victory of Apocalypse was not a labored one: it flowed out of the experience of Bible, preaching, prayer, and circumstance, and it meant service, discipline, and sacrifice.[85] While caught in the cauldron of racial terror and draconian punishment, white men thought of sex, purity, profanation, self-justification, immanence, and justice imposed in the acts they inflicted, while black people thought of suffering, service, sacrifice, transcendence, and justice yet to be realized in the predicament they bore. Sacrifice implied victory, even as Christ's sacrifice had brought victory. Here was not a people awaiting Moses to lead them out of bondage, but a people taking on the life of Christ, sloughing off the despair that afflicted those who had placed their faith in mankind — even the whites — and understanding that the only victory "worth winning was to follow Christ, even though it led to his cross."[86] The victory lay within them as they took on the power of Christ not to receive heaven as compensation for the cross they bore, but to achieve victory through it. The power of the language that bespoke a "race of sorrows and acquainted with grief" came out of a community that had experienced solidarity and hope in Christ before being attacked by white terror; the promise of victory from the experience of past redemption from slavery could not be believed by a people whose faith was a ramshackle, sometime thing. The experience of being the suffering servant with the promise of redemption sealed by emancipation and Christ's crucifixion was a true experience of the whole community, not the compensatory nonsense of an imaginary heaven.

The souls of black folk seemed to find salvation in a distinctly different way from the self-righteousness and blanched holiness of a segregated white community. This is not to say that black people were not afflicted by the same flaws inherent in any religious community: hypocrisy, tribalism, and spiritual pride. But the Christian narrative seemed precisely to fit the African American community's situation in the midst of white supremacy. Identifying with the crucified Savior, African Americans affirmed the moral sublimity of Christ for having lived his life amid persecutions like their own and having—through his life, death, and resurrection—become the redeemer of the world. It thus seemed natural for a prophetic woman addressing her people in the Methodist *Star of Zion* to insist that Christ had experienced African American life; it was the kind of recapitulation that a church father made in the second century of the Common Era.[87] In fusing African American experience and Christian salvation, Mary Louks identified with the agony in which Christ prayed for release from the sacrificial meaning of his destiny just as black men had confronted the horror of their deaths at the hands of a mob hastening them to their own Golgotha. Remembering the terror with which Christ was faced, Louks linked Gethsemane, the seething mob, the shout of "crucify Him," the mock trial, and the final sacrifice to African American experience. God appeared to forsake his suffering son as Jesus cried, "They know not what they do!"—as if those who hanged him on the tree were crazed by their own blindness and thirst for blood. It would be impossible to separate the participation by Louks's readers in Christ's suffering from their own experience of white terror. When she repeated the familiar words, "For us He died—startling thought," Louks allowed the imagination broadly to range from myth to history to the immediate present, stained with its own terror and awful possibilities. The same people who could read her familiar words and imagine the salvation that had been sealed in sacrifice could on the same page read Bishop Henry McNeal Turner's insistent message that African Americans "honor black,"[88] and they could reflect on what that could possibly mean. Such messages were obviously not about postponing until death the reception of victorious life. The pie-in-the-sky caricature imagined by those who are contemptuous of African American folk religion fails to engage the meaning of sacrifice and discipleship that believers had sketched out for each other under slavery and later under a more bloody, erratic, and terrifying oppression.

If preachers and women speakers preached the Christ vicariously bleeding on a cross out of love for them, they knew that through accepting the cross with him their work, exhaustion, and despair could become meaningful, for he had accepted the same on their own behalf.[89] Like them, Christ had been "despised and rejected of men" (Isaiah 53:3), and this rejection had made him one of them; being one of them, he then made them like unto himself. The Incarnation was not an abstract and strange doctrine, but a living reality that transformed the persecution of black folk into a means of salvation through the sacrifices of community.[90] Being like-minded with Christ meant that from despair and anguish could come the peace of one who had experienced the same despair and had become victorious; as Christians, they too would be enabled to become victorious through identification with him.[91] Through this taking on of Christ in the process of making their own religious lives, African Americans confounded the logic of lynching mobs and those who defended them.

If whites thought that lynching blacks would teach African Americans a lesson, as so many of them repeated ad nauseam, they failed to understand that the lesson taught would be the opposite of what they had intended. Lynchers believed that they enacted a just vengeance that dramatically punished guilt by terrorizing African Americans. They were incapable of understanding that in selecting a body to represent in their own minds the African American community of potential criminals, they had made the person thus embodied and subjected to their wrath in hideous punishment into a martyr. By shaming the subject through their engine of death, they had transformed him into an innocent.[92] Even in the case of a confessed murderer like Thomas Wilkes, African Americans saw the terrible death in blood and fire as the making of a martyr in the same way as the early Christians had been made martyrs by Roman persecution. In making this very point, one minister added that the Romans had been more merciful; but in remembering the victory of Christian martyrs, the implication was clear that African Americans, too, would be victorious.[93]

Martyrdom, both as a sacred reference and as an immediate danger, both as the familiar image of the cross and as the hideous possibility of lynching, meant sacrifice. The martyr is also literally a witness, so that in donning the mantle of martyrdom one witnessed to the belief for which he was being martyred. Black people knew that when one of their own was selected for punishment, it was not for the crime specified, but for the crime of being black, since the law already prescribed penalties for the former.[94] To make sense of an act imposed by people who renounced their own laws in senselessness, African Americans came to understand that the implied testimony of the martyr was of African American sacrifice. They knew that as martyrdom meant sacrifice, sacrifice in some way meant gain! At the end of the nineteenth century, writes a student of "the science of sacrifice," "sacrifice" came to be the narrative that scholars, essayists, religionists, and social scientists used to define the fundamental "sacrament" of a volatile, mobile society. Sacrifice was more than a subject of scholarly interest with regard to alien and familiar peoples, and it was more than an "overworked" metaphor. Sacrifice was an essential structure in discourse about the nature of society during the years when lynching was becoming the haunting representation of southern horror. Sacrifice was associated with spiritual loss, the cost of progress, the fortification of social boundaries, and the justification of in-equities by making them appear to be essentially "natural."[95] Sacrifice became humanized, points out one of its students, as writers thought of the natural "costs of human progress." One writer actually insisted that "progress every-where waits on death—the death of the inferior individual—and nowhere more so than in racial problems." This comment reveals the reservation by defin-ition and act, as critic René Girard says, of "whole categories of human beings" for "sacrificial purposes to protect other categories." Southern whites had iden-tified African Americans—just as their northern counterparts had identified immigrants and laborers—as victims of social transformation "uniquely wor-thy of sacrificial treatment."[96] White southerners had engineered segregation to define who stood most squarely in the way of progress. By pushing a whole cat-egory of persons to the margins, both in discourse and in law, the powerful had reserved a class of people to be punished as payment for the failures of white people in the complex transition to modernity.

If the sacrificial mentalité required both Romans and martyrs, African Amer-icans knew which was which, and the sensibility was not merely a dumb defer-ence to Rome or Caesar, but a positive affirmation of African American innocence, courage, and determination in its different forms, from the chants of apocalyp-tic hope of country preachers to the sophisticated understanding of W. E. B. Du Bois. Du Bois knew, as one of his students points out, that American blacks had their "own forms of sacrificial agency."[97] In *The Souls of Black Folk*, he re-minded white Americans of the gifts of story and song that black people had given to American culture, and he urged them not to forget the third gift: the "gift of the Spirit." He wrote:

> Out of the nation's heart, we have called all that was best to throttle and sub-due all that was worst; fire and blood, prayer and sacrifice, have billowed over this people, and they have found peace only in the altars of the God of Right. Nor has our gift of the Spirit been merely passive. Actively we have woven ourselves with the very warp and woof of this nation—we fought their bat-tles, shared their sorrow, mingled our blood with theirs, and generation after generation have pleaded with a headstrong careless people to despise not Justice, Mercy, and Truth, lest the nation be smitten with a curse.[98]

In the midst of terror, "sacrificial agency" did not surrender self and commu-nity to the logic of the narcissistic white world of segregation and lynching. Sacrificial agency empowered African Americans to make from both the Chris-

tian narrative and hope a strategy—one that relied on internal solidarity, forbearance, fortitude, and the capacity to endure pain—to break the power of
white violence to subdue them.

RELIGION AS A LIVED experience is not merely about the ways in which beliefs
that engage the meaning of the world shape daily life. It is also about how people find in a religious experience or the imagined dimensions of the transcendent a way to place everything in a perspective that salvages as much personal
and communal dignity as possible from the clutches of the satanic—powerlessness, hostility, pain, alienation, and death. The human predicament that spawned
lynching, like slavery, presents religious historians with an opportunity to study
religion beyond the confines of institutions and creeds and at the same time to
tease out the ways in which institutions, creeds, and the experiences encouraged by them through the words of sacred writ do indeed illuminate past lives.
In the racial crisis of the 1880s and 1890s, white supremacy was obviously secured
by religious faith.[99] The religion that whites inherited and the religion that they
fabricated allowed them the illusion of purity and righteousness. It was an illusion that encouraged a white man to say that lynching was part of the religion of
his people. But in contemplating the meaning of lynching, it is also necessary to
understand it as part of the religion of African Americans.[100] Lynching seemed
to dramatize in blood the suffering and despair with which slavery had burdened black people; that these feelings profoundly shaped the sensibility and
the music that flowed from it into the blues should come as no surprise. The
"blues lyric tradition," writes Adam Gussow, reflected "anxieties about encirclement, torture and dismemberment"—precisely the terrors that flowed from
lynching. Against this "oppressive [ghostly] presence," blues enabled African
Americans to transcend terror through the artistic genius of their music. They
did the same thing in their religion, which made the death of Christ a sacrifice
through which to transcend the terror inflicted upon them. All that Christ experienced demonstrated his oneness with African Americans. The Christian
religion of black southerners could encourage them to believe ultimately that
they would overcome all things. As believers, they saw that God was not a God
of white purity, as segregation implied and as lynchers insisted, but of black
sacrifice and eventual resurrection. During the terror of lynching, African Americans experienced suffering and sacrifice, which many of them bore through a

religious understanding identified with the life, death, and resurrection of the Christ. White terror had demanded a savage sacrifice before, when the very Son of God was lynched. The mystery of such a cosmic event could not explain why such things happened, but its outcome in resurrection could offer hope that God's children would prevail.

This hope—flowing from suffering and sacrifice—is not what many people think of when they think of American religion, but it is time that they did. In thinking of religion in America, we need to think of Americans not only as white and powerful, but also as people of color who have experienced suffering and sacrifice. For Christians, it is especially important to learn this lesson, because the supreme Christian narrative of salvation hangs on the cross, and no amount of liberal demystification can explain away that fact. For everyone who must understand religion in order to understand history, an understanding of the experiences of people caught up in the social and cultural totality that could erupt into such rites as lynching must include both the articulated traditions of formal religious institutions and values (the incorporation of sacred narrative into everyday life) and also the ways in which social and cultural facts express a religious sensibility that lies beyond those institutions and values (segregation and lynching). As we come to understand more about the ways in which people from differing perspectives responded to illegal white violence through the discourse of religion, we shall see the ethically deadening effect of a religion that supported a narcissistic confirmation of righteousness and renounced any meaningful confession of sin. Such was the flaw of a white evangelicalism that assumed absolutely no responsibility for the violence inherent in its obsession with purity and danger. The sacrificial agency of which W. E. B. Du Bois wrote helps us see the power of African Americans' Christian faith, but the full meaning of religion and lynching may not be understood until we seriously confront the meaning of punishment itself, the status of those punished, the complicity of the punishers in defining what is punishable, and the full ramifications of punitiveness. The cultural permission to punish and the capacity of the punished to suffer invite the analysis of those who seek to understand history through understanding religion. Students should neither ignore nor restrict themselves to obviously holy things and sacred discourse, but explore the full ramifications of the religious, both in the evil that humans do and in their capacity to survive it.

Notes

1. See John Boles, "The Discovery of Southern Religious History," in *Interpreting Southern History: Historiographical Essays in Honor of Sanford W. Higginbotham*, eds. John Boles and Evelyn Nolen (Baton Rouge: Louisiana State University Press, 1987): 510–48; Catharine C. Cleveland, *The Great Revival in the West, 1797–1805* (Chicago: University of Chicago Press, 1916); Wesley M. Gewehr, *The Great Awakening in Virginia, 1740–1790* (Durham: Duke University Press, 1930); Hunter D. Farish, *The Circuit Rider Dismounts: A Social History of Southern Methodism* (Richmond: Dietz Press, 1938); and Walter Brownlow Posey, *Frontier Religion: A History of Religion West of the Southern Appalachians to 1861* (Lexington: University Press of Kentucky, 1966) and *Religious Strife on the Southern Frontier* (Baton Rouge: Louisiana State University Press, 1965).

2. Emily Bingham, *Mordecai: An Early American Family* (New York: Hill & Wang, 2003); Ellen Eslinger, *Citizens of Zion: The Social Origins of Camp Meeting Revivalism* (Knoxville: University of Tennessee Press, 1999); Sylvia R. Frey and Betty Wood, *Come Shouting to Zion: African American Protestantism in the American South and British Caribbean to 1830* (Chapel Hill: University of North Carolina Press, 1998); Paul Harvey, *Redeeming the South: Religious Cultures and Racial Identities among Southern Baptists, 1865–1925* (Chapel Hill: University of North Carolina Press, 1997); Christine Leigh Heyrman, *Southern Cross: The Beginnings of the Bible Belt* (New York: Alfred A. Knopf, 1997); Beth Barton Schweiger, *The Gospel Working Up: Progress and the Pulpit in Nineteenth-Century Virginia* (New York: Oxford University Press, 2000); Jon F. Sensbach, *A Separate Canaan: The Making of an Afro-Moravian World in North Carolina, 1863–1840* (Chapel Hill: University of North Carolina Press, 1998).

3. Richard Carwardine, *Evangelicals and Politics in Antebellum America* (New Haven: Yale University Press, 1993).

4. See especially Heyrman, *Southern Cross*, and Cynthia Lynn Lyerly, *Methodism and the Southern Mind, 1770–1810* (New York: Oxford University Press, 1998).

5. Students may begin with Peter L. Berger, *The Sacred Canopy: Elements of a Sociological Theory of Religion* (New York: Doubleday, 1967), and Thomas Luckmann, *The Invisible Religion: The Problem of Religion in Modern Society* (New York: Macmillan, 1967).

6. Mary Douglas, *Purity and Danger: An Analysis of Concepts of Pollution and Taboo* (London: Routledge & Kegan Paul, 1966; Pelican Books, 1970), 40.

7. Clifford Geertz, *Interpretation of Cultures: Selected Essays* (New York: Basic Books, 1973), 90.

8. Ibid., 94.

9. Robert G. Hamerton-Kelly, *Sacred Violence: Paul's Hermeneutic of the Cross* (Minneapolis: Fortress Press, 1992), 15.

10. Arthur Raper, *The Tragedy of Lynching* (Chapel Hill: University of North Carolina Press, 1933), 6, 11, 15–18, 20–39, 53–54, 74–84, 119–24, 129–38, 145–71, 191–202, 211–32, 249–60, 281–301, 312–16, 347–55, 367–68, 378–83.

11. Walter White, *Rope and Faggot: A Biography of Judge Lynch* (1929; reprint, New York: Arno/The New York Times, 1969), 40.

12. Edwin Taliaferro Wellford, *The Lynching of Jesus: A Review of the Legal Aspects of the Trial of Christ* (Newport News, Va.: Franklin Printing, 1905).

13. René Girard, *The Girard Reader*, ed. James G. Williams (New York: Crossroad, 1996); James G. Williams, *The Bible, Violence, and the Sacred: Liberation from the Myth of Sanctioned Violence* (San Francisco: HarperSanFrancisco, 1991).

14. Stewart E. Tolnay and E. M. Beck, *Festival of Violence: An Analysis of Southern Lynchings, 1882–1930* (Urbana: University of Illinois Press, 1995).

15. James Allen, Hilton Als, John Lewis, and Leon F. Litwack, *Without Sanctuary: Lynching Photography in America* (Santa Fe: Twin Palms Publishers, 2000).

16. Richard Slotkin, *Regeneration through Violence: The Mythology of the American Frontier, 1600–1860* (Middletown, Conn.: Wesleyan University Press, 1973). I do not address the endemic violence of American history and culture. Despite Slotkin's corpus of work and that of Richard Maxwell Brown, Orville Vernon Burton, and others, U.S. historians still have not engaged the ways in which violence has shaped American values and history and the ways in which we historians have managed to hide that process from our students and audiences.

17. Some readers will be put off by my belief, based on reading Walter White and African American weekly periodicals, that African Americans thought that white people (especially men) were "crazed by a fascination with purity and profanation" that frequently focused on sex. White men themselves could sometimes justify their lynching of blacks by a kind of holy madness (righteous provocation) in the face of black profanation. There was a logic to the narrative they assumed, to be sure; but they employed appeals to emotions in which madness (being crazed, in my understanding) allowed men to do things because the sacred had been profaned. I suspect that some whites developed this rationalization to compound their terrorizing of blacks. Feigning madness disorients opponents and can be used in a calculating manner, but it still is the madness to which one responds.

18. Mark Twain [Samuel Clemens], "The United States of Lyncherdom," August 1901, in *Collected Tales, Sketches, Speeches, and Essays, 1891–1910* (New York: Library of America, 1992): 484–86.

19. Edward Ayers, *The Promise of the New South: Life after Reconstruction* (New York: Oxford University Press, 1992), 160–82.

20. *Star of Zion*, February 21, 1889, 2; June 13, 1889, 2; June 14, 1894, 2.

21. Mrs. J. J. Ansley, *History of the Georgia Women's Christian Temperance Union from Its Organization 1883 to 1907* (Columbus: Gilbert Printing Company, 1914); Paul Isaac, *Prohibition and Politics: Turbulent Decades in Tennessee, 1885–1920* (Knoxville: University of Tennessee Press, 1977); James Benson Sellers, *The Prohibition Movement in Alabama, 1702 to 1943* (Chapel Hill: University of North Carolina Press, 1943); Daniel Jay Whitener, *Prohibition in North Carolina, 1715–1945* (Chapel Hill: University of North Carolina Press, 1946).

22. Harold Mann, *Atticus Greene Haygood: Methodist Bishop, Editor, Educator* (Athens: University of Georgia Press, 1965); Louis D. Rubin Jr., ed., *Teach the Freeman: The Correspondence of Rutherford B. Hayes and the Slater Fund for the Negro* (Baton Rouge: Louisiana State University Press, 1959); David F. Godshalk, "William J. Northen's Public and Personal Struggles against Lynching," in *Jumpin' Jim Crow: Southern Politics from Civil War to Civil Rights*, eds. Jane Dailey and Glenda Gilmore (Princeton: Princeton University Press, 2000), 140–61.

23. White, *Rope and Faggot*, 40.

24. When White attributed the emotional compulsion (as opposed to the political and economic reasons) to lynch to undisciplined emotions evoked by clever, religious hysterics, he was obviously not writing as a dispassionate social scientist. He was responding to a stereotype of revivalistic preaching that seemed to him to be based as much on unleashed emotion as were the maddened crowds he associated with lynching. Not that he attributed lynching to emotions alone, but he did believe that "fanaticism" sparked the fires of both camp meetings and lynchings. Other emotions, interests, and fears stoked those fires to burn more fiercely. That White relied on stereotype to begin thinking about the religious nature of lynching does not mean he was mistaken; his Rorschach-type response reveals a lot about the ways in which observers saw the ineffectual nature of white southerners' piety.

25. "Social equality," he wrote, could always evoke an "insane rage" (ibid., 52).

26. Ibid., 48.

27. Carol Zisowitz Stearns and Peter N. Stearns, *Anger: The Struggle for Emotional Control in America's History* (Chicago: University of Chicago Press, 1986), 36–68.

28. Christopher Waldrep, "Word and Deed: The Language of Lynching, 1820–1953," in *Lethal Imagination: Violence and Brutality in American History*, ed. Michael A. Bellesiles (New York: New York University Press, 1999), 241–43; Bertram Wyatt-Brown, *Southern Honor: Ethics and Behavior in the Old South* (New York: Oxford University Press, 1982), 306, 388–89.

29. See press responses to the murder of "Sam Hose" by a mob in Newnan, Georgia, April 23, 1899, in *Newnan Herald and Advertiser*, April 28, 1899, 6. See also article by Judge L. E. Bleckley taken from the *Forum* of November 1893 and printed in the *Newnan Herald and Advertiser*, August 13, 1897, 1.

30. *Newnan Herald and Advertiser*, April 28, 1899, 6, quoting a Macon, Georgia, newspaper.

31. Bleckley in *Newnan Herald and Advertiser*, August 13, 1897, 1.

32. "He Goes to Death without an Outcry," *Atlanta Journal*, April 24, 1899, 1.

33. Steven M. Stowe, *Intimacy and Power in the Old South: Ritual in the Lives of the Planters* (Baltimore: Johns Hopkins University Press, 1987): 167, 252–53.

34. Ibid., 1–2.

35. Wyatt-Brown, *Southern Honor*, 362–401, 435–61.

36. The fact that the argument could be made at all rested on the folk-cultural stereotype of the hot-tempered "Southron" gentleman. But he could act coolly once he had been spurred to action by the perceived combination of blasphemy, lese majesty, and af-

front to honor in whatever crime could be attributed to the focus of his wrath. The point is not that provocation was irrational, but that it unleashed a holy fury.

37. Ansley, *History of the Georgia Women's Christian Temperance Union*; Isaac, *Prohibition and Politics*; Sellers, *Prohibition Movement in Alabama*; Ted Ownby, *Subduing Satan: Religion, Recreation, and Manhood in the Rural South, 1865–1920* (Chapel Hill: University of North Carolina Press, 1990), 170–73, 208–9; Whitener, *Prohibition in North Carolina*.

38. On controlling the black workforce, see John W. Cell, *The Highest Stage of White Supremacy: The Origins of Segregation in South Africa and the American South* (New York: Cambridge University Press, 1982), 134; William Cohen, *At Freedom's Edge: Black Mobility and the Southern White Quest for Racial Control, 1861–1915* (Baton Rouge: Louisiana State University Press, 1991); and C. Vann Woodward, *The Strange Career of Jim Crow* (New York: Oxford University Press, 1974). On purifying the people, see Cohen, *At Freedom's Edge*, 214–15. On purifying politics, see Ayers, *Promise of the New South*, 52–54, 67–68, 121–27, 136–49, 269, 175–78, 289–90, 298–99, 304–9, 409–13, 429, 433–34; and Woodward, *Strange Career of Jim Crow*, 67–109.

39. Philip Alexander Bruce, "Evolution of the Negro Problem," *Sewanee Review* 19 (October 1911): 385–99, reprinted as "In Defense of Southern Race Policies" in *The Development of Segregationist Thought*, ed. I. A. Newby (Homewood, Ill.: Dorsey Press, 1968): 70–78.

40. Douglas, *Purity and Danger*, 145.

41. Ibid., 67.

42. Lillian Smith, *Killers of the Dream* (1949; reprint, New York: W. W. Norton, 1961), 83.

43. Ibid., 88–90, 101, 224–52.

44. In *Crucible of Race: Black-White Relations in the American South since Emancipation* (New York: Oxford University Press, 1984), Joel Williamson puts the matter this way: "In their frustration white men projected their own worst thoughts upon black men, imagined them acted out in some specific incident, and symbolically killed those thoughts by lynching a hapless black man. Almost any vulnerable black man would do" (308).

45. *Newnan Herald and Advertiser*, February 22, 1895.

46. *Griffin Daily News*, February 27, March 2, 10, June 18, 21, 1901.

47. Bishop Atticus Green Haygood of the Methodist Episcopal Church, South, as reported in Williamson, *Crucible of Race*, 118.

48. Ibid., 115–24.

49. "Hose is a 'Will,'" *Atlanta Constitution*, April 16, 1899, 2.

50. "Capture of Sam Hose," *Atlanta Constitution*, April 15, 1899, 2.

51. *Atlanta Constitution*, April 15–23, 1899; *Atlanta Journal*, April 16–23, 1899.

52. *Sparta Ishmaelite*, November 22, 1901, quoted in Eric Tabor Millin's fine master's thesis, "Defending the Sacred Hearth: Religion, Politics, and Racial Violence in Georgia, 1904–1906" (University of Georgia, 2002), 60. The cannibalism of inhaling the aroma of burning flesh is emphasized by Orlando Patterson in *Rituals of Blood: Consequences of Slavery in Two American Centuries* (Washington, D.C.: Civitas Counterpoint, 1998), 194–202.

53. Ida B. Wells, *Southern Horrors: Lynch Law in All Its Phases* (New York: New York Age, 1892), reprinted in *Southern Horrors and Other Writings: The Anti-lynching Campaign of Ida B. Well, 1892–1900*, ed. Jacqueline Jones Royster (Boston: Bedford Books, 1997), 50–57.

54. Martha E. Hodes, *White Women, Black Men: Illicit Sex in the Nineteenth-Century South* (New Haven: Yale University Press, 1997); Victoria E. Bynum, *Unruly Women: The Politics of Social and Sexual Control in the Old South* (Chapel Hill: University of North Carolina Press, 1992).

55. Ida B. Wells, *A Red Record: Lynchings in the United States* (Chicago: privately printed, [1894]), in Royster, *Southern Horrors*, 77.

56. John Crowe Ransom, *God without Thunder: An Unorthodox Defense of Orthodoxy* (New York: Harcourt, Brace, 1930), 32.

57. Ibid., 325.

58. Wilbur J. Cash, *The Mind of the South* (New York: Vintage Books, 1969), 59.

59. Robert Lewis Dabney, "Vindicatory Justice Essential to God (Southern Pulpit, April 1881)," in *Discussions of Robert L. Dabney, D.D., Ll.D.*, ed. C. R. Vaughn (Richmond: Presbyterian Committee of Publication, 1890), 1:466.

60. George C. Rable, *But There Was No Peace: The Role of Violence in the Politics of Reconstruction* (Athens: University of Georgia Press, 1984); Allen Trelease, *White Terror: The Ku Klux Klan Conspiracy and Southern Reconstruction* (New York: Harper & Row, 1971).

61. Wyatt-Brown, *Southern Honor*, 436.

62. Ibid., 444, quoting Natalie Zemon Davis, "The Reasons of Misrule: Youth Groups and Charivaris in Sixteenth-Century France," *Past and Present* 50 (February 1971): 43, 55.

63. Wyatt-Brown, *Southern Honor*, 436–37.

64. Ibid., 453–61.

65. Donald G. Mathews, "The Southern Rite of Human Sacrifice," *Journal of Southern Religion* 3 (August 2000), ⟨http://jsr.as.wvu.edu⟩; Wyatt-Brown, *Southern Honor*, 434–51, 190–91. For a discussion of the scapegoat mechanism and its effects with regard to ritual and violence, see (to begin with) Williams, *Girard Reader*, esp. 9–29, 69–106. See also Brian K. Smith, "Capital Punishment and Human Sacrifice," *Journal of the American Academy of Religion* 68 (March 2000): 3–25.

66. See, for example, Hamerton-Kelly, *Sacred Violence*, 59–87.

67. See René Girard in Williams, *Girard Reader*.

68. "Capture of Sam Hose," *Atlanta Constitution*, April 15, 1899, 2; "God's Righteous Wrath Is Never Slow to Avenge the Christian Home," *Newnan Herald and Advertiser*, May 12, 1899, 3, referring to the lynching of "Sam Hose." In another section, referring to Thomas Wilkes's supposed rape of Mrs. Cranford, the man wrote: "God ordains it just and right to avenge this hellish crime" (quoting from *Atlanta Constitution*, 3). See also the actions of a Baptist preacher in organizing and leading the lynching of Mack Charles

Parker in 1959, recounted in Howard Smead, *Blood Justice: The Lynching of Mack Charles Parker* (New York: Oxford University Press, 1986), 33–36.

69. William Fitzhugh Brundage, *Lynching in the New South: Georgia and Virginia, 1880–1930* (Urbana: University of Illinois Press, 1993), 195–97, 201–2; Ralph Luker, *The Social Gospel in Black and White: American Racial Reform, 1885–1912* (Chapel Hill: University of North Carolina Press, 1991), 91, 100; Williamson, *Crucible of Race*, 287–91. See also references to black men as rapists in discussions of lynching in the *Nashville Christian Advocate*, October 15, 19, 1906, and the *Wesleyan Christian Advocate*, August 29, 1888, May 3, 10, 1899.

70. Wells, *A Red Record*, 80, 92, 119–20.

71. Minutes, Atlanta Evangelical Ministers Association, April 1, 1907, Atlanta History Center, Atlanta, Ga.; Godshalk, "William J. Northen."

72. W. H. Crogman to Mrs. Atticus Green Haygood (copy), June 6, 1896, Atticus G. Haygood Papers, 138, Special Collections, Robert Woodruff Library, Emory University, Atlanta, Ga. See also Haygood, *Our Brother in Black* (New York: Phillips & Hunt, 1881).

73. When faced with the mythic canon of immaculate protection, both men at least once in their lives justified lynching for rape. Northen created a storm for having done so in Boston after the Thomas Wilkes lynching of April 1899. See Godshalk, "William J. Northen."

74. See Herbert Shapiro, *White Violence and Black Response from Reconstruction to Montgomery* (Amherst: University of Massachusetts Press, 1988); Trelease, *White Terror*; and W. Fitzhugh Brundage, "The Roar on the Other Side of Silence: Black Resistance and White Violence in the American South, 1880–1940," in *Under Sentence of Death: Lynching in the South*, ed. William Fitzhugh Brundage (Chapel Hill: University of North Carolina Press, 1997), 271–91.

75. *Georgia Baptist*, May 17, 1900, 1, 4.

76. Ibid., May 31, 1900, 4.

77. Ibid.

78. Ibid., June 7, 1900, 1, 4; June 14, 1900, 4; June 21, 1900, 4.

79. The following account is based on Brundage, *Lynching in the New South*, 133–37, and "The Darien 'Insurrection' of 1899: Black Protest during the Nadir of Race Relations," *Georgia Historical Quarterly* 74 (Summer 1990): 234–53.

80. *Georgia Baptist*, August 31, 1899, 1.

81. Ibid.

82. Darien citizens were not alone in acting to prevent lynching. On July 21, 1892, for example, the *Star of Zion* reported that black crowds did the same in Paducah, Kentucky, and in a Florida county (1). These were not unique events.

83. Charles Colcock Jones, *The Religious Instruction of the Negroes in the United States* (Savannah: Thomas Purse, 1842); Donald L. Grant, *The Way It Was in the South: The Black Experience in Georgia* (Athens: University of Georgia Press, 1993), 128, 147.

84. E. M. Brawley wanted Georgia's black Baptists to free themselves of northern white

connections and to establish institutions free from all white influence, northern or southern. He was active in statewide affairs and was fearless in agitation for autonomous and independent African American institutions.

85. *Georgia Baptist*, December 1, 1898, 1, 8.

86. Ibid., February 2, 1899, 1. See also *Star of Zion*, April 27, 1893, 2, about "taking up the cross" as a way of suffering with Christ who suffers with us.

87. See Eric Francis Osborn, *Ireneus of Lyons* (New York: Cambridge University Press, 2001), 97–140. One of the great fathers of the second-century church, Ireneus, Bishop of Lyons (Lugdunum), developed a complex theology of the Incarnation and a soteriology, emphasizing that "everything that God does is part of his economy and every part of his economy is defined in relation to its recapitulation." That is, Christ came to live the perfect life of man. In doing so, he healed all the brokenness created by sin. By taking on every man's experience and through his death on the cross becoming victorious (*Christus Victor*) over sin and death, he saved those who received him in faith. The moral elements of this recapitulation of Christ were his "love, magnanimity or long suffering, his reason and his justice . . . as he gave his life for our life and his flesh for our flesh." In effect, "God became what we are so that we might be what he is." Identifying with his perfect life by accepting the work of the cross, the Christian received salvation. This taking on of Christ was familiar language to every Christian; the language of the cross was essential when thinking of salvation. A God who humbled himself in love to create and who took the risk of Incarnation by taking on the violence of humankind in the cross certainly offends those who despise victims and a slave morality. To those experiencing the human predicament as victims of terror, however, the narrative of Christ's victory heard against the threatening narratives of immaculate protection and righteous provocation provided a perspective that broke whites' power to have the last say about African American lives. The point is simply that the identification of the believer with the crucified Lord (a major scandal, to be sure) has been a part of the Christian narrative for centuries, and to the student who has confronted the narrative in two such disparate locales as second-century Lugdunum and nineteenth-century Georgia, the similarity is transhistorical.

88. *Star of Zion*, September 10, 1886, 1.

89. Miss A. Kelley, "Sin and Its Reward," speech reprinted in *Star of Zion*, March 24, 1887, 1.

90. *Star of Zion*, March 28, 1898, 2.

91. "Religious Life the Christian Religion," *Star of Zion*, March 24, 1887, 1. See also January 30, 1890, 1, and April 27, 1893, 2.

92. James Gilligan, *Violence: Our Deadly Epidemic and Its Causes* (New York: G. P. Putnam, 1996), 113, 185. Gilligan points out that punishing subjects transforms them into innocents in their own conceptions of self; draconian punishment would seem to intensify the effect. Defenders of lynching were frustrated by how their acts transferred public focus from the crime for which a person was lynched to the lynching in itself, and yet they seem never to have thought seriously about why this transformation might have taken

place. The incident associated with an Augusta, Georgia, crowd's fury at the *Washington (D.C.) Bee*'s comment about the martyrdom of the young black man lynched in spring of 1900 for defending the honor of a young black woman (see above) demonstrates the feeling of blacks and whites in regard to martyrdom.

93. J. J. Kearney, untitled article, *Star of Zion*, May 11, 1899, 2. See also *Star of Zion*, November 9, 1893, 1. In July 1893, Bishop Henry McNeil Turner and 300 others called for a meeting to protest the persecutions, which they compared to those of Queen Mary of England; they clearly appropriated Foxe's *Book of Martyrs* for African Americans, but they insisted that the sixteenth-century burnings were not so numerous as what they were experiencing then. See also *Georgia Baptist*, May 18, 1899, 7; this article appeared after the Wilkes lynching, when the International Sunday School lesson was John 18:28, 40 and 19:4. The people who delivered Jesus to Pilate "[did] not know that the true Passover Lamb was being put to death by them and that their Passover, like their Sabbaths and all their feasts, was a mere form—a husk without a kernel." In the familiar story, the crowd shouts for and receives the release of Barabbas. The lesson ends with Pilate saying, "Behold, your king!" to which the crowd responds, "We have no king, but Caesar" (John 19:14–15). In the context of the time, it would not take a genius to know whom African Americans thought it was that cried for Barabbas, that Jesus might die.

94. I am grateful to Kurt Berends for discussing this matter with me. I am not sure he would appreciate the way I have, possibly, twisted what he said, but the conversation continues.

95. Susan L. Mizruchi, *The Science of Sacrifice: American Literature and Modern Social Theory* (Princeton: Princeton University Press, 1998), 25–27. The phrase "key social sacrament" is Mizruchi's, 25.

96. Ibid., 31, quoting Charles Ellwood's review of William Benjamin Smith, *The Color Line*, in the *American Journal of Sociology* (November 1905): 574. The second quotation is Mizruchi's report of René Girard's observation, and the last quotation is from Mizruchi herself.

97. Ibid., 354.

98. W. E. B. Du Bois, *The Souls of Black Folk* (1903; reprint, New York: New American Library, 1969), 375–76.

99. The source of this faith was partially Christian, but Christian ideals of purity were mixed with racist fears that attributed a demonic danger to whites from blacks. Blackness, however, was not about color. It was, rather, the sum total of everything that threatened the purity, sanctity, and self-understanding of people who believed that defining themselves as white was essential. Furthermore, this was not merely about power. Sex, gender, purity, danger, and politics are all implied in everything that white people said to justify themselves; these statements were expressions of an ontological reality—the very nature of good and evil. Whites created the demons that haunted them in dialectic with their understanding of the meaning of their historical interaction with African Americans, to whom they then attributed profanation and danger. The process continues in the "politics of terrorism" that now grips the nation.

100. The following discussion is based on Adam Gussow, *Seems Like Murder Here: Southern Violence and the Blues Tradition* (Chicago: University of Chicago Press, 2002), 23–39 and throughout. Most blues, Gussow writes, were "unconscious transformations rather than intentional codings of lynching tropes and scenarios." Gussow believes that "the 'blues subject' emerged out of a forced daily confrontation with the possibility of annihilation" and that it "spoke back to that threat in song," that is, "in the blues lyric tradition." "Anxieties about encirclement, torture and dismemberment" remained as "an oppressive phantasmic presence" that chased the subject, Gussow argues. Most were "unconscious transformations rather than intentional codings of lynching tropes and scenarios." They "express[ed] the 'pressured, nightmare-strewn subjectivities'" that whites intended to produce. But Gussow absolutely denies that such a creativity was capitulation to terror; he sees it as a "creative response to it which offered a 'liberating catharsis'" by distancing and artistic creation. Lynching was not a theme, but the "ontological ground out of which blues expressiveness arose: an overhanging threat of nonbeing, at once personal and highly phantasmic."

For Further Reading

Allen, James, Hilton Als, John Lewis, and Leon F. Litwack. *Without Sanctuary: Lynching Photography in America*. Santa Fe: Twin Palms Publishers, 2000.

Ayers, Edward L. *The Promise of the New South*. New York: Oxford University Press, 1992.

Berger, Peter L. *The Sacred Canopy: Elements of a Sociological Theory of Religion*. New York: Doubleday, 1969.

Brundage, William Fitzhugh. "The Roar on the Other Side of Silence: Black Resistance and White Violence in the American South, 1880–1940." In *Under Sentence of Death: Lynching in the South*, edited by William Fitzhugh Brundage, 271–91. Chapel Hill: University of North Carolina Press, 1997.

———. *Lynching in the New South: Georgia and Virginia, 1880–1930*. Urbana: University of Illinois Press, 1993.

———. "The Darien 'Insurrection' of 1899: Black Protest during the Nadir of Race Relations." *Georgia Historical Quarterly* 74 (Summer 1990): 234–53.

Bynum, Victoria E. *Unruly Women: The Politics of Social and Sexual Control in the Old South*. Chapel Hill: University of North Carolina Press, 1992.

Cash, Wilbur J. *The Mind of the South*. New York: Random House, 1941; Vintage Books, 1969.

Cell, John W. *The Highest Stage of White Supremacy: The Origins of Segregation in South Africa and the American South*. New York: Cambridge University Press, 1982.

Cohen, William. *At Freedom's Edge: Black Mobility and the Southern White Quest for Racial Control, 1861–1915*. Baton Rouge: Louisiana State University Press, 1991.

Douglas, Mary. *Purity and Danger: An Analysis of Concepts of Pollution and Taboo*. London: Routledge & Kegan Paul, 1966; Pelican Books, 1970.

Du Bois, W. E. B. *The Souls of Black Folk.* 1903. Reprint, New York: New American Library, 1969.

Geertz, Clifford. *Interpretation of Cultures: Selected Essays.* New York: Basic Books, 1973.

Gilligan, James. *Violence: Our Deadly Epidemic and Its Causes.* New York: G. P. Putnam, 1996.

Girard, René. *The Girard Reader.* Edited by James G. Williams. New York: Crossroad, 1996.

Godshalk, David F. "William J. Northen's Public and Personal Struggles against Lynching." In *Jumpin' Jim Crow: Southern Politics from Civil War to Civil Rights*, edited by Jane Dailey and Glenda Gilmore, 140–61. Princeton: Princeton University Press, 2000.

Grant, Donald L. *The Way It Was in the South: The Black Experience in Georgia.* Athens: University of Georgia Press, 1993.

Gussow, Adam. *Seems Like Murder Here: Southern Violence and the Blues Tradition.* Chicago: University of Chicago Press, 2002.

Hamerton-Kelly, Robert G. *Sacred Violence: Paul's Hermeneutic of the Cross.* Minneapolis: Fortress Press, 1992.

Hodes, Martha E. *White Women, Black Men: Illicit Sex in the Nineteenth-Century South.* New Haven: Yale University Press, 1997.

Luckmann, Thomas. *The Invisible Religion: The Problem of Religion in Modern Society.* New York: Macmillan, 1967.

Luker, Ralph. *The Social Gospel in Black and White: American Racial Reform, 1885–1912.* Chapel Hill: University of North Carolina Press, 1991.

Mathews, Donald G. "The Southern Rite of Human Sacrifice." *Journal of Southern Religion* 3 (August 2000), ⟨http://jsr.as.wvu.edu/mathews.htm⟩.

Millin, Eric Tabor. "Defending the Sacred Hearth: Religion, Politics, and Racial Violence in Georgia, 1904–1906." Master's thesis, University of Georgia, 2002.

Mizruchi, Susan L. *The Science of Sacrifice: American Literature and Modern Social Theory.* Princeton: Princeton University Press, 1998.

Osborn, Eric Francis. *Ireneus of Lyons.* New York: Cambridge University Press, 2001

Ownby, Ted. *Subduing Satan: Religion, Recreation, and Manhood in the Rural South, 1865–1920.* Chapel Hill: University of North Carolina Press, 1990.

Patterson, Orlando. *Rituals of Blood: Consequences of Slavery in Two American Centuries.* Washington, D.C.: Civitas Counterpoint, 1998.

Rable, George C. *But There Was No Peace: The Role of Violence in the Politics of Reconstruction.* Athens: University of Georgia Press, 1984.

Ransom, John Crowe. *God without Thunder: An Unorthodox Defense of Orthodoxy.* New York: Harcourt, Brace, 1930.

Raper, Arthur. *The Tragedy of Lynching.* Chapel Hill: University of North Carolina Press, 1933.

Royster, Jacqueline Jones, ed. *Southern Horrors and Other Writings: The Anti-lynching Campaign of Ida B. Wells, 1892–1900*. Boston: Bedford Books, 1997.

Shapiro, Herbert. *White Violence and Black Response from Reconstruction to Montgomery*. Amherst: University of Massachusetts Press, 1988.

Slotkin, Richard. *Regeneration through Violence: The Mythology of the American Frontier, 1600–1860*. Middletown, Conn.: Wesleyan University Press, 1973.

Smead, Howard. *Blood Justice: The Lynching of Mack Charles Parker*. New York: Oxford University Press, 1986.

Smith, Brian K. "Capital Punishment and Human Sacrifice." *Journal of the American Academy of Religion* 68 (March 2000): 3–25.

Smith, Lillian. *Killers of the Dream*. 1949. Reprint, New York: W. W. Norton, 1961.

Stearns, Carol Zisowitz, and Peter N. Stearns. *Anger: The Struggle for Emotional Control in America's History*. Chicago: University of Chicago Press, 1986.

Tolnay, Stewart E., and E. M. Beck. *Festival of Violence: An Analysis of Southern Lynchings, 1882–1930*. Urbana: University of Illinois Press, 1995.

Trelease, Allen. *White Terror: The Ku Klux Klan Conspiracy and Southern Reconstruction*. New York: Harper & Row, 1971.

Waldrep, Christopher. "Word and Deed: The Language of Lynching, 1820–1953." In *Lethal Imagination: Violence and Brutality in American History*, edited by Michael A. Bellesiles. New York: New York University Press, 1999.

White, Walter. *Rope and Faggot: A Biography of Judge Lynch*. 1929. Reprint, New York: Arno/The New York Times, 1969.

Williams, James G. *The Bible, Violence, and the Sacred: Liberation from the Myth of Sanctioned Violence*. San Francisco: HarperSanFrancisco, 1991.

Williamson, Joel. *Crucible of Race: Black-White Relations in the American South since Emancipation*. New York: Oxford University Press, 1984.

Woodward, C. Vann. *The Strange Career of Jim Crow*. New York: Oxford University Press, 1974.

Wyatt-Brown, Bertram. *Southern Honor: Ethics and Behavior in the Old South*. New York: Oxford University Press, 1982.

ANTHEA D. BUTLER

7

Church Mothers and Migration in the Church of God in Christ

Mother Mary Mangum Johnson's journey north to Detroit from Memphis in 1914 was a reluctant one. Soon after she married her second husband, Brother W. G. "Ting-a-ling" Johnson, Brother Johnson was impelled to write a hand-written message in an unknown language after a Church of God in Christ prayer meeting. Ting-a-ling (nicknamed for the sweetness of his singing voice) took the message to church leader and spiritual avatar Charles H. Mason. Mason interpreted the writing as a call from God for the Johnsons to move to the state of Michigan to preach. Mary wanted no part of it and brushed the prophetic message off. That worked for a few days, until she felt compelled by the Holy Ghost during her household chores to write down a similar message in an unknown handwriting. The message was interpreted again, this time by her husband, as the call for them to move to Michigan. Mother Johnson remained unconvinced until the following Sunday, when she prayed at service for peace about the calling. Feeling freed, she agreed to move to Michigan, leaving a much prized mule in the front yard for the prospective buyer to retrieve.[1]

The story of the Johnsons' migration from Memphis to Michigan combines the pragmatic with the supernatural. This unlikely combination characterized the everyday lives of African Americans who embraced Pentecostal or Holiness faith during the Great Migration. Pentecostalism and its antecedent, Holiness, were forms of religious belief that focused on the power of the Holy Spirit to enable individuals to live a "sanctified" life dedicated to Christian service. For Pentecostals and the members of some Holiness groups, various religious practices such as dreams, visions, tongues speaking, and tongues writing (also known as the "unknown handwriting") played an important role in both belief systems and the construction of religious identity. For African American women within Pentecostal churches like the Church of God in Christ (COGIC) during the migratory period from 1914 to 1940, this spiritual framework coupled with southern cultural practices to ground their displaced lives. By linking their identities as black southern women to their identities as "Saints" within the Pentecostal tradition, the southern customs and piety they carried into northern cities served both as a marker and as a boundary. Migration affirmed their unique religious identities as bearers of the southern-based religious traditions of ecstatic worship, hospitality, and evangelical fervor, which continue within the church to this day. Combining Pentecostal spirituality, southern domesticity, and practical sensibilities, the older women of COGIC, often referred to as "church mothers," established a firm foundation for COGIC migrants and converts across the United States.

The Church of God in Christ is one of the religious institutions that benefited immensely from the Great Migration, experiencing rapid growth in membership from 1914 until after World War II. Founded in 1896 by expelled Baptist ministers Charles Harrison Mason and Charles Price Jones, COGIC began as a Holiness group, with its first church in a cotton gin house in Lexington, Mississippi. The church later split over the doctrine of baptism in the Spirit in 1907.[2] Its pairing of Holiness teachings, commonly referred to as the "the sanctified life," with the Pentecostal practice of speaking in tongues created a rigorous, experiential faith that attracted members throughout the southern states.[3] COGIC drew many African Americans and white people who felt disenfranchised by their lack of wealth and status, although congregations included people of all social classes.[4] Women, and African American women in particular, found in Pentecostalism a welcoming, protective community that allowed them to participate in the charismatic practices of the faith while sheltering them from a southern society that did not honor them as women. Within COGIC, a network of Bible bands—church-based Bible study groups—provided women with leaders who were already well versed in both the study of Scripture and evangelistic activities.[5] Mason, noting the numbers of women within COGIC, established a separate Women's Department in 1911. Women who were already accustomed to traveling around the South selling Bibles and working as missionaries looked upon migration as an opportunity to be free to evangelize and to be freed from the burdens of southern life. Migration provided freedom for COGIC women who wanted a fresh start.

Previous studies of African American women and migration have focused on work, family, vice, and relationships.[6] The religious beliefs and practices that migrant women nurtured during their journeys away from the South remain shrouded in obscurity. Their religious ties, however, offer an important means of understanding women's lives in the urban areas of the northern and western United States. This essay emphasizes how migrant women sustained their southern customs and piety and argues that southern religiosity, hospitality, and gender reshaped the urban topography. The storefront churches full of plainly dressed church mothers that stood squarely in the midst of neighborhood jook joints and gambling dens created church communities that were grounded in a distinctive southern religious identity.[7] As Milton Sernett observed in *Bound for the Promised Land*, women transferred southern religious practices to the urban north.[8] The migration of COGIC church mothers like Mother Johnson transmitted southern religious sensibilities and practices to the city.

THE CHURCH MOTHER or "mother in Israel" is a ubiquitous figure in southern black churches who is usually the most spiritually mature member of the congregation.[9] "Mother," as C. Eric Lincoln and Lawrence Mamiya have observed, was "an honorific title usually reserved for the wife of the founder or for the most experienced female members of the church." The phenomenon of the church mother, they claim, has no parallel in white churches: it is derived from the kinship networks found in black churches and black communities.[10] The office operates informally, and sometimes formally, in church hierarchy. Although a critical leader in African American churches, the church mother has been ignored by religious historians. Perhaps the most notable discussion of church mothers is found in the work of the sociologist Cheryl Townsend Gilkes. In a series of articles, she examined what she termed the "dual sex roles" of pastors and church mothers. Gilkes wrote:

> The most distinctive aspect of dual-sex church politics is the role of the Church Mother. While most black churches in the Baptist, Methodist and "Sanctified" (Pentecostal, Holiness, Apostolic) denominations have a woman to whom all members refer as the "church mother," her position varies. In almost all cases, she is an older woman, often elderly, who is considered an example of spiritual maturity and morality to the rest of her congregation. Her career as a Christian is usually exemplary and long, and most members know of her various activities in the missionary unit or on the deaconess board. Perhaps she is the widow of a pastor or bishop or a deacon, but not necessarily. She is one of the few people whose seat in the congregation is formally

or informally reserved. When she dies, her seat may be draped in black. Most important, she is publicly addressed by the pastor, the bishops, and members of the congregation as mother.[11]

A church mother is everything from a busybody to an administrator. She is aware of the newcomers and the old-timers, and she has veto power over the pastor if she thinks he has violated Scripture. She is sought after for both spiritual and temporal advice. She is, in a sense, the queen mother, the source of power in each individual church.[12] Within COGIC, the office of the church mother was institutionalized by the formation of the Women's Department in 1911. The first national church mother of COGIC, Elizabeth (or Lizzie) Robinson, neé Woods, was appointed general overseer of the women at the national convocation of the church that year.[13] Robinson, a migrant herself, moved to Nebraska around 1914 with her third husband.[14]

By taking the traditional role of the church mother and combining it with an evangelical thrust, church mothers like Robinson maintained both southern community and religious continuity, and they recruited women members by emphasizing sanctified church practices. Unlike their counterparts in black Baptist and African Methodist Episcopal (AME) churches, who espoused racial uplift and shunned ecstatic worship practices, COGIC church mothers emphasized southern church customs and slave antecedents. Shouting, protracted services, and tongues speaking combined with evangelical fervor, hospitality, and piety to help church mothers unify their secular and sacred lives in the North. Their multiple identities as church planters, teachers, and fictive mothers helped COGIC retain its southern identity by spreading black southern religious culture nationwide. They were an important cultural conduit for practices and beliefs rooted in southern identity and African-based religious culture. Although they were often criticized by northern black people as backward, their southernisms provided the means for their survival, connecting them to communities, practices, and families far away. These women were good, but not altogether gone from the South. Anecdotes from the lives of migrating mothers and records related to their role at the yearly southern "pilgrimage" to the denominational convocation in Memphis demonstrate how church mothers were both guardians and teachers of southern religious practices. But what exactly was "southern" about these church mothers?

The southern accent, politeness, hospitality, attachment to land and family, folk culture, and superstition have all been called marks of a true southerner.[15]

Southern culture, fodder for many a joke or tall tale, was ridiculed but also irrepressible. When paired with a biblical worldview that centered on sanctified or holy living, southern traditions—Sunday dinners, storytelling, and dressing up for church—became sacred. Coupled with evangelical fervor, such practices became sacred and immovable. Womanhood, and even more importantly motherhood, was essential to the religious transmission of the southern culture. Women were the priestesses of the southern cultural practices that sustained belief and worship. COGIC church mothers made these sacralized southern practices elemental to what it meant to be a sanctified woman, and their transmission became part of the mission and religious work of COGIC women.

Not all southern customs were taken north. Lynching and Jim Crow laws made the South untenable for many African American men and women. The Klan, racial discord, and the boll weevil made the migration northward a necessity for others. The mother held families together in these perilous times. As white southerners dehumanized the African Americans they tried to subdue with violence and Jim Crow, southern black women endured suffering in an effort to maintain the quality of their lives. COGIC women, therefore, were more than qualified to uphold southern traditions related to family, food, piety, and purpose when they relocated from the South. They combined a southern identity with their religious identity to become Saints.

"Saint" was the term used by sanctified church members when they greeted each other; they also used it to identify exemplary members of the church who embodied the sanctified life. The term "Saint" was an important marker used by migrants from the South to separate the members of COGIC and other sanctified churches from other churches' members or city dwellers.[16] Saints embraced renunciatory practices, including dress codes, fasting, and protracted prayer, that gave them distinctive identities within their communities and also marked them as southerners. Church mothers made members of the church community into a family of saints who retained their distinctively southern religious practices. Mother Mary Johnson's call to Michigan, therefore, provides a lens through which to interrogate the efficacy of church mothers in keeping the southern practices of the Saints alive.

MOTHER MARY JOHNSON exemplifies the saintly church mother. Johnson, a former state mother of Michigan, wrote her memoirs some time after completing her evangelistic work in Detroit and throughout the state of Michigan. It is not clear what compelled her to tell her story, but the text is a fascinating piece that illuminates the life of a transplanted southern Pentecostal woman. A member of COGIC since 1901, Mother Johnson lost her first husband to tuberculosis. Her father died when a bullet pierced the Holiness tent where he was preaching. After one of the Saints visited her store in Memphis, her second husband, Ting-a-ling Johnson, began to write in an "unknown handwriting." Tongues writing, a little known and uncommon practice among early Pentecostals, involved the belief that one could write in another language under the direction of the Holy Spirit. That Ting-a-ling took the writing to Mason suggests that he believed it was just another manifestation of baptism in the Holy Spirit. By interpreting the unintelligible message as a "call to Michigan," Bishop Mason helped to spread the church beyond the South. Mason sent both men and women across the nation to establish COGIC churches. He usually sent out either church elders who had traveled as part of an evangelistic band or women who had come under the auspices of the Women's Department. In sending the Johnsons to Michigan, Mason combined the pragmatic with the spiritual. Tongues writing, dreams, and visions thus both appropriated southern folklore and extended the boundaries of the church.

Mother Johnson's call to Michigan placed her in a network of women in COGIC who had been organizing throughout the South since 1912.[17] Mother Robinson, the head of the Women's Department, was a former Baptist who had worked in the Bible band movement under American Baptist missionary Joanna P. Moore. Upon her appointment as the overseer of the Women's Department, Robinson set out to "systematize and organize" the women of COGIC. During the first two years of her appointment, she traveled through Tennessee, Arkansas, Louisiana, and Texas and appointed local church mothers to the positions of state mother or overseer.[18] State mothers organized local church mothers and the prayer and Bible bands. Prayer and Bible bands taught the doctrines of the church and conducted daily Bible studies and prayer groups. Some of the prayer bands met in "shut-ins" for twenty-four-hour periods devoted to prayer. These meetings created spaces in which women could practice shouting, tongues speaking, and healing outside of the regular church services. They kept alive the women's identity as Pentecostals and also ensured that COGIC members were versed in church beliefs.

Mother Robinson also sent out women as missionaries to plant new COGIC churches. By 1916, Robinson had appointed women to leadership positions in the states of Georgia, Arkansas, Louisiana, Mississippi, Tennessee, Illinois, Missouri, Texas, and Oklahoma.[19] Robinson's organizational skills and her ability to choose women who were leaders belies the traditional view of Pentecostals as otherworldly and uninterested in organizations. On the contrary, Mother Robinson's organizing was part of an intentional evangelical thrust that would become the basis on which COGIC members planted churches around the United States. Mason, a traveling evangelist himself, was adept in choosing people who were loyal and industrious and who could take on their duties without much supervision.

Mother Robinson took to her duties so well that the rapid influx of women into the ranks of COGIC caused tension between female and male members of the church. Annual meetings in the first few years of her appointment were consumed by detailed discussions of the differences between women's and men's work and of the role of women in "teaching" or "speaking" rather than "preaching." Women were not officially banned from ordination in COGIC, but they were not allowed to preach. Their role was to teach and to evangelize.[20] Industrious women, however, knew that they could be in the service of the Lord if they left home to plant a church in an urban area. Mother Johnson was just such a woman, eager to serve both the Lord and her household.

What Mother Johnson and her husband did on their arrival in Detroit was called "digging out a church." Digging out, sometimes referred to as "plowing the field" or "working the ground," involved preaching and holding healing services on street corners, in houses of ill repute, in tents, or anywhere else in cities where converts might be gained. The agricultural metaphors are biblically appropriate and evoke the agrarian culture of the South. While digging out a church, male and female COGIC members could conduct open-air or indoor services until their converts created a critical mass, at which point they required a pastor. Pastors were generally not recruited from the local area; instead, a letter would be "sent down south" to Memphis for a pastor, ensuring the continuity of southern leadership. Women often requested men that they knew, but Bishop Mason appointed pastors as well. Johnson's husband was actually ordained by Elder Whittie, one of the white Holiness ministers in the city, at the request of Bishop Mason.[21]

Mother Mary Johnson's first official digging out enterprise was held on Elliot Street in front of a house called a "Bear Trap . . . because of the class of people who lived within." In Detroit, bear traps were boardinghouses that charged tenants low rent; they were havens for illicit activities such as prostitution and gambling.[22] Rather than avoid these areas, COGIC members saw bear traps and boardinghouses as places rife with potential converts and evangelistic opportunities. Johnson remarked that her husband "preached" and she "spoke" from the sixth chapter of Romans. The distinction between preaching, teaching, and speaking would prove to be problematic in urban areas. After beginning evangelistic meetings, women were expected to turn over control to ordained men as soon as a congregation's numbers increased. In Mother Johnson's case, this was perhaps less difficult than it was for other women, as she turned the congregation over to her husband. She remarked in her memoirs: "I was my husband's helper, stayed in my place, and let God do the work." By following biblical admonitions and upholding traditional gender roles, COGIC church mothers presented an example to their neighbors. Describing an occasion on the first night after she and her husband arrived in Detroit when they prayed in the middle of the street, Mother Johnson recalled: "Many people ignored us; considered us as southerners, who did not have good sense. But God's wisdom confounded the wisdom of both the great and the wise of this world."[23]

Mother Johnson's perseverance gained them enough converts to dig out a small storefront church. She and her husband rented a storefront, making it both their church and their home. She used percale fabric from Memphis to cover the pulpit, and she had her husband "gather chicken giblets, heads, and feet" on Saturday nights from the butchers so that she could prepare dumplings for Sunday dinners to serve to the visitors to the Sunday service. As in the South, Sunday was a day of worship and fellowship—a day to spend together. By cooking on Saturday nights, Mother Johnson ensured that the service and worship would be uninterrupted on Sundays.[24] Although Johnson used her skills as a homemaker to bring people into the church, she also lamented the loss of her southern comforts:

> Since this rented storefront had to be both our house and church, Elder Johnson erected a partition within the building by means of a post, and some of the cotton material we had bought from Memphis. We had in our little "home-made" room, a roll-away bed, a monkeys-stove, which we used for both heat and cooking purposes. . . . Although I had given up and left a comfortable and well furnished home in Memphis to do God's will in Detroit, there were no rugs on the cold floor of our room, until I made a rug of burlap cloth which was generally used as a wrapping for bulk of cloth material. This piece of burlap was sold to me by a man for the price of seventy-five cents.[25]

Keeping to such southern housekeeping practices helped the Johnsons to win over both those who were transplants and those who were lifelong urbanites. The dinners they gave in their home for the members of the prayer and Bible bands were welcoming to transplants as well. Mother Johnson partitioned her home into sacred space and living space. The homey touches she added to the storefront space strengthened the bonds between the members of the domestic family of God. The connections Mother Johnson made between the work of the Lord and the creation of a neat home paralleled the strong connections between domesticity and spirituality for southern women. It was not enough simply to have a space in which to live and worship; she wanted a space that would be pleasing both to the eye and to God. The "politics of domesticity" for migrant women was partially a response to the limited opportunities for African American women to work, but it also lifted these women's status, as urban northerners customarily believed that slovenly living was common in the agrarian South. The witness of a clean storefront church and home, therefore, was of importance in testifying to what the life of a Saint should be.[26] Anthropologists and sociologists would later remark that the storefront churches were able to attract converts because of the family feeling that they engendered. The combination of domestic and public piety, Sunday dinners, and the frequent references to church members as sisters and brothers all combined to blend religious and secular practices into a seamless whole. The down-home feeling and good food helped to start the Johnsons' small COGIC church in Detroit off on a good footing. Mother Johnson and her husband continued to plant churches in Detroit and the surrounding cities, culminating in her appointment as Detroit state mother in 1920.

Mother Johnson and her husband forged connections with white Holiness groups in Detroit. Many of the early visitors to the Johnsons' Sunday services were white people, perhaps members of other Holiness churches. Mother Johnson recounts in her memoirs that in the first marriage ceremony her husband performed after his ordination there was a "colored man and a white woman, both members of our church." The Johnsons overcame traditional southern mores and opened their home and church to whites. Their willingness to embrace an interracial couple and the white people who comprised one-third of their congregation suggests that they made a conscious effort not to replicate southern racial customs in their church. The proximity of whites and blacks was perhaps crucial to their decision to be open to whites in Detroit, as they lived without the legalized segregation that prevailed in the South.

Despite the success of the Johnsons' church, some Detroiters found the couple strange and believed that their strangeness stemmed from their southern heritage. Many Detroiters regarded praying in the street or eating the leftover parts of chickens as backward. The shouting, shudders, and jerks of the body that could be witnessed during the long services held by COGIC and other Pentecostal denominations provided ample reason for criticism. Coupled with that, fears of race mixing drove the critique of storefront churches in Detroit.[27] Historian Victoria W. Wolcott has noted that "all of the African American church leaders and members of the Detroit Urban League lumped all storefront churches together as a cohesive and reprehensible group."[28] That southerners were unwilling or unable to embrace the urban worship styles of northern churches marked them for the ridicule and disdain of those who considered themselves to be the arbiters of respectability. Anthropologists and sociologists later echoed such views.

IN OTHER AREAS of the country, southern women fared better with the locals. The women who founded Saint's Home Church in Los Angeles, California, were an intrepid group of street missionaries who gathered up converts. Mother Millie Crawford and Mother Martha Armstrong started a mission in a tent at Fourteenth and Woodson in Los Angeles. The southern-style revival services started at 9 A.M. and continued all day, stopping for lunch and resuming in the afternoon. Men were also involved, but the women "[stood] out as beacon lights" in the leadership of the group.[29] Just as they were in the Johnson's Detroit mission church, the services were racially mixed, and this caused consternation for Elder Eddie Driver, the first pastor called to the Los Angeles church. Driver was sent to pastor in Los Angeles after receiving a vision in which the "Lord told him to go to California." Upon his arrival, Driver was surprised to find a mixed-race congregation. A man with a "strong personality," Driver soon clashed with the women who had dug Saint's Home out through their tent ministry. According to COGIC bylaws, women were not allowed to lead the churches they had founded. This ruling spurred some women to start their own churches.[30]

Mother Emma Cotton, who migrated to California from Louisiana, was one of the first state mothers in California. She began evangelistic work with her husband in Los Angeles, and they subsequently moved to the Oakland area. Cotton, described by Aimee Semple McPherson as "a little woman with a mighty halleluiah—neatly dressed, unprepossessing and a firebrand," copastored with her husband in the Oakland area, a fact that did not go unnoticed by one COGIC visitor from Memphis.[31] Elder McKinley McCardell, arriving from Texas as a young migrant, boarded at Mother Cotton's home in Oakland for a time. He remarked: "As I approached the door, there was a sign, Elder H. C. Cotton, Pastor and Mrs. Emma Cotton, Assistant Pastor; that startled me—looking and thinking; because I had just left a state where women did not pastor churches."[32]

COGIC women like Mother Cotton, who eventually broke ranks with the denomination, posed a unique challenge to its expansion. Debates raged in this early period as women leaders challenged traditional gender roles. The leaders in the Women's Department often attempted to reinforce tradition. Mother Robinson, in her role as overseer of women, moved to dissuade the women from taking on the role of preacher: "The women were turned over to me and I asked, how many preachers are there? Thirty-two stood up. I asked, who told you to preach? I took them right down to the bible. One said that God had spoken to her out of the air, I said, well, the devil is the prince of the air and no one told you to preach but the devil. You are no preacher."[33]

Holiness churches like COGIC provided a network of stable environments that called members to shun the vices of the city. The idea of living a sanctified life as a Saint held great appeal for young women who were displaced and without spouses. This cohort provided a ready source of converts to COGIC.[34] It was no accident that COGIC church mothers targeted the slum areas of the major migration cities like Detroit, Philadelphia, and Chicago. New arrivals from the South found limited options in these cities. The influx of women who filled the pews of the storefronts coupled with the nervousness of COGIC's male leaders may have threatened the delicate working balance between the Women's Department and the male pastorate. Various admonitions at the yearly meetings, such as the exhortation to women's overseers to be "obedient and hear the male overseers," suggest that the growing numbers of women in the church sparked disagreements between men and women in leadership.[35]

THE CONSERVATIVE values of COGIC were deeply challenged during the 1920s. American women embraced a new dress code that included fancy clothing, shorter skirts, feathers, and baubles designed to enhance attractiveness and catch the eye. The fancy clothing of African American women and men in the cities during the 1920s threatened COGIC churchgoers' carefully constructed repudiation of the world and its ills. Mother Robinson considered the new garments to be signs of a sinful lifestyle. Guidelines helped women learn that proper dress would demonstrate holiness. Robinson devised a code for women evangelists and missionaries that was eventually applied to all women church members. The first dress code appeared in the rules for women's work in the early 1920s: "Rule #4. All members and missionaries must not wear hats with flowers or feathers nor Short Dresses, Split Skirts or Short Sleeves. . . . Rule #5. All members and missionaries must dress in modest apparel as becometh holiness, professing Godliness with good work."[36] There were pragmatic reasons for developing a dress code. Evelyn Brooks Higginbotham, in her landmark work on the Baptist women's conventions, has suggested that black women developed a politics of respectability in their dress so that when they were traveling or working men would be deterred from accosting them. Plain dress indicated they were churchwomen and allowed African American women to avoid constant harassment from both black and white men who considered them to be easy sexual prey.[37]

COGIC women used their dress code not only to embrace the politics of respectability, but also to engage in the visual politics of disseminating belief and distinction. Dresses that were the antithesis of 1920s mainstream fashions were in vogue for the sanctified woman. Following a basic formula that stated what a Saint should look like, a sanctified dress was plain; keeping with the biblical admonitions of 1 Timothy 2:9–10 and 1 Peter 3:3, which encouraged "dressing as becometh holiness," it had no adornment.[38] This manner of dress eschewed ornate garments, feathers, and the like for a plain template of colors such as blues, blacks, whites, and browns. Mother Robinson's usual attire was a starched, ankle-length black skirt and a white blouse that covered her arms down to the wrists.[39] This type of attire was worn by most of the southern rural women's membership of COGIC in the early days. Though dressing up for church was important, it was equally important that one's dress did not overshadow the worship. Makeup was prohibited, and the use of Madame C. J. Walker's new processes for straightening hair was forbidden.[40]

Southern women migrating to the urban areas of Detroit, Chicago, and Philadelphia were tempted to appear citified, and their desires violated the standards of clothing befitting holiness. If COGIC women looked like other fashionable urban women, they would lose their distinctiveness, and their respectability would be called into question. Mother Robinson believed they would be mistaken for urban blacks who frequented social clubs and lodges, both expressly prohibited by COGIC. Her calls to holiness, therefore, were more pronounced to members of the storefront COGIC churches in the cities:

> In Isaiah 20, God told Isaiah to walk naked before the people for three years for a sign and wonder upon Egypt and Ethiopia. He said the Assyrians would come up and take the Ethiopians barefoot and naked, captive with their buttocks showing. Well, this is the time to teach about the buttocks. When the women stoop down you can see their buttocks. We are living in that day right now. So, the women must put their dresses down. The people must be taught. They are getting away from God. Do you not see the women losing their modesty? Don't you see it as a lust breeder? The word says, if a man looks on a woman to lust after her he has already committed adultery in his heart. So, a man just looks at a woman, and would like to be with her, he sees her legs and sees how she looks; he has committed adultery without touching her. The women should keep their dresses down. My nephew is a wicked young man but he said to me, Aunt Lizzie, the mothers ought to get the ankles to give a party and invite the dresses down to it because you can't tell the church-women from the street women now.[41]

The directness of this quotation from Mother Robinson demonstrates that the denomination's sexual prohibitions were based not only in southern ideals of womanhood, but also in the nexus of the images of African American women in the South. If one was not a Mammy, then one was a Jezebel, a loose, lascivious woman. It became paramount for churchwomen's dress to visually affirm for outsiders the link between purity and holiness. If churchwomen were not dressed "holy," sexual sins were certain to become prevalent in the church. The progression of sight, covetousness, and desire in Mother Robinson's exposition could only lead to sin. By reining in the women's dress, both men and women would once again become subject to restraints upon their sexual behavior. Even the armpits were seen as areas that might arouse sexual excitement, and long sleeves were thus required even in summertime.[42] Perhaps onerous by today's standards, the dress codes were viewed as a necessary protection against the purported ills of the day. Poems like the one below were recited in church to reinforce the importance of these regulations.

> When I come to church look what I see, real short dresses, slit skirts and
> rusty knees.

Change the style,

Sometimes that skirt's split front, side and back,

Somebody pass that sister a pin or a tack

When they walk that slit gaps open wide, anyone can see everything inside.

Sometimes that slit is cut up so high, it goes past the knee and you can see
the thigh.

Then some dresses are cut so low at the top, all the contents nearly fall out
plop.[43]

Hymns also reinforced the dress code. In a hymnbook used from the 1930s to
the 1950s, a hymn entitled "The Florida Storm" (subtitled "Nahum 1 and 2")
incorporated a verse in which dress was a focus:

Short Skirts and Filthy Dances

Have caused my heart to bleed

And now our country is filled up

With every wicked deed,

But Ah, that's all right,

God's going to visit you one night

And will pour out his judgment upon man.[44]

If dress codes could be instituted as a sexual deterrent, church leaders also
showed concern for members' sexual behavior in other ways. Those who were
unmarried, male or female, were expected to be celibate. As a result, the "purity class" was created in 1926. This class, as described in its handbook, was
"created to preserve in Christian youth a high moral standard of living, because
. . . the moral decay of the 1920's was destroying the basic principles of Christian living the church had been upholding." Discussions of dress, sexual behavior, and marriage were repeated in the curriculum early and often, and by
the time children were of marriageable age they were encouraged to marry
only within the COGIC denomination.

By the mid-twenties, the number of women converts and leaders in COGIC
had grown. The 1918 minutes stated that COGIC women had been appointed as
women overseers of states attracting a significant migrant population: California, New York, Illinois, Arizona, New Mexico, and Colorado. Leaders of the rapidly growing denomination were convinced that the way to maintain their southern heritage was to hold an annual denominational convocation in Memphis.

THE CONVOCATION WAS the yearly meeting of the denomination, held in Memphis at 392 South Wellington Street, COGIC's home base.[45] In the tradition of Holiness camp meetings, this yearly meeting of prayer and revival that occurred from November 25 to December 14 was virtually mandatory for COGIC members. The concept of the convocation was taken from the Old Testament; Leviticus 23:2–4 called for "holy convocations which ye shall proclaim in their seasons." These meetings provided a time of separation and consecration to church members, a time to pray, to hear preaching, and, most importantly, to settle church business that had come to various state overseers during the year. The period of the convocation was considered to be sacred time; it reinforced the teachings of the church as well as a southern sense of time. Coming just after the fall harvest, it connected urban members with a slower southern rhythm that followed the crops and seasons. For those who returned yearly, it was a way to get back in step with what mattered most. The most important function of the convocation, however, was to draw members back into the nexus of ecstatic worship, reminding them of the richness of piety and fervor. Long services, close quarters, and fellowship acted together to connect displaced COGIC women and men, giving them a place where they were once again in the majority.

Gathering the members of COGIC was a difficult task. The southern members who were not sharecroppers could leave to travel to Memphis after the harvest. Others from urban areas had to either forego employment or make special arrangements. The trip to Memphis presented its own set of problems, including Jim Crow laws that restricted the mobility of African Americans, the threat of lynching, and the unpredictability of segregated train travel. The length of the convocation was also a problem for some of the faithful. Women who attended did not qualify for the clergy discounts offered to the men who were pastors or elders in the church, and this increased the financial burden on them. It was important for the women to be present, as many of the duties of the convocation were entrusted to them, and they had to ensure that it ran smoothly. Jim Crow also presented a problem in worship for COGIC members, as white Church of God in Christ members could not sit in the same sections of the church with their fellow black Saints. White Saints were seated in a special roped-off section during the convocation, but invariably the altars would fill with blacks and whites in the midst of ecstatic worship.[46] Jim Crow also affected the lodging of church members. Due to the lack of available rooms in the black sections of Jim Crow Memphis, COGIC adopted a system of sharing rooms in the homes of local church members. With visiting brethren sleeping in eight-hour shifts, the convocation would run services almost twenty-four hours a day to accommodate their schedules. Women attending the convocation were admonished to "send along bedding, as the meeting [was] still growing larger each year, and the demand for more cover [was] necessary."[47]

Convocation attendees also had to be fed. In the 1910s and 1920s, attendees ate at members' homes, and cooking was, of course, done by the women. Leila Byas, daughter of founder Charles H. Mason, remarked in an interview that the "members depended on the praying Church mothers to take care of the needs of the sick, poor and indigent."[48] Those church mothers who had money and other resources took care of those who came to the convocation in need of food and a place to sleep. Homemade soup and cornbread were served to all of the Saints, and the cooking was done in various homes. Byas later went on to supervise the free food program and to become the convocation's dietitian, creating the menus for the convocation meetings. Over the years, increasing attendance necessitated bigger facilities. In 1925, the "Tabernacle" was built to provide the Saints with a place to both worship and eat together.[49] Though it entailed intricate planning, COGIC members looked forward to the convocation, where they could immerse themselves in a protracted three weeks of Sundays filled with fervor, prayer, fellowship, and rest.

The convocation's major purpose, however, was to provide spiritual renewal. Pentecostal practices of fasting, protracted prayer, lengthy services, and testimony were integral to the marking of sacred and secular time. Scripture was used to both justify and set the tone for the convocation, as in the following passage: "Blow the Trumpet in Zion, sanctify a fast, call a solemn assembly. To sanctify means to set apart for god—a fast to consecrate ourselves for the work He has given us to do, to humble ourselves before God, and to repent of all sin and disobedience in our lives. Joel 2:15, Exodus 34:38, Leviticus 23:27, Deuteronomy 9:9, Samuel 7:6."[50]

Mason claimed that he wanted a church meeting that was focused on "sacred and sanctified gatherings for the Saints" where they could "have communion with one another."[51] Members rushed to Memphis to participate in the first three days and nights of the convocation, which were devoted to prayer and fasting. By requiring them to refrain from food and water for the first three days, the stringent fasting ritual acted as a cleansing process that allowed members to focus clearly on garnering spiritual strength and subduing their carnal desires. The practice of fasting, prayer, and repentance was believed to allow the

Spirit to enter the services. Members believed, in the words of Bishop Mason, "that the presence of the Lord was great to bless and heal."

Members and nonmembers packed the convocation services to see the demonstration of miracles and healings occur. Within a charged environment of continual prayer, singing, shouting, and fervor, there was no reason not to anticipate power encounters of various kinds. Mason's ministry of healing by prayer and the laying on of hands was critical to the convocation services, so much so that nonmembers attended the convocation hoping for a touch from him. Holy Ghost power was not limited to the denominational leadership, however, but was available to all who fasted and prayed. Members shouting, dancing, and testifying during the service were "under the power." These behaviors linked the experience of worship to the remembrance of worship styles from the days of slavery, a period that many of the members could literally recall. Unlike many black Baptists, who shunned enthusiastic forms of spiritual expression in the hopes of gaining respectability, COGIC members imbued the ecstatic worship of the convocation services with an outpouring of the Spirit, which they believed was referred to in the Old Testament Book of Joel and was connected to their former identity as slaves. The emotionally charged environment encouraged members to get back in touch with the sacred and to touch the not-so-distant slave past.

The ecstatic worship allowed men to experience what COGIC women were already experiencing in their prayer and Bible band circles. Prayer shut-ins during which participants prayed and fasted all night were a regular practice of the convocation that had its beginnings in the Women's Department. The convocation allowed both men and women to engage in spiritual practices that were reserved primarily for women during the rest of the year. The intentional connection between COGIC women's practices and the practices of the convocation allowed women to model what it meant to be a sanctified person, or Saint, at these gatherings. Women's knowledge of the appropriate responses in prayer, in worship, and in ecstasy, therefore, helped the men to become open to the "move" of the spirit. Women became focal points of the convocation. As they addressed the convocation about the works of the Women's Department, their exhortations, prayers, and testimonies developed into a separate, day-long service that was later known as "Women's Day." Mother Robinson led these prayers and conducted a Bible lesson, after which reports of the work and monies raised by the Women's Department during the year were tallied.

New missionaries and evangelists for the Women's Department were also appointed on this day. Migration's effect on those traditional roles of southern women were reflected in these appointments. The newly appointed women were expected to uphold the examples of southern pietistic practices in regions not as densely evangelized by COGIC members. Evangelists and missionaries, along with the unseen prayer partners and altar workers, reminded members how to pray, sing, shout, and dress. If the local church members were not following the prescriptions of sanctified life, a COGIC missionary or evangelist might be sent in to "fire up" the Saints. The commissioning of these cultural missionaries was crucial in ensuring that appropriate practices were reinforced both at home and abroad.

The business session of the convocation often gave way to the consideration of more intimate issues related to family life among those who had migrated. As much as a stringent moral code was important for the members, it was even more important for those who had been appointed to positions of spiritual and temporal authority within the church. For COGIC women in leadership roles as missionaries, evangelists, or church mothers, rules related to marriage were stringent. The policy of most early Pentecostal denominations was that divorced men and women could not remarry until their former spouse died, and divorce permanently prohibited both men and women from ministry. COGIC policy was a unique twist upon the remarriage policy; it focused not on divorced persons, but on those who did not bother to obtain a divorce before remarrying. Mason's teaching on what he called "double marriage" was rooted in both a biblical and a pragmatic perspective: "Now You women that have other women's husbands or men that are not yours, and husbands that have other men's wives will have to tell the truth when you meet Jesus. It may be at the well, or on your dying bed, but you will have to tell the truth. The Lord says let not the wife depart from her husband and let not the husband put away his wife. . . . Jesus said whosoever shall put away his wife and marry another committeth adultery against her, and [if] a woman shall put away her husband and marry another, she committeth adultery."[52]

The issue of double marriage had nothing to do with the practice of marriage, divorce, and remarriage common among other Pentecostals. The policy was designed to address bigamy. It was not uncommon for migrants to simply leave one spouse and take up with another without having secured a legal divorce.[53] The practice had its roots in slave families, which were repeatedly broken up when members were sold apart from one another. Legal marriages among African Americans increased during the eras of Reconstruction and the Great Migration, but these were for the most part between middle-class and upper-class black people who could afford to marry. Among lower-class and impoverished African Americans, common-law marriages or serial relationships were the norm. Migration exacerbated the issue, as spouses left home to find work in the North or West and remarried in their new locales. Unless someone notified the previous spouse, chances were that the unsuspecting new spouse would never know that he or she was involved with a bigamist. Such domestic issues occupied a major portion of the convocation business meetings during the 1920s. For COGIC men and women, marriage to someone who had another spouse could mean the termination of their positions as evangelists, missionaries, or church mothers. COGIC leaders who were found to be in a double marriage were supposed to be stripped of their credentials, but women suffered more often from this rule than men did. The double marriage issue was hotly contested at the annual convocations; the story of evangelist Cora Stevens provides a case in point.

Cora Stevens was a licensed evangelist in the Women's Department. Her marriage to COGIC Elder R. H. Stevens was declared invalid when it was discovered that Stevens was still married to his first wife. According to the minutes of the 1922 convocation, Elder Stevens was instructed to "put Cora away" so that he could continue to serve as an elder within the church. Cora, however, was stripped of her evangelist's license and accused of having taken another man's wife. Cora fought the ruling. At the 1924 convocation, she brought charges of unlawful removal against women's leader Mother Robinson. Convocation committee members sided with Mother Robinson's decree, and the decision to revoke Cora's license was upheld. Yet ten years later, Cora was still causing problems for the Women's Department. In a 1934 issue of the denominational newspaper, *The Whole Truth*, a two-line statement regarding Cora Stevens appeared: "This is to let you know that Sis. Cora Stevens of Texas is not doing mission work in the Church of God in Christ. License revoked by Mother Robinson."[54]

In Elder Stevens and Sister Cora's case, both parties were in positions of spiritual authority within COGIC. The minutes are not clear as to why Elder Stevens was allowed to retain his position after returning to his first wife while Cora was forsaken of her position as an evangelist. Perhaps Mother Robinson's stringent rules regarding missionaries and evangelists were to blame. More likely, the double standard imposed upon the women of COGIC, which insisted that they be chaste and irreproachable sanctified women, was at fault in her removal. When double marriages were investigated, no details about the bigamists' sexual relationships were recorded. An argument from silence could be made that the church considered these sexual relationships irrelevant. In cases of bigamy, women bore an extraordinary burden both materially and sexually. Having lost the spousal support that they counted on, women were often turned out and left with sole responsibility for the children who were the fruit of their relationships. In many cases, the women themselves had been unaware that their spouses had already taken wives. When word of their double marriages emerged, not only was the family disrupted, but their ministries were disrupted as well. Cora Stevens's contestation of the removal of her license, therefore, was motivated by her concerns about her rank and her livelihood. Without Elder Stevens's support, Cora could not afford to lose her evangelist's license, which allowed her to provide for herself. She continued to pass herself off as an evangelist for a number of years by speaking in churches under the auspices of that revoked license.

The issue of double marriages illustrates the fluidity of marriages and common-law relationships; the social and economic status of many lower-class whites and blacks alike precluded them from involving the legal system in matters of the heart. Divorces were expensive and time consuming, and tracking an errant spouse could be virtually impossible. That the convocation minutes record interest only in cases of double marriage among prominent licensed clergy and leaders in the Women's Department shows that ministers within the church were held to high standards—and their marriages subjected to close scrutiny—compared to lay members of the church. The women of COGIC, like southern women, were expected to uphold a stringent policy that protected an ideal of the sanctity of marriage and of womanhood. The convocation, therefore, was not only a spiritual meeting, but also a family reunion at which the spiritual family of Saints' concerns were placed alongside the temporal concerns of family life.

IT IS CLEAR THAT church mothers' embodiment of domestic and familial ties to the South were crucial both in the growth of the Church of God in Christ and to the religious commitment of many COGIC members. Even more than preachers, church mothers were able to connect church members and converts to a sacred world where women were central to the faith; they provided examples for new members to emulate of how to live the sanctified life in the unsanctified cities. Holding on to their southernisms, the church mothers of COGIC managed to extend the core values of their lives into the urban North and West. In the interplay between the traditional roles of African American women and the patriarchal black church structure, these church mothers influenced the placement of pastors, church planting, convocation meetings, and the development of a nationwide network of women; they served the church as they traveled across the country and reinforced a southern sanctified lifestyle in the cities. Like Mother Mary Johnson in Detroit, no matter how far these COGIC women traveled, they were good, but not altogether gone from the South.

Notes

1. Mother Mary Mangum Johnson, *Life and Labors* (n.p.: n.d.).

2. Ithiel C. Clemmons, *Bishop C. H. Mason and the Roots of the Church of God in Christ* (Bakersfield, Calif.: Pneuma Life Publishing, 1996).

3. Its teachings differed from other Pentecostal groups of the time that did not place as strong an emphasis on the necessity of the experience of sanctification for speaking in tongues. See Donald W. Dayton, *Theological Roots of Pentecostalism* (Metuchen, N.J.: Scarecrow Press, 1987).

4. Grant Wacker, *Heaven Below: Early Pentecostals and American Culture* (Cambridge, Mass.: Harvard University Press, 2001). Wacker shatters the mythology of deprivation that has haunted the study of Pentecostalism.

5. These groups have their origins in Baptist/Holiness organizations of the latter half of the nineteenth century. See Joanna P. Moore, *"In Christ's Stead": Autobiographical Sketches* (Chicago: Women's Baptist Home Mission Society, 1902), and Anthea Butler, "A Peculiar Synergy: Matriarchy and the Church of God in Christ" (Ph.D. diss., Vanderbilt University, 2001).

6. Joe William Trotter Jr., ed., *The Great Migration in Historical Perspective: New Dimensions of Race, Class, and Gender* (Bloomington: Indiana University Press, 1991).

7. Milton C. Sernett, *Bound for the Promised Land: African American Religion and the Great Migration* (Durham: Duke University Press, 1997), 195.

8. Ibid. Sernett refers to the work of COGIC mother and eventual women's supervisor Lillian Brooks Coffey, who was one of the first COGIC members in Chicago. She is credited with planting more than twelve churches in the area.

9. C. Eric Lincoln and Lawrence H. Mamiya, *The Black Church in the African-American Experience* (Durham: Duke University Press, 1990), 65–66; Cheryl Townsend Gilkes, *If It Wasn't for the Women: Black Women's Experience and Womanist Culture in Church and Community* (Maryknoll, N.Y.: Orbis Books, 2001).

10. Lincoln and Mamiya, *Black Church in the African-American Experience*, 275.

11. Cheryl Townsend Gilkes, "The Politics of 'Silence': Dual-Sex Political Systems and Women's Traditions of Conflict in African-American Religion," in *African American Christianity: Essays in History*, ed. Paul E. Johnson (Berkeley: University of California Press, 1997), 92.

12. Butler, "A Peculiar Synergy," 3.

13. "The Voice of Mother Robinson, Overseer of the Women's Department," *The Whole Truth*, February 1968, 3.

14. National Register of Historic Places, Lizzie Robinson Home, Douglas County, Nebraska, Continuation Sheet (1993), sec. 8, 3.

15. Benjamin Schwartz, "The Idea of the South," *Atlantic Monthly*, December 1997, 122.

16. Cheryl J. Sanders, *Saints in Exile: The Holiness-Pentecostal Experience in African American Religion and Culture* (New York: Oxford University Press, 1996), 58.

17. Butler, "A Peculiar Synergy."

18. There is some confusion about how women were initially addressed. "Overseer" meant bishop, but these women were leading only women and were not ordained. "State mother" became more common in the late teens and into the 1920s.

19. Minutes of the Church of God in Christ, 1917, in Lucille J. Cornelius, *The Pioneer History of the Church of God in Christ* (Memphis: n.p., 1975), 51–55.

20. This difference between teaching and preaching was contested among COGIC members. Women could teach women and men, but they were not allowed into the pulpit of the church. They were encouraged to address the Saints in exhortations or testimonials in the churches, but they could not stand in the pulpit. This policy is still in effect in some COGIC churches today.

21. Johnson, *Life and Labors*, 15.

22. Victoria W. Wolcott, *Remaking Respectability: African American Women in Interwar Detroit* (Chapel Hill: University of North Carolina Press, 2001), 59. The Urban League tried to close up the bear trap on Elliot.

23. Johnson, *Life and Labors*, 15–16.

24. Ibid., 12–13.

25. Ibid., 12.

26. Wolcott, *Remaking Respectability*, 22–30.

27. Ibid., 117.

28. Ibid., 115.

29. Rose Marie Duff, *The Ethnohistory of Saint's Home Church of the Church of God in Christ, Los Angeles, California* (Sacramento: California State University, 1972), 20.

30. Ibid., 39.

31. "Mother Cotton Sounds Bugle," *Foursquare Crusader* 2, no. 46 (May 13, 1936): col. 1.

32. "Biography of Elder McKinley McCardell," 1944, reprinted in *Twenty-Fifth Silver Anniversary, Women's Department of California Northwest Jurisdiction, COGIC, May 1982* (n.p.: [1982]), 11.

33. "The Whole Truth," reprinted in *Women's Page*, February 1968, 3.

34. Charlotte Perkins Gilman, "Surplus Negro Women," in *Radicals and Conservatives, and Other Essays on the Negro in America*, ed. Kelly Miller Smith (1908; reprint, New York: Schoken Books, 1968). Gilman argues that black women outnumbered available single black men in migration to the North.

35. Minutes of the National Convocation of the COGIC, December 12, 1916, in Cornelius, *Pioneer History*, 51–55. Women were instructed to be obedient and to hear their overseers.

36. Lillian Brooks Coffey, comp. *Yearbook of the Church of God in Christ for the Year 1926* (Memphis: privately printed, 1926), 148, Assemblies of God Archives, Springfield, Mo.

37. Evelyn Brooks Higginbotham, *Righteous Discontent: The Women's Movement in the Black Baptist Church, 1880–1920* (Cambridge, Mass.: Harvard University Press, 1993), 98–100.

38. Both Scriptures advocate modest apparel, non-braided hair, and the putting away of gold.

39. Sherry Dupree, interview by the author, June 1996. Dupree once interviewed an older COGIC mother who had ironed garments for Mother Robinson. The church mother complained about the heavy starching she had to do to Robinson's white blouses and black skirts so that Mother Robinson would be satisfied.

40. *Memphis Corporate Salute to COGIC* (Memphis: COGIC Publishing House, 1996), 21.

41. *The Whole Truth*, February 1968, 3.

42. COGIC church mothers frowned upon short sleeves or sleeveless dresses because armpits were considered to be suggestive of female genitalia. The analogy was lost upon me until I realized that shaving of underarms and legs for American women became a common grooming ritual only after World War II.

43. Lucy Flagg, "Lord, Change the Style," n.d., n.p., Dupree African-American Pentecostal and Holiness Collection, Schomburg Center for Research in Black Culture, New York Public Library, New York, N.Y. Other interesting lines include, "We used to be too modest to show under the arm, but now we expose our pits and call it charm."

44. *Sing unto the Lord a New Song: Songs of Inspiration, Revelation, and Doctrine of the Church of God in Christ from the 1930's to 1950's* (n.p.: Gospel in Reach Ministries, n.d.).

45. Bobby Bean, *This Is the Church of God in Christ* (Atlanta: Underground Epics, 2001), 47.

46. Ibid., 48.

47. Minutes of the COGIC Convocation, 1916, in Cornelius, *Pioneer History*, 51–55.

48. Lelia Mason Byas with Jack T. Hunt, *From Priors Farm to Heaven: Bishop C. H. Mason, a Biography of His Life* (n.p.: Hunt Family Publishing Company, 1995), 72.

49. Bean, *This Is The Church of God in Christ*, 48.

50. Dr. Sister Pearl Page Brown, *Sewing Circle Artistic Fingers* (n.p.: Church of God in Christ, n.d.), 15, Dupree Collection. These are earlier reprints on prayer and fasting.

51. Byas, *From Prior's Farm to Heaven*, p. 70.

52. Bishop C. H. Mason, "The Whole Truth about Double Marriages," in Coffey, *Yearbook*, Assemblies of God Archives.

53. Hortense Powdermaker, *After Freedom: A Cultural Study in the Deep South* (New York: Viking, 1939), 156–57. Powdermaker notes that legal divorce in the town of

Bronzeville was something "more than a luxury," because "it savor[ed] of pretensions and extravagance."

54. *The Whole Truth*, March 1934, 4.

For Further Reading

Bean, Bobby. *This Is the Church of God in Christ*. Atlanta: Underground Epics, 2001.

Butler, Anthea. "A Peculiar Synergy: Matriarchy and the Church of God in Christ." Ph.D. diss., Vanderbilt University, 2001.

Clemmons, Ithiel. *Bishop C. H. Mason and the Roots of the Church of God in Christ*. Bakersfield, Calif.: Pneuma Life Publishing, 1996.

Dayton, Donald W. *Theological Roots of Pentecostalism*. Metuchen, N.J.: Scarecrow Press, 1987.

Gilkes, Cheryl Townsend. *If It Wasn't for the Women: Black Women's Experience and Womanist Culture in Church and Community*. Maryknoll, N.Y.: Orbis Books, 2001.

———. "The Politics of 'Silence': Dual-Sex Political Systems and Women's Traditions of Conflict in African-American Religion." In *African American Christianity: Essays in History*, edited by Paul E. Johnson. Berkeley: University of California Press, 1997.

Higginbotham, Evelyn Brooks. *Righteous Discontent: The Women's Movement in the Black Baptist Church, 1880–1920*. Cambridge, Mass.: Harvard University Press, 1993.

Lincoln, C. Eric, and Lawrence H. Mamiya. *The Black Church in the African-American Experience*. Durham: Duke University Press, 1990.

Powdermaker, Hortense. *After Freedom: A Cultural Study in the Deep South*. New York: Viking, 1939.

Sanders, Cheryl J. *Saints in Exile: The Holiness-Pentecostal Experience in African American Religion and Culture*. New York: Oxford University Press, 1996.

Sernett, Milton C. *Bound for the Promised Land: African American Religion and the Great Migration*. Durham: Duke University Press, 1997.

Trotter, Joe William, Jr., ed. *The Great Migration in Historical Perspective: New Dimensions of Race, Class, and Gender*. Bloomington: Indiana University Press, 1991.

Wacker, Grant. *Heaven Below: Early Pentecostals and American Culture*. Cambridge, Mass.: Harvard University Press, 2001.

Wolcott, Victoria W. *Remaking Respectability: African American Women in Interwar Detroit*. Chapel Hill: University of North Carolina Press, 2001.

JERMA JACKSON

8

Sister Rosetta Tharpe and the Evolution of Gospel Music

> Now don't you hear me swinging,
> Hear the words that I'm singing,
> Moist my soul with water from on high.
> While the world of love is around me,
> Evil thoughts do bind me,
> Oh if you leave me, I will die.
> —Sister Rosetta Tharpe, "Rock Me"

In the fall of 1938, Sister Rosetta Tharpe, accompanying herself on guitar, sang this modified version of "Hide Me in Thy Bosom."[1] Some music reviewers referred to the song as a spiritual, but it was actually part of a new form of sacred music—known as "gospel"—that emerged in African American communities over the course of the twentieth century. Tharpe, a Pentecostal evangelist, began using gospel to reach the unregenerate as a young child in churches and at revivals, as well as on city streets. By October 1938, however, Tharpe had found new terrain on which to save souls. As her performance at New York's Cotton Club attested, this Pentecostal evangelist had turned to nightclubs and theaters. One black newspaper reported that Tharpe explained her decision this way: "She sings in a night club because she feels there are more souls in the nighteries that need saving than there are in the church."[2] Moving from churches and revivals to nightclubs and theaters, Tharpe helped to secure a place for gospel in the commercial arena. Four years later, when Arna Bontemps published one of the earliest articles on gospel, he noted that the music enjoyed enormous popularity both inside and outside the church. Bontemps maintained that the music stretched back to the depression years, when "a wave of fresh rapture came over the people" as "Negro churches, particularly the Sanctified groups and the shouting Baptists, were swinging and jumping as never before." Enthusiasm for gospel songs soon swelled beyond church settings altogether. "In

Negro communities," Bontemps explained, "school children sing them on the streets." Chicago taxicab drivers tuned in to church services broadcast over the radio. The songs, he said, had become so popular by the early forties that they were beginning to rival secular music. "Here indeed," he wrote, "is church music that can hold its own against anything on the hit parade."[3] Tharpe's Cotton Club appearance demonstrates how widespread gospel had become during the late thirties. The popularity that contemporary gospel singers such as Kirk Franklin and Yolanda Adams enjoy among black audiences attests to the pull that the music continues to have.

The movement of gospel from churches to radio waves, record charts, and nightclubs marked the expansion of a consumer-oriented society in which money and popularity became measures of worth. Tharpe's popularity marked a corresponding shift in the ways in which millions of African Americans practiced religion. The aura surrounding money and material consumption gave secular values enormous power. Poised between religion and commerce, gospel emerged as an arena where African Americans used religion to make sense of the world and at the same time to secure a place for themselves in a commercial society. Tharpe's trajectory from Pentecostal evangelist to national celebrity supplies us with a lens for examining the evolution of gospel over the course of the twentieth century. Moving from the 1890s, when the Holiness and Pentecostal movements took shape, through the half century up to 1960, we will use the context in which Tharpe operated to explore how a mode of worship coalesced into the discrete music style we know as gospel.

The evolution of gospel provides historians with an opportunity to examine religion as a social and cultural process. The trajectory of Tharpe from Pentecostal evangelist to national celebrity calls our attention to the shifting contours of religion in African American communities over the course of the twentieth century. Whether she was in the church, on the street, or in the market, Tharpe held on to the tenets of her religious upbringing, especially to the notion that music was a divine gift. Over time, Tharpe modified the way she conveyed these sentiments to audiences. In the Pentecostal community where she evangelized as a child, music gave voice to what believers felt in their hearts and souls. When she moved to the market, Tharpe's attention to skill and craft rendered the religious sources of her music diffuse and murky.

This essay offers a fresh perspective on popular religion. In recent years, a growing number of scholars have moved beyond matters of theology and religious institutions to examine popular religion. Few, however, have explored the religious dimensions of mass-produced culture. In her journey from church to nightclub, Tharpe was instrumental not just in moving gospel beyond the church, but in transforming a mode of church worship into a popular religion deeply entrenched in the commercial realm.

BONTEMPS LOCATED THE origin of gospel in the depression years, when it gained recognition as a legitimate style. Yet the music can be traced back to the late nineteenth century, specifically to the emergence of Holiness and Pentecostalism. Embedded in turn-of-the-century social and cultural politics, these movements developed out of debates about the meaning religion ought to assume in a secularizing society. The debates, which transcended racial boundaries, acquired a distinctive meaning among African Americans, who, in the wake of emancipation, established separate congregations in order to govern their own religious lives. The Holiness and Pentecostal movements nurtured a distinctive worship style, supplying critical elements that later blossomed into the distinctive body of sound we know as gospel.[4]

The Pentecostal movement flourished in Arkansas, where Tharpe was born. Her mother, Katie Bell Nubin, was a missionary for the Church of God in Christ, a black Pentecostal denomination that began to take shape in the Mississippi Delta region during the first decade of the century. Tharpe gained critical music skills from her spiritual affiliation, as this religious community fashioned singing and instrumental accompaniment into modes of worship. The musical sensibilities Tharpe developed remained with her throughout her life. For example, Tharpe always accompanied herself on guitar both on stage and in her recordings, whether she was a vocalist with a swing band or singing duets with Marie Knight. Since the instrument was widely used in the community where she grew up, Tharpe used her recordings to pay homage to the array of guitarists who persisted in the Church of God in Christ.[5]

Guitar-accompanied singing, which would later become Tharpe's trademark, distinguished gospel from other forms of sacred music. In the hymns and spirituals that prevailed in most late-nineteenth-century black churches, either a leader sang lines that were repeated by the congregation or choirs led the congregation in song. Both performance styles featured slow-metered tempos. Conversely, gospel emphasized solo rather than either congregational or choral singing. Instrumental accompaniment, a critical component of gospel, lent an upbeat tempo to the music that also distinguished it from hymns and spirituals.[6]

The politics of the Holiness and Pentecostal movements sheds light on how gospel acquired these elements. The Holiness movement among African Americans began in the 1890s when disgruntled members of Baptist congregations expressed dismay over what many perceived to be the capitulation of congregations and church leaders to secular values. The men and women who established the Church of God in Christ separated themselves not only from Baptist congregations, but also from an array of secular values that they referred to as "worldliness." These men and women pointed to the loss of religious fervor in everyday life and the willingness of congregations across the denominational spectrum to prize decorum over religious expression as reasons for forming their new church.[7]

Pentecostal denominations like the Church of God in Christ, in which Tharpe grew up, stressed the importance of religion as a corporeal experience in which the physical and emotional reinforced one another. As parishioners spoke in tongues—a practice that was considered to be the most sacred divine gift— they made external an experience that was private and internal, and in the process they helped to generate a community. Maudelle Oliver, who experienced conversion in 1922 at the age of fourteen, related how the corporeal experience of the Holy Ghost moved believers to dance:

> MO: The Spirit would come on you and you would do things. And we just enjoyed what the Lord did. And we'd dance you know what I mean. Do you know what the holy dance is?
>
> JJ: I've heard of it. I was wondering if you could tell me what it is.
>
> MO: Oh Lord have mercy. You just rejoice instead of wrestling may I say. You know some churches the folks be happy, and the folks hold them. But we never held nobody, just keep them from hurting anybody else if they would probably to fall down. You know in those days we would see the Lord knock people out and purge them. Well we just enjoyed seeing the Lord work.[8]

As believers consecrated their bodies to God, they celebrated God's presence.

The same corporeal experience that urged parishioners to shout, dance, and rejoice in the Spirit also inspired songs that emphasized rhythm and individual singing. More than a few observers commented on how the emphatic rhythms that laced the music made for a distinctive sound. The blues guitarist T-Bone Walker noted that he first heard boogie-woogie piano playing in the sanctified church in his Texas hometown.[9] Music comprised an integral part of Pentecostal religious worship. One man described how Pentecostals of the twenties and thirties transformed music and dancing into mediums for praising God: "Our music was tambourines and sometimes a guitar. The Holy Ghost would come and we would dance for hours and hours. . . . We praise God in the dance and plays music."[10]

Even as music served as a vehicle for collective celebration, it also became a forum for individual expression. In a community where the physical manifestation of religious devotion assumed vital importance, Pentecostals used music and singing to offer public testimony about the presence of God in their lives. Describing a religious experience he had in 1907, Charles H. Mason conveyed how collective and individual singing could reinforce one another: "More light came, and my heart rejoiced! . . . Some said, 'Let us sing.' I arose and the first song that came to me was, 'He Brought Me Out of the Miry Clay; He Sat My Feet on the Rock to Stay.'"[11] Moved by the Spirit, Mason arose from his seat to deliver the song that came to him. As Mason stood amidst the congregation delivering his song, he departed from the lining-out tradition in which a designated individual led the community in congregational singing. Yet the sight of someone so moved by the Spirit did not offend those who had assembled, many of whom probably felt inspired to catch the song and join him in the singing.

Mason later established the Church of God in Christ, and he encouraged individuals to testify in song during its worship services. Out of that testimony came Tharpe's career; she was one of the many possessed of the Spirit who would sing the songs of God. Horace Boyer, who grew up in the Church of God in Christ, recalled that the members of the community understood music as more than just a skill an individual possessed. They considered it a divine gift. He remembered being told: "The Lord gives each person some kind of gift. He gives some the gift of smiling, some the gift of talking soothingly to people, some the gift of praying, some the gift of preaching . . . some the gift of singing."[12] Tharpe affirmed the personal meaning of possessing the divine gift of music in "What He Done for Me," a song she recorded in 1942:

He took my feet out of the miry clay,
What He done for me.
He put them on the rock to stay,
What He done for me.
He put a song in my soul to stay,

What He done for me,

I never shall forget, for he set me free.[13]

Tharpe seems to have built on the song Mason delivered in 1907. In his version, Mason pointed to his delivery from trying, uncertain circumstances to a more secure foundation as evidence that God had an active and tangible presence in the world. Significantly, Tharpe added musical skills to the list of ways God could actively shape daily life.

The concept of music as a divine gift turned singers into divine mediums. Consider the experience of Mason in 1907. Raising himself from the chair as the song came to him, Mason had become a vessel of God. Tharpe had similar experiences. Marie Knight, who performed with Tharpe during the fifties, described how Tharpe's creative process worked:

> It was a gift. Sound. If she could hear it, she could play it. Sometimes she would be up, like 2 or 3 in the morning. She'd be downstairs at the piano. And she would say, "You gotta come down, cause we got a song—I got a song that's coming through." . . . She would get the guitar and I would play the piano, and she'd sit there and we'd word it out. She'd word it out. And that's how we did our recordings. She would hear the songs as they came through. And she would sit there and pick them out on the guitar. The keys and what not. And that's the way she did it. It had to come to her by sound.

Knight, who also grew up in the Church of God in Christ, later explained that all gifts come from divine sources. "You see, we all have a gift," Knight pointed out. "See all person's gifts come from God." "We don't," she emphasized, "make them ourselves."[14] The sentiments Knight expressed echoed those voiced by Boyer. Both understood the divine as having an active and tangible presence in daily life, so that the songs they sang were God's songs.

In Pentecostal communities, those who showed musical promise were encouraged to develop their talents. Tharpe was one such individual. Stories abound in Pentecostal circles about the extraordinary talent she displayed as a child. During the thirties, Tharpe spent some time in Chicago. One woman remembered the local reputation Tharpe enjoyed in the city before her tenure on the concert and nightclub stage. "Everybody, people would just be amazed at how she could play that guitar and sing," the resident recalled.[15] Tharpe's talent held religious significance in a setting where music assumed importance as a divine gift. Pentecostal audiences believed they witnessed God at work through Tharpe.

"They would call on her for a number in the church," a Chicago resident explained, "and then she would get up and begin to sing and minister to the people."[16] Experiences such as these, together with the missionary work her mother pursued, encouraged and may have even compelled Tharpe to use her music to evangelize.

Whereas other African American children passed their early lives attending school or helping out with farmwork, Tharpe spent her youth as an itinerant missionary. Throughout the twenties and thirties, Tharpe traveled across the country doing religious programs and revivals. Richard Cohen, whose family lived in Miami, Florida, remembered seeing Tharpe and her mother when Tharpe was a teenager. "She played the guitar," Cohen recalled, "and the mother played the mandolin."[17] The mother–daughter team traveled up until 1934, when Tharpe married Thomas J. Tharpe, a minister in the Church of God in Christ. The marriage did not, however, end Tharpe's missionary work. She continued to travel, but she now worked alongside her husband: while he preached the Word, Tharpe evangelized with her music.

Tharpe never received formal musical training, but Pentecostal churches and revivals gave her rich opportunities to practice and share her gifts. Richard Cohen reflected on the education her missionary work provided in 1992. "When you think of Tharpe's music," he was asked, "what comes to mind?" In addition to citing her clear diction and expressiveness, Cohen mentioned Tharpe's ability to reach inside her audiences and propel them to another domain: "When things were kind of . . . draggy, you know, she had that inner thing that she could just pull it up. I've seen her on programs with other groups and [the audience would] be kind of dead, and she would get up and talk to them, you know. She'd get to talking and strike her guitar, you know, and talk to them about things, and every now and then would strike the guitar. And the next thing you know, the folk would be up, you know. And they would really get with her." According to Cohen, Tharpe developed "that inner thing" from her mother, who enjoyed a reputation as one of the most dynamic evangelists in the Church of God in Christ. Cohen explained that Tharpe "was trained to give a show. Because her mother, you know, her mother could give you a show."[18]

Neither Tharpe nor her Pentecostal contemporaries envisioned themselves as pioneers of gospel music during the years between 1890 and 1930. Many Pentecostals surely recognized that their music differed from the music that prevailed in mainline churches, but they were unlikely to dwell on such distinctiveness, because they regarded their music as synonymous with religious feeling and worship. Histories produced by the Church of God in Christ underscore this perception. These sources, which focus on the development of denominational organization, give scant attention to the subject of music. References to music are most often found in testimonies that describe religious experiences.[19]

BLACK PENTECOSTALS envisioned themselves as restoring old-time religion. Yet their modes of worship, especially music, seemed refreshing to many who joined the movement. Equating musical virtuosity with evidence of divine agency, black Pentecostals placed no constraints on how an individual approached music. For this reason, gospel shared much with newly emerging secular styles, especially blues. Nowhere was this overlap more evident than in the use of the guitar. While commonly associated with blues, the instrument assumed an important place in Pentecostal worship services. Primarily, however, the relationship between gospel and blues stemmed from two factors: the aggressive proselytizing efforts Pentecostals used to reach the unregenerate; and their understanding of religion as a celebration, both emotional and physical, of the divine.[20]

Aggressive proselytizing strategies transformed the Church of God in Christ from a small fellowship to one of the nation's fastest-growing denominations. During the first decade of the twentieth century, the name "Church of God in Christ" referred to a small church in Lexington, Mississippi. Thanks to a dedicated corps of evangelists and missionaries, the church soon blossomed into an independent denomination. Intent on spreading the message of sanctification, these men and women, who approached their spiritual work with steadfast commitment, engaged in a broad range of activities that included healing the sick, preaching the Word, organizing prayer bands, and building missions. During the twenties and thirties, some Pentecostals converted radio and recordings into vehicles for saving souls. Many more, like Tharpe and her mother, turned to city streets to reach the unregenerate. Initially, churches sprang up in the Delta regions of Mississippi and Arkansas. As African Americans moved to the metropolis, so did the evangelists and missionaries so instrumental in building the denomination. By the mid-fifties, the Church of God in Christ, once regionally based, had emerged as a national denomination with churches across the country.[21]

The work of saving souls offered opportunities to women such as Tharpe. Most men who heard a divine call directed their spiritual work toward pastoring churches, a trend especially evident in the twenties and thirties. Women took a particularly active role in proselytizing because the Church of God in Christ restricted them from preaching and pastoring. Unwilling to deny the power of the Spirit, male church leaders enlisted women in a special work. George Hancock, who lived in Michigan, described how the work of female missionaries and evangelists during the teens and twenties proved indispensable to the growth of the denomination there: "I know you're not going to like what I'm getting ready to say. But in 'those days' the women started this thing." Women were prohibited from the pulpit, but Hancock explained that "the only way that a church got built was a woman missionary went out and built it."[22]

Tharpe's mother, Katie Bell Nubin, did not pastor a church, but, like the women in Michigan, she was instrumental in building the Church of God in Christ. So was Maudelle Oliver. Recalling her venture to Crawfordsville, Arkansas, from Memphis with a group of women in 1922, Oliver said that enthusiasm for holiness and sanctification compelled them to take initiative: "Well see as I said we were just inclined to do. We weren't sent by nobody. But when the people found out what we had, then they wanted to use us."[23] Women like Oliver traveled all over the South, while Nubin and Tharpe turned to the North, following the tens of thousands of black migrants who embarked for the northern metropolises with the onset of World War I. A member of one Pentecostal congregation in Chicago remembered that Tharpe and her mother led revivals at a congregation on the west side of the city that P. R. Favors pastored. The itinerant life that Oliver, Nubin, Tharpe, and other women led attested to their unswerving commitment to the Lord's work.[24]

As public space, the street helped to distinguish the metropolis from the countryside. The street, while not sacred, could be transformed into an ephemeral, sacred space through prophecy and music. Such divine possibilities turned the street into a space where evangelists and missionaries could confront potential converts. The use of music to reach the unregenerate was so commonplace that commercial recording companies coined the term "guitar evangelists" to distinguish sacred musicians from their secular blues counterparts. Although many of these musicians were men operating independently of churches and denominations, female missionaries also seized the street to save souls. In contrast to guitar evangelists, female missionaries often maintained ties to specific denominations and churches. Among these women were Nubin and Tharpe, who held memorable street meetings.[25] Gospel singer Marion Williams recalled hearing Tharpe singing on the streets of Miami when she was a child.[26] Likewise, Agnes Campbell remembered hearing Tharpe on the streets of Chicago in the summers. Tharpe "would play her instrument and sing," Campbell related, "and then her mother would teach."[27]

Evangelizing on city streets offered Tharpe vital lessons about the ways of the world. The street was an intermediate space between the church, where individuals made up a community, and the market, where human interactions were governed by forces beyond their control. On the street, especially in the commercial districts where African Americans congregated, strangers interacted with one another in a host of different ways. Vendors peddled their wares. People, especially the young, socialized. Different styles of music—sacred and secular—vied with each other as Pentecostals held street meetings while secular musicians sang about the carnal pleasures of life.[28] The street was the world, but it could be claimed for God. Street meetings differed from regular worship services and even from the more periodic revivals and tent meetings. As men and women stopped to watch and listen to evangelists like Tharpe and her mother, they became spontaneous congregations distinct from the more stable communities of church members that dominated revivals and worship services. Like worship services, tent, street, and revival meetings included praying, testifying, and singing. Street meetings, however, were far shorter than worship services and revival and tent meetings, all of which generally lasted somewhere between two and three hours. Without chairs or any protective covering, street meetings usually lasted about one hour.[29]

The spontaneous congregations emanating from street meetings provided a pool of potential new church members. Agnes Campbell, who grew up in Chicago, remembered street meetings as a recruitment device. She led street meetings in the city with her father, William Goodwin, sometime between 1927, when he started a church, and 1945, when he moved to Michigan. They held their meetings close to the church so that members could share fellowship with potential recruits. After the meetings, Campbell noted, "people would come and meet us at the church."[30]

Tharpe and her mother combined the type of institutional affiliation maintained by Campbell with the complete independence of guitar evangelists. Although affiliated with the Church of God in Christ, they may not have been members of a congregation. The extensive distance the women covered in their travels between Chicago and Florida suggests that their meetings may have provided them with a source of monetary support, especially during the depression years. The two may have followed up their singing and teaching with requests for free-will offerings, a practice common among guitar evangelists like Blind Willie Johnson as well as among secular musicians such as Blind Blake and Tampa Red.[31]

Those who spent considerable time evangelizing on the street—often guitarists—developed a distinctive style of play. The way Tharpe combined voice and guitar provides perhaps the most concrete evidence of her street work. Most evangelists who accompanied themselves on guitar when recording sacred songs featured chords rather than individual notes, so that the instrument supplied a vital source of background rhythm. Those who remember hearing Tharpe before the late thirties, however, recall her ability to pick the instrument. One Chicago woman related: "[Tharpe] could pick that box, baby. Oh she could pick that box."[32] Another recalled how Tharpe "would just make that guitar talk."[33] Gussie Hamilton, who met Tharpe at a Florida convocation in 1935, recalled that her uncle had met Tharpe years before at an annual Pentecostal convocation in Memphis. On his return to Florida, Hamilton remembered, "[He would] tell us about this young lady who could really pick the guitar and sing."[34] By making her guitar a source of melody instead of rhythm, Tharpe made it speak.

The picking style Tharpe used was common among guitar evangelists such as Rev. Gary Davis, Blind Willie Johnson, and others who played extensively on the street. Only through hearsay can we ascertain what Tharpe sounded like before 1938. Johnson, however, recorded during the late twenties and early thirties. Singing alone, he fashioned string melodies to create a second voice. This distinctive style probably emerged to meet the conditions of the street. The need for a second voice was less common in worship services and tent and revival meetings, where congregational singing prevailed. The social dynamics of the street may also have inspired evangelists like Tharpe to play single notes rather than chords; the picking style these evangelists embraced was common among blues guitarists generally. Such cross-fertilization was inevitable on the street, where the worldly and the sacred could influence each other.[35]

Additional evidence of the similarity between gospel and blues comes from the piano. While the enormous size of this instrument made it stationary and therefore impractical for use on the street, significant overlap existed between playing styles found in Pentecostal and Holiness congregations and those that prevailed among blues piano players. T-Bone Walker alluded to this overlap when he likened the music he heard in a Dallas, Texas, sanctified church to barrelhouse piano. No doubt Walker could have been referring to Arizona Dranes, who lived in nearby Forth Worth, Texas. This blind Pentecostal singer adopted a boogie-woogie piano style and turned to recordings to reach the unregenerate. During the twenties, commercial recording companies, eager to reach black consumers, made a concerted effort to record black singers and musicians. Dranes was among the host of men and women from the Church of God in Christ who availed themselves of the opportunity to record.[36]

Together, the experiences of both Tharpe and Dranes indicate how integral music was to the sanctified worship experience. As individuals made manifest the presence of the divine, they transcended the self. The emphasis on transcendence took precedence over any particular music one played, so that blues musicians, moved by the Spirit, were encouraged to bring their music into the church. Moreover, transcendence stemmed from a celebration of emotional power that helps to account for the similarities between blues and gospel. Blues musicians did not typically direct their instruments to divine subjects. Yet they did celebrate the power of emotion. As blues musicians used their instruments and voices to reflect on the pain and misery of life, the power they elicited through personal expression created the possibility of conquering pain and misery. Whereas blues musicians used music to create an existential experience, gospel singers and musicians directed emotion toward creating a religious experience.[37]

We have come to view both the street and the recording studio as incubators of secular values. The experience of Tharpe, however, serves as a reminder that during the twenties and thirties evangelists and missionaries seized these spaces to confront potential converts. The aggressive strategies Pentecostal denominations used to reach the unregenerate led Tharpe to evangelize on city streets, where commerce and religion coexisted. Indeed, those same strategies persuaded Tharpe to appear at the Cotton Club in 1938, where she gained access to the music business. But she would discover that the sacred possibilities of the music industry and the market culture of which it was a part were muffled in that setting relative to the street.

IN OCTOBER 1938, Tharpe brought the gospel songs she had sung on city streets and in churches and revivals to New York's Cotton Club. The appearance brought Tharpe national acclaim, transforming her life so dramatically that one journalist likened her to Cinderella. In the postwar era, gospel would come to enjoy enormous mass appeal, and singers would routinely achieve stature as national celebrities. Since no such trend prevailed in the late thirties, however, the trajectory of Tharpe from evangelist to celebrity helped situate gospel at the center of the music business. Pentecostal songsters who made recordings during the twenties had used the commercial arena to disseminate gospel. Since these individuals had focused their efforts on making commerce conducive to their religious ends, gospel lingered on the margins of the music industry. Tharpe, however, moved gospel music in a new direction by securing a space for the music in the realm of commercialized entertainment. In the process, she reconfigured gospel, creating an overall smoother sound than that of her Pentecostal predecessors and camouflaging her religious convictions. The national attention and success she enjoyed inevitably inspired Tharpe to forge new ways of comprehending her faith.[38]

Tharpe realized that she was venturing into uncharted terrain when she accepted an invitation to sing on a nightclub stage. According to Richard Cohen, she shrouded her decision in secrecy, refusing to tell her husband about the engagement: "She was very deceptive about it because she told her husband . . . she was going home to see about her mother."[39] The deception suggests the ambivalence Tharpe may have felt. The engagement, which revolved around her sacred songs, did not require Tharpe to abandon gospel and establish herself in a secular field. Nevertheless, Pentecostals stood aloof from spaces like the Cotton Club, dismissing these venues of commercialized leisure as nothing more than incubators of sin.

Changes in the music industry during the depression made the experiences of those like Tharpe who recorded in the late thirties very different from the experiences of those who had recorded just a few years earlier. The music industry had been a diffuse operation during the twenties and early thirties. Radio networks, record companies, and nightclubs constituted distinct entities. In addition, the array of companies that made race recordings attested to the fierce competition that existed. Companies looked beyond vaudeville and show business for recording artists. As a result, many took an interest in religious subjects that ranged from gospel, or what many in the industry then called "sacred music," to sermons. The devout, especially among Baptists and Pentecostals, recognized that recordings could evangelize, and they welcomed the opportunity to record. Such opportunities significantly withered during the depression, however, as many race recording companies went out of business, allowing a small number of record companies to dominate the industry.[40]

The music business had consolidated by the late thirties thanks to a small corps of managers who forged connections between radio stations, recording companies, and venues of commercialized leisure. Music publisher and impresario Irving Mills used the Cotton Club to forge such connections, transforming the club from a little-known cabaret into a preeminent institution for showcasing African American talent to mass audiences. The Cotton Club catered exclusively to an elite white population. An appearance at the club, however, assumed a level of importance far beyond what could be conferred by those in attendance. Mass-circulation newspapers from both the trade and black presses routinely reported on the club's seasonal productions. One station broadcast a weekly radio show from the club that featured the swing bands that performed there, giving access to the performances to African Americans, who were barred from patronizing the theater. Many in the industry watched the acts that performed at the Cotton Club, and Tharpe captured widespread attention.[41]

Almost overnight, Tharpe had a flood of opportunities. Mills published a collection of her songs as sheet music. Decca Records, a leading label during the thirties and forties, offered her a recording contract. John Hammond, a white independent producer, set out to introduce white audiences to the broad spectrum of African American music by bringing black singers and musicians from across the country to perform in "From Spirituals to Swing," a concert held at Carnegie Hall. The sensation Tharpe generated at the Cotton Club led Hammond to invite her to participate in the concert in 1938 and again in 1939. In addition to white audiences, the Cotton Club performance gave Tharpe access to black audiences who were unfamiliar with gospel. She appeared at nightclubs and theaters where African Americans congregated throughout New York and across the country, including the Apollo and Paramount theaters.[42]

The scale of the attention Tharpe received was greater than anything she had ever experienced before. To be sure, African American Pentecostals from Miami to Chicago had heard about Tharpe before she ventured onto the market. Yet few African Americans outside of Pentecostal circles were familiar with her. Consequently, when two black newspapers first reported on her activity, they were indifferent to her earlier career. The *Washington Afro-American* described her previous life as having been confined to "a small out of the way Pentecostal church in Miami."[43] The *Pittsburgh Courier* did not make any reference to her career prior to her appearance at the Cotton Club.[44] Singing in churches and on the streets, she had reached individuals on a local level, but this local reputation had come to assume national proportions.

The Cotton Club engagement moved Tharpe into the unfamiliar and, for her, completely new domain of the music industry, where a market culture nurtured decidedly secular values. The music industry revolved around the market, a "boundless and timeless phenomenon" that presumably operated outside of society according to "natural," immutable laws such as the law of supply and demand.[45] Over the course of several interviews, Marie Knight, who began singing with Tharpe in 1943, never invoked the term "market," but she did capture how market culture worked in incisive discussions about the music business. Knight related how money organized human interactions in the music industry. She explained: "There's more to recording than just walking in the studio. . . . Every minute is counted." And "all the minutes you burn up," she pointed out, cost money. "If you got a group," she went on to say, "all the time that's wasted come out of the leader's check."[46]

The aura of money enabled those with access to it to wield considerable authority. Knight alluded to this fact in a description of the role managers played in the music business. The success or failure of any singer or musician did not rest solely on skill; the fate of an artist also hinged on the willingness of managers to invest in the music. "It's not what you know," she reiterated on several occasions, "it's who you know." Managers wielded power because they possessed capital, or what Knight referred to as "financial background." She explained: "[With] . . . music, you must have a background. You got to have it. If you expect to go anyplace, you got to have a background." Knight maintained that the popularity Tharpe enjoyed stemmed from the managers—booking agents, publishers, promoters, record men, and independent producers—who took interest in her. Over the course of her career, Tharpe worked with an array of different managers. Moe Gale booked her concerts in 1941, but ten years later she was working with Irving Feld. Tharpe worked with different record men during her long tenure at Decca Records. Given the engagement at the Cotton Club, Tharpe may have worked with Irving Mills when she initially entered the music business. Knight recalled that when she teamed up with Tharpe in 1943, "Rosetta was already with the musical center—with the Jews, with the Italians that have the money."[47] Certainly, the willingness of managers to invest in her brought significant payoffs for Tharpe. Available sources do not detail how much money Tharpe made at the Cotton Club, but Marie Knight recalled that during their tenure, together they earned weekly salaries ranging between five and six thousand dollars.[48]

Market culture gave managers a perspective on the meaning of music significantly different from that held by evangelists and missionaries like Tharpe. For Mills, music was a commodity from which investors like him could make money. Consequently, he had little interest in any souls Tharpe might save. In the Pentecostal community where she grew up, on the other hand, music had no relevance as a commodity, but it served as an integral part of religious fellowship. From this fellowship, Tharpe had received the gift to "move" audiences, namely, the power to enable them to transcend self; it was a religious gift, and it was power. These different perspectives underscore the competing notions of power that helped to distinguish the sacred arena from the commercial realm. In market culture, where power revolved around money, managers like Mills were interested in absorbing audiences, enticing them with images and lifestyles they could consume. In the domain of the sacred, where power centered on the divine rather than on money, individuals placed a high premium on interacting with audiences because the interplay afforded an opportunity to display one's power.[49]

Mills had little, if any, interest in gospel music. Having previously devoted his attention to jazz, Mills took an interest in Tharpe primarily because he sought to broaden the market for African American music and talent. Perhaps he reasoned that attracting a broader market would increase his profits, especially if that market encompassed the white middle-class audience considered by managers in the industry to be the most lucrative. The success he enjoyed managing swing bands led by Duke Ellington and Cab Calloway must have confirmed for Mills that African American talent could draw white middle-class audiences. Now eager to capitalize on the growing interest of the white middle class in swing, Mills turned to Tharpe to sell black sacred music as the bedrock of swing.[50]

Mills conveyed his strategy in *Eighteen Original Negro Spirituals*, a sheet music collection of Tharpe's songs that he published in 1938. He used the preface of the collection to explain the connection between black sacred music and swing: "Countless numbers of people both in this country and Europe have become interested in American music and Negro spirituals—so much so in fact, that they have created a market for a type of standard rhythmic music which might almost be said to have been wholly inspired by the Negro spiritual."[51] Here, Mills used "standard rhythmic music" to refer to swing. To entice enthusiasts of the music, he argued that spirituals comprised the roots of swing. None of the songs in the collection, however, were spirituals, the body of songs created during slavery. This misnomer hardly mattered to Mills. Since "gospel" at that time enjoyed currency among only black audiences, Mills never invoked the term. Instead, he referred to Tharpe's songs as "spirituals." The spate of college choirs, concert artists, and songbooks featuring these nineteenth-century folksongs gave them enormous currency among both black and white audiences throughout the twenties and thirties. If the term "spirituals" attracted a wider audience than did "gospel," its widespread recognition also ultimately posed a problem. "Swinging spirituals," as the songs came to be known, would later provoke considerable controversy among African American audiences.[52]

Since Mills and other managers had more interest in making money than in saving souls, gospel stood little chance of securing a seat at the center of the music industry without Tharpe's drive and talent. On the nightclub stage and in the recording studio, she downplayed her religious convictions. Virtually all the songs Tharpe sang during the period between 1938 and 1941 were familiar to religious communities. Many of them had been recorded during the late twenties and early thirties. Tharpe reinterpreted the songs by making their references to religion decidedly ambiguous. This ambiguity is clear in her rendering of "Hide Me in Thy Bosom," whose lyrics appear at the beginning of this chapter. Thomas Andrew Dorsey, the song's composer, had intended the song to be a prayer to God for divine protection. Tharpe altered the lyrics of the song so that it lost its status as a prayer. Dorsey had stressed the world of sin that surrounded him, but Tharpe spoke of the world of love that surrounded her. Tharpe was careful, however, not to eliminate the divine altogether and thereby turn the song into a reflection about a man who had left her.[53]

To secure a space for gospel in the entertainment industry, Tharpe emphasized the music skills she possessed rather than her religious convictions. She created a smooth sound by using open vocals to deliver her songs, departing from the throaty, textured vocals that had emerged as a common idiom among gospel singers and groups. Even as she featured open vocals in most of her songs, Tharpe deployed textured vocals at particular intervals, retaining the idiom but using it for punctuation and effect.[54] In the process, she produced a sound familiar yet also different. For urban white audiences, Tharpe's guitar gave her sound a distinctly southern flavor. At her death in 1973, one critic insisted that her guitar style stemmed from the blues: "The qualities of that potent swinging vocal style and blues-soaked guitar were very real and very lasting."[55]

The same vocal-guitar combination that felt fresh to urban audiences felt familiar to southern, rural audiences. Curtis Lyles maintained that Tharpe's guitar accompaniment resonated with black southerners like himself: "During that time you had a lot of what they call black troubadours: black guitar players who would play at house parties. So her music reflected that and it reflected more sophistication." Lyles, who grew up in the rural South, found Tharpe's guitar familiar but pointed to her bright, clear vocals as distinctive. "There was something striking about her voice," he recalled. "It was strong, clear and decisive. It was different."[56]

Many black southerners seem to have endorsed the sentiments of Lyles. In the years following World War II, Tharpe embarked on a tour of small southern towns, where capacity crowds came out for her concerts. Abner Jay, a promoter and radio disc jockey in Macon, Georgia, described the pandemonium that erupted in 1949 when Tharpe came to town to perform: "Five thousand tickets were sold, that was the seating capacity. It's estimated that they turned away 6,000. I had never seen nothing like it or heard nothing like it. Downtown near the auditorium the whole streets were full of people, not cars. People—standing room only—trying to get to the auditorium two and three blocks away. I never seen nothing like it, nowhere." A similar scene transpired in other southern towns. Jay, who would later book her concerts, explained the difficulty he had in finding spaces large enough to accommodate the throngs of southerners, black and white, who would show up to hear Tharpe. The largest available facilities consisted of ballparks and stadiums. Large indoor facilities were more difficult to get at the time, since many auditoriums refused to accommodate black audience members. Jay recalled that, faced with this dilemma, he sometimes had to stage her concerts in remote locations. Yet people came from miles around to hear Tharpe.[57]

Tharpe's emergence onto the national stage marked the expansion of a consumer culture in which material wealth and possessions became measures of success. The prominence she enjoyed also placed Tharpe among an expanding corps of black music professionals who comprised a new generation of heroes in black America. Experiencing fame once confined to educated elites, this new generation included growing numbers of singers and musicians. A disproportionate number of women who gained stature as symbols of black achievement were gospel singers like Tharpe. These women, having been prohibited from the pulpit, gained recognition that extended far beyond the church.[58]

Tharpe adapted her faith to lend meaning to her new circumstances. In a 1939 interview, the gospel singer pointed to religion, specifically to the faith she possessed, as the source of her success. A reporter said of Tharpe: "She has a firm belief that her faith is the cause of her amazing overnight popularity, [and she] believes that nothing else can supplant belief in the Lord."[59] Even as she regarded her success as a reward for her faith, religion remained a physical experience for Tharpe and a critical component of her creative process. Yet over time she placed more and more emphasis on the material rewards of her faith, and in the process she embraced religious rituals significantly different from those that prevailed in the Church of God in Christ. Abner Jay, who traveled with Tharpe during the forties and fifties, described her unusual displays of generosity: "And money, money, money, money, money, money, she gave away more than anybody." He explained that Tharpe would stop at street corners to give money to strangers and appear at schools to give children money. On concert tours, especially in the South, Tharpe often boarded in private homes. Jay recalled an incident in South Carolina when Tharpe purchased kitchen appliances for one hostess. "Mama, you need a new stove and refrigerator," Tharpe told the woman before taking her downtown to make the purchase.[60]

The commercial arena, particularly the entertainment industry, was instrumental in facilitating consumer values. In the music business, where Tharpe now worked, money prevailed as the critical medium of exchange, and it assumed an aura that easily rivaled the divine. Yet, for her, money was derived from God, and it had no inherent value. Tharpe needed only to turn to her music to find confirmation of her outlook. Since she regarded her music as a divine gift, Tharpe needed little reassurance that the monies it generated also came from divine sources. When a song came to her at two o'clock in the morning, Tharpe understood that experience as the manifestation of the divine. With her gestures of kindness, then, Tharpe shared the blessings she received from God with those less fortunate, participating in an age-old ritual of Christian charity.

Even as faith continued to be a vital component of her life, Tharpe began to articulate her faith in new ways. Her acts of charity suggest that while the Spirit continued to move Tharpe, she placed more and more emphasis on the rewards of her faith. The circumstances that prompted this shift make it particularly significant. Tharpe, a national celebrity and model of success, generously shared the blessings she received. Yet her charity, which stemmed from her stature, hinged on Tharpe's ability to deliver gospel songs with a decided ambiguity that obscured her religious convictions. The ambiguity Tharpe infused into her songs helped obfuscate the divine, and thus her performances became markedly different from those of her youth, in which gospel had served as a vehicle for displaying the presence of the Spirit.

The ambiguity of the role she embraced, which fell between evangelizing and entertaining, disturbed some African Americans. Richard Cohen, whose family hosted Tharpe and her mother when they traveled to his hometown of Miami, felt uncomfortable with the feelings and motivations that infused Tharpe's popular music. Was her behavior an expression of mere showmanship—the manipulation of outward appearances—or did it stem from sincere religious convictions? Cohen remained uncertain whether she "really actually truly deep down within felt [them]."[61] A similar uncertainty led some African Americans to disavow Tharpe, insisting that she had sacrificed gospel and abandoned religion altogether.

If some African Americans objected to the modifications Tharpe made in her music, others found them deeply meaningful. Together, the controversy and popularity she generated make Tharpe a pivotal figure for understanding the changing parameters of religion among African Americans. Detractors dismissed Tharpe's new form of evangelizing, insisting that she was nothing more than an entertainer posing as an evangelist. Supporters, deeply moved by her music, reached new levels of spiritual existence. In these competing responses, African Americans voiced divergent views about just what constituted religious experience. Did it revolve around the divine, or did it center on experience, specifically transcendence, that could spring from sources other than the divine? As she moved from churches and revivals to nightclubs, Tharpe abandoned neither gospel nor her religious convictions. Instead, she carved out a niche for gospel in a mass-consumer society and helped to forge new modes of practicing religion.[62]

OVER THE COURSE of the twentieth century, a mode of worship coalesced into the discrete music style we know as gospel. In the Pentecostal community where Tharpe grew up, music served as a vehicle for both sharing fellowship and displaying the presence of God. The emphasis Pentecostals placed on celebrating the Spirit led them to pursue evangelizing activities that took them to the recording studio, the street, and the radio station. The music business, however, significantly differed from the church or even the street, where Tharpe had evangelized. In the market culture that dominated the music business, human relations were governed by money. In this context, a mode of worship became a discrete music style and ultimately a commodity capable of being mass-produced and disseminated across the nation. The Cotton Club engagement propelled Tharpe to the center of the entertainment industry. With access to the market, Tharpe became instrumental in popularizing gospel beyond the church, situating the music between religion and commerce.

Tharpe's music and her career trajectory underscore the importance of religion as a vibrant arena that African Americans fashioned to give meaning to daily life. The solo singing and infectious rhythms that became foundational elements of gospel emerged inside communities like the Church of God in Christ at the turn of the century precisely because believers used singing, dancing, and shouting to give testimony to the presence of God in their lives. Pentecostals regarded the talents and skills members possessed as evidence of sacred power. A half-century later, Tharpe did not assert that any spiritual directives compelled her to move to the nightclub circuit. Instead, she pointed to the influence commercial venues wielded, and she conveyed just how much secular values had taken hold in America: "There were more souls in the nighteries that needed saving," she asserted, "than there were in the church." Departing from her predecessors, who made the church the cornerstone of their evangelical work, Tharpe pointed gospel in a new direction and worked to secure a place for the music on the nightclub circuit.

The popularity and controversy Tharpe generated signaled the emergence of a new social order in which local music styles like gospel became part of a national, mass-produced culture. Whether gospel prevailed in local black communities or entered mainstream American culture, the music remained a vibrant form of religious expression. During the late thirties, it certainly struck some as outrageous that Tharpe was singing gospel on a nightclub circuit dominated by jazz bands. Yet such activity became commonplace in the postwar era, when gospel emerged as a leading form of popular music. By the fifties, African Americans across the nation were congregating in theaters and baseball parks to have church. The appeal the music generated among southerners rendered gospel a critical vehicle for disseminating a national culture in the South.[63]

Notes

1. This song originated with Thomas Andrew Dorsey, who wrote the music and lyrics and titled it "Hide Me in Thy Bosom." On stage and in the recording studio, however, Sister Rosetta Tharpe slightly altered the lyrics. In addition, she gave her rearranged version the distinctive title "Rock Me." For a recorded version of the song, see *1938–1941*, vol. 1 of *Sister Rosetta Tharpe: Complete Recorded Works 1938–1944 in Chronological Order*, reissue compact disk, DOCD-5334 (Vienna: Document Records, 1995). My sincere gratitude goes to the many individuals who generously shared their gospel experiences in oral interviews. I would also like to thank friends and colleagues whose comments and support enhanced this work: M. Jacqui Alexander, Consuella Brown, William Dargan, Pamela

Grundy, and Carmen Whalen. Finally, I wish to extend a special thanks to the editors of this volume, Donald Mathews and Beth Barton Schweiger, whose substantive comments made revising this article an invaluable learning experience.

2. "Night Club Soulsaver," *Baltimore Afro-American*, January 11, 1941, 14.

3. Arna Bontemps, "Rock, Church, Rock!" *Common Ground*, Autumn 1942, 77.

4. See Horace Clarence Boyer, *How Sweet the Sound: The Golden Age of Gospel Music* (Washington, D.C.: Elliott & Clark Publishing, 1995), and Lawrence Levine, *Black Culture and Black Consciousness: Afro-American Folk Thought from Slavery to Freedom* (New York: Oxford University Press, 1977), 174–89. For an alternative perspective that examines the later development of gospel in black Baptist churches, see Michael W. Harris, *The Rise of Gospel Blues: The Music of Thomas Andrew Dorsey in the Urban Church* (New York: Oxford University Press, 1992).

5. Viv Broughton, *Black Gospel: An Illustrated History of the Gospel Sound* (Poole, England: Blandford Press, 1985); Anthony Heilbut, *The Gospel Sound: Good News and Bad Times*, 3d ed. (New York: Proscenium Publishers, 1989), 189–96.

6. For an excellent overview of the lining-out tradition, see William Dargan, *Long Black Songs: Dr. Watts, Hymn Singing, and the Music of African Americans* (Berkeley: University of California Press, forthcoming). For a discussion of the evolution of choirs and how the music produced in that context differed from gospel, see Harris, *The Rise of Gospel Blues*.

7. Bishop J. O. Patterson, Rev. German R. Ross, and Mrs. Julia Mason Atkins, *History and Formative Years of the Church of God in Christ with Excerpts from the Life and Works of Its Founder—Bishop C. H. Mason* (Memphis: Church of God in Christ Publishing House, 1969); Charles Pleas, *Fifty Years of Achievement, from 1906–1956: A Period in History of the Church of God in Christ* (Memphis: Church of God in Christ, 1956; reprint, 1991). Since Holiness and Pentecostalism stemmed from tensions among African Americans over the meaning of education and religion in daily life, gospel music provoked considerable controversy during its formative years. I explore these issues in greater detail in *Singing in My Soul: Black Gospel Music in a Secular Age* (Chapel Hill: University of North Carolina Press, 2004).

8. Maudelle Oliver, interview by the author, April 30, 1993, by telephone, tape recording.

9. Nat Hentoff, *Hear Me Talkin' to You: The Story of Jazz as Told by the Men Who Made It* (New York: Dover, 1955; reprint, 1966), 249–51.

10. Lucille J. Cornelius, *The Pioneer: History of the Church of God in Christ* (Memphis: Church of God in Christ Publishing, 1975), 69.

11. Patterson, Ross, and Atkins, *History and Formative Years of the Church of God in Christ*, 19.

12. Horace Boyer, interview by the author, January 23, 1992, by telephone, tape recording.

13. Sister Rosetta Tharpe, "What He Done for Me," on *1938–1941*.

14. Minister Marie Knight, interview by the author, November 14, 1996, New York, tape recording.

15. Agnes Campbell, interview by the author, April 26, 1993, by telephone, tape recording.

16. Musette Hubbard, interview by the author, April 29, 1993, by telephone, tape recording.

17. Richard Cohen, interview by the author, January 22, 1992, Miami, tape recording.

18. Ibid., January 29, 1992.

19. For an example of this pattern, see Cornelius, *The Pioneer*; Patterson, Ross, and Atkins, *History and Formative Years of the Church of God in Christ*; and Pleas, *Fifty Years of Achievement*.

20. The similarities between blues and gospel have led scholars in recent years to pose new questions about these music styles. Some have examined the religious dimensions of blues; see Jon Michael Spencer, *Blues and Evil* (Knoxville: University of Tennessee Press, 1993). Others have explored the influence of blues techniques on gospel music. For example, Michael Harris coined the term "gospel blues" to refer to gospel. See Harris, *The Rise of Gospel Blues*.

21. "Fastest-Growing Church," *Ebony*, August 1949, 59–60; Paul Oliver, *Songsters and Saints: Vocal Traditions on Race Records* (New York: Cambridge University Press, 1984), 169–98; Pleas, *Fifty Years of Achievement*.

22. George Hancock, interview by Patricia Wells, February 1988, quoted in Patricia Wells, "Historical Overview of the Establishment of the Church of God in Christ" (Ph.D. diss., International Seminary, 1989), 93.

23. Maudelle Oliver, interview.

24. For an overview of the role women played in the Holiness and Pentecostal movements, see Cheryl Townsend Gilkes, "'Together and in Harness': Women's Traditions in the Sanctified Church," *Signs: Journal of Women in Culture and Society* 10 (Summer 1985): 678–99.

25. Oliver, *Songsters and Saints*, 169–98.

26. Terry Gross, producer, "Interview with Marion Williams," *Fresh Air* (National Public Radio, December 6, 1993).

27. Agnes Campbell, interview.

28. For a discussion of the importance of the street, and of commercial districts more generally, within black urban communities, see Elsa Barkley Brown and Gregg D. Kimball, "Mapping the Terrain of Black Richmond," *Journal of Urban History* 21 (March 1995): 296–346; Tera W. Hunter, *To 'Joy My Freedom: Southern Black Women's Lives and Labors after the Civil War* (Cambridge, Mass.: Harvard University Press, 1997), 45–73, 145–67; and Earl Lewis, *In Their Own Interests: Race, Class, and Power in Twentieth-Century Norfolk, Virginia* (Berkeley: University of California Press, 1991), 89–109.

29. Agnes Campbell, interview. Campbell contrasted street and tent meetings in this interview:

JJ: Now I'm curious, what's the difference between a tent meeting and a street meeting?

AC: . . . A street meeting you have no covering, you just there on the corner. But a tent, you know what a tent is? Well, you'd have a tent and people would come into the tent and have a seat. . . .

JJ: But how long would a street meeting last?

AC: About an hour.

JJ: How long would a tent meeting last?

AC: Oh, two or three hours. Maybe we'd start at 8:00 and get out at 10:30, 11:00.

30. Ibid.

31. Paul Oliver, *Blues off the Record: Thirty Years of Blues Commentary* (New York: De Capo Press, 1988), 88–94, 99–102, and *Songsters and Saints*, 208.

32. Musette Hubbard, interview.

33. Agnes Campbell, interview.

34. Gussie Hamilton, interview by the author, January 15, 1993, Miami, tape recording.

35. For a discussion of the music that guitar evangelists recorded, see Oliver, *Songsters and Saints*, 206–28.

36. Malcolm Shaw, "Arizona Dranes and Okeh," *Storyville*, February 1970, 85–89; Arizona Dranes, *Arizona Dranes, 1926–1928*, reissue LP, Herwin 210 ([Glen Cove, N.Y.?]: Herwin Records, [197-?]).

37. Albert Murray, *Stomping the Blues* (New York: McGraw Hill, 1976; reprint, Random House, 1982), 3–76; Larry Neal, "Ethos of the Blues," in *Sacred Music of the Secular City*, ed. Jon Michael Spencer, special issue, *Black Sacred Music: A Journal of Theomusicology* 6, no. 1 (Spring 1992): 36–46.

38. Leighla W. Lewis, "Sister Tharpe Swings Hymns at Cotton Club," *Washington Afro-American*, January 14, 1939, entertainment section, 10. Thomas Andrew Dorsey, regarded as the "Father of Gospel Music," was instrumental in disseminating gospel. For an extensive discussion of his role in popularizing the music, see Harris, *The Rise of Gospel Blues*.

39. Richard Cohen, interview.

40. For an overview of race records, see Robert M. W. Dixon and John Goodrich, *Recording the Blues* (New York: Stein & Day, 1970), 41–61, and Ronald Clifford Foreman, "Jazz and Race Records, 1920–1932: Their Origins and Their Significance for the Record Industry and Society" (Ph.D. diss., University of Illinois, 1968), 265–75. For a discussion of sacred race records, see Evelyn Brooks Higginbotham, "Rethinking Vernacular Culture: Black Religion and Race Records in the 1920s and 1930s," in *The House That Race Built: Black Americans, U.S. Terrain*, ed. Wahneema Lubiano (New York: Pantheon, 1997), 157–77, and Oliver, *Songsters and Saints*, 140–228.

41. Leonard Feather, "Mills: A Life of Being in Swing," *Los Angeles Times*, April 28, 1985, calendar section, 88; Jim Haskins, *The Cotton Club* (New York: Random House, 1977).

42. Jerma Jackson, "Testifying at the Cross: Thomas Andrew Dorsey, Sister Rosetta

Tharpe, and the Politics of African-American Sacred and Secular Music" (Ph.D. diss., Rutgers, The State University of New Jersey, 1995), 263–78.

43. Lewis, "Sister Tharpe Swings Hymns at Cotton Club."

44. "Sister Tharpe, Psalm Singer Signed by Mills," *Pittsburgh Courier*, October 15, 1938, 13.

45. Quoted in Charles L. Ponce de Leon, "Idols and Icons: Representations of Celebrity in American Culture, 1850–1940" (Ph.D. diss., Rutgers, The State University of New Jersey, 1992), 14–15.

46. Minister Marie Knight, interview by the author, March 20, 1997, New York, tape recording.

47. Ibid.

48. Horace Boyer, "Contemporary Gospel Music," *The Black Perspective in Music* 7 (Spring 1979): 7; Heilbut, *The Gospel Sound*, 189–96; "Musical Empire of Felds Has Capital in Back Room," *Washington Post*, September 30, 1956, copy consulted in Clipping File, Feld Family, Washingtonian Collection, Public Library, Washington, D.C.; Maurice Zolotow, "Harlem's Great White Father," *Saturday Evening Post*, September 27, 1941, 37, 40, 64, 66, 68.

49. For market culture, see Jean-Christophe Agnew, *Worlds Apart: The Market and the Theater in Anglo-American Thought, 1550–1750* (New York: Cambridge University Press, 1986), and T. J. Jackson Lears, "Introduction," in *The Culture of Consumption*, eds. Richard Wightman Fox and T. J. Jackson Lears (New York: Pantheon, 1983).

50. Cab Calloway and Bryant Rollins, *Of Minnie the Moocher and Me* (New York: Thomas Y. Crowell, 1976), 110–11; James Lincoln Collier, *Duke Ellington* (New York: Oxford University Press, 1987), 64–74; John Hammond with Irving Townsend, *John Hammond on Record: An Autobiography* (New York: Ridge Press, 1977; reprint, Penguin Books, 1981), 123–39; David W. Stowe, *Swing Changes: Big Band Jazz in New Deal America* (Cambridge, Mass.: Harvard University Press, 1994), 94–140.

51. Sister Rosetta Tharpe, *Eighteen Original Negro Spirituals*, sheet music collection (New York: Mills Music, 1938).

52. For a discussion of the popularity spirituals enjoyed, see Tim Brooks, "'Might Take One Disc of This Trash as a Novelty': Early Recordings by the Fisk Jubilee Singers and the Popularization of 'Negro Folk Music,'" *American Music* 18, no. 3 (Fall 2000): 278–316, and John Lovell Jr., *Black Song: The Forge and the Flame* (New York: Macmillan, 1972; reprint, Paragon House, 1986). For a discussion of the controversy around swinging spirituals, see "Dr. Harvey's Article on Insidious Evil of Swinging Spirituals Brings Many Letters," *Pittsburgh Courier*, March 18, 1939, 15; "Fight against Defilement of Negro Spirituals Continues," *Pittsburgh Courier*, April 22, 1939, 15; "Must Stop Desecration of Spirituals," *Pittsburgh Courier*, March 25, 1939, 15; "Says Swinging Spiritual Is Disgrace to Race," *Pittsburgh Courier*, March 11, 1939, 15; "Teachers, Song Writers, and Choir Singers Join in Protest against Swinging Spirituals," *Pittsburgh Courier*, April 1, 1939, 15.

53. Thomas A. Dorsey, "Golden Years of Music," [1970], Thomas Andrew Dorsey Collection, box 6, Fisk University, Nashville, Tenn.

54. Boyer, "Contemporary Gospel Music"; Heilbut, *The Gospel Sound*, 189–96.

55. Max Jones, "Sister Rosetta Tharpe: Queen of Gospel," *Melody Maker* 40 (October 27, 1973): 40.

56. Curtis Lyles, interview by the author, April 14, 1994, Brooklyn, tape recording.

57. Abner Jay, interview by the author, May 25, 1993, by telephone, tape recording.

58. During the early decades of the twentieth century, the vast majority of black Americans regarded educated elites, specifically those who made inroads for the race, as symbols of success. In the twenties, these symbols began to include singers, musicians, and also athletes. The pattern accelerated during the thirties and forties. For evidence of the new pattern, see *Ebony*, a magazine directed toward black audiences that began publication in the mid-forties.

59. Lewis, "Sister Tharpe Swings Hymns at Cotton Club."

60. Abner Jay, interview.

61. Richard Cohen, interview.

62. I explore the controversy Tharpe sparked and the diverse experiences her music generated in *Singing in My Soul*. For a discussion of the religious dimensions of popular culture, see Eric Michael Mazur, *God in the Details: American Religion in Popular Culture* (New York: Routledge, 2001), and Spencer, *Blues and Evil*.

63. For evidence of how the popularity gospel enjoyed during the postwar era prompted changes in how audiences engaged the music, see "20,000 Watch Wedding of Sister Rosetta Tharpe," *Ebony*, October 1951, 27–28, 30; "15,000 Attend Sister Tharpe's Wedding," *Richmond Afro-American*, July 14, 1951, 1–2; B. Dexter Allgood, "Black Gospel in New York City and Joe William Bostic, Sr.," *The Black Perspective in Music* 18 (1990): 101–15; Lee Hildebrand and Opal Nations, introduction to brochure notes for *The Great 1955 Shrine Concert*, reissue compact disk, SPCD-7045-2 (Berkeley: Specialty Records, 1993); and Thermon T. Ruth, *Gospel: From the Church to the Apollo Theater* (Brooklyn: T. Ruth Publications, 1995). For an alternative perspective that dismisses the changes in gospel as examples of crass commercialism, see George T. Nierenberg's film *Say Amen Somebody!* (New York: GTN Productions, 1983).

For Further Reading

Gilkes, Cheryl Townsend. *If It Wasn't for the Women: Black Women's Experience and Womanist Culture in Church and Community*. Maryknoll, N.Y.: Orbis Books, 2001. In this collection of essays, Gilkes devotes considerable attention to the experiences of women in African American Holiness and Pentecostal churches. Since some of the most important innovators in gospel were women, this book provides important background about the music.

Harris, Michael W. *The Rise of Gospel Blues: The Music of Thomas Andrew Dorsey in the*

Urban Church. New York: Oxford University Press, 1992. In this biography of a legendary gospel composer, Harris examines the rise of gospel in black Baptist churches. He traces the controversy that surrounded the music during the twenties and the eventual acceptance of gospel music during the late thirties.

Higginbotham, Evelyn Brooks. "Rethinking Vernacular Culture: Black Religion and Race Records in the 1920s and 1930s." In *The House That Race Built: Black Americans, U.S. Terrain*, edited by Wahneema Lubiano, 157–77. New York: Pantheon Books, 1997. This article provides an insightful exploration of sacred race records produced during the twenties. Focusing on black Baptist preachers who recorded, Higginbotham insists that the focus on black secular music distorts the appeal that sacred recordings enjoyed among African Americans.

Hinson, Glenn. *Fire in My Bones: Transcendence and the Holy Spirit in African American Gospel*. Philadelphia: University of Pennsylvania Press, 2000. Hinson provides an insightful exploration of the religious dimensions of gospel by chronicling the anniversary celebration of a gospel group based in North Carolina. With this focus, he explores how the sanctified experience the holy across time and space.

Levine, Lawrence. *Black Culture and Black Consciousness: Afro-American Folk Thought from Slavery to Freedom*. New York: Oxford University Press, 1977. Levine explores the transformation of African American culture in the transition from slavery to freedom and situates the emergence of gospel within the context of this important social process.

Lornell, Kip. *"Happy in the Service of the Lord": African-American Sacred Vocal Harmony Quartets in Memphis*. 2d ed. Knoxville: University of Tennessee Press, 1995. Gospel music consists of two traditions: the quartet tradition, often dominated by men, and the solo tradition, often dominated by women. Lornell, who focuses on gospel quartets in Memphis, Tennessee, examines how the commercialization of gospel helped transform the music within one local community.

9

LYNN LYERLY

Women and Southern Religion

Imagine Sunday morning in a colonial Virginia parish. The parson has already started the service, but outside, a circle of gentlemen lingers to discuss the prices of land, tobacco, and slaves. They enter the church late, parading together down the aisle to their family pews. They expect a short, erudite sermon, and since they control the clergyman's salary and tenure, it is unlikely he will disappoint.[1]

Such is the indelible scholarly image of early American Anglican worship and, by implication, practice. It is one that focuses on elite white men: their power, their public posture, and their tepid interest in worship. The image also reflects the tendentious memory of Bishop William Meade, who recalled a colonial clergy more interested in hunting foxes than in saving souls.[2] If we imagine faithful women, however, Anglican piety looks radically different. Women (who were in the pews before services began) made up the majority of communicants; if their husbands, brothers, and fathers ruled the church through the vestry, they themselves were in charge of the sacred lives of families. They readied their homes for baptisms, marriages, and funerals, reared their children in the faith, pondered devotional literature, and supported their churches with gifts and bequests. They could also be, insisted an optimistic clergyman, a "powerful Means to win Men from Heathenism to Christianity."[3] Women among the New Lights, too, and later among the Wesleyans, made the church possible in the American South; indeed, one could transpose Ann Braude's reference to American religious history to say that southern women's history *is* southern religious history.[4] Focusing on women transforms our view of southern religion; focusing on women and religion transforms our view of southern history; and doing so suggests ways in which southern honor was contested by women early in the republic[5] and later in the twentieth century.[6] Moving from a base that seemed perfectly respectable—the hearth and the churches—women developed their capacity for nursing and nurturing into public benevolent action; in the process, they often transformed their roles. Women's innovative work in home missions, for example, prepared the way for a surprising and vibrant Social Gospel.[7] Through religion, African American women contested racism in a myriad of ways as they held the church together. White women used their culture's glorification of mothers and wives to carve out larger spheres of responsibility in religious and public affairs. In their interracial work, churchwomen challenged segregation and lynching. Even those beliefs and values that were shared by men and women often had different meanings for each sex.

Scholarship on southern women and religion challenges models of understanding structured upon institutions and men. Two terms used frequently— "church" and "ministry"—must be redefined when women are foregrounded. Churches were (and are) more than the sum of their trustees, clergy, theological discourse, and denominational bureaucracies. In almost every era, in almost every religious body in the United States, women have outnumbered men in membership and attendance at services. Women's ministries have included much work they shared with pastors, such as visiting the sick and elderly, rearing children in the faith, comforting the bereaved, helping to bring others to God, and practicing prayer. Women also led the way in interracial, charitable, reform, and children's educational work. Women's missionary societies were surely a key part of the church as well as an important ministry. Beyond the formal women's societies were also the noninstitutional, parallel, and even "shadow" churches of believers who stretched the notion of heresy perhaps to the breaking point by harboring beliefs and insights that were reassuring and meaningful to women and never submitted to men for approval. In the 1870s, women who held such beliefs might have found solace in a lingering spiritualism that they fabricated from pain, suffering, and the death of loved ones.[8] Even a Georgia novelist of the next generation, famous for her attachment to traditional religion and piety, could, through the very process of writing, discover and broadcast religious insights decidedly different from those of male orthodoxy.[9]

Putting southern women at the center of attention has required scholars to rethink some timeworn historical constructions. As women's historians now understand a previous century's gendered "spheres" and the continuum from private to public in increasingly sophisticated ways, they discover that women's religious experience and history demonstrates the complexity of women's thought and action.[10] Religion is public and private, communal and personal, horizontal as well as vertical. Women attended public services and joined church organizations; they formed their own associations, which sustained them as they participated in family devotions, prepared the home for religious celebrations and rituals, and instructed their children in the faith. This description reflects a functional interpretation of what women did, but they also had personal, interior religious lives that could not be contained. They communed with God, prayed, read Scripture, pored over devotional literature, and searched their hearts for godliness and sin. To further complicate matters, some women made public their private religious lives through testimony or the written word. The terms "public" and "private" are still useful, but the study of women and religion must encompass both and envision a spectrum from private to public rather than a division between the two.

The private-public life of Frances Bumpass suggests the intellectual resources that religion provided to women who might not have taken the North/ South divide as seriously as politicians did and who could expand the power given to them by the indwelling of the Holy Spirit into the foundation of a women's constituency. Bumpass repudiated the ideology of women's rights while asserting the prerogatives of faithful disciples in Christ—female or not—to express the power of God publicly, privately, and persistently. Her Methodist-birthed journal, the *Weekly Message*, attracted male as well as female readers, but it was the latter whom she attempted to cajole, push, and preach into taking up a more assertive Christian discipleship that alone would justify their public proclamation that they were perfecting their lives and faith. Through her "Dove"— the symbol of the Holy Spirit and her name for the *Message*—Bumpass brought to her readers a transatlantic constituency of women who were as inspired by Phoebe Palmer of New York City as they were by Bumpass's own pastoral care and homiletic urgency. Bumpass used this pulpit to promote and consolidate what she and her constituents considered to be a "sisterhood" of holy women who desired nothing less than the social and spiritual transformation of the world. Perhaps this was a lot to expect from a small-circulation journal edited by a minister's widow in Guilford County, North Carolina, from the mid-1850s to the 1870s. But the eschatological hope and the self-confidence it elicited represented the ways in which the substance—not the function—of religion filled the minds of women whose granddaughters would continue to proclaim the *Message* through missionary societies and an inchoate Social Gospel.[11]

A survey of the historical literature also confirms that we need to bridge the divide that still exists between scholars who ask what religion did *to* women and those who ask what religion did *for* women. These are loaded questions; the first presupposes patriarchal oppression and the second female empowerment. But there are examples of religious oppression and empowerment in any single congregation and in any woman's experience. One recurring pattern in women's religious history has been that whenever women's religious organizations became too powerful, male church leaders attempted to take them over, limit their power, seize their assets, or dissolve them entirely. Which should be emphasized: women's organizational power or men's efforts to limit it? Women's religiosity cannot be reduced to what they were or were not allowed to do by male clergy and deacons. Religion fills the mind with a language that can be used to understand goals, disappointments, responsibilities, and deferred victory; it shapes perception, orders the world, provides meaning. It comforts and disquiets, rewards and punishes. By widening the scope of the questions we ask of the sources, we can better analyze the extraordinarily rich views of experience, culture, and ideology that religion provides, and, in turn, we can better understand the South.

Evelyn Brooks Higginbotham reminds us that "too often, 'minister' functions as a metonym for church."[12] Religious life did not begin with the presence of ministers nor cease with their absence, and, as any number of ministers learned, they held no patent on religious influence. The shortage of both Anglican and Catholic priests increased the moral authority of colonial women, who assumed responsibility for catechizing their children and passing on their faith.[13] Evangelical women in the colonial and early republican South acted as spiritual guides and counselors. Women's influence within the churches was profound; they led others to convert, resisted ungodly patriarchs, contested the male culture of honor, and provided the primary spiritual and material support for fledgling churches and their preachers. Pious African American women have long been recognized as "mothers of the church," and trouble awaited a pastor who did not defer to them.[14] Nor have women been, in all times and in all churches, excluded from church governance and formal leadership. Early Baptist women voted and served as deaconesses in some churches; early Methodist women served as class leaders and exhorters.[15] Mary Lee Cagle was one of many New Testament Church of Christ women who, in the 1890s, preached and organized new congregations.[16] Women as energetic and innovative as she founded the majority of black Spiritual churches in New Orleans and the first Spiritual church in Nashville.[17]

In public services, women have played important roles. Women have never been absolutely silent in southern churches. Early Baptist and Methodist women prayed in public, exhorted, and on rare occasions preached.[18] In the early nineteenth century, although male evangelical leaders began to emphasize their support for patriarchy and slavery, they could not prevent insistent women from testifying.[19] Indeed, even after it was clear that the patriarchy would attempt to silence women through disapproval, intimidation, and ridicule, a woman such as Virginian Martha Hancock Wheat could frequent protracted meetings, annual conferences, and prayer meetings to pray at great length, celebrate the power of the spirit, proclaim sanctification, and receive thanks from the newly ordained that they could never have received such grace but through her ministrations.[20] Evangelical women continued to pray in public and to testify in antebellum Mississippi.[21] In the post–Civil War Southern Baptist Convention, controversy arose over women's testimony precisely because some male leaders believed women were using testimony time to preach and teach,[22] but this did not prevent Southern Baptist women from mounting their own independent movement under the symbolism provided by Charlotte "Lottie" Digges Moon to create the Women's Missionary Union.[23] Even in churches led by men otherwise insistent that women "keep silence," women were never barred from singing; otherwise, the silence would have been deafening. Gospel star Willie Mae Ford Smith was one of many women whose gift of song was a form of ministry. Her singing revived, inspired, and enriched the spirituality of her listeners.[24]

Some women preached despite denominational prohibitions. Sarah Ann Hughes served as pastor in Fayetteville and Wilson's Mills, North Carolina. Luzerne Chipman, who was white, drove her buggy between Raleigh and Goldsboro and back, spreading the holiness gospel before the Civil War; she also published her theological musings.[25] When Hughes, along with five other African Methodist Episcopal (AME) preaching women, appealed to the General Conference in 1884, the hierarchy decreed that women could not be given pastorates, though it did allow preaching women to serve as "evangelists."[26] Within a decade, an African Methodist Episcopal Zion (AMEZ) bishop could justify the itinerant role for women by saying that men simply could not do the job! Men may have opposed ordaining women—and some women may have done so, too —but by the late 1890s black women were presenting themselves to be thus consecrated.[27] Southern women have, in each generation, pushed the boundaries of what churchmen thought permissible. In the colonial and antebellum South, for the vast majority of women, churches were the only public arenas in which they had voice and influence, usually without official office, always without universal approval, and persistently with determination and courage. The power of the Spirit and the conviction born of knowing the Bible's liberating implications did not create the variety of secular reform movements identified with northern women, perhaps, but there were nonetheless movements led by tough, pushy, and insistent women. In the late nineteenth century, when growing numbers of southern women began carving out larger public roles, they did so primarily through church societies such as the Women's Missionary Union and the Women's Missionary Society or through organizations not associated with the church such as the Woman's Christian Temperance Union, the Young Women's Christian Association, and the Federation of Women's Clubs.[28]

Congregational life was not determined by the actions of clergy or male administrators. A wide variety of women's religious activity—Sunday schools, fairs, potlucks, guilds, prayer meetings, benevolent societies, sodalities, visits to shut-ins or the sick—took place independently of services.[29] And in those services, women's imprint was everywhere. From the altar cloths they sewed to the carpets and stained glass windows they purchased, the statues they cleaned, and the music they provided, women shaped and enriched the experience of worship. For eighteenth-century Anglicans, the home was a center of religious activity, for many baptisms, marriages, and funerals took place there.[30] In the early republic, women began developing a parallel church through sewing circles, missionary organizations, Sunday schools, and benevolent societies. Women's fundraising activities enhanced parish life through gifts to the church or its causes and provided social outlets for parishioners in rural communities, towns, and cities. Church architecture began to reflect the parish life women had created, as parlors and kitchens were added to church buildings. Women ministered to the sick in hospital beds and to prisoners in their cells; they ministered to orphans and paupers, and they donated their time, their skills, and (as Elizabeth Turner has so beautifully shown) their aesthetic sensibility to a church desperately in need of it. Women's organizations evolved and developed local, conference, diocesan, and national levels of structure, paralleling those of the institutional church. The parallel church enriched the social lives of congregations and expanded religious ministries.[31]

For Roman Catholic laywomen, devotional societies and confraternities offered opportunities for spiritual growth and service. The Ladies Congregation of the Children of Mary in French colonial New Orleans, for example, served the Blessed Virgin with prayer and benevolence; in the 1730s, more than one-third of the city's free women—from the wealthiest to the poorest—belonged. Members had to meet the strictest moral standards and were required to perform a regimen of devotions, prayers, and recitations of the rosary. Women of the confraternity were more active in proselytizing slaves than any other organization in the colony. Despite the shortage of priests, French colonial Catholics were not, as some have claimed, indifferent to the faith. As with colonial Anglicans, scholars have generalized from the behavior of men.[32]

The route to leadership and influence for women was often through a separate organization. Religious orders and congregations offered Catholic women a respectable alternative to marriage and motherhood. The first order in the South was that of the Ursulines, who came to New Orleans in 1727. They established a girls' school for elite boarders and day students of more modest means and held free classes for African Americans and Native Americans. The Ursuline convent functioned as a center of the Catholic community in the city, especially for women; it sheltered abused wives, protected orphans, and trained young women in the faith. The sisters also provided nursing care at the military hospital. By 1860, there were more than nineteen congregations serving in the South. Nursing, caring for orphans, and teaching were their primary ministries, and they pursued them as befitted white southerners.[33] White women religious had adapted to southern mores quickly: order after order, by means of either novitiates' dowries or North American sponsors, came to own slaves. The Ursulines, given slaves in their contract with the Company of the Indies, came to view assaults on their independence in ways historians have associated with revolutionary-era planters. During their lengthy fight to keep a Jesuit confessor, the order's mother superior protested the effort to force a Capuchin on them, using rhetoric that certainly had more resonance in slaveholding Louisiana than in France: "It would be vain for them to wish to enslave us. We have not given up the liberty of conscience we enjoyed in France to come to place ourselves in slavery."[34] The Ursulines understood absolute power when applied to themselves, perhaps, but how they understood their stewardship when they were the enslavers is unclear; scholarship on women religious in the South too often borders on hagiography. The story of slaveholding nuns, for example, has yet to be told with analytical sophistication. How women religious understood their roles, what they expected of slaves, and how they received emancipation is still unknown. Investigations of Catholicism among slaves belonging to women's communities, the impact of this presence upon the nuns' understanding of faith, and the moral dilemmas nuns faced could shed light on Catholic history, women's history, and the history of slavery.[35]

The Oblate Sisters of Providence, the first order of black nuns in the South, played a central role in the black Catholic community of Baltimore. Formed in 1828, the Oblates operated a school for girls, ran night schools for adults, staffed homes for widows and orphans, and organized sodalities for laymen and laywomen.[36] When the Pope recognized the order in 1831, its members vowed to "renounce the world to consecrate themselves to God and to the Christian education of young girls of colour." In several ways, the Oblates challenged prevailing racial thinking. Simply by professing, these women proclaimed their chastity and sanctity; their habits were visual reminders that they rejected white notions of black women's impurity. Their rule restricted the mother superior's power to correct a sister's faults in front of others, thus ensuring that discipline in the convent would not mirror the humiliation blacks suffered outside convent walls. And in a stunning racial reversal, in 1837 the Oblates reserved the rear six benches of their chapel for whites who attended services there.[37]

Protestant women, except for those who belonged to a few short-lived but dedicated orders of specially consecrated deaconesses, organized in lay associations to exercise a ministerial function.[38] In the early nineteenth century, Protestant women in towns and cities formed denominational benevolent, missionary, temperance, and mite societies.[39] Considering how few women had independent control of family resources, the financial contributions of these societies could be substantial. In 1845, the year the Southern Baptist Convention was organized, women actually provided one-third of all monies for foreign missions.[40] Women, through benevolence, provided a central (and sometimes the only) source of social services in the antebellum South. In Petersburg, Virginia, as Suzanne Lebsock observes, "voluntary, organized charity was the exclusive province of women" until 1858.[41]

In the late-nineteenth- and early-twentieth-century South, missionary societies were the most significant Protestant women's organizations.[42] These societies met a range of women's needs and provided a wide variety of services. Meetings often opened with prayer and devotions, creating a space for women's spiritual life between Sabbath worship and private religiosity. Some societies, such as the Baptist Women's Missionary Union, issued prayer cards to members, who would pray each month for a specific mission need; thus the society encouraged women to incorporate church work abroad into their daily spirituality. The goals of mission work were threefold. Evangelism and charity went hand in hand. Yet just as important was women's desire to widen their sphere of church work.[43] Through missionary societies, women learned how to run meetings, set agendas, manage budgets, advertise, and raise funds. From organizing children's bands to establishing missionary training schools, women shaped the priorities of their churches and carved out increasingly larger areas for their ministry and leadership. Foreign missions, publicized in periodicals, connected southern women to the world outside the United States. Some local and state organizations supported specific missionaries, enabling women to have a more personal connection to evangelism abroad. Female missionaries, whose roles were similar to those of pastors, widened women's sense of the kinds of service open to them. A number of women who rose to prominence in southern churches first felt called to ministry as foreign missionaries.[44]

Women's work in home missions is a vital chapter in southern women's religious history and in southern history generally. Historians looking for a Social Gospel movement in the South initially examined the efforts of male church leaders only to conclude that the Social Gospel had relatively little influence in the region.[45] The picture changes dramatically when women's home missions become the focus. Methodist women used the language of the Social Gospel (they were building "the kingdom of God on earth"), read the works of Social Gospel theologians, and emphasized the dignity and worth of each individual. The original purpose of the Methodist Woman's Department of Church Extension, established in 1886, was to build and repair parsonages in the American West, but women in that organization became involved in a wide range of reforms from temperance to child labor laws. Women in home missions gradually —and with increasingly radical insights into the nature of capitalism—turned from treating the effects of social ills to identifying and eliminating their causes.[46] Southern Methodist (MECS, for Methodist Episcopal Church, South) women never lost sight of the importance of saving souls, but for them salvation entailed a broader vision of social progress than changing individuals' personal orientation; social and cultural context was important, too.

Women may have viewed home missions as a form of service, and, indeed, Baptists called their home missions work "Personal Service," but it was clearly a ministry, too. Texas Baptist women in home mission societies received a yearly questionnaire that asked how many visits they had made to hospitals, prisons, and shut-ins, how many tracts and Bibles they had distributed, how many jobs they had secured for the unemployed, and how many "groceries" they had given to the poor.[47] Through home missions, women extended the definition of "church" beyond the membership and became involved in controversial causes. While a few male clergy with theoretically progressive views who envisioned a "New South" were urging manufacturers to move South by touting the region's cheap labor, laywomen were trying to ameliorate the working conditions of women and children. They established day nurseries, kindergartens, and boardinghouses for young women in industry and became politicized. By the early twentieth century, the Methodist Woman's Home Mission Society fought for state and national legislation that mandated better wages and working conditions, shorter hours, and restrictions on child labor.[48] In 1881, Methodist women mused about the "ignorance, degradation, oppression, slavery and superstition of woman in heathen lands" and compared it with women's condition in the United States. They wondered at "the wrongs of many women, in [their] highly favored land and [asked] who but an enemy [Satan] could have done all this!"[49] Twenty-three years later, the journal that continued to express the concerns of Methodist women demanded as the extension of the Gospel good education, adequate food, decent housing, a living wage, reasonable working hours, and efficient and honest government for all.[50] Language that evoked the wrongs inflicted upon women by Satan had been transposed into the language of the welfare state without any demonstrable loss of piety or zeal.

Black women's mission work differed in some crucial respects from that of white women. White women often depended on African American domestics to provide them with the leisure time to undertake volunteer work. Many black women were employed outside their homes in jobs with long hours and low wages, and they still contributed monies and time to religious associations. In Memphis, close to two-thirds of the black women who served as leaders in benevolent societies worked as washerwomen or domestics, while the other 33 percent came from more privileged positions. The majority of the black women who performed mission work were former slaves or the daughters of former slaves, and their goals were to uplift the race, provide sorely lacking social welfare services for the members of their communities, and enlarge the sphere of women's religious work, which meant expanding the social services of the church. Black churchwomen identified and then met practical needs in their communities or congregations, as the Daughters of Zion did in 1867 when they hired a physician to tend sick members of their Memphis AME congregation. Black women's benevolence was spiritual as well as pragmatic, and considered alongside the similar activities of a few white women, it challenges the simplistic division between sacred and secular. Colored Methodist Episcopal (CME) women spoke of benevolence and mission work as a way of "Christianizing" their people; "Christianization," for these women, was a "one word code" for the introduction of piety, economic security, education, self-esteem, and civil rights.[51]

Churchwomen—black and white—were in the vanguard of interracial relations in the South. At the historic 1920 meeting in Tuskegee of leaders of the National Association of Colored Women and the white Methodist home missions, the anxieties of both groups ran so high that it took an hour of prayer and Bible reading before the women could talk with each other.[52] The suspicions fabricated by generations of miseducation, exploitation, self-righteousness, political brutality, and mutual antagonism seemed a lot to overcome until someone began to sing a hymn that both the black and the white women had learned as children. Religious expression was their common ground and common language; they tried to build from that common ground a better understanding, but it was not easy.[53] Early interracial efforts focused on providing or improving sanitation, health care, and education. In the 1930s and 1940s, under the guidance of African Americans, white Methodist women began to radicalize. Motivated by a commitment to "make real and effective the teachings of Jesus," they worked for black voting rights and lobbied state and national legislators in favor of antilynching and school funding bills. During the decades of school desegregation, the Woman's Division of the United Methodist Church encouraged members to arrange interracial workshops and prayer groups. These women integrated their offices and colleges, too, and they did so earlier than the United Methodist Church.[54]

Activist MECS women had given impetus and intellectual grounding to the process by which whites were beginning to understand their responsibility for racial alienation. They committed themselves to the Paine Institute as a symbol of how black and white could come together when they discovered how half-hearted and incomplete the commitment of MECS men to the academy had been. The Paine Institute had been conceived as a joint enterprise of the Colored Methodist Episcopal Church and the Methodist Episcopal Church, South in 1882; a white Methodist minister was usually president, but when MECS women discovered how poorly the young women of the institute were served, they assumed responsibility for improving the support the institute received from its founding organizations. When president John Hammond brought his wife, Lily Hardy Hammond, to live in Augusta, he brought a dedicated publicist who made it her life's work to tell white people about the history, achievements, and claims that African Americans had established by being ripped from Africa by Europeans and thrust into New World slavery. By 1914, Lily Hardy Hammond was inviting southern white women to think of African Americans in radically new ways. She encouraged them to capitalize the "N" in "Negro" (a major achievement, actually); to confess that white people, not black people, were responsible for the poverty, anguish, despair, and desperation of African Americans; and to approach African Americans empathically. Hammond wrote: "The same things poison the minds and bodies of white and of black alike; the same elements nourish both." During the prior fifty years, she argued, whites had acted in such a way as to make African Americans distrust them. The lynching that disgraced the South was not the fault of blacks—as so many men had said—but of whites. Instead of probing the many causes of lynching like a social scientist, she spoke like a prophet. She knew that whites were ultimately responsible, and she pleaded with them to repudiate the vengeance that men seemed to "cherish" as a "sacred and inalienable right." Striking at the self-righteousness of whites, she insisted that punishment, whether in lynching or in legal penalty, had to be surrendered as the appropriate posture of whites toward even those African Americans who were in fact guilty of crime. Crime and poverty were the responsibility of comfortable white people, she emphasized with the homiletic urgency of a preacher, and their punitiveness, she believed, reflected "a useless and frightful sacrifice" to "blindness and folly." Hammond knew she was asking a lot; it was the way of the cross, which included the self-sacrificing love that meant pain. Few other white women appealed to their sisters to bear the pain of justice for black people.[55]

Black women knew, moreover, that there were few white women like Lily Hammond; their own experiences were with the women whom Hammond was attempting to convert to a new way of relating to them. Black women's experiences were primarily with white women who were convinced of their own superiority because they had been relating to black women as servants for many years; theirs was the female side of southern paternalism. Black women, therefore, cleverly exploited white women's "maternalism" and desire to see themselves as the senior partners in interracial work. The joint efforts of CME women and MECS women were typical. Both groups described white women's role as "giving, teaching, aiding, assisting, and supporting" and black women's role as "learning, receiving[,] aiding[, and] appreciating the assistance they were given." But black women identified the needs in their communities and implemented the projects and missions funded by whites. Black women set the priorities and advanced their own goals. In the process, MECS women gradually realized they were learning more than they were teaching; how well they learned the limitations of their own racism is unknown.[56] Women's interracial work usually preceded that of the churches to which they belonged. For many women, embracing the civil rights movement meant questioning their denominations or opposing members of their own congregations.[57] When working with black women to improve housing, white members of the Christian Women's Interracial Fellowship of Denton, Texas, discovered that some of the poorly maintained rental units they wished to improve belonged to elders of their own church.[58] Sue Thrasher had learned about Christian brotherhood as a Methodist, yet her conversion to civil rights activism was inspired by a white Methodist church's rejection of a black woman for membership. Lily Hammond would have approved of Thrasher's new resolve.[59] Then, sisterhood became powerful.[60]

Black women saw their civil rights activism as a ministry. In sheltering, feeding, and caring for young civil rights workers, women continued the kind of social ministry they had begun in their churches. Older black women, using their influence as mothers of the church, persuaded others to register to vote, introduced Student Nonviolent Coordinating Committee (SNCC) and Congress of Racial Equality (CORE) workers to their neighbors, and pressured their preachers and deacons to support the cause.[61] Fannie Lou Hamer used song and testimony, two traditional forms of women's religious voice, in her movement work. Through song, she turned the audience into a rhetorical community, put the suffering of African Americans into the context of Judeo-Christian history, and, as many movement people attested, inspired others to persevere in spite of their fears. Through the retelling of her experiences, she testified to the need for racial justice.[62] Like the public expressions of countless women before her, Hamer's testimonies were actually sermons constructed from the fusion of memory, spiritual authority, and expectation. She could quickly move from reciting a Bible verse from memory to telling of her personal experience to making a call (often expressed in biblical language) for her listeners to join the struggle.[63] The easy movement of thought, prayer, anticipation, and voice from the silence of sacred communion into the eloquent and evocative cacophony of familiar pleas to action anticipating victory was not the possession of men alone; Fannie Lou Hamer was a true mother in Israel, a true mother of the church.

Scholars have yet to sufficiently appreciate movement women's theology, which illuminates the ministry of civil rights activism. Mary McLeod Bethune's public work, like her private life, was premised on a radical interpretation of the Golden Rule. "Loving your neighbor," she explained, "means being interracial, interreligious and international."[64] Fannie Lou Hamer's gospel was a blend of emancipatory Christology, radical forgiveness, and apocalypticism. For Hamer, Christ's central message was that of freedom; true Christians would act to liberate themselves and others. She bluntly acknowledged the suffering that whites had inflicted on African Americans but warned against the self-destructive luxury of hating whites. To forgive did not mean, for Hamer, to accept the status quo. Forgiveness purified the activist for the struggle that was sure to be long and difficult. If America did not embrace social justice, Hamer cautioned, God would mete out punishment accordingly. Her biblical exegesis fused past and present and mandated activism in the future. Because Jesus was a "radical" who always sided with the poor, because God had led the Israelites out of slavery, the only action a Christian could take was to side with the movement.[65] Ella Baker's vision of "participatory democracy," in which decision making and leadership were shared by all members of a group, bears an unmistakable religious imprint. She likened this form of empowerment, in which people would not "look to salvation anywhere but to themselves," to a "crusade."[66]

Like the men who decided that women's testimony had become too much like preaching, the ministers who led the civil rights movement also distinguished women's official and unofficial places in it, and they were reluctant to concede leadership positions to women. Over the centuries, churchmen have been wary of the power of women's organizations and of the roles women in these organizations assumed. In antebellum Petersburg, Virginia, amid growing concern about women's influence in churches and in public life, Methodist men took control of an orphanage that women had run for over a decade.[67] Southern Protestant men traditionally had drawn careful distinctions between "preaching" and "teaching," and they further emphasized that women could not teach adult men. The Southern Baptist Convention did not allow women to speak from behind a pulpit when delivering addresses or reports.[68] Southern Methodist men decided to merge the women's home and foreign mission societies without the consent or input of the women leaders of those groups. Southern Presbyterian leaders thwarted women's efforts to organize a regional missionary board until 1912 because they feared women would, if given more authority in the church, demand it in society outside the church.[69]

One of the more lively and polarized debates in southern women's religious history has been about the extent of men's authority over women in nineteenth-century Baptist churches. Jean Friedman, in her study of Georgia and North Carolina, maintained that Baptists enforced a "sexual double standard" in their disciplinary proceedings. Although men were almost three times more likely to be tried by their churches, sexual misconduct accounted, in Friedman's findings, for 6 percent of the charges against white men and 44 percent of those against white women. Obviously, many more men than women were beyond the reach of the church, and women could not hide the results of their sexual activity as well as men. Once charged, women were more likely than men to suffer suspension or exclusion.[70] Stephanie McCurry also argues that "congregational discipline of women focused inordinately on sexual transgressions."[71] By contrast, Randy Sparks found that in Mississippi churches white women were almost twice as likely as men to be tried for offenses in "sex and family life" but that fewer than 10 percent of women's disciplinary cases were in this category.[72] Gregory Wills's examination of Georgia Baptist churches reveals that white men and women were disciplined at approximately the same rate for sexual offenses and that women were slightly more likely to be excommunicated for sexual sins than men.[73] Frederick Bode found that in a thirty-two year period four of the six white women disciplined in Georgia Baptist churches were charged with sexual offenses compared to nine of sixty-four white men. While Bode's percentages (66 versus 14) come close to Friedman's, he draws quite different conclusions. He argues that we cannot posit a sexual double standard, because the sheer number of cases was so small, and because women had every reason to embrace evangelical sexual mores: only churches held men accountable for their sexual misconduct, whereas both churches and secular society held women accountable for theirs.[74] If we focus on numbers instead of percentages, Friedman's study still shows an "inordinate" focus on women's sexual conduct (103 cases) in comparison with men's (38 cases). Still, these 103 cases come from fifteen different churches over a fifty nine-year period. Trials of women for sexual misconduct, in these churches, were quite infrequent. Stephanie McCurry's contention that evangelical leaders engaged in a "constant battle to police female sexuality" presupposes that women struggled with evangelical sexual mores, and that supposition is not borne out by the statistical evidence.[75]

Bode's analysis of his data is instructive, for he argues that evangelical churches more frequently disciplined men than women, especially for fighting, physical abuse, and drunkenness. Churches, he suggests, provided women with limited protection against "male violence and disorder."[76] McCurry agrees on this point, contending that "yeoman women found more protection for their persons and interests in evangelical than secular society."[77] Yet men's misbehavior and women's faithful adherence to church norms were ideologically recast in ways that profoundly affected evangelical women. Churches expected white men to lapse, and some were frequently lenient when they did. White women were expected to be more pious, and churches were comparatively unforgiving when they were not.[78] Evangelical men were lauded for their "heroic resistance to the powerful temptations that confronted them in the world"; women who sinned were thought to be pathetic. Equally important, male sinners could embrace the code of honor and suffer no public reproach beyond the church. Women who were ostracized by their churches had no alternative public culture in which to participate.[79]

Studies of African American church discipline are not as divergent as those of church discipline among whites; Sparks and Friedman both found that black women were approximately twice as likely to be charged with sexual offenses as black men. Betty Wood puts such statistics in perspective. Although offenses related to sex and family life outnumbered other offenses blacks were charged with in the early South, very few black members were brought up on such charges. Moreover, as Wood cogently reminds us, slaves wanted secure marriages and families; the churches' prosecution of sexual violations was at least a recognition that slaves were moral agents with obligations to spouses and children, a not-so-subtle reminder to whites of slavery's devastating impact on black marriages and families. For black women, church courts offered some limited protection against sexual abuse, and evangelical churches did, in some proceedings, take the word of black women over that of white men, even of white ministers.[80]

Future studies of Baptist church discipline must take several factors into account. First, the findings about discipline and gender must consider the gender balance of congregations. We would also benefit from a study that examines cases in which both the man and the woman involved in a sexual offense were members of the same congregation. Third, we need studies that factor in subregion and change over time. We know that disciplinary proceedings became increasingly rare over the course of the nineteenth century, but we do not know the full impact of this decline on women. If, as so many scholars contend, churches protected women from male violence and unpredictability in the early nineteenth century, the decline in discipline may represent a weakening of women's influence on congregational leaders. If Ted Ownby is correct, however, it is possible that church discipline declined because churches were more adept politically at imposing church-sponsored social discipline upon society through laws designed to make men sober and susceptible to public and domestic, if not ecclesiastical, discipline. Such victories would have been the victories of women over men—and some men certainly felt they had been vanquished.[81] The record is ambiguous. Turn-of-the-century efforts to attract more men to churches and to project a muscular version of Christianity reflected anxieties about the influence of women in the churches on one hand and about many men's disinterest in religion on the other. How southern churches responded to this perceived crisis is just beginning to be explored, but it is quite possible that the decline of church discipline was part of the southern response to modernity and to the need to domesticate and cleanse public space.[82] We also need studies that balance aggregate figures against specific congregational rates. Bode's study of Stone Creek Baptist Church is illuminating in this respect. He found ninety-seven disciplinary hearings in a thirty-two-year period—an average of three church trials each year. Only six of the seventy members who were tried in this period were women. Last, we need studies that explore women's response to church discipline. Did women hold themselves to a higher standard? Were women, like churches, less forgiving of female lapses, no matter how small? And how did women react to church trials? There is a danger in relying so heavily on records that involve errant church members to explain the attitudes and behavior of the majority of church members who, we should not forget, were women.

The best work on the question of what the churches did *to* women critically examines the rhetoric of official male leaders and, when possible, seeks to explore what that rhetoric meant for churchwomen.[83] In the mid- to late eighteenth and early nineteenth centuries, when evangelicals were marginalized and competing for converts, they exalted women's submission to God over their submission to patriarchs, especially nonevangelical patriarchs. Women were praised for being influential, wise, and assertive for the faith. Evangelicalism created an identity for women apart from that of daughter, wife, or mother. Conversion, as Donald Mathews observes, "provided [women] a sense of social distance from the matrix of group relationships previously valued." Evangelicals, moreover, extolled the feminine virtues of humility and meekness and, in confirming the authenticity of the conversion experience, prized emotion over reason. As evangelical leaders sought respectability, and as they moved from the margins to the mainstream, they began to place more emphasis on women's role in families. Such an emphasis grew in part from patriarchs' failure to create households of Christian nurture and in part from women's numerical dominance in churches. To assure southern men that evangelicals were no longer a threat to patriarchy or slavery, clergymen promoted hierarchical households—households tempered by Christian love, to be sure, yet households in which the lines of authority were nonetheless clear. Proslavery spokesmen connected white supremacy and patriarchy, making every white man a master.[84]

The tension between women's duty to God and their duty to submit to patriarchs could be painful as women internalized the conflict between Christ and the world. Sarah Jones, who was extraordinarily influential in the Methodist Church of early-nineteenth-century Virginia, could not persuade her planter husband, Tignal, to emancipate their slaves despite the fact that she feared God would violently punish slaveholders in this world and the next.[85] Louisa Maxwell Cocke objected when her husband bought, sold, and hired out his slaves, and she despised his decision to put the children from his first marriage into dancing school, but she could not prevent him from doing these things. Cocke reconciled her church's insistence that she was morally autonomous with its exhortations to wifely submission, but not without enduring psychological turmoil that could not be assuaged by the simple knowledge that she was victorious in Christ. Evangelical religion did, as Frederick Bode argues, create a "common sphere in which men and women frequently acted together to save souls, nurture children, and perform works of benevolence," but in the common sphere of the household, women usually had less power to act on their beliefs than did their husbands.[86]

Fathers were deemed heads of Christian families, but mothers were accorded the primary responsibility for rearing godly children. Catholic women in particular may have linked childrearing with Christian responsibility, for they had in Mary a model for sacralized motherhood.[87] In the exaltation of motherhood, southern women of faith again faced a contradiction: a proper mother was strong, influential, and authoritative, while a proper wife was submissive and subservient. For Protestant women in the late nineteenth century, these domestic ideals had import in church polities, for while women were prohibited from speaking to mixed assemblies and from having authority over men, they were encouraged to teach and evangelize among women and children. They were expected to provide their households with an orderliness, decorum, and implicit moral ambience that only the most insistently pious, if gracious and self-disciplined, women could provide. This implicit and almost sacred decorum resulting from the example and dignity of accomplished Christian women gave women a power neither formal nor ineffectual. Frederick Bode demonstrates how women were able to exercise this implicit power by influencing important decisions within the life of the church, even influencing the calling of pastors although they held no offices and cast no votes.[88] As they had learned in their marriages, women could manipulate, cajole, guide, exemplify, and perhaps even tease the most agreeable men into behaving as women hoped they would behave. Such power was the public achievement of domestic negotiation between two people living in intimacy. If sometimes husbands could be as brutal as historians have discovered them to be, the example of "good women" had its effect. Not surprisingly, Gregory Vickers has found that when Baptist men described the Christian woman, they depicted her as an ideal wife.[89]

The ideal—since it was so ambiguous and capable of carrying so many different, if positive, connotations among Christians, at least—allowed southern women to manipulate nineteenth- and twentieth-century discourse about motherhood and womanhood in order to expand their roles and even challenge prevailing gender norms. The antebellum Methodist women's magazine, *Southern Lady's Companion*, criticized men for not fulfilling their roles as Christian husbands. In return for godly submission, women demanded respect from their husbands, an implicit bargain that could sustain the notion that women did not owe obedience to disrespectful husbands.[90] In the domestic sphere, antebellum evangelical women were subordinate, but as church members they also viewed themselves as "heirs of immortality," and in that role they accepted confinement neither to the home nor to inferior status.[91] Baptist women in the Women's Missionary Union embraced their responsibilities as wives and mothers, but they also advanced a place for women as religious workers and transformed the roles of mother and homemaker into public ones. A good mother cared not only for her own children, but for all children; a good homemaker helped keep schools safe and streets clean.[92] Methodist women turned the clergy's stock praise of female piety into an argument for laity rights. Women had long been told they were more devout than men, and gradually they came to claim a voice and a vote in church government.[93]

The Women's Christian Temperance Union, with its advocacy of suffrage —controversial among some clergymen—as a means to purify the public sphere, allowed some southern women to view the vote as an extension of their moral influence rather than a radical departure from their traditional social role. Although scholars have not yet thoroughly analyzed the relationship between the fights for laity rights and those for woman suffrage, there is evidence that some southern women were introduced to the idea of suffrage first in their struggle for laity rights. When Methodist women learned that the hierarchy did not respect them enough to consult them about the merger of the home and foreign missions, they responded by petitioning, beginning in 1910, for voting privileges in the denomination. As successive conferences rejected proposals to give laity rights to women, local missionary societies began discussing "the relationship between women's suffrage and world evangelization."[94] Because home mission societies had supported child labor laws and local improvements in sanitation and schools, society members began to connect political suffrage to their home missions agenda; as voters, they would be better able to influence local, state, and national lawmakers.[95] Southern Methodist and Baptist women finally won the right to represent their local churches in conferences and conventions in 1918.[96]

Nowhere were the ideals of wife and mother more contested than in the debates over woman suffrage in the South. Presbyterian theologian Robert Lewis Dabney believed that young women ought to stay home, take care of the house, and give birth: the home was their kingdom, he argued, albeit a kingdom under the thumb of their imperial masters.[97] Like so many antisuffragists, Dabney predicted that woman suffrage would ruin families and children, pervert Christianity, and destroy civilization. Dabney could not separate the question of whether women should preach with that of whether they should vote, which suggests that the church was politicized and gender roles sacralized.[98] A number of southern women also joined the antisuffrage cause, and like Dabney they proclaimed that God had destined women to be subordinate to men. If women voted, antisuffragists argued, they would put their own interests before their families'; soon the wife would be the head of the husband, and women would lose moral influence in the home.[99] Southern suffragists wisely avoided attacking or challenging the Bible, and they tried to make their cause respectable by asking for ministers' support, using Bible passages as mottoes for their organizations, and opening rallies and meetings with prayer. Instead of challenging southern evangelical ideals of womanhood, suffrage leaders tried to make the vote a cause that an ideal evangelical southern lady could support.[100] That only Tennessee of all the southern states ratified the Susan B. Anthony Amendment suggested the relative weakness of southern women's position within the masculine arena of electoral politics, but the battle was nonetheless important for rallying women beyond the churches and preparing them for such battles as the fight against lynching. That a Texas organizer for woman suffrage should have been recruited to rally women to fight lynching was not surprising; neither was it surprising that her appeal should be to churchwomen, the natural constituency from which to enlist the vanguard in the fight against the violent crimes associated with southern honor.[101]

While the relationship between suffrage and religion has been explored, the ways in which southern religious women have engaged feminism and resisted it have not received enough attention. That is, scholars seem to favor studying the protofeminism and feminist implications of the fusion of women and religion rather than the full range of responses to the transformation of women's roles. A number of studies show how conservatism with regard to gender roles was central to the fundamentalist movement and later to the Religious Right. There is still much to be done with regard to understanding the ways in which conservative religion has enabled women both to resist embracing feminism and at the same time to sustain a sense of self-esteem commensurate with the personal and collective responsibility associated with their religious commitments. We continue to need an empathic understanding of conservative female activists in the South, their networks, and their local politics.[102] The struggle for the Equal Rights Amendment in the 1970s galvanized conservative religious women, who saw the amendment as an endorsement of homosexuality, secular humanism, abortion, and of course feminism. The androgynous ideal that attracted supporters to the ERA seemed almost demonic to its opponents, who believed that traditional values of womanhood were the only safe foundation in a society where gendered rules of personal identity were under attack. Opponents of the proposed amendment viewed sex and gender as inseparable; for them, the anatomical body prescribed social roles and defined subjectivity. To tinker with what anti-ERA women believed had been designed and intended by God was to risk moral decay and pollution. If their rhetoric was frequently emotional and apocalyptic, it reflected a fear at the impending loss of an agreement —once presumed to be socially consensual—about the sacred distinctions between men and women.[103] The intricate patterns of relationships and expectations sustained by the many ways of expressing religion, value, and self still await analysis as they relate to sex, gender, abortion, evolution, and sex education.

Four recent studies offer models for future scholars of women's religious history. The most sophisticated analysis of women's resistance to institutional sexism through the parallel church is Evelyn Brooks Higginbotham's examination of turn-of-the-century black Baptist women. Their female leaders formulated a feminist theology that legitimated their church work and redefined women's place in Christian history. Black Baptist women took pride in a number of biblical mothers but stressed that these mothers had fulfilled more than a biological role: they had raised and guided "the Sons who would deliver Israel from its oppressors." As Higginbotham has noted, these women did not attempt to break with their church or all of its traditions. Instead, they acted within the institution from a position of "radical obedience," arguing for a wider sphere for women and a feminist theology that worked within Baptist biblical orthodoxy.[104] Black Baptist women also contested racism by advocating a "politics of respectability." This politics simultaneously denied the validity of white Americans' negative views of African Americans and upheld a middle-class standard of morality and behavior that conformed to white Victorian norms. Yet respectability was not exclusive to the middle class; black Baptist women leaders praised poor and working-class women who were sober, industrious, dignified, and upright. While Baptist women occasionally spoke and wrote in ways that depicted some blacks much as white racist stereotypes did, their exhortations to cleanliness and temperance were premised not on a belief in black inferiority but on a commitment to "full inclusion and equal justice."[105] Baptist women challenged racism and sexism, broadened the scope of their church's mission, and carved out a wider role for women's leadership and service in the church. This story would still be untold if scholars had focused only on male clergy or on the prohibition of female preaching. Higginbotham's study challenges us to question our assumptions about male-run churches, especially in the era of women's church organizations. For black Baptist women, "church" referred not only to the local congregation and the denomination; "church" also meant the Women's Convention and its institutions, meetings, and literature.

Laura Hobgood-Oster's study of antebellum women's Sabbath journals shows the value of close analysis of women's religious writing. What preachers said from the pulpit and what women heard could be quite different. One woman attended a sermon on the theme of women's domestic role and heard a call to a more active religious life. Because women viewed the preacher as God's mouthpiece, he did not embody only male authority. Women were not passive listeners; they believed that they were obliged to act on and grow under what they heard. They routinely admitted to being taken by a feeling of "transport" when they heard the preached Word; they were taken to a "liminal place, at a threshold between 'heaven' and 'earth.'" Preaching thus extricated them from their earthly subordination and allowed them to focus on their personal, unmediated relationship with God.[106] Hobgood-Oster's study reminds us, as do references to the forgotten words of Frances Bumpass and Lily Hardy Hammond, that scholars should pay more attention to the copious religious writings of southern women, who have transformed what they have heard in preaching, prayer, and meditation into a voice that carries a timbre recognizably female.

Thomas Tweed's study of Cuban Americans' practices at the Our Lady of Charity shrine in modern Miami is an exemplary analysis of gender in the noninstitutional church. The shrine and the Virgin in it are for diasporic Cubans powerful symbols of nationalism and of hope for Cuban liberation. But men's and women's devotions differ in crucial respects. Men most often come to the shrine during collective public rituals. Women outnumber men at these public events and form the majority of those who come for "private unscheduled devotion." Women's deeply personal attachment to the Virgin is also demonstrated by the fact that they are two times more likely to call her "my mother" than men, who usually call her "our mother." Women ask the Virgin for help in healing illness, in conceiving a child and having a healthy delivery, and in marital and family matters. Finally, women pass on devotion to Our Lady of Charity to their children. While women devotees share in the politicized Cuban American identification with the Virgin, she is equally important as a force in their personal lives.[107]

The fourth study is Emily Bingham's *Mordecai: An Early American Family*, which contains the elegantly written stories of three generations of Jews who settled in the South and engaged the Christian evangelization of that region in varied ways over the course of a hundred years.[108] Of course, they confronted other things as well, but this family discovered America in the South, and because of the roles that women played in sustaining the family through letters, personal relationships, and religion, they presented historians with treasure troves from which to recreate the past. Networks constructed through both kinship and religion reveal the ways in which Mordecai women thought about their lives and constructed identities, whether Jewish or Christian; the relationships Bingham discovered are similar to those that made Frances Bumpass so important to reflective, religious women in evangelical venues at much the same time. The networks are both private and public; they reveal people struggling with responsibility and identity; they reveal also that religion is not separable from daily life. And in daily life, the Mordecais found different solutions to the problem of being engulfed by a culturally aggressive and frequently arrogant evangelicalism. Some ignored their own religious tradition, some did so and then reclaimed it, and others unself-consciously blended into the larger culture by privileging personal relationships. Still another wrestled profoundly with her sense of self within the context of female relationships that provided the emotional and social background for the final resolution of her relationship with God in profoundly personal and intensely fulfilling ways. The anguish and drama and resolution took place within the South. The pressures that created the anguish were southern, but the intellectual world within which it took place was Anglo-American and spanned the Atlantic (just as Frances Bumpass's experience did). Bingham notes that in the end this southern family was an American family.

Her point is well taken, but it presents historians of the South with a problem. How is the Mordecai family a venue for writing southern religious history? How southern is the Virgin? How southern are the Cuban exiles who appeal to her? How southern was Frances Bumpass when she called to Southern Methodist women to feel free in the Spirit to voice their discipleship? How southern was Lily Hardy Hammond, who was raised in New Jersey, when she called southern women to confession, or Fannie Lou Hamer when she preached freedom? The Mordecais wrestled with their Jewishness in the South as Jews did in the North; when, after hearing of President Lincoln's call to arms, Major Alfred Mordecai resigned his commission rather than fight against his southern family or his Yankee son, his principled stand was American. But it was peculiarly southern, too. That the Virgin is revered in Goldsboro, North Carolina, as well as in Miami, and that Hispanics in both cities are transforming the South as well as America, suggest the duality with which students of the South as well as southerners wrestle. The South is an idea for some. It is home for others, even though "home" is also locality, and no one locale is "the South." As we continue to study southern women's religious history, the trend will be away from studies that merely document women's religious activities or that border on hagiography and toward scholarship that is nuanced, theoretically sophisticated, and analytically rich.[109] Historians must seek to uncover women's community ministries and women's influence on local congregational life; they must explore the private dimensions of women's religiosity as well as they have investigated the public and the collective. They must provide greater topical and chronological coverage, especially of High Church women, of nonevangelicals, and of women in the colonial and twentieth-century South. Because work in the field is burgeoning, it will become increasingly difficult for historians to write about southern religion without considering the women who have over the course of the South's history comprised the majority in churches, synagogues, and meetinghouses. As the South becomes more Roman Catholic and more ethnically diverse—as the South becomes more like the rest of the country, and as the southern family becomes an American family—how will the writing of southern religious history be affected? Perhaps answering that question is the next assignment.

Notes

1. Rhys Isaac, *The Transformation of Virginia, 1740–1790* (Chapel Hill: University of North Carolina Press, 1982).

2. William Meade, *A Brief Review of the Episcopal Church in Virginia from Its First Establishment* (Richmond: Southern Literary Messenger, 1845).

3. Richard Allestree, "The Special End of Woman's Creation," in *The Colonial and Revolutionary Periods*, vol. 2 of *Woman and Religion in America*, eds. Rosemary Radford Ruether and Rosemary Skinner Keller (San Francisco: Harper & Row, 1983), 207.

4. Ann Braude, "Women's History Is American Religious History," in *Retelling U.S. Religious History*, ed. Thomas A. Tweed (Berkeley: University of California Press, 1997), 87–107.

5. See, for example, Cynthia Lynn Lyerly, *Methodism and the Southern Mind, 1770–1810* (New York: Oxford University Press, 1998).

6. Jacquelyn Dowd Hall, *Revolt against Chivalry: Jessie Daniel Ames and the Women's Campaign against Lynching* (New York: Columbia University Press, 1979; reprint, 1994).

7. John Patrick McDowell, *The Social Gospel in the South: The Woman's Home Mission Movement in the Methodist Episcopal Church South, 1886–1939* (Baton Rouge: Louisiana State University Press, 1982).

8. Sarah Chilton wrote to Loly [Mrs. L. N. Brown, New Orleans, La.] on October 31, 1875: "I am glad that you feel some comfort in the communications which I sent you about our dear dear Charlie. I am sure I do feel myself infinitely comforted. . . . He has a talk with me every day." Mrs. Chilton communicated with her son by writing on paper. She was discovering that being a medium was not a miracle, but a "science" with its own rules. Norton-Chilton-Damcron Papers, Southern Historical Collection, University of North Carolina, Chapel Hill, N.C.

9. In *The Happy Pilgrimage* (Boston: Houghton Mifflin, 1927), 277, Corra White Harris challenged theologians to complain of her "little homemade creed," which she believed was much more manageable and appropriate to understanding suffering, love, and death than the "patented formulas of faith they impose[d]." Theologians simply wasted time in contending about doctrine, Harris argued. She dismissed materialists as well as theologians; the former, she continued, would be amused at her because she was inconsistent and illogical. She was not deterred. The issue, she insisted, was value. The materialist valued things that animals valued and shared their fate. Who knew what happened to theologians?

10. Linda K. Kerber, "Separate Spheres, Female Worlds, Woman's Place: The Rhetoric of Women's History," *Journal of American History* 75 (June 1988): 9–39.

11. See Cheryl Fredette Junk, "'Ladies, Arise, the World Has Need of You': Frances Bumpass, Religion, and the Power of the Press, 1851–1860" (Ph.D. diss., University of North Carolina at Chapel Hill, in progress).

12. Evelyn Brooks Higginbotham, *Righteous Discontent: The Women's Movement in the*

Black Baptist Church, 1880–1920 (Cambridge, Mass.: Harvard University Press, 1993), 49.

13. Dolores Egger Labbe, "'Helpers in the Gospel': Women and Religion in Louisiana, 1800–1830," *Mid-America: An Historical Review* 79 (Summer 1997): 153–75; Leslie J. Lindenauer, "Piety and Power: Gender and Religious Culture in the American Colonies, 1630–1700" (Ph.D. diss., New York University, 1997); Joan R. Gundersen, "The Non-institutional Church: The Religious Role of Women in Eighteenth-Century Virginia," *Historical Magazine of the Protestant Episcopal Church* 51 (1982): 347–57; Timothy M. Matovina, "Lay Initiatives in Worship on the Texas *Frontera*, 1830–1860," *U.S. Catholic Historian* 12 (Fall 1994): 107–20.

14. Alonzo Johnson, "'Pray's House Spirit': The Institutional Structure and Spiritual Core of an African American Folk Tradition," in *"Ain't Gonna Lay My 'Ligion Down": African American Religion in the South*, eds. Alonzo Johnson and Paul Jersild (Columbia: University of South Carolina Press, 1996), 8–38; Cheryl Townsend Gilkes, "The Roles of Church and Community Mothers: Ambivalent Sexism or Fragmented African Family-hood?" *Journal of Feminist Studies in Religion* 2 (1986): 41–60.

15. Harry Leon McBeth, "The Role of Women in Southern Baptist History," *Baptist History and Heritage* 12 (1977): 3–25; Charles W. Deweese, "Deaconesses in Baptist History: A Preliminary Study," *Baptist History and Heritage* 12 (1977): 52–57.

16. Robert Stanley Ingersol, "Burden of Dissent: Mary Lee Cagle and the Southern Holiness Movement" (Ph.D. diss., Duke University, 1989).

17. Hans A. Baer, "The Limited Empowerment of Women in Black Spiritual Churches: An Alternative Vehicle to Religious Leadership," *Sociology of Religion* 54 (1993): 65–82.

18. Sylvia R. Frey and Betty Wood, *Come Shouting to Zion: African American Protestantism in the American South and British Caribbean to 1830* (Chapel Hill: University of North Carolina Press, 1998); Lyerly, *Methodism and the Southern Mind*; Barbara R. Allen, "Early Baptist Women and Their Contribution to Georgia Baptist History," *Viewpoints: Georgia Baptist History* 9 (1984): 31–42; Patricia Summerlin Martin, "Hidden Work: Baptist Women in Texas, 1880–1920" (Ph.D. diss., Rice University, 1982), chapter 4.

19. Christine Leigh Heyrman, *Southern Cross: The Beginnings of the Bible Belt* (New York: Alfred A. Knopf, 1997).

20. Martha Hancock Wheat Diary, 1–7, 66, 68, esp. November 25, 1859, Miscellaneous Papers 517.58, Southern Historical Collection, University of North Carolina, Chapel Hill, N.C.

21. Randy J. Sparks, *On Jordan's Stormy Banks: Evangelicalism in Mississippi, 1773–1876* (Athens: University of Georgia Press, 1994).

22. Martin, "Hidden Work."

23. Catherine B. Allen, *A Century to Celebrate: History of the Woman's Missionary Union* (Birmingham: Woman's Missionary Union, 1987); Regina Sullivan, "Woman with a Mission: Remembering Lottie Moon and the Women's Missionary Union" (Ph.D. diss., University of North Carolina at Chapel Hill, 2001).

24. William Thomas Dargan and Kathy White Bullock, "Willie Mae Ford Smith of St.

Louis: A Shaping Influence upon Black Gospel Singing Style," in *This Far by Faith: Readings in African-American Women's Religious Biography*, eds. Judith Weisenfeld and Richard Newman (New York: Routledge, 1996), 32–55.

25. Luzerne Chipman, *Earnest Entreaties and Appeals to the Unconverted* (Raleigh: Press of the Weekly Post, 1852).

26. Jualynne Dodson, "Nineteenth-Century A.M.E. Preaching Women: Cutting Edge of Women's Inclusion in Church Polity," in *Women in New Worlds: Historical Perspectives on the Wesleyan Tradition*, vol. 1, eds. Hilah F. Thomas and Rosemary Skinner Keller (Nashville: Abingdon Press, 1981), 276–89; Stephen Ward Angell, "The Controversy over Women's Ministry in the African Methodist Episcopal Church during the 1880s: The Case of Sarah Ann Hughes," in Weisenfeld and Newman, *This Far by Faith*, 94–109.

27. *Star of Zion*, September 20, 1894, 2, and July 7, 1898, 3.

28. McDowell, *Social Gospel in the South*; Anastasia Sims, *The Power of Femininity in the New South: Women's Organizations and Politics in North Carolina, 1880–1930* (Columbia: University of South Carolina Press, 1997). In "A Place to Speak Our Minds: The Southern School for Women Workers" (Ph.D. diss., University of North Carolina at Chapel Hill, 1981), Mary Frederickson also shows how the YWCA could spawn radical spaces for women that were certainly beyond the expectations of the founding mothers.

29. For Sunday schools, see Sally G. McMillen, *To Raise Up the South: Sunday Schools in Black and White Churches, 1865–1915* (Baton Rouge: Louisiana State University Press, 2001).

30. Gundersen, "The Non-institutional Church."

31. Joan R. Gundersen, "Women and the Parallel Church: A View from the Congregations," in *Episcopal Women: Gender, Spirituality, and Commitment in an American Mainline Denomination*, ed. Catherine M. Prelinger (New York: Oxford University Press, 1992), 111–32; Elizabeth Hayes Turner, *Women, Culture, and Community: Religion and Reform in Galveston, 1880–1920* (New York: Oxford University Press, 1997).

32. Emily Clark, "'By All the Conduct of Their Lives': A Laywomen's Confraternity in New Orleans, 1730–1744," *William and Mary Quarterly* 54 (1997): 769–94. See also Lois Stanford, "The Hijas des Maria," *Password* 39 (1994): 113–23. Remarkably, there is only one scholarly study of devotion to Our Lady of Guadalupe. See Jeanette Rodriguez, *Our Lady of Guadalupe: Faith and Empowerment among Mexican-American Women* (Austin: University of Texas Press, 1994).

33. Jane Frances Heaney, *A Century of Pioneering: A History of the Ursuline Nuns in New Orleans, 1727–1827* (New Orleans: Ursuline Sisters of New Orleans, 1993). See also Frances Jerome Woods, "Congregations of Religious Women in the Old South," in *Catholics in the Old South: Essays on Church and Culture*, eds. Randall M. Miller and Jon L. Wakelyn (Macon: Mercer University Press, 1983), 99–123; Jean Marie Aycock, "The Ursuline School in New Orleans, 1727–1771," Sally K. Reeves, "The Society of the Sacred Heart in New Orleans," and Patricia Lynch, "Mother Katherine Drexel's Rural Schools: Education and Evangelization through Lay Leadership," all in *Cross, Crozier, and Crucible: A Volume Celebrating the Bicentennial of a Catholic Diocese in Louisiana*, ed. Glenn R. Con-

rad (New Orleans: The Archdiocese of New Orleans, 1993); Patricia Byrne, "Sisters of St. Joseph: The Americanization of a French Tradition," *U.S. Catholic Historian* 5 (Fall 1986): 241–72; Joseph G. Mannard, "Converts in Convents: Protestant Women and the Social Appeal of Catholic Religious Life in Antebellum America," *Records of the American Catholic Historical Society of Philadelphia* 104 (1993): 79–90; Priscilla Ferguson Clement, "Children and Charity: Orphanages in New Orleans, 1817–1914," *Louisiana History* 27 (1986): 337–51; and Judith Metz, "The Founding Circle of Elizabeth Seton's Sisters of Charity," *U.S. Catholic Historian* 14 (Winter 1996): 19–34.

34. Heaney, *A Century of Pioneering*, 80.

35. One especially rich article is Robert Emmett Curran, "'The Finger of God is Here': The Advent of the Miraculous in the Nineteenth-Century American Catholic Community," *Catholic Historical Review* 73 (1987): 41–61. See also Emilie Dietrich Griffin, "The Louisiana Years of Cornelia Connelly: A Paradigm of Conversion," in Conrad, *Cross, Crozier, and Crucible*, 404–16.

36. M. Reginald Gerdes, "To Educate and Evangelize: Black Catholic Schools of the Oblate Sisters of Providence, 1828–1880," *U.S. Catholic Historian* 7 (Spring/Summer 1988): 183–99.

37. Thaddeus J. Posey, "Praying in the Shadows: The Oblate Sisters of Providence, a Look at Nineteenth-Century Black Catholic Spirituality," in Weisenfeld and Newman, *This Far by Faith*, 73–93, quote on 79. See also M. Boniface Adams, "The Gift of Religious Leadership: Henriette Delille and the Foundation of the Holy Family Sisters," in Conrad, *Cross, Crozier, and Crucible*, 360–74. For a full discussion of the Oblate Sisters of Providence, see Diane Batts Morrow, *Persons of Color and Religious at the Same Time: The Oblate Sisters of Providence, 1821–1860* (Chapel Hill: University of North Carolina Press, 2002).

38. Mary E. Frederickson, "Shaping a New Society: Methodist Women and Industrial Reform in the South, 1880–1940," in Thomas and Keller, *Women in New Worlds*, 345–61; Dodson, "A.M.E. Preaching Women"; Barbara Brandon Schnorrenberg, "Set Apart: Alabama Deaconesses, 1864–1915," *Anglican and Episcopal History* 63 (1994): 468–90; *Wesleyan Christian Advocate*, April 30, 1903, 8, and May 21, 1903, 1. Bishop Eugene Hendrix, who presided over a consecration service for deaconesses and some Southern Methodist ministers, seemed to believe it was the beginning of the end times. The service appeared to be an ordination service to some alarmists; the costume that the young women wore looked to some to be a special "habit." It reeked of Catholicism, women's ordination, and who knew what else.

39. Whittington B. Johnson, "Free African-American Women in Savannah, 1800–1860: Affluence and Autonomy amid Diversity," *Georgia Historical Quarterly* 76 (1992): 260–83.

40. Helen Emery Falls, "Baptist Women in Missions Support in the Nineteenth Century," *Baptist History and Heritage* 12 (1977): 26–36; Labbe, "Helpers in the Gospel."

41. Suzanne Lebsock, *The Free Women of Petersburg: Status and Culture in a Southern Town, 1784–1860* (New York: W. W. Norton, 1984), 215.

42. Bobbie Sorrill, "Southern Baptist Laywomen in Missions," and Carolyn De Armond Blevins, "Patterns of Ministry among Southern Baptist Women," both in *Baptist History and Heritage* 22 (1987): 21–28, 41–49.

43. Southern Baptist women edited the *Heathen Helper, Our Missionary Helper, Missionary Talk*, the *Texas Baptist Worker*, and the *Orphan's Friend*, among other publications. See Evelyn Wingo Thompson, "Southern Baptist Women as Writers and Editors," *Baptist History and Heritage* 22, no. 3 (1987): 50–58; T. Laine Scales, "'All That Fits a Woman': The Education of Southern Baptist Women for Missions and Social Work at the Missionary Union Training School, 1907–1926" (Ph.D. diss., University of Kentucky, 1994).

44. See, for example, Ingersol, "Burden of Dissent," and Gregory Vickers, "Models of Womanhood and the Early Woman's Missionary Union," *Baptist History and Heritage* 24, no. 1 (1989): 41–53.

45. Gregory Vickers, "Southern Baptist Women and Social Concerns, 1910–1929," *Baptist History and Heritage* 23, no. 1 (1988): 3–13; McDowell, *Social Gospel in the South*.

46. See, for example, Owen R. Lovejoy, "What Legislation Has Done for Children," *Missionary Voice* 4 (February 1914): 145–46. Lovejoy discusses the importance of age and hours legislation; the next article is on "Juvenile Court" (146–48). See also the list of recommended readings for women leaders in the Methodist Episcopal Church, South, "Approved by the General Sunday School Board of the Methodist Episcopal Church, South," in *The Program of the Christian Religion*, ed. John W. Shackford (Nashville: Lamar & Whitmore; New York: Methodist Book Concern, 1917). The list included George Coe's *Education in Religion and Morals* and *The Spiritual Life*; Shailer Mathews, *The Church and the Changing Order* and *The Social Teachings of Jesus*; Francis G. Peabody, *Jesus Christ and the Social Question*; Walter Rauschenbusch, *Christianizing the Social Order*; and Harry Ward, *A Yearbook of the Church and Social Service in the United States, Poverty and Wealth*, and *The Social Creed of the Churches*.

47. Martin, "Hidden Work," 144. See also Sorrill, "Southern Baptist Laywomen," and McBeth, "The Role of Women."

48. Frederickson, "Shaping a New Society"; Anastasia Sims, "Sisterhoods of Service: Women's Clubs and Methodist Women's Missionary Societies in North Carolina, 1890–1930," in Thomas and Keller, *Women in New Worlds*, 196–210.

49. See Frances M. Bumpass, "Enmity between Thee and the Woman," *Women's Missionary Advocate* (February 1881): 6.

50. "What Is Social Justice?" *Missionary Voice* 4 (January 1914): 9.

51. Kathleen C. Berkeley, "'Colored Ladies Also Contributed': Black Women's Activities from Benevolence to Social Welfare, 1866–1896," in *Church and Community among Black Southerners, 1865–1900*, ed. Donald G. Nieman (New York: Garland, 1994), 327–49; Mary E. Frederickson, "'Each One is Dependent on the Other': Southern Churchwomen, Racial Reform, and the Process of Transformation," in *Visible Women: New Essays on American Activism*, eds. Nancy Hewitt and Suzanne Lebsock (Urbana: University

of Illinois Press, 1993), 296–324; Anne Firor Scott, "Most Invisible of All: Black Women's Voluntary Organizations," *Journal of Southern History* 56 (1990): 3–22.

52. Arnold M. Shankman, "Civil Rights, 1920–1970: Three Southern Methodist Women," in *Women in New Worlds: Historical Perspectives on the Wesleyan Tradition*, vol. 2, eds. Hilah F. Thomas, Rosemary Skinner Keller, and Louise L. Queen (Nashville: Abingdon Press, 1981), 157–78; Glenda Elizabeth Gilmore, "'A Melting Time': Black Women, White Women, and the WCTU in North Carolina, 1880–1900," in *Hidden Histories of Women in the New South*, eds. Virginia Bernhard, Betty Brandon, Elizabeth Fox-Genovese, and Elizabeth Hayes Turner (Columbia: University of Missouri Press, 1994), 153–72; Carolyn L. Stapleton, "Belle Harris Bennett: Model of Holistic Christianity," *Methodist History* 21 (1983): 131–42; Vickers, "Southern Baptist Women and Social Concerns"; Arthur Ben Chitty, "Women and Black Education: Three Profiles," *Historical Magazine of the Protestant Episcopal Church* 52 (1983): 153–65; Hall, *Revolt against Chivalry*. See, for the antebellum era, Elizabeth R. Varon, "Evangelical Womanhood and the Politics of the African Colonizationist Movement in Virginia," in *Religion and the Antebellum Debate over Slavery*, eds. John R. McKivigan and Mitchell Snay (Athens: University of Georgia Press, 1998), 237–59.

53. Wilma Dykeman and James Stokely, *Seeds of Southern Change: The Life of Will Alexander* (Chicago: University of Chicago Press, 1962), 90–92.

54. Alice G. Knotts, *Fellowship of Love: Methodist Women Changing American Racial Attitudes, 1920–1968* (Nashville: Kingswood Books, 1996), quote on 139.

55. Lily Hardy Hammond, *In Black and White: An Interpretation of Southern Life* (New York: Fleming H. Revell, 1914), 3–40, 60, 152–79 (esp. 153), 228, 230–44. See also Hammond, *In the Vanguard of a Race* (New York: Council of Women for Home Missions and Missionary Education Movement of the United States and Canada, 1922).

56. Frederickson, "Each One is Dependent on the Other." See also Nancy Marie Robertson, "Deeper Even Than Race? White Women and the Politics of Christian Sisterhood in the Young Women's Christian Association, 1906–1946" (Ph.D. diss., New York University, 1997).

57. Joanna Bowen Gillespie, "Sarah Patton Boyles's Desegregated Heart," in *Beyond Image and Convention: Explorations in Southern Women's History*, eds. Janet L. Coryell, Martha H. Swain, Sandra Gioia Treadway, and Elizabeth Hayes Turner (Columbia: University of Missouri Press, 1998), 158–83.

58. Richard W. Byrd, "Interracial Cooperation in a Decade of Conflict: The Denton (Texas) Christian Women's Inter-racial Fellowship," *Oral History Review* 19 (1991): 31–54.

59. Hammond, *In Black and White*, 228.

60. Sara Evans, *Personal Politics: The Roots of Women's Liberation in the Civil Rights Movement and the New Left* (New York: Vintage Books, 1980), 35.

61. Vicki Crawford, "Race, Class, Gender, and Culture: Black Women's Activism in the Mississippi Civil Rights Movement," *Journal of Mississippi History* 58 (1996): 1–21.

62. Janice D. Hamlet, "Fannie Lou Hamer: The Unquenchable Spirit of the Civil Rights Movement," *Journal of Black Studies* 26 (1996): 560–76.

63. On Hamer, see also Kay Mills, *This Little Light of Mine: The Life of Fannie Lou Hamer* (New York: Plume, 1993), and Charles Marsh, *God's Long Summer: Stories of Faith and Civil Rights* (Princeton: Princeton University Press, 1997), chapter 1.

64. Clarence G. Newsome, "Mary McLeod Bethune as Religionist," in Thomas and Keller, *Women in New Worlds*, 102–16, Bethune quoted on 114. See also Grace Jordan McFadden, "Septima Clark and the Struggle for Human Rights," in Weisenfeld and Newman, *This Far by Faith*, 301–12.

65. Bernice Johnson Reagon, "Women as Cultural Carriers in the Civil Rights Movement: Fannie Lou Hamer," and Jacquelyn Grant, "Civil Rights Women: A Source for Doing Womanist Theology," both in *Women in the Civil Rights Movement: Trailblazers and Torchbearers, 1941–1965*, eds. Vicki Crawford, Jacqueline Anne Rouse, and Barbara Woods (Bloomington: Indiana University Press, 1993), 30–55, 153–76.

66. Carol Mueller, "Ella Baker and the Origins of 'Participatory Democracy,'" in Crawford, Rouse, and Woods, *Women in the Civil Rights Movement*, 177–200.

67. Lebsock, *Free Women of Petersburg*.

68. Scales, "All That Fits a Woman."

69. Virginia Shadron, "The Laity Rights Movement, 1906–1918: Woman's Suffrage in the Methodist Episcopal Church, South," in Thomas and Keller, *Women in New Worlds*, 261–75; Jean Friedman, *The Enclosed Garden: Women and Community in the Evangelical South, 1830–1900* (Chapel Hill: University of North Carolina Press, 1985), 117–18.

70. Friedman, *Enclosed Garden*, 14–15, 131–34.

71. Stephanie McCurry, *Masters of Small Worlds: Yeoman Households, Gender Relations, and the Political Culture of the Antebellum South Carolina Low Country* (New York: Oxford University Press, 1995), 182. For a similar argument, see Timothy J. Locidey, "A Struggle for Survival: Non-elite White Women in Lowcountry Georgia, 1790–1830," in *Women of the American South: A Multicultural Reader*, ed. Christie Anne Farnham (New York: New York University Press, 1997), 26–42.

72. Sparks, *On Jordan's Stormy Banks*, chapter 9. See also Janet Moore Lindman, "A World of Baptists: Gender, Race, and Religious Community in Pennsylvania and Virginia, 1689–1825" (Ph.D. diss., University of Minnesota, 1994).

73. Gregory A. Wills, *Democratic Religion: Authority and Church Discipline in the Baptist South, 1785–1900* (New York: Oxford University Press, 1997).

74. Frederick A. Bode, "The Formation of Evangelical Communities in Middle Georgia: Twiggs County, 1820–1861," *Journal of Southern History* 60 (November 1994): 711–48.

75. McCurry, *Masters of Small Worlds*, 184.

76. Bode, "Formation of Evangelical Communities," 737. See also Ted Ownby, *Subduing Satan: Religion, Recreation, and Manhood in the Rural South, 1865–1920* (Chapel Hill: University of North Carolina Press, 1990).

77. McCurry, *Masters of Small Worlds*, 194.

78. Wills, *Democratic Religion*.

79. Bode, "A Common Sphere: White Evangelicals and Gender in Antebellum Georgia," *Georgia Historical Quarterly* 79 (Winter 1995): 775–809, quote on 798. See also Lebsock, *Free Women of Petersburg*.

80. Betty Wood, "'For Their Satisfaction or Redress': African Americans and Church Discipline in the Early South," in *The Devil's Lane: Sex and Race in the Early South*, eds. Catherine Clinton and Michele Gillespie (New York: Oxford University Press, 1997), 109–23. Lindman found black men twice as likely to be charged with sexual offenses as black women ("A World of Baptists").

81. Ownby, *Subduing Satan*.

82. When Methodist women pushed for laity rights, one of the arguments used against them was that men were already less interested in church work than women. Should women be allowed to help govern the church, opponents feared, more men would avoid church altogether. See McDowell, *Social Gospel in the South*.

83. For the colonial and early national South, see Cynthia A. Kierner, *Beyond the Household: Women's Place in the Early South, 1700–1835* (Ithaca: Cornell University Press, 1998); Gundersen, "The Non-institutional Church," 348; Jon Sensbach, "Interracial Sects: Religion, Race, and Gender among Early North Carolina Moravians," in Clinton and Gillespie, *The Devil's Lane*, 154–67; and Johanna Miller Lewis, "Equality Deferred, Opportunity Pursued: The Sisters of Wachovia," in Farnham, *Women of the American South*, 74–89.

84. Donald G. Mathews, *Religion in the Old South* (Chicago: University of Chicago Press, 1977), 105; McCurry, *Masters of Small Worlds*; Heyrman, *Southern Cross*; Lyerly, *Methodism and the Southern Mind*.

85. Lyerly, *Methodism and the Southern Mind*.

86. Bode, "A Common Sphere," 779. See also Anne Firor Scott, *The Southern Lady: From Pedestal to Politics, 1830–1930* (Chicago: University of Chicago Press, 1970).

87. Dolores Egger Labbe, "Mothers and Children in Antebellum Louisiana," *Louisiana History* 34 (1993): 161–73.

88. Bode, "Formation of Evangelical Communities" and "A Common Sphere."

89. Vickers, "Models of Womanhood." See also Martin, "Hidden Work."

90. James L. Leloudis, "Subversion of the Feminine Ideal: The *Southern Lady's Companion* and White Male Morality in the Antebellum South, 1847–1854," in Thomas, Keller, and Queen, *Women in New Worlds*, 51–76.

91. Laura Hobgood-Oster, "'Anticipating the Rich Gospel Feast': Gender Construction through the Ritual of Preaching and Response among Antebellum Evangelical Protestant Women in the South" (Ph.D. diss., Saint Louis University, 1997).

92. Vickers, "Models of Womanhood."

93. McDowell, *Social Gospel in the South*; Mary E. Frederickson, "Laity Rights and

Leadership: Winning Them for Women in the Methodist Protestant Church, 1860–1900," in Thomas and Keller, *Women in New Worlds*, 345–61.

94. Shadron, "The Laity Rights Movement," quote on 269. See also Paul E. Fuller, *Laura Clay and the Woman's Rights Movement* (Lexington: University Press of Kentucky, 1975).

95. Chapter 8 of Anne Firor Scott's *The Southern Lady* is suggestive on this point, because the legislation that enfranchised women supported has much in common with the home missions agenda.

96. Gundersen, "Women and the Parallel Church," 119.

97. Robert Lewis Dabney, "The Public Preaching of Women," in *Discussions of Robert Lewis Dabney*, ed. C. R. Vaughn (Richmond: Presbyterian Committee of Publication, 1891), 2:106. See also 1 Tim. 5:14.

98. Rick Nutt, "Robert Lewis Dabney, Presbyterians, and Women's Suffrage," *Journal of Presbyterian History* 62 (1984): 339–53.

99. Elna Green, *Southern Strategies: Southern Women and the Woman Suffrage Question* (Chapel Hill: University of North Carolina Press, 1997).

100. Evelyn A. Kirkley, "'This Work Is God's Cause': Religion in the Southern Woman Suffrage Movement," *Church History* 59 (1990): 507–22. See also Pat Brewer, "Lillian Smith on the Southern Patriarchy and the Paradox of Religion," *Proceedings of the Georgia Association of Historians* 8 (1987): 122–36, and Cheryl Townsend Gilkes, "'Together and in Harness': Women's Traditions in the Sanctified Church," *Signs* 10 (1985): 678–99.

101. Hall, *Revolt against Chivalry*. See also Mary Jane Brown, *Eradicating This Evil: Women in the American Anti-lynching Movement, 1892–1940* (New York: Garland Publishing, 2000).

102. Betty A. DeBerg, *Ungodly Women: Gender and the First Wave of American Fundamentalism* (Minneapolis: Fortress Press, 1990); Margaret Lamberts Bendroth, *Fundamentalism and Gender, 1875 to the Present* (New Haven: Yale University Press, 1993); Rebecca E. Klatch, *Women of the New Right* (Philadelphia: Temple University Press, 1987).

103. Donald G. Mathews, "'Spiritual Warfare': Cultural Fundamentalism and the Equal Rights Amendment," *Religion and American Culture* 3 (1993): 129–54; Mathews and Jane Sherron DeHart, *Sex, Gender, and the Politics of ERA: A State and the Nation* (New York: Oxford University Press, 1991).

104. Higginbotham, *Righteous Discontent*, 129.

105. Ibid., 97.

106. Hobgood-Oster, "Anticipating the Rich Gospel Feast," 207.

107. Thomas A. Tweed, *Our Lady of the Exile: Diasporic Religion at a Cuban Catholic Shrine in Miami* (New York: Oxford University Press, 1997).

108. Emily Bingham, *Mordecai: An Early American Family* (New York: Hill & Wang, 2003).

109. We still need more research on Mormon, Lutheran, Presbyterian, and Jewish women; Latina Catholics are also underexplored. For Jewish women, see Jean E. Fried-

man, "The Politics of Pedagogy and Judaism in the Early Republican South: The Case of Rachel and Eliza Mordecai," in Farnham, *Women of the American South*, 56–73; Beth Wenger, "Jewish Women of the Club: The Changing Role of Atlanta's Jewish Women (1870–1930)," *American Jewish History* 76, no. 3 (1987): 311–33; Turner, *Women, Culture, and Community*; Solomon Breibart, "Penina Moise, Southern Jewish Poetess," and David T. Morgan, "Eugenia Levy Phillips: The Civil War Experience of a Southern Jewish Woman," both in *Jews of the South: Selected Essays from the Southern Jewish Historical Society*, eds. Samuel Proctor, Louis Schmeir, and Malcolm Stern (Macon: Mercer University Press, 1984), 31–43, 95–106; William Toll, "A Quiet Revolution: Jewish Women's Clubs and the Widening Female Sphere, 1870–1920," *American Jewish Archives* 41, no. 1 (1989): 7–26; Helen Jacobus Apte, *Heart of a Wife: The Diary of a Southern Jewish Woman* (Wilmington: SR Books, 1998); and Stanley Bray, "The Jewish Woman, 1861–1865," *American Jewish Archives* 17, no. 1 (1965): 34–75. For Latina Catholics, see Vicki Ruiz, "Dead Ends or Gold Mines? Using Missionary Records in Mexican American Women's History," in *Unequal Sisters: A Multicultural Reader in U.S. Women's History*, 2d ed., eds. Vicki Ruiz and Ellen Carol Dubois (New York: Routledge, 1994), 298–315, and Kay F. Turner, "Mexican American Home Altars: Towards Their Interpretation," *Aztlan* 13 (1982): 309–26. See also Joanna Bowen Gillespie, *The Life and Times of Martha Laurens Ramsay, 1759–1811* (Columbia: University of South Carolina Press, 2001), and Richard Rankin, *Ambivalent Churchmen and Evangelical Churchwomen: The Religion of the Episcopal Elite in North Carolina, 1800–1860* (Columbia: University of South Carolina Press, 1993).

For Further Reading

Bingham, Emily. *Mordecai: An Early American Family*. New York: Hill & Wang, 2003.

Crawford, Vicki, Jacqueline Anne Rouse, and Barbara Woods, eds. *Women in the Civil Rights Movement: Trailblazers and Torchbearers, 1941–1965*. Bloomington: Indiana University Press, 1993.

Frey, Sylvia R., and Betty Wood. *Come Shouting to Zion: African American Protestantism in the American South and British Caribbean to 1830*. Chapel Hill: University of North Carolina Press, 1998.

Friedman, Jean. *The Enclosed Garden: Women and Community in the Evangelical South, 1830–1900*. Chapel Hill: University of North Carolina Press, 1985.

Heyrman, Christine Leigh. *Southern Cross: The Beginnings of the Bible Belt*. New York: Alfred A. Knopf, 1997.

Higginbotham, Evelyn Brooks. *Righteous Discontent: The Women's Movement in the Black Baptist Church, 1880–1920*. Cambridge, Mass.: Harvard University Press, 1993.

Hobgood-Oster, Laura. "Anticipating the Rich Gospel Feast: Gender Construction through the Ritual of Preaching and Response among Antebellum Evangelical Protestant Women in the South." Ph.D. diss., St. Louis University, 1997.

Isaac, Rhys. *The Transformation of Virginia, 1740–1790*. Chapel Hill: University of North Carolina Press, 1982.

Lyerly, Cynthia Lynn. *Methodism and the Southern Mind, 1770–1810*. New York: Oxford University Press, 1998.

Mathews, Donald G. *Religion in the Old South*. Chicago: University of Chicago Press, 1977.

McDowell, John Patrick. *The Social Gospel in the South: The Woman's Home Mission Movement in the Methodist Episcopal Church South, 1886–1939*. Baton Rouge: Louisiana State University Press, 1982.

Rankin, Richard. *Ambivalent Churchmen and Evangelical Churchwomen: The Religion of the Episcopal Elite in North Carolina, 1800–1860*. Columbia: University of South Carolina Press, 1993.

Sparks, Randy J. *On Jordan's Stormy Banks: Evangelicalism in Mississippi, 1773–1876*. Athens: University of Georgia Press, 1994.

Thomas, Hilah F., and Rosemary Skinner Keller. *Women in New Worlds: Historical Perspectives on the Wesleyan Tradition*. Vol. 1. Nashville: Abingdon Press, 1981.

Thomas, Hilah F., Rosemary Skinner Keller, and Louise L. Queen. *Women in New Worlds: Historical Perspectives on the Wesleyan Tradition*. Vol. 2. Nashville: Abingdon Press, 1981.

Turner, Elizabeth Hayes. *Women, Culture, and Community: Religion and Reform in Galveston, 1880–1920*. New York: Oxford University Press, 1997.

Tweed, Thomas A. *Our Lady of the Exile: Diasporic Religion at a Cuban Catholic Shrine in Miami*. New York: Oxford University Press, 1997.

Weisenfeld, Judith, and Richard Newman, eds. *This Far by Faith: Readings in African-American Women's Religious Biography*. New York: Routledge, 1996.

10

God and Negroes and Jesus and Sin and Salvation

Racism, Racial Interchange, and Interracialism in Southern Religious History

> God and Negroes and Jesus and sin and salvation are baled up together in southern children's minds and in many an old textile magnate's also.
> —Lillian Smith, *Killers of the Dream* (1949)

> Negro entered into white man as profoundly as white man entered into Negro—subtly influencing every gesture, every word, every emotion and idea, every attitude.
> —W. J. Cash, *The Mind of the South* (1941)

> We stood up. Me and God stood up.
> —Ethel Gray, Greenwood, Mississippi, civil rights activist

Religion in the post–Civil War American South has been both priestly and prophetic. If white southern theology generally sanctified southern hierarchies, the belief and practice of Christians could also subtly undermine the dominant tradition. This essay examines three central themes of southern religious history since the Civil War: racism, racial interchange, and interracialism. I will explore the ways in which the theologically and culturally grounded Christian racism pervasive among white southern Christians eventually faltered, giving way to the more inclusive visions espoused by black Christians in the civil rights movement. One way came in those moments of racial interchange in southern religious practice, which coexisted with southern racism. Another came from the black and white southern prophets who formed a southern evangelical counterculture.

White supremacy was an ideology of power that enveloped white southerners in an imagined community, a theological regime grounded in conservative notions of hierarchy. Nineteenth-century white southern theologies of class and blood—sometimes expressed formally but more often disseminated in everyday speech, Sunday sermons, self-published tracts, and pamphlets—buttressed white southern practice. Southern theological figures from James Henley Thornwell, the nineteenth-century South Carolina Presbyterian divine, to W. A. Criswell, the combative pastor of First Baptist Church in Dallas (the largest congregation in America in the 1950s and 1960s), preached that God ordained inequality. They espoused a southern conservative tradition that emphasized one's place and station in life. By the 1960s, however, southern whites had lost much of this theological undergirding, and they increasingly defended Jim Crow more on practical ("tradition") and constitutional ("states' rights") grounds. In doing so, they lost the battle to movement activists who inspired a generation to deconstruct Jim Crow. Since the civil rights movement, the conservative argument has resurrected itself as a defense of gender hierarchy and subordination.

My second theme is racial interchange (or, alternately, biracialism) in southern religious culture. Long before the civil rights movement, black and white evangelicals met together in settings outside of the institutional church. White and black southerners attended separate churches, organized into racially defined denominations, baptized their converted in separate pools, and buried their dead in segregated cemeteries. Their normal religious expressions took place in separate institutions. But there is another more hidden part of the story: the narrative of racial interchange in this world of segregated southern religion. White and black southerners—Christians, spiritual seekers, curiosity hounds, socializers, village atheists—gathered outside the prescribed Sunday morning times to celebrate, observe, question, and mock their common evangelical heritage. They jointly attended special community occasions, including the performances of child evangelists and other novelty acts; they gathered at town-wide revivals and river baptisms; they convened to hear visiting preachers and choirs and biracial itinerant evangelical teams; they exchanged religious songs and pulpit styles; and they met together to create new religious traditions. Early-twentieth-century Holiness and Pentecostalism involved such moments of tactile and cultural connection between black and white, as did southern music, with its deep biracial roots. The common evangelical tradition of white and black southerners, the biracial cultural forms of evangelicalism, unintentionally created openings that could be exploited by interracial activists to demolish segregation.

Third is the theme of southern Christian interracialism. Through the twentieth century leading up to the civil rights movement, believers concerned with racial justice struggled toward mutual respect, desegregation, and a politics (if not exactly a culture) of interracialism. In the interwar years, groups such as the Fellowship of Southern Churchmen established a religiously based challenge to the southern social order. In the 1950s and 1960s, civil rights activists in the Southern Christian Leadership Conference (SCLC) and the Student Nonviolent Coordinating Committee (SNCC) emerged from black churches to tear down the legally mandated segregation that was defended by conservative white Christians and opportunistic politicians. While religious institutions were resistant to change, many religious folk devoted themselves to a racial revolution precisely because they perceived God to be the author of it.

Racism in Southern Religious Thought

The dominant understanding of evangelicalism in the South, the so-called cultural captivity thesis, explains how religious institutions and practices in the nineteenth- and twentieth-century South reflected and reinforced racism. Slumbering in a reactionary form of evangelicalism, southern whites faltered before the moral challenges posed to them, from the challenges of abolitionism through those of Reconstruction and, later, the civil rights movement. Black religious institutions, dormant until their revitalization in the 1950s and 1960s, primarily served to console parishioners who were worn out by the travails of life under segregation.

There are obvious and important truths here. Writing in the midst of the civil rights revolution, scholars such as Samuel Hill and John Lee Eighmy could not help but see cultural captivity when stiff-necked deacons and ushers stood cross-armed at church house doors defending segregation now, segregation forever. More recently, scholars have pointed out that prominent black ministers avoided association with the movement and that some of them were clearly complicit in the oppressive system. In this sense, the cultural captivity thesis damns both white and black churches. Compelled to choose between Christ and culture, southerners chose culture.

Yet throughout history, the dominant classes have rarely espoused theologies of equality. More commonly, they adopt theologies that sanctify inequality. "We do not believe that 'all men are created equal' . . . nor that they will ever become equal in this world," a prominent Southern Baptist cleric said in the 1880s.[1] The white southern theology of class, blood, and sex was premised on God-ordained inequality. It was an unstable foundation in the context of American liberal democracy, but one common in human history.

White supremacist Christians in the South were not necessarily hypocrites. To classify them as such implies that true Christianity would have required its believers to accept racial equality—an important point theologically, but a dubious mode of analysis for historians. The insistence that Christianity mandates social equality has a history itself, and it has remained a difficult argument to make in most societies. White southern religious ideas of the social order of the races, moreover, could be intellectually grounded in a conservative vision of the role of hierarchy in preserving order and staving off anarchy. These notions were not merely hypocritical cant intended to void a clear biblical message, for particular biblical passages clearly explained why spiritual equality does not (and must not) imply temporal equality. The reasoning went like this: God created the world. If inequality exists, then God must have a reason for it. Without inequality—without rulers and ruled, without hewers of wood and drawers of water—there could be only anarchy. Men cannot govern themselves on a plane of equality. Realizing this, God sanctioned himself to head the church, men to lead women and children, owners to direct the lives of slaves, and white people to guide the destiny of black people.

Using such logic, and with plentiful references to biblical texts, antebellum white southern ministers sanctified slavery and defined southern theology. They borrowed heavily from a national tradition of conservative theology outlined by Federalist theologians. Godly societies were orderly societies, conservative southern divines said, and orderly societies required such hierarchies as God clearly had ordained—of class, blood, and gender. Presbyterian elders, Episcopalian divines, and even Baptist and Methodist preachers aspiring to the status of "gentleman theologians" understood that formulating a distinctive theological tradition for their section constituted part of their calling as apostles of respectability.[2]

The ideology of racism required Christian underpinnings for the brutal exercise of power in an evangelically devout society. The proslavery argument filled this void. Post–Civil War southern theologians responded to defeat in the Civil War by emphasizing human weakness, fallibility, and dependence on God. For many white southern theologians, defeat in the Civil War also shored up orthodoxies of race and place. The Negro—as a beast, a burden, or a brother—was there to be dealt with by whites, who were the actors in the racial dramas. After the Civil War, by using the term "redemption," white southerners expressed a deeply religious understanding of the tumultuous political events of the 1870s. The divinely ordained social and racial hierarchy had been restored by southern martyrs and the South atoned, renewed. The *New Orleans Advocate* (Louisiana's white Methodist newspaper) crowed in 1879: "Not a Negro at the polls. This is just as it should be. . . . Let the Negroes and Chinamen and Indians suffer the superior race of white men to whom Providence has given this country, to control it."[3]

For biblical literalists, defending slavery was a relatively simple proposition. The Bible spoke clearly of spiritual equality and temporal inequality. Fighting for political redemption was equally justified. In the twentieth-century South, however, constructing a theological defense of segregation was more complicated. After World War II, the American creed required white southern theologians to mouth the words that all men were created equal. To justify the state-mandated inequality of segregation, they resorted to constitutional arguments ("interposition"), appeals to tradition, and outright demagoguery. They dug up references to "render unto Caesar" and distorted Old Testament passages by imposing on the text mythologies such as the story of "the Son of Ham."

During the mid-twentieth century, religious segregationists peopled the white churches of the region, but they were difficult to prompt to concerted action. A segregationist folk theology was more pervasive among southern laymen and laywomen and among ministers outside the denominational hierarchy than in the circles of denominational leadership. More so than ministers, many of whom either were relatively silent during the civil rights crises or attempted to use the language of moderation to paper over differences, white laymen in the South articulated, defended, and enforced the theology of segregation. The work of deacons, laymen's associations, and church auxiliaries in the church world paralleled the efforts of businessmen's groups and citizens' councils in the workaday world. In many cases, the membership rolls of the religious and secular groups overlapped heavily, and both issued similar defenses of the theology and practice of segregation.

This folk theology of segregation was what made the white South so puzzlingly obstinate, so obsessed with purity. Only a proper ordering of the races would maintain white southern purity against defilement: the sexual metaphors behind the race politics were obvious and restated endlessly. The phobia of impurity, seen in the frequent references to "filth" and "social disease" that pervaded segregationist literature, clarifies that belief in the necessity of segregation was something deeper than custom, that it had been sanctified. When W. A. Criswell said, in a reference to segregation, that he did not want to be "forced to go into those *intimate* things" that he did not "wish to go [into]," he captured perfectly the link between race and sex, the obsession with purity, that haunted white southern conservatives.

Carey Daniel, pastor of the First Baptist Church of West Dallas, Texas, and active in the White Citizens' Council in his region, authored a widely reprinted and distributed pamphlet entitled "God the Original Segregationist" that articulated themes common to much of this literature. "Anyone familiar with the Biblical history of those cities during that period can readily understand why we here in the South are determined to maintain segregation," he wrote, introducing a familiar litany of arguments drawn from the already exhausted "Son of Ham" tradition. According to Daniel's view, the Canaanites ("the only children of Ham who were specifically cursed to be a servile race") had been allowed temporarily to occupy a narrow strip of the promised land along the Mediterranean, including the fateful lands of Sodom and Gomorrah. The children of the servant people were to live in a different part of the country from the children of Shem, the ancestors of white people, but "when they later dared to violate God's sacred law of segregation by moving into and claiming the land farther east," God had commanded the chosen people to destroy them. "We have no reason to suppose that God did not make known to Noah and his children His divine plan for racial segregation immediately after the flood," Daniel argued, although three generations later the segregated peoples were living together. The burden of proof, Daniel concluded, rested with those who would say that Jesus was not a segregationist, since he never specifically repudiated the system.[4]

Daniel's folk theology of segregation may be found recycled throughout the ephemeral literature of the era in letters to editors, newspaper columns, and frequently in private correspondence. White supporters of civil rights quoted Acts 17:26: "Of one blood has God made all nations." Segregationists, in response, explicated the second half of the verse, which referred to God assigning to his creatures the "bounds of their habitation." For biblical literalists such as most southerners were, passages such as Acts 17:26 correlated to the specific social customs of God's Zion, the American South. "The plan of God is for diversity of races to continue through earthly time and into eternity," wrote a Baptist editor, meaning that those who would "try to break down or obliterate racial distinctions and bring in a mongrel race or mongrel races [went] contrary to this plan of God." This editor repeated the familiar folklore of how God had divided the world between Noah's sons, giving Africa and the burden of servitude to Ham and his descendants. The Israelites had been chosen to be God's people and forbidden to intermarry; this law provided the religious sanction for America's own miscegenation laws. Denominational ethicists and theologians pleaded that such ancient stories in no way justified the specific social system of segregation in the twentieth-century South. But this was beside the point, for the folk theoreticians of Jim Crow were by definition suspicious of officially sanctioned modes of biblical interpretation on the race issue. In endorsing the *Brown v. Board of Education* decision, after all, the southern church leadership had betrayed them.[5]

To these dubious biblical exegeses were added more secular arguments that ultimately took center stage in the civil rights debate. In the context of the Cold War, white southerners could also seize upon the fight against communism, just as those in favor of black civil rights did. In the heart of Dixie, *Alabama Baptist* newspaper editor Leon Macon carried on the segregationist fight throughout his tenure, which ended only in 1964. "Integration is nothing but Communism, and it is strictly against God's Holy Word," he intoned in his state denominational newspaper. He found "strong evidence that world Communism [was] stirring the segregation problem in America," and he also pointed to the "definite dread in the hearts of people relative to losing the identity of their races through inter-marriage and amalgamation." Some Christian segregationists simply combined both strands of the argument. A rural pastor named T. J. Preston, for example, inveighing against school desegregation, argued: "In the first place the Bible teaches segregation and in the second place what the Supreme Court did is political and our Conventions had no right to try to deal with it. . . . If the Lord had wanted us to all live together in a social way, why did he separate us in the beginning? . . . what the Supreme Court did would finally bring us under a dictatorship." That integration would produce intermarriage and a mongrel race, that blacks themselves preferred segregation, that Negroes were unclean and socially inferior, that civil rights organizations (notably the NAACP) were communist inspired: religious segregationists used a plethora of arguments in defense of a social system that they had regarded, mistakenly, as timeless.[6]

Southern Christian defenders of segregation fought on in the 1960s but suffered serious ideological setbacks. If they were to continue as self-proclaimed defenders of law and order, they now faced the troubling reality that the law was on the side of desegregation while blame for disorder increasingly lay squarely with fellow segregationists who had been complicit with the violent terrorism of radical white supremacists. Many continued to believe that segregation was right in God's eyes but conceded that as a Christian citizen one must submit to the powers that be. During the period when Congress was debating the Voting Rights Act, the editor of the *Alabama Baptist* attacked President Lyndon Johnson's efforts to enlist clergymen in his behalf; the move "[turned] our pulpits into political rostrums to advance the ideas of one man, or group of men," Macon argued. Civil rights legislation, wrote Macon, represented yet another step toward "an all-powerful centralized Federal government," one that would "out-socialize the Socialists" and destroy personal freedom. Likewise, the insistence by church authorities that local congregations open the church doors to all violated the principle of the autonomy of the local church. Macon's final argument was his most important: "The basic fear and cause of the opposition to the integration which the Civil Rights Bill intends to bring about has been the mongrelization of our society through intermarriage," he wrote, as it was God's desire that humankind keep its "races pure" rather than tamper with the "difference and variety in His creation." Following the passage of the civil rights legislation of the mid-1960s, however, obedience to the laws required acquiescence to desegregation in public institutions. Rendering unto Caesar had trumped rendering unto God.[7]

By the 1960s, the raw exercise of power that white supremacy entailed appeared naked, increasingly without any compelling theological justification. Eventually, southern theologians chose to focus their efforts on more successful conservative themes such as family values, the defense of life, and millennialist visions. Since the 1960s, the standard biblical arguments against racial equality, now looked upon as an embarrassment from a bygone age, have found their way rather easily into the contemporary religious conservative stance on gender. A theology that sanctifies gendered inequalities has become, for our generation, arguably what whiteness was to earlier generations of believers. Behind the recent battle for control of the Southern Baptist Convention, won by theological conservatives after a nasty denominational fracas that lasted over a decade, has been the deep divide between those for whom human equality and autonomy reign as fundamental principles and those for whom communal norms and strictures and a divinely ordained hierarchy remain determinative of social values. For contemporary southern religious conservatives, patriarchy has replaced race as the defining principle of God-ordained inequality.[8]

Racial Interchange in Southern Religious Cultures

July 10, 1895: E. B. Ingram, a general merchandise store owner and a church member in Darlington, South Carolina, sorted through his impressions of going to see "the Negro Girl Preacher" visiting his town. That evening, as he recorded in his diary, there was a "crowded house white and [colored] about 300 mourners"; he wrote that he "[didn't] know what to say" about them. The next week, he "went to hear the Mulattoe 12 year old girl Preach," and while he "[didn't] know what to think" about her, either, he described the "Big crowd white & [colored] white ladies and all sorts" that had attended the event. There was at least "good behaviour there," he commented, knowing how often young men disrupted church services. When a "colored girl preacher" came to North Carolina and preached in the local African Methodist Episcopal Zion church in New Bern, whites and blacks sat across from each other in the church. The whites remained for a revival service after the star performance. In Selma, Alabama, African Methodist Episcopal (AME) pastor and bishop Winfield Henry Mixon led a camp meeting in 1903, preaching on the theme "seek ye first the Kingdom of God." There was, he recorded, a "great crowd," and "many white friends out." In May of that year, AME bishop W. J. Gaines also had visited town, lecturing to a "very good crowd, white and colored."[9]

From the late nineteenth century, Holiness churches, traveling evangelists, and other religious novelties attracted biracial crowds. Female evangelist and faith healer Maria Woodworth-Etter conducted meetings in Louisville, Kentucky, in 1888, welcoming all classes and colors. White leaders attempted to dissuade her, but Woodworth-Etter had "no desire to drive [the Negroes] away, but felt glad to have the privilege of leading them to Christ." She remembered: "God came in such wonderful power it was not long till they seemed to forget the color. The altar was filled with seekers, white people on one side and colored on the other." Even in moments of spontaneous religious passion, the rules of segregation were not forgotten, but in this case the worshippers ignored the spirit, if not the letter, of the segregation laws. A black female evangelist visiting a Woodworth-Etter gathering graced one meeting with a spontaneous prayer that "took hold of God in such a way as to shake every member of the congregation," and it "came near raising them all on their feet."[10]

Segregation laws and customs governed such informal biracial gatherings with rigid rules and norms. The turn-of-the-century South, moreover, was hardly an auspicious place and time for racial interchange. White southerners, having just fought bitterly over Populism, campaigned in nearly every state to enshrine segregation and disenfranchisement into state constitutional law. Whites viscerally feared the "new Negro," the first generation of blacks born after slavery, and they expressed those fears in lynchings, "whitecappings" (extralegal violence to drive black landowners off their property), and petty daily racial harassment. For many black southerners, it was a time of degradation and terror.[11]

Yet even during this nadir of race relations, a common evangelical heritage attracted white and black southerners and led them to the same events, whether for curiosity's sake, for entertainment, or for a meaningful worship experience. What did biracial evangelical events signify in the Jim Crow South? What was the meaning of racial interchange in religious gatherings in the context of this de facto and de jure segregation?

Segregation in post–Civil War southern religion was normal. Only in those liminal moments—during novelty acts, revivals, and the creation of new religious and musical traditions—did the bars of race come down, and then only temporarily. When they did come down, however, they opened up possibilities for cultural interchange that fed into the "shared traditions" outlined by historian and anthropologist Charles Joyner. Like Huck and Jim on the raft, black and white southerners, Joyner argues, "continued to swap recipes and cultural styles, songs and stories, accents and attitudes." He continues: "Folk culture simply refused to abide any color line, however rigidly it may have been drawn."[12] White and black southern religious folk cultures drew from common evangelical beliefs and attitudes and swapped musical and oratorical styles and forms. On occasion, they shared liminal moments of religious transcendence before moving back into a Jim Crow world where color defined and limited everything.

The possibility of biracial worship raises the long-lived discussion about whether black evangelicalism has African or American roots.[13] Scholars skeptical about biracialism in southern religion have raised important questions. Even if whites and blacks worshipped in the same place, they have asked, how much did that—could that—really mean? In antebellum churches, white clergymen preached the expected message—submission, obedience, contentment with one's lot in life—to a (literally) captive audience of slaves and their masters. The slave narratives address both directly and slyly the soul-deadening nature of such pious rationalizations for power. The slaves knew the drill: the insufferably pious white man pretended to preach, and they pretended to listen. But whites and blacks in the nineteenth-century South often approached God together, sometimes in the stilted and tense settings of the antebellum biracial church, and other times in more informal ways.

In the post–Civil War era, missionaries, travelers, reporters, and early anthropologists perceived believers in the region as culturally other—whether exotically primitive, pathetically backward, folkishly quaint, or heroically resistant to the homogenizing trends of corporate, capitalist America. For these observers, southern religion was emotion: overwrought, anti-intellectual, too given to personal experience over formalized understandings of faith. In short, it was too "Negro." In national publications such as *Harper's* and *Lippincott's*, and in regional ones such as the *Southern Workman* and the *South Atlantic Quarterly*, they recounted their observations of southern religious services, white and black. Some were missionaries intent on converting southern Christians to respectability; others were northern reporters dabbling in exotica; still others were anthropologists collecting material in the field, and this group included black reporters sent out by William Armstrong of the Hampton Institute to collect folkloric data before the old folkways passed away with the slave generation.

There were obvious differences—including class distinctions—in white and black traditions, yet a regional style persisted. Southern evangelical enthusiasm provided ample opportunity for ridiculing primitive whites so backward as to practice customs tinged with folk negritude. Solomon Conser, a Methodist cleric in Reconstruction-era Virginia, described the "extravagant devotions" of freedpeople, how they fell "into trances and cataleptic fits and professed to see visions of angels and demons." Such "spasmodic excesses," he pointedly added, punctuated worship services among both white and black believers. This religious "fanaticism" was, he believed, "encouraged by a class of zealots and divines of limited physical learning." Myrta Avary, an unsympathetic chronicler of southern life after Reconstruction, sniffed that southerners could not believe a conversion was genuine unless it was "ushered in by a good, strong unmistakable fit of hysterics." Another reporter observed of an 1885 camp meeting in Augusta, Georgia, "Southern people think nothing is done unless there is a gale of excitement, and they do not think they can seek pardon or purity without this." In the 1930s, an ex-slave witnessed "both white and colored people responding to preaching in much the same way as in his early life," with preachers appealing "to the emotions of their flock."[14]

Such observations fit the tradition of viewing southern religious expression as peculiarly emotional and sometimes entertaining. In the nineteenth century, whites from both South and North flocked to hear John Jasper, an "old-time" black preacher in Virginia known regionally for his funeral orations, preach his famous sermon "De Sun Do Move." Yet at least some of these cultural tourists recognized a spiritual movement in themselves that shook up their initial ironic bemusement. Jasper's white contemporary in the Virginia Baptist ministry, William E. Hatcher, eulogized the orator in *John Jasper: Unmatched Negro Philosopher*, a genuine but hopelessly paternalistic effort to afford the "old-time" preacher his due: "His sermons had the ring of the old gospel preaching so common in the South. He had caught his manner of preaching from the white preachers and they too had been his only theological teachers. . . . Wherever he went, the Anglo-Saxon waived all racial prejudices and drank the truth in as it poured in crystal streams from his lips." Whites who heard his funeral sermons were, Hatcher reported, "stirred to the depths of their souls[,] and their emotion showed in the weeping." This is not entirely imagined. Even minstrel shows in northern cities, with their cruel parodies of slaves and free blacks, sometimes moved white audiences to tears in ways much like Jasper, who was also a figure both of parody and empathy, did.[15]

References both explicit and cryptic suggest the frequency and hint at the meaning of biracial religious events. Elizabeth Johnson Harris, a mother of nine and a devout Colored Methodist Episcopal Church member in Georgia from her girlhood in the 1870s until her death in 1942, provides one example. In her life story, scrawled out in the 1920s, she recounted the aid from both white and colored that built her beloved home church, the Rock of Ages Colored Methodist Episcopal Chapel, in Augusta after the Civil War. In 1876, when she was nine, she desired immersion, but the Methodist pastor convinced her to "be baptized in the usual way of the Methodist faith." She remembered: "I was young, but proud to be a member of the Church by true conversion and always proud to fill my seat in Church at every opportunity." Her faithfulness earned her the appellation "little pastor." She recalled when the Chicago-based mass revivalist Dwight Moody preached in town. Moody acceded to local custom when he traveled, preaching to all-white crowds or to mixed ones depending on the preference of the organizers. In this case, white and black Augustans gathered together to hear a Christian crusader who was, according to Johnson, "perfectly free and friendly as a man of God, with both white and colored." Johnson described the event: "He extended a free invitation to one and all, to these services. The audience was sometimes mixed, the crowds were great, and the Holy Spirit seemed to be in such control over the house that the color of skin was almost forgotten for the time being."[16]

Harris devoted her life to extending God's Kingdom on her postage stamp of soil in Georgia. Accordingly, she seized on any indication of evangelical cooperation and said little about racial conflicts. Yet her account suggests that biracial religious gatherings provided, on occasion, communal spaces for worship, spectatorship, and entertainment.

A twentieth-century example comes from Eli Evans's account of growing up Jewish in Durham, North Carolina. Evans felt himself an outsider—white, but not really white—and identified closely with black worship. His friends, however, "didn't seem to see any distinction; black and white Christianity was all mixed up in their minds." His friends saw the emotion in the black church as "primitive." It reaffirmed their presumption of the "supremacy of the white culture." Evans saw it differently. As a teenage boy, he "did what most other white boys did on the weekends," going to rural black churches "just to see the holy rollers shake and chant." He recalled: "We bathed in the 'Oh tell it . . . tell it' magic of hypnotic stimulation between preacher and congregation, each driving the other on to mounting excess of singsong sermonizing and jump-up conversions and twitching moments of 'cain't-stand-it-no-more' spiritual release and liberation. For us white boys clustered way in the back where we had to stand to see anything, it was more like going to a performance than to a religious service. It was a special experience for me to immerse myself in a kind of Christianity without fear." For once, he could rest assured that none of his chums "would get swept away and go down front to be saved, and leave [him] as the only unwashed outsider at the service." After the service, he could join in imitating "the Negro preacher, moaning and crying out the 'praise de Lawd' accents of the panting sermons." If white fundamentalist churches, in Evans's young eyes, "churned up resurrection and retribution," black churches "conveyed a sense of gentleness and consolation."[17] Evans respected the African American liturgy more than his white counterparts did, but even his rowdy friends came back for more. In the very act of mockery, they recognized the passionate theater of southern religious performances.

Racial interchange figured importantly in early Holiness and Pentecostalism. A faith not born in the South, but which attracted white and black southern folk disaffected by the embourgeoisement of dominant urban religious institutions, early Pentecostalism functioned much like early national camp meetings. In both cases, mobile common folk created a democratic religious impulse that impelled them to form close bonds, adopt a strict moral code forbidding worldly pleasure, and embrace hypnotic worship practices that made bodies receptive to the Spirit. Whites and blacks drank in the Spirit together, and blacks delivered a message that, for a time, whites eagerly embraced. Once these initial enthusiasms settled into institutional routines, white and black believers moved into separate and (usually) distinct religious organizations.

The notion of Spirit possession had long been attractive to plain-folk southern believers; it drew converts to the eighteenth-century Baptists and to the early-nineteenth-century Methodists. Indeed, if Pentecostal fatalism about the irredeemable fallenness of this world came from traditions of white southern belief, Pentecostal faith in personal transformation through the power of the Spirit closely paralleled common African American beliefs that arose from both slave religion and the remnants of African practices.

Pentecostalism was an offshoot of the Holiness movement, a northern evangelical revival and reform tradition that emphasized total sanctification of believers and their accompanying "enduement" for Christian service. Holiness made little headway in the South until the 1880s, when southerners disenchanted with the increasing worldliness of respectable southern denominations turned to Holiness sects. By the 1890s, Holiness sects had sprouted like mushrooms throughout the South. More sectarian than their northern counterparts, southern Holiness preachers emphasized the importance of a second work of grace that produced an instantaneous sanctification of the believer's soul. Southern Holiness churches demanded total abstinence from alcohol, tobacco, worldly entertainments, and fashionable frills.

One of the most significant examples of racial interchange in southern religious culture can be found in the early Holiness group called the Fire-Baptized Holiness Church. Adherents held that God's spirit would baptize the believer with fire, purifying the body and soul of sin, with emotional rapture following. Those in this proto-Pentecostal church did not assign importance to speaking in tongues as evidence of fire baptism, but it was a short step from Fire-Baptized Holiness beliefs to this basic tenet of Pentecostalism. "It seems clear to us that history is repeating itself and that in these last days we are being permitted to witness the same marvelous and miraculous displays of divine power which the early disciples witnessed in those first days," wrote an early believer.[18]

The apocalyptic imagery of fire baptism induced the fervent emotionalism that later characterized Pentecostal meetings. "When we use the word 'Fire' in our name we use it as a symbol of the uncompromising God," explained the original manifesto of the Fire-Baptized Holiness Church. At one gathering in Beniah, Tennessee, in 1899, a church evangelist recorded: "The Lord put the holy dance upon a number of the saints. . . . Such jumping, and screaming, and shouting, and dancing before the Lord, we have seldom seen." From there, this Holiness minister traveled to Abbeville, South Carolina, at the invitation of William E. Fuller, ruling elder of the Colored Fire-Baptized Holiness Association. Leaders of the white community in the region scorned Holiness in part for its theology and in part precisely because of the class of people its attracted: lower-class whites, factory workers, and ordinary black farmers and laborers. "In this country," the evangelist wrote, "the proud, supercilious, ungodly whites look upon us with scorn and contempt because we hold meetings for the colored people, and preach the gospel to their former slaves." White mill workers also flocked to the services. "These poor and needy people are hungry for the pure gospel," he commented, because the "big, proud, worldly church, and the unsaved preachers . . . have no real interest in them, and do not want them in their 'heathen temples.'" Black seekers met in a ramshackle building on the outskirts of town, but the impoverished setting could not offset the rich spirit: "Such singing, such shouting, such dancing, such praying, it has never before been our privilege to hear," he wrote. He found that the colored people "dance[d] before the Lord differently than . . . white people," a feature of the meeting "peculiarly fascinating" to the brother leading the service, who was the only white man there. The minister then traveled to Kingstree, South Carolina, where he joined Isaac Gamble, a black Holiness evangelist. The two held meetings there conjointly and constructed a tent for biracial worship, dividing the salvation altar into white and black sections. The services, by their account, came off harmoniously, with a "profound interest manifested among the people, both white and colored, and a real Holy Ghost awakening." Gamble later led some camp meetings in which blacks and "some of the leading white people of the community came out, and showed much interest."[19]

Frequent reports in the Holiness and Pentecostal press, in books, and in diaries illuminate the hidden world of biracial services that coexisted with the dominant and segregated religious practices in the region. In North Carolina, even as white political leaders engineered a racial massacre in Wilmington in 1898 and defeated the Populist and fusionist challenge to white supremacist rule, white and black Holiness people met together to celebrate their release from sin. A. B. Crumpler, a powerful preacher and contentious newspaper editor, pioneered Holiness in Dunn, North Carolina. One convert remembered camp meetings Crumpler led in 1896: "Some said the preacher had powder and scattered on the folks and that they fell like dead men and lay for hours. They fell, it was true, but it was by the mighty power of God. . . . Brother Crumpler brought several workers with him, men and women filled with the Holy Ghost. . . . They soon had the town and surrounding country in a stir. Brother Crumpler could be heard preaching on a still night fully two miles, and the Lord was on him so the people could not stand it." Reporting from a colored Holiness convention in North Carolina, one writer noted the effect Crumpler's ministry had on the black Saints, who were not "bound down by conventionalities," but full of "blessed liberty." If this represented a fair sample of black holiness, he concluded, then whites would have to "spur up or they'[d] find themselves behind in this blessed race." He entreated: "May God pour out his Spirit on both the white and colored people in our state." In 1903, the "colored saints" in Dunn invited white Holiness minister Gaston B. Cashwell to preach to them on a Sunday evening. "The house was packed with both white and colored," he recorded, "and the Spirit of the Lord was there, the people rejoiced and God blessed them." He commented: "They seemed to be filled with the Spirit, and the white people of the community say they live it."[20]

Early white and black southern converts to Holiness and Pentecostal churches experienced the second baptism in similar ways. After the Azusa Street revivals in Los Angeles in 1906, many believers accepted tongues speech as the initial evidence of the baptism of the spirit. Theologically, that is, they became Pentecostals. Charles Fox Parham was a key theological innovator. Leading a Bible school in Kansas at the turn of the century, Parham preached that tongues speech would appear as evidence of the baptism of the Holy Spirit. Parham taught his doctrines to a group of seekers in Houston in 1905 and 1906, and among his students were a black Louisianan named William J. Seymour, who would lead early Pentecostals in Los Angeles, and Lucy Farrow, the niece of Frederick Douglass and another key black Pentecostal figure. The second baptism of sanctification, which Holiness theologians described as the ultimate cleansing of sin from the soul, was necessary but not sufficient, he preached. Only the Holy Spirit baptism, sometimes called the third blessing, could complete the initiate's spiritual quest. Tongues speech (glossolalia) was its true signifier, for it proved that God's power had suffused the human vessel.[21]

Howard Goss, a native of rural southern Missouri, was one early convert to the new doctrine. His autobiography provides a glimpse at what Pentecostals called the "baptism of the Spirit." After a youth spent working in mines, he sold his worldly possessions and followed Charles Parham to Houston, where several early converts gathered to experience the latter-day Pentecost. As Goss witnessed fellow mourners lining up, being touched, and speaking in tongues, all under the guidance of Lucy Farrow, his "heart became hungry again for another manifestation of God." He recounted: "So I went forward that she [Farrow] might place her hands upon me. When she did, the Spirit of God again struck me like a bolt of lightning; the Power of God surged through my body, and I again began speaking in tongues. From that day to this I have always been able to speak in tongues at any time I yielded to the Spirit of God." He remembered the transformation of Addison Mercer, formerly a black Baptist deacon in Texas: "Such spectacular conversions as his . . . were all deeply sincere; they covered up nothing, and held back nothing. This brought everyone under conviction and packed the building." Unlike more established evangelicals, Goss endorsed fervent bodily exhibitions: "I have never seen dancing that was of God that did not touch someone in the audience." Public religious dance in white Holiness and Pentecostal churches, he acknowledged, was "drawn from the colored work": "their freedom from inhibition, one of their most attractive traits[,] made its appeal." Such joyous expressions were, he assured his (perhaps discomfited) readers, "entirely controlled by the pastor, and stopped or started at his signal." He explained: "As does any other pastor, he knew his congregation, no doubt, and allowed only what was beneficial."[22]

These early believers—southerners, northerners, and westerners—embraced Pentecostal worship practices along with strict behavioral codes. The Reverend Charles Harrison Mason, a former black Baptist minister in Mississippi, who converted to Pentecostalism during the Azusa Street revivals, founded the Memphis-based Church of God in Christ (COGIC) as a Holiness band in the 1890s. In his early days, Mason was a tireless itinerant evangelist. In Conway, Arkansas, in 1904, Mason's preaching overpowered a white man named James Delk, one of a substantial crowd standing around a cotton wagon listening spellbound to Mason's sermons and songs. "That day Brother Mason made an impression on me that I have never forgotten and can never forget," Delk later wrote. He described the man who brought about his spiritual transformation: "Brother Mason attended college very little but has a wide experience with human nature and an understanding of his fellow man such as no other man seems to have.

. . . I doubt if there ever has been a minister who has lived since the day of the apostles who has shown the sweet spirit to all people, regardless of race, creed, or color, or has preached with greater power than Brother Mason." Delk founded a COGIC church in Madisonville, Kentucky, suffering harassment there for his work.[23]

In 1906, Mason made his Pentecostal pilgrimage to Los Angeles. There, he heard the new doctrines of Pentecostalism from ex-slave and early tongues speech apostle William Seymour, who himself had been tutored (seated on the other side of a curtain from the white students) by the eccentric future racist demagogue Charles Fox Parham. Seymour's preaching and the tumultuous services that resulted had been publicized in the *Los Angeles Times* as well as in Holiness and Pentecostal publications. Word spread quickly, and seekers from around the country (and the world) converged in the humble location in south central Los Angeles. Mason joined a number of other southerners, including the white North Carolinian Gaston B. Cashwell, who in the next few years helped to found the Pentecostal Holiness Church.

At the Azusa Street revival, along with Lucy Farrow and other white and black southerners, the Mississippian Charles Harrison Mason received "all three operations of divine grace: regeneration, sanctification, and spiritual baptism." He then traveled back home to Memphis. From his pulpit, he dispensed supernatural cures and the Pentecostal gospel to crowds primarily of black, but also of some white, seekers. He quickly developed a reputation for possessing the spiritual gift of interpreting "sounds, groans, and any kind of spiritual utterance." He worked closely with early white Pentecostals and, indeed, for a time led the only officially incorporated church in which Pentecostal ministers could be credentialed. (Credentials were important, for they gave ministers access to clergy rates for rail passes.) Mason spoke to the founding Assemblies of God convention in 1914, blessing this new (white) alliance of Pentecostal groups. In his sermon, he employed roots and strangely shaped plants as folk homiletic devices, a practice he employed throughout his career.[24] During these years, Mason traveled with a white minister named W. B. Holt, and the two were jailed at times for breaking Jim Crow laws. In Nashville in 1916, Mason preached to a sizable crowd at a city auditorium. "Many of the best white people of the city attended the meeting. The Holy Spirit through me did many wonderful things," he later recounted. A series of services in Little Rock in 1919 purportedly had the same effect, as "God so wonderfully wrought His power among both white and black, sanctifying, baptizing, and healing." In 1933, the paper of the church,

The Whole Truth, reported that "both white and colored testified of the wonderful healing power of God" at the COGIC annual convention in Rocky Mount, North Carolina.[25] Until his death in 1961, Mason reigned over the Church of God in Christ, the most significant black Pentecostal denomination in twentieth-century America.

The relationship between whites and blacks in early Pentecostalism sometimes incited violence, a reminder to Pentecostals of the trouble they could invoke by violating the white South's treasured theological maxims and social customs. At an annual state encampment in Hearne, Texas, blacks built a brush arbor as an add-on to accommodate the white people who wanted to attend a camp meeting. People flocked to the meeting, having never heard the full gospel of Pentecostalism before. Because they could not bring themselves to "seek Baptism at a colored altar," whites requested a white Pentecostal teacher to come and "help them into the Baptism." A young minister came, preaching to crowds of whites and blacks in separate services. At his next appointment, he met men with pistols who threatened to shoot him for putting them "on a level with the d—— niggers." While he waited to take the train out of town, another crowd of men beat him with clubs, fracturing his wrist. The young minister proudly reported his Pentecostal martyrdom.

Like the "Negro Girl Preacher" seen by E. B. Ingram in the 1890s and the traveling ministry of William E. Fuller from 1898 to 1907, black Pentecostal evangelists proved to be popular in the 1910s and 1920s. Numerous white and black Pentecostal evangelists, songsters, faith healers, and itinerant preachers combed the southern countryside, attracting racially diverse crowds, sometimes arousing the ire of authorities for their departures from the dominant institutions of southern religion. E. N. Scippio was a class leader of an African Methodist Episcopal church. After claiming that he had experienced sanctification and the divine healing of his cataracts in 1914, he preached for two decades for both white and black listeners in the Southeast. At one meeting in Georgia, he recounted, "white and colored were at the altar. Seeking for Salvation." "The meeting was so powerful," he said, "that men seemingly could not stay on their jobs." Later, in Jacksonville Heights, Florida, he discovered that "the white people throughout that place had great faith in the gospel that was preached to them, until they would send handkerchiefs to the meeting, and God would manifest his power through the prayer of faith." He continued preaching through the 1920s and 1930s, still with what he described as "large gatherings, white and colored" greeting him. In one service in South Carolina, he remembered,

"God began to work, and the power began to fall; one night it fell so, until it fell on a white girl outside the tent, and she began to shake, so they carried her away."[26]

Sister Mary Magdalena Tate, another itinerant black Pentecostal apostle, founded the Church of the Living God, the Pillar and Ground of Truth, Inc. Tate felt moved to preach the gospel in 1903. Along with her two sons, she began her work in Steele Springs, Tennessee. From there she preached in Paducah, Kentucky, where "her call to the ministry and commission to go and preach the Gospel was more forcibly shown and made plain to her." Soon she accepted invitations from many churches to "teach and preach what was hailed as a 'new gospel[,]' for many people had not heard of true holiness and the baptism of the fire and Holy Ghost which she advocated." She was invited "to the homes of both white and colored and invited to preach in a Temple of a Presbyterian Church, colored." A church historian described the experience: "Never will it be forgotten how the power of God lifted physically strong men as well as women from off their seats while she preached and taught the people that night in that Temple of the Presbyterian Church in Paris, Tennessee. Grown men shouted, leaped, and wept for joy." In such experiences, the shared traditions of evangelical emotional expression, spirit possession, and holy dancing were unmistakably present.[27]

Energetic white Pentecostals created small empires of competing churches, publishing houses, academies, and denominational structures. As the churches grew, white Pentecostals increasingly separated from black Pentecostals such as William E. Fuller, who had written for a white readership in Holiness publications and had been instrumental in spreading the new gospel but who later was forgotten in church annals. Early Pentecostalism represented a liminal moment. Gradually, the everyday world of the segregated South shaped Pentecostal culture; it simply was not possible to build new denominations that were not segregated. Early biracial groups later separated into white and black church organizations. Fuller, a native South Carolinian and pioneer black Holiness preacher in the Southeast, attended the organizing session of the Fire-Baptized Holiness Association of America in 1898 in Anderson, South Carolina. A few years later, it organized more officially into the Fire Baptized Holiness Church of God. "We were connected with the white people for ten years," Fuller later recounted, but "owing to the growing prejudice that began to arise among the unsaved people, it was mutually agreed that we have separate incorporations."

In 1908, Fuller formed a separate black organization in South Carolina, the Fire Baptized Holiness Church of God of the Americas. He served as this church's overseer until his death in 1958, his early biracial preaching services forgotten.[28]

But Pentecostal cultural forms were indelibly affected by the racial interchange that was a part of the early history of the new religious movement. The vivid encounters evident in Pentecostal experience strongly influenced southern evangelical music. From the early intermingling of Protestant hymns and African styles in spirituals to the mixing of white and black country and gospel sounds on radio dials, two streams of musical religious culture flowed beside each other, never merging, but often intersecting. As rural southerners made their treks from countryside to town in the early twentieth century, and as many of them found their way to northern cities later in the century, they carried their Holiness and Pentecostal churches with them, marking them for the derision of their urban neighbors. Later in the twentieth century, however, Pentecostalism became one of the fastest-growing religious movements in America, confounding a generation of interpreters who had condemned it as the opiate of the dispossessed. These primitives instead provided much of the soundtrack and many of the expressive forms that reshaped American cultural styles later in the twentieth century. Like the black Pentecostal COGIC, white Pentecostal churches served as training grounds for a remarkable number of figures (such as Elvis Presley, Johnny Cash, and Oral Roberts) who deeply imprinted American popular culture.

Twentieth-century southern gospel music illustrates how these traditions were shared. The gospel music business, according to historian Bill Malone, evolved from shape note singing schools and evangelical revivals "but drew much of its dynamism and much of its personnel from the Holiness-Pentecostal movement of the late nineteenth century and early twentieth century." "By 1900," Malone has explained, "a great stream of religious songs, fed by the big-city revivals of the era, flowed into American popular culture." Publishing houses, both within and outside denominations, cranked out paperback hymnals for church meetings and singing schools. White gospel singing groups learned from hearing the shape note hymns, from instruction in singing schools, and from barbershop and black gospel quartets that toured the region and received wide regional radio airplay. And beyond church walls, white and black secular and religious performers traded licks, vocal styles, and lyrics. Bluegrass pioneer Bill Monroe incorporated black quartet singing into his own gospel renditions, while the white gospel hymn tradition handed down from the nineteenth century was revivified by black gospel music innovators such as Thomas Dorsey (a native Georgian) and Lucy Campbell.[29]

Holiness and Pentecostalism provided fertile ground for musical interchange among white and black southerners, just as the great camp meetings of the early nineteenth century had provided a similar forum for cultural interchange. Guitars, tambourines, and other rhythmical instruments, once seen as musical accompaniments for the Devil, found their way into black Pentecostal churches in the early twentieth century. Charles Harrison Mason's Church of God in Christ congregations immediately adopted them. White Pentecostals soon picked them up, and the two groups shared hymns and holy dancing. Not bound by respectable conventions, white Pentecostals borrowed freely from all traditions. Howard Goss remembered the singing in early Pentecostal services as "entirely unpretentious." He said that "the very artlessness of these songs . . . created no barriers of antagonism." He recounted how styles borrowed from black Pentecostal brethren (Goss was rather unusual in his free acknowledgment of this borrowing) insinuated themselves into white musical performance. The songs came in at "break-neck speed," Goss recalled: "We didn't notice the accelerated tempo. Anyway, everyone was jubilantly dancing inside, whether it showed outwardly or not. . . . We were the first, so far as I know, to introduce this accelerated tempo into Gospel singing. . . . 'Jazzed-up hymns' they were sometimes designated by the critical, because this joy of the Lord was so built up on our young people that when they got a chance to sing, they exploded. Every particle of their being was poured into worship as they sang, nothing slowed them down." The derisive term "holy roller music" referred to gospel hymns, refrains, and chants belted out in an enthusiastic and syncopated style. White and black Pentecostal musical styles remained distinct, but they intersected at many points. Both employed rhythmical accompaniments, enthusiastic hollers, and holy dancing.[30]

Holiness and Pentecostal preachers and singers were among the most culturally innovative and entrepreneurial of twentieth-century plain-folk southerners. As Bill Malone explains, "Whether black or white, Pentecostal evangelists . . . armed with guitar and Bible, accompanied perhaps by a mandolin-strumming or tambourine-shaking wife, and preaching on street corners, under brush arbors, in tents, or in storefront churches, took their places alongside the shape-note teachers and gospel quartets as major agents in the fashioning of the southern gospel music repertory." Brother and Sister George Goings, black Pentecostal singing evangelists, took their Holiness message through Tennessee and Kentucky in the last years of the nineteenth century. They introduced audiences to songs such as "There's a Little Black Train A Coming," a tune that found its way into black churches and rapidly became a gospel music warhorse. It became a staple of a black minister in Atlanta named J. M. Gates, who recorded more than three hundred sides of his preaching and singing from 1926 to 1941. White and black gospel songs by the hundreds worked over the infinitely malleable metaphor of the train, a vehicle that took sinners to hell, saints to heaven, pilgrims to rest, and prodigal sons home.[31]

As white Pentecostals organized the Pentecostal Holiness Church (centered in the Southeast), the Church of God (Cleveland, Tennessee), and the more conservative and carefully institutionalized Assemblies of God (centered in the midsection of the country and now headquartered in Springfield, Missouri), they seized on the opportunities provided by mass media to spread their message. So did black Pentecostals. Gospel music publishing companies, led by the Tennessee-based Vaughan empire and its numerous offshoots, profited from marketing their tunes by sending out gospel quartets that sang the copyrighted songs in appealingly innovative styles. In this way, plain-folk southerners learned new songs (such as the 1930s hit "I'll Fly Away") that addressed their millennial hopes and daily struggles during the depression. Among whites, the Vaughan family in Tennessee and their rivals the Stampps-Baxter Company introduced a whole new catalog of southern religious songs that could be adapted by white gospel groups, by bluegrass musicians such as Bill Monroe, or by black gospel soloists, quartets, and choirs. Black publishers and composers were just as aggressive. Many of the black gospel pioneers came out of the Baptist and Methodist churches, but the influence of Holiness and Pentecostal performance styles broke through the stranglehold of "respectable" music that had defined urban bourgeois black services. Black gospel during these years developed its own tradition, its favorite touring quartets and choirs, its first star soloists (such as Mahalia Jackson), and its own fierce internal competitions among publishing outfits, composers, and traveling singing groups. In gospel, then, the streams of southern religious music, white and black, flowed alongside one another, exchanging tunes and lyrics and styles while remaining distinct. Radio became gospel's most effective medium, for it reached out-of-the-way places.

Later in the twentieth century, those raised in the context of this racial interchange in religious expression entered the public world of broadcasting and performing. Radio orators, barnstorming evangelists, gospel singers, bluegrass pioneers, and pop stars—nearly all with roots in the Low Church southern religious traditions—permanently changed American popular culture. Any number of country and soul singers and black gospel stars, from Hank Williams and Bill Monroe to Ray Charles and Sam Cooke, come to mind. Hank Williams's "Honky-Tonk Angels" bore a marked resemblance to the white gospel classic "Great Speckled Bird," made famous by Roy Acuff; Bill Monroe's innovative jamming on mandolin often backed gospel crooning that was obviously influenced by black quartet singing; Ray Charles's "Baby What I Say" was little more than a gospel vamp backing Charles's eroticized refrain; and Sam Cooke became a model for later singers such as Al Green in his move from gospel to soul and back again. Perhaps more than anyone else, however, Elvis Presley illustrates this point.

The young Elvis borrowed freely from sacred performers in creating his own musical persona. Elvis committed to memory an entire catalogue of church music from both the white and black traditions, and he could produce on command church songs of all sorts. Along with his friends in Memphis, Presley enthusiastically sampled African American religious culture both in person and on the radio. Unlike the rowdies (both white and black) who made sport of southern religious solemnities, Presley was affected by these encounters and particularly by his encounter with African American Pentecostalism, recognizing its kinship to his own Assemblies of God tradition. He listened to black religious orator Herbert Brewster on the radio and visited local meetings of the Church of God in Christ.

Presley's cultural pastiche emerged from a larger cultural transmission from black to white and back again, seen most clearly in the early history of Holiness and Pentecostalism and its relationship to the evolution of southern religious music. In both cases, whites and blacks borrowed theologies, performance styles, and cultural practices freely (if often unwittingly) from one another. Presley, for example, absorbed the sounds, the rhythms, and the stage manner (including the leg shake) that shaped his own electric performances. By Presley's time, white and black teenagers were eager to break down the rope lines that segregated them at rhythm and blues events, and white teenagers found black styles alluringly imitable. White secular and religious performers learned from—some might suggest they stole—the doo-wop style (which had its own roots in black gospel quartets), religious "holy-roller" dancing, and the melismatic singing that coursed through African American church music. In the process, they created sacred entertainments that shaped American popular culture. Sacred passion, expressed most obviously in white and black southern Pentecostalism, was at the heart of R & B, as well as of rock and roll.[32]

Racial interchange in southern religious culture could not override racism, and it rarely even mitigated it. Biracial attendance at religious events was not a necessary or sufficient step to interracialism. Racial separation in southern religion was the norm, obvious to anyone who attended church on Sunday. Yet even outside observers sensed that white and black southerners carried on religious cultures that bound them together, somehow, even as they marked their separateness. The religious expressions of southern common folk emerged from an entangled racial and cultural history.

Interracialism

White converts to interracialism adopted African American theological understandings, even if the black community never adopted the white converts in quite the same way. Churches as institutions were conservative, but progressive Christians drew different lessons from southern spirituality than regional religious leaders often intended. The actions of individual churchmen and churchwomen outstripped the cautious defensiveness that marked the public stance of the religious institutions. As Mary King, an idealistic Methodist and a SNCC activist in the early 1960s, wrote in her memoir, the civil rights movement "abounded in the biblical ethos of the Southland, black and white, and [it] was part of the climate in which the movement was working."[33]

Early interracialism drew from a carefully delimited, middle-class, painfully respectable model of biracial civility, a courteously negotiated set of rules for segregation. In 1919, sickened by that violent Red Summer, Will W. Alexander, a Methodist minister in Nashville, organized the Commission on Interracial Cooperation (CIC). Alexander hoped to bring together the "best men" of the region, white and black—defined as those who were racial moderates—to forge a new racial compromise. The CIC investigated and publicized lynchings and other particularly egregious abuses. Alexander worked through southern social agencies such as churches and YMCAs to cultivate racial goodwill. Walter White of the NAACP frequently called on Alexander's resources to investigate particular lynchings, beatings, and economic fraud perpetrated on sharecroppers. In the 1930s, state women's CIC committees gathered more than forty thousand signatures asking that southern sheriffs restrain mob violence against black suspects.[34]

The legacy and limitations of white southern reform are well documented, notably by John Egerton in his recent chronicle *Speak Now against the Day: The Generation before the Civil Rights Movement in the South*. Most in the CIC looked upon the organization "as an instrument of fairness and conciliation vital to the maintenance of 'separate but equal' segregation." Alexander's personal views, however, ranged far beyond those publicly ascribed to him, as Egerton makes clear. As early as 1926, Alexander publicly opposed segregation, nearly losing his job in the process. Subsequently, he worked behind the scenes. The CIC thus "developed a curious image of liberal activism within the bounds of cautious and proper respectability," explains Egerton. Some black observers held a less charitable view. They saw biracial cooperation among so-called moderates as smoothing over rather than challenging racial oppression. While "racist demagogues plied their trade [and] Ku Klux Klaners surged to power," one African American charged, CIC personnel "quibbled over the nuances of working and used their positions as mediators between the black community and the white power structure to impose their own interpretations of what was strategic and timely on even the most cooperative of black leaders."[35]

The CIC collapsed in the 1930s; Alexander accepted a job with the New Deal, and black allies realized the organization's inherent limitations. Alexander himself publicly condemned segregation—not just in its worst aspects, but also as a system—in a 1944 issue of *Harper's* magazine. He had come a long way from his boyhood on a Missouri farm and his well-meaning charitable efforts in the Nashville neighborhood where he first pastored after receiving theological training at Vanderbilt. His work with the CIC, moreover, provided a limited but crucial precedent for interracial cooperative efforts, one a later generation would expand on considerably.[36]

From the Great Depression to *Brown v. Board*, progressive southern Christians pursued interracial justice largely outside the public eye. They took up where Alexander and his cohorts left off. Writing about the rise of southern liberalism, John Egerton explains that churches and universities were wellsprings "for the intellectual and philosophical stimulation out of which some reform movements came"; he explains, however, that "when the institutions themselves shrank from joining the fray, it was often their sons and daughters, acting in new alliances or as individuals, who moved the dialogue and the action to a higher plane."[37] Here, a few narratives will have to suffice to illustrate the growth of Christian interracialism in the pre–civil rights movement South.

One remarkable individual, who challenged his own white Southern Baptist tradition, was Clarence Jordan. In the 1930s, Jordan attended Southern Baptist Theological Seminary in Louisville, fully intending to pursue a standard ministerial career path in the denominational bureaucracy. His encounter with professors who shocked students with progressive ideas started him on a different path, one intensified by the worsening poverty he witnessed in the depression-era rural South. Jordan sought to bring both a progressive gospel and progressive farming to the desiccated theologies and worn-out lands in the rural southern countryside. Like the young Tom Watson, he saw that poor white and black farmers were in the ditch together, facing common problems not solved by the rampant white demagoguery about the black beast rapist. Jordan's initiative resulted in the opening of Koinonia Farm near Americus, Georgia, in 1942. It was an experiment in Christian communal living and progressive farming that stood as an embattled but remarkable witness to radical southern Christianity.

Problems with communalist experiments together with quandaries inherent in Koinonia's attempt to rebuke the regional racial orthodoxy continually plagued the farm. Attempts by local authorities and vigilantes to drive Jordan out of Sumter County eventually frayed the small community. Jordan's communalist economic dream conflicted with his equally treasured vision of whites and blacks working together peaceably. Local blacks needed economic opportunity and stability, and they could ill afford to dump their meager resources into a community pot, a reality that Jordan understood. National church groups assumed that the farm served as a base for civil rights activities despite Jordan's insistence that Koinonia was foremost an experiment in Christian communalism and that it was involved in politics as part of a larger radical Christian witness. In the early 1960s, the farm harbored black activists such as Charles Sherrod and other SNCC members engaged in the Albany campaign. Yet Clarence Jordan shied away from SNCC's philosophy of active nonviolence. He hewed instead to a Quaker-like faith in nonresistance and a progressive farmer's belief in economic independence.[38]

While Jordan patiently toiled away in rural Georgia in the 1960s, known mainly for his *Cotton-Patch Gospels*, other racial justice advocates took up the mantle. Charles Jones was a Presbyterian minister in North Carolina from the 1940s into the 1960s. He was eventually excommunicated for theological heterodoxy. His contemporaries remembered him for his courage in challenging Chapel Hill residents to forsake segregation. A complex individual, Jones was averse to institutional traditions, whether the segregationist straitjacket or Presbyterian orthodoxy. A Chapel Hill editor, calling Jones "the most profane preacher

I've ever met in my life," recalled: "Some of our people have conferred sainthood on him, other people feared him, some of our people hated him." Black North Carolinians admired him. "He could explain what segregation felt like, from the inside," remembered one resident. "He'd say suppose you had a shoe that didn't fit and it hurts your heel." Black ministers in the area told young people to be wary and not to get involved in civil rights. Jones encouraged them to "go ahead and do it," the resident remembered: "And they cheered because they had heard this behave yourselves, do like we've been doing for 100 years. And so they followed his advice." Black minister and author Henry H. Mitchell remembered his personal admiration for Charlie Jones, who ate at the same table with his domestic servants: "He insisted his children should not grow up seeing or being involved in any arbitrary discrimination."[39]

In 1947, Bayard Rustin, along with other idealists and pacifists, embarked on the Journey of Reconciliation. This foreshadowed the later Freedom Rides. Both exercises tested segregation laws in interstate travel. Given the university town's reputed liberalism, the riders expected little trouble when they arrived in Chapel Hill, but they soon faced attacks from local roughs. Intervening quickly, Jones secreted these early-day Freedom Riders into his house. The following day, he smuggled them out of town. When they eventually served prison time on road gangs for violating state law, Jones and others in the Fellowship of Southern Churchmen (FSC) saw to their welfare. Later, Bayard Rustin wrote to Jones's secretary, the future feminist theologian Nelle Morton, "When I think of the ease with which certain types of progress can be made in New York as compared with the more serious problems that southern Christians and liberals face, I always feel that I should take off my hat to those of you who continue in the struggle."[40] After being forced from his Presbyterian charge, in the early 1950s Jones founded the Community Church of Chapel Hill, which experimented in integrated worship. He was a controversial figure in local politics, debating local racists over the *Brown* decision and participating in local civil rights protests in the 1960s.

Jones was a member of the Fellowship of Southern Churchmen, organized by Howard Kester. "Buck" Kester spent a remarkable, if ultimately disappointing and frustrating, career in ministering, agitating, and organizing. He grew up in West Virginia in the 1910s, where he witnessed firsthand the bitter lives of southern working-class families. After attending Lynchburg College in the early 1920s and matriculating at Princeton (which he found too conservative for his tastes), he finally found academic satisfaction at Vanderbilt. After serving a stint as a YMCA worker in the 1920s, he subsequently entered Union Theological Seminary in New York in the early 1930s. At Union, he studied with Reinhold Niebuhr and formed friendships with fellow southern-born radicals and pacifists such as James Dombrowski and Myles Horton. In the mid-1930s, Walter White, executive secretary of the NAACP, asked Kester to investigate the notorious lynching of Claude Neal in Florida. For Kester, the young Social Gospel idealist, it was a harrowing experience. Whites spoke to him freely until his cover was exposed and he was forced to flee. Kester's analysis of lynching as a mechanism of economic control drew nationwide attention when White distributed Kester's work across the country. Increasingly influenced by Niebuhrian realism, with its goal of a "rough approximation of justice," by the mid-1930s Kester had left behind his youthful YMCA-influenced Social Gospel idealism as well as the idealistic pacifism common to his contemporaries. Both paled beside the squalor and terror that he saw (and experienced) while organizing southern working people, which he detailed in his 1934 exposé of the violent repression of labor-organizing efforts among poor southern farmers, *Revolt among the Sharecroppers*.[41]

The Fellowship of Southern Churchmen originated at a conference in 1934 at Monteagle, North Carolina. It was the brainchild of Howard Kester and other protégés of Reinhold Niebuhr, including Dombrowski and Horton. Kester wrote to a Fisk University faculty member at the time: "My mind has been drawn increasingly toward the necessity of instilling a deep and powerful religious motivation of a revolutionary nature among those individuals and organizations which offer some hope for the future. I am extremely anxious to see the Fellowship of Southern Churchmen act as such an instrument and to express its faith in creative terms in whatever areas of life are open to them." In "We Affirm," the original FSC manifesto, Kester explained: "We seek to identify ourselves with the emerging minority of prophetic Christians who are trying to discover and give practical expression to the historic redemptive mission of our religion. . . . We thus commit ourselves to the task of creating, by the power of God and in the brotherhood of man, liberated from poverty, ignorance and insecurity, healed from the wounds of hatred, exploitation, and strife, laboring together in love and peace." Kester's pamphlet suggested that "the redemption of the individual and of society are one and inseparable." Kester's allies in the FSC saw their job as spearheading "radical Christianity within their churches and denominations." "Each member," they believed, had to "be a creator of a cell within his own orbit of work." In *Prophetic Religion*, a mimeographed newsletter distributed to a few thousand subscribers, David Burgess of the Board of Missions of the Congregational Church asked, "Will the churches of the South, whose denominational roots are revolutionary and whose Holy Book is not a stick of candy but a stick of dynamite, do as much [as the FSC] to bring to the farm and factory worker a good wage, a decent house, a free assembly, a brotherhood enfolding all races?"[42]

A small group of mostly white and middle-class southern radicals, the FSC helped to bring together scattered and often iconoclastic individuals interested in awakening a prophetic white southern Christianity and in providing a sense both that its members were not alone and that the South might not be as solid as it seemed. In the 1950s, fellowship members sought to capitalize on what they perceived as the existence of a body of sympathetic Christians who pursued justice over southern tradition. Kester wrote to the Field Foundation in 1952: "Due to the changed and changing situation in the region during the past twenty years, there are a great many Southerners who can and should be harnessed to liberal and progressive movements such as the Fellowship. Hundreds of these Southerners are unrelated to any movement and are without any sort of spiritual or social home." The FSC organized interracial conferences and pushed for the opening up of church-affiliated colleges to African American students. Kester pointed out the new dangers that would arise from the *Brown* decision, which he believed had "crystallized the fears of [the] pseudo-democratic majority," and from the power that congregations had exercised to deny jobs to eminently qualified pastors who had taken pro–civil rights stands. "We will keep hammering away in the church, at the church, with the church, in the knowledge that we stand on solid ground and with the ages," he concluded.[43]

In the 1950s, as the revolution its members had long sought appeared, the FSC collapsed. A loner in temperament, relatively unskilled at selling projects to donors, Kester proved incapable of persuading potential supporters (especially liberal foundations) to commit resources to the FSC. Black organizations such as the SCLC were far more attractive to those interested in supporting racial justice causes. As many in the FSC came to realize by 1955, its time had come and gone. Everett Tilson, a Vanderbilt professor in the 1960s who authored the antiapartheid *Segregation and the Bible*, was concerned that historians would overplay the influence of white liberalism on the civil rights movement. If left up to the "fellowship of upper-middle class professionals" (as he referred to the FSC) and "other white organizations of this sort," he argued, "there would [have been] no civil rights movement. . . . It took a black light really to bring the blacks together."[44]

Kester eventually accepted a teaching post at a small religious college in Illinois. His successor, the radical Southern Baptist preacher Will Campbell, attended the organizing meetings of the Southern Christian Leadership Conference while ministering to Klan members and southern religious racists. He served as a gentle icon of white religious populist radicalism, eventually returning to a theology that distrusted all institutions and relied on a personal witness. More so than Social Gospel idealism or even the neo-orthodox radicalism of Kester and his fellows, Campbell's anti-institutional theology—expressed in his aphorism "We're all sons of bitches but God loves us anyway"—moved white southern Christians to consider and question their race privilege.

Most southern religious men who questioned Jim Crow did so outside of institutional church bounds through groups such as the FSC. Denominational bureaucracies run by men remained, for the most part, obstinate in their defense of segregation. To the extent that progressivism entered the institutional church at all, it was primarily through women, especially white Methodist women. Will Alexander felt that Methodist women constituted "the most progressive and constructive religious group of the South." Imbued with an optimistic Wesleyan theology that emphasized free will, Methodist women brought the politics of racial justice to the door of the church.[45]

From their beginnings in the 1880s, Methodist women's home and foreign mission societies had attracted about sixty thousand members by 1910. By 1939, when southern and northern Methodists merged, they numbered nearly three hundred thousand. Begun mainly to raise money to build parsonages at home and to convert the heathen abroad, in the early twentieth century the societies moved swiftly into advocating the Christian Social Gospel. Early leaders Belle Bennett (a patrician Kentuckian) and Bertha Newell argued that the state was necessary as "God's ministry of organization, through which he must work." In 1914, Lily Hammond, an early organizer of the Woman's Home Missionary Society of the Methodist Church, South, published *In Black and White: An Interpretation of Southern Life*, a study guide for women's missionary organizations that implored Methodist women to move beyond charity and explore interracial friendships. Hammond complained: "[The] pulpits of the South rarely speak of those problems which press upon us all, and for which there is no solution outside the teachings of Christ."[46]

Methodist women deeply influenced the course of twentieth-century civil rights activism. In 1919, Will Alexander persuaded white Methodists Carrie Parks Johnson and Estelle Haskin to meet together with black progressive reformer Lugenia Burns Hope, wife of the president of Morehouse College. Their discussions led to a seminal conference in Memphis in 1920, the delegates to which included Margaret Murray Washington (wife of Booker T. Washington) and Charlotte Hawkins Brown, a North Carolina educator. At the meeting, as the black women entered from the back of the room, Belle Bennett sang out the opening lines to "Blessed Be the Tie That Binds." Emotions flowed freely as the women engaged in dialogue that by the standards of the time was frank. Charlotte Hawkins Brown told the white women about being expelled from a railroad car while she traveled to this conference for racial understanding. Brown later praised the conference as "the greatest step forward since emancipation." Jesse Daniel Ames believed the gathering demonstrated that "the common ground upon which these two groups of women could meet and plan for the common good was that of religion." She recalled: "Other ways were tried but all failed." The black women present "helped us to see some things in a different light," Carrie Johnson remembered, and she took it upon herself to spread the spirit of the interracial dialogue. In a subsequent speech before the Woman's Missionary Council, she informed her Methodist sisters that the nation had "not only been unjust to a race of people in her power, but [had] practiced barbarism, which [was] scarcely surpassed by any of the most barbarous and pagan peoples of the world."

In 1922, seven white and seven black women formed the Women's General Committee of the Commission on Interracial Cooperation. Local white and black committees formed separately. The CIC used its Methodist connections to spread information and discussion of racial problems. The women discovered that emotional dialogue had its limits; friendship and charity would only go so far. In the late 1920s, Ames, an independent and forthright Texan, took over the reins of the Women's General Committee. At the expense of addressing segregation as a total social system, she soon focused all the committee's energies into a regionwide antilynching campaign spearheaded by her new organization, the Association of Southern Women for the Prevention of Lynching (ASWPL). While the organization was effective in generating sentiment and shaming some southern sheriffs, Ames refused to throw the ASWPL's support behind federal antilynching legislation, gutting the association's political effectiveness.[47]

Prior to the depression, most white southern progressives advocated uplift, not integration. They looked to ease the strictness of segregation rather than to lift the veil entirely. By the advent of World War II, however, movements to reject segregation altogether animated progressive women. Methodists Louise Young and Thelma Stevens charted such a path for white southern Christians struggling to move beyond Jim Crow. Young grew up near Memphis, was educated at an Episcopal school for girls, and later earned her B.A. at Vanderbilt and did graduate work at the University of Wisconsin and Bryn Mawr. From 1925 to 1957, she chaired the Department of Sociology and Social Work at Scarritt College for Christian Workers in Nashville, a school established by the Southern Methodists for training female lay workers. During those years, she also directed the Methodist Woman's Missionary Council, and she was an early member of the Association of Southern Women for the Prevention of Lynching. Her male counterparts, she remembered, primarily pursued statistical growth in churches, whereas women "were after [growth] in terms of social work almost totally. Social work and teaching." Working at Paine College in Augusta from 1919 to 1922, a Colored Methodist Episcopal school for black students supported primarily with white Methodists' money, she boarded in a white home but was "literally living in a Negro world." Young worked closely with Charles Johnson, an African American sociologist at Fisk. There was "very little color between us," she later reminisced. Young also mediated the sometimes tense relationship between Jesse Daniel Ames, a forthright "organization person" (in Young's words), and Will Alexander, who "was really a persuader." Through her association with the Tennessee Council for Human Relations, she also worked with Eleanor Roosevelt.[48]

Young's biggest influence was on her protégé at Scarritt College, Thelma Stevens. This native Mississippian toiled tirelessly for racial justice in church and society. As a young schoolteacher in the Magnolia State, she witnessed a particularly brutal lynching and made a decision: "If the Lord would let me live long enough . . . I would do something to bring a little bit of relief from fear and a little human dignity to black people in Mississippi." After graduating from Hatticsburg State Teacher's College, Stevens attended Scarritt, and in the 1920s she succeeded Young as director of the Bethlehem Center in Augusta. Believing that the church was too "isolated from life," she conceived her work at Bethlehem as community development, not settlement house charity. She sought to move beyond the paternalistic "for the Negroes" model, realizing that in their dealings with black Methodist women whites "weren't working on a horizontal level."[49]

In 1938, Thelma Stevens organized the first truly interracial Methodist conference. Held at Paine College, it was designed to cultivate closer contact between white and black Methodist women. In the same year, Stevens also attended the founding meeting of the Southern Conference for Human Welfare in Birmingham, where more than a thousand southern reformers, New Dealers, and radicals made plans to attack endemic southern problems. Over the next several decades, Stevens provided a significant integrationist southern voice in a major American denomination. Combined with the Social Gospel idealism that spread into southern church organizations, evangelical resolve to cleanse the region energized racial justice politics.[50]

The southern writer, social critic, and activist Lillian Smith exemplifies another evolution from a conservative and evangelical southern childhood to social critique and activism. Smith was, as Morton Sosna has argued, an anticaste missionary: "[Smith] fought segregation with the fervor of a fundamentalist preacher attacking sin. She believed that somewhere, deep inside the souls of white southern Christians, there surely must have lurked the recognition that Jim Crow was a sin." Born in 1897 and raised in Florida and Georgia, she taught music for three years at a Methodist mission school in China. In the mid-1920s, she moved back to Georgia to serve as a counselor at a Methodist women's camp established by her father, a Methodist layman. For the next four decades, she penned articles and books that dissected southern racial mores and hypocrisies; a strongly Freudian element underpinned her analysis. Her 1944 novel *Strange Fruit*, which garnered considerable public attention, probed an interracial affair in a fictional small southern town. Smith's collection of essays, *Killers of the Dream*, published in 1949, explored the ways in which evangelical religion reinforced white supremacy: "Nowhere else, perhaps, have the rich seedbeds of Western homes found such a growing climate for guilt as is produced in the South by the combination of a warm moist evangelism and racial segregation," she wrote. The revivals central to her childhood experience were "a source of enormous terror and at the same time a blessed respite from rural monotony." Smith explained: "Nothing but a lynching or a political race-hate campaign could tear a town's composure into as many dirty little rags or give as many curious satisfactions." Smith shocked students at Morehouse College with her straight talk about segregation. As editor of the *South Today* (formerly called the *North Georgia Review* and before that *Pseudopodia*), she published eminent black authors such as W. E. B. Du Bois. From the 1950s until her death in 1966, she enthusiastically endorsed the *Brown* decision, corresponded with and advised movement leaders, and used her pen and energy in support of racial justice politics.[51]

The contrast between the institutional church—a largely conservative force—and progressive church people and Christians unaffiliated with the church such as Smith illuminates the complicated interrelationship of churches, racism, and interracialism. Keen observers recognized that white southern progressives, members of the so-called silent South, remained too few and too weak to bring about the end of racial inequality in the South. When Myles Horton, founder of the Highlander Folk School in Tennessee, received a well-meaning suggestion in the 1950s that he employ revivalism as an organizing tool, he thought: "[The] last thing I wanted [was] a revival. I don't care how radical it is; it could be right out of Karl Marx. . . . Education is one thing, a revival is another." Unlike Kester and others, Horton never saw "religion as a stepping stone" to social activism. Rather, he perceived that churches hindered civil rights and labor organizing: "Even though they preached the right thing, they wouldn't practice it; wouldn't back you up when you're on a picket line, they were against it, because they were against violence." Charles Jones noted that in the 1950s and 1960s a supposedly progressive town such as Chapel Hill was racially open "so long as it wasn't made public and it didn't make a fuss." The so-called radicalism of university and religious folk in the town involved "insight but little action." Churches "would issue their papers and so forth, but there was no implementation for it," Jones said. "It was sort of like the Creed. If you repeat the Creed, you're okay," he concluded.[52]

Horton and Jones understood the limitations of southern religious progressivism, but work pursued by committed individuals outpaced the conservative organizations from which they sprang. Groups such as the FSC nurtured believers and activists. Nelle Morton later said that her time with the Fellowship of Southern Churchmen "saved" her: "I just couldn't believe that there were that many people who felt about things like I did." It was "deeply satisfying" work because, she said, "you felt you could put everything you have in this, because this is the way it ought to be." Anne Queen, born white, southern, and working-class, studied at Yale Divinity School and joined the Fellowship of Southern Churchmen. "It's been a sense of religious community that's kept us going in period of defeat," she said of the group's experience during the years of massive resistance and White Citizen's Councils. Randolph Taylor, the first moderator of the reunited southern and northern Presbyterians (PCA-USA), remembered southern white Christians involved in the movement as a "thin but tough community of folk" whose job was not just to lance the boil, "but to see to the healing that's involved." "It's painful," he said, "but it's a very important discipline." Martin Luther King Jr. provided his own testimonial on this point: "When you can finally convert a white Southerner, you have one of the most genuine, committed human beings that you'll ever find. Did you ever notice that?"[53]

White supremacist hatred could be converted to racial goodwill, a kind of "racial conversion narrative" recently traced by southern literary scholar Fred Hobson. Hobson writes that the civil rights movement "had always been, for participating whites, in part about saving their own souls—about willing themselves back into a religion they could believe in—and their feelings of rejection within the movement in its latter days suggested they were not worthy after all." James McBride Dabbs, a Presbyterian providentialist, experienced his racial conversion in the 1930s following the death of his wife. Dabbs recalled: "[I] had finally to oppose all division and separation, both within myself and within that outer picture of myself, the world. When finally I realized what a division segregation was, I had to oppose it too." Like many other white southern Christians, he saw the African American as a savior and the black church as a potential redeemer of the national soul. Reflecting on the role of song in the civil rights movement, Pat Watters described his own experience in terms of a religious conversion brought about by freedom songs, writing of the "mystical, ecstatic experience" that he found through the sacred songs of the movement. As objects rather than agents in this version of the conversion narrative, black southerners evinced considerably more skepticism, but even for them the evangelical mythology deeply pervaded how they interpreted the movement. Fannie Lou Hamer told a group of Mississippi schoolchildren: "They ain't gonna be savin' *you*. You gonna be savin' them." Throughout the course of the 1960s, such conversions had to withstand a pervasive white disillusionment with the breakdown of the apparent white-black unity implied in the term "beloved community."[54]

The contrast between the institutional church and individual churchmen and churchwomen also emerges when looking at black churches and the civil rights movement. Ralph Abernathy, King's ally and close associate in SCLC, spoke charitably but critically of clergymen who theoretically favored social change but "were willing for it to come about slowly, when white society was ready to accept it." He recalled: "They preached a strict adherence to the law and peace at any price. The last thing they wanted to see destroyed was the precarious credibility among white leaders, who occasionally gave them minor posts of honor in the community in order to keep the rest of us in line." Privately, blacks expressed anger at whites, but publicly "they would say nothing to incur the wrath of those they privately denounced." When one looks beyond the black church and its leaders—more often conservative than prophetic—the empowerment provided by religious belief appears more clearly than ever. Those on the movement's front line, as one activist expressed it, had to "have that something on the inside," which she attributed to the black southern evangelical tradition: "It's not the denomination, it's the spirit. I think religion is kind of the way we use it, you know." Susie Morgan joined the freedom movement in Mississippi one Sunday when, as she later expressed it, "something hit [her] like a new religion." As Charles Payne has written, "Faith in the Lord made it easier to have faith in the possibility of social change," even if in the Delta towns he studied, such as Greenwood, the movement grew despite ministerial recalcitrance.[55]

Many civil rights workers, especially radicals in SNCC, hailed from backgrounds far removed from the black southern evangelical ethos: they were from families associated with universities, or they were Jewish radicals, or they were idealistic students inspired by the free speech movement. Whether religious themselves or not, they had to draw on what moved the people: prayer, song, and testimony. They learned of the black evangelical traditions that especially emboldened older movement members. Meetings in Greenwood, Mississippi, during the black freedom struggle surged with feelings evoked by prayer and music. One activist remembered: "The religious, the spiritual was like an explosion to me, an emotional explosion. I didn't have that available to me [before]. It just lit up my mind. The music and the religion provided a contact between our logic and our feelings. . . . And gave the logic of what we were doing emotional and human power to make us go forward." Parishioners at the meetings began attacking conservative and timid preachers, who responded by trying "to build their images and redeem themselves," as a contemporary observer put it. The followers in the movement, inspired by an evangelical vision of justice, led the leaders. Ethel Gray had rattlesnakes thrown on her porch but said proudly: "We stood up. Me and God stood up." Women such as Fannie Lou Hamer "placed Jesus where his experiences, as passed through the traditions of the Black church, could be used in the freedom struggle."[56]

For Gray, Hamer, and many others, nothing else could have sufficed to gird them to sacrifice themselves for what appeared to others a hopeless cause. Robin D. G. Kelley has argued that "we need to recognize that the sacred and the spirit world were also often understood and invoked by African Americans as weapons to protect themselves or to attack others." He asks: "Can a sign from above, a conversation with a ghost, a spell cast by an enemy, or talking in tongues unveil the hidden transcript?" To which one might add, can one's private and communal prayer when facing down racist sheriffs, voting registrars, or snakes thrown on one's front porch embolden resistance and serve as the antidote to the opiate fed to the people by Jim Crow's spokesmen? In Mississippi, Alabama, and other places in the 1950s and 1960s, the "hidden transcript" came to the surface. Whites who bombed the Sixteenth Street Baptist Church in Birmingham and dozens of other ecclesiastical buildings through these years recognized this as clearly as anyone.[57]

SNCC organizers, many with evangelical or Vatican II–era Catholic heritage, felt a higher power suffusing them in the movement, and for this they earned the respect of the deeply evangelical "local people" with whom they worked. Early black SNCC workers—John Lewis, Diane Nash, and others—combined their black evangelical heritage with lessons in radical nonviolent politics learned from James Lawson at Vanderbilt during the 1950s. For Lewis, it was like a "holy crusade," with the blood of civil rights martyrs redeeming the South from its former self-professed Redeemers. The young students who integrated lunch counters in Greensboro and inspired the original SNCC organizing conference also came from the church world. Many whites in SNCC came from churches as well. SNCC's "distinctively idealistic belief that fortitude, determined action, and fearlessness would result in momentous social change," Mary King has explained, "stemmed to a great degree from the Protestant upbringings of most of its workers." She connected her vision specifically to Wesleyan theology, the idea that "through grace and redemption each person can be saved"; this view, she recalled, "reinforced our belief that the good in every human being could be appealed to, fundamental change could correct the immorality of racial segregation, and new political structures could be created." Belle Bennett, Louise Young, and Thelma Stevens had expressed the same reasoning in a very different context before the movement began.[58]

The central event of twentieth-century southern history, the civil rights movement, took on an evangelical Protestant cast itself and became a sort of region-wide revival movement. Civil rights leaders, as well as their opponents, spoke the language of evangelicalism and understood the history of their times as part of sacred (albeit competing and contradictory) narratives about God's intent and purposes in history. The moment of supreme spiritual freedom for black Mississippian Bee Jenkins came when she was facing down a group of state troopers. Confronting the possibility of death in deciding whether to join a civil rights march, she "walked outta the house, looked up, said a prayer, and went and got in the marching." Despite the presence of law enforcement, she was not afraid. She said: "I know I had somebody there who was on my side. And that was Jesus; he was able to take care of me. That's who I can depend on and put my trust in." The African American freedom movement looked, to some white southern believers, like a plot to take away freedom, hence the ferocity of the anti-civil rights movement. If the Freedom Summer of 1964 was "God's long summer," as theologian and historian Charles Marsh has memorably described it, the era from the Civil War to the civil rights movement might be described for the South as God's long century, for it was in the South during this time that American Christianity was at its most tragic and its most triumphant.[59]

Conclusion

In Thomasville, Georgia, in the mid-1990s, a young white woman named Jaime L. Wireman gave birth to a child she named Whitney after the contemporary black singer Whitney Houston. Wireman's husband, an African American man named Jeffrey Johnson, worked odd jobs locally, and the two lived together in a trailer just outside the southwest Georgia town. The child, born with a skull not fully formed, died after just nineteen hours. Jaime Wireman wanted the baby to be buried with her maternal grandfather in the cemetery of the Barnetts Creek Baptist Church. After the burial, however, deacons of the church, who had not known previously that the father was black, asked the family to remove the child from the historically all-white cemetery. When the embarrassing incident came to light, church members criticized the deacons' action and permitted the child to remain in the cemetery. After some prodding from Whitney's maternal grandmother, the deacons and the pastor of the church, the Reverend Leon VanLandingham, met the family, apologized for their actions, and asked for forgiveness. "Our church family humbly asks you to accept our apology," the chairman of the deacon board told the family. "I believe people are sorry," the child's grandmother concluded. "She was just a baby."[60]

This story of race and religion in the contemporary South is almost allegorical in its retelling of the familiar themes of southern religious history: racial separation, sin, forgiveness, and an ambiguous healing. The tale contains the elements of the southern gothic religious romance: racial division, religious bigotry, biracial sex, innocent childhood disrupted by the intrusion of an unjust social world, and a culmination that, on the face of it, brings healing to the parties. Just as importantly, the story puts into relief a paradox of southern, and American, religious history, namely, the deep contradiction between human spiritual equality in the eyes of God and divinely ordained social inequality in the everyday world. Lillian Smith expressed it best in a letter to Martin Luther King Jr. in 1956: "I, myself, being a Deep South white, reared in a religious home and the Methodist church realize the deep ties of common songs, common prayer, common symbols that bind our two races together on a religio-mystical level, even as another brutally mythic idea, the concept of White Supremacy, tears our two people apart."[61] From Reconstruction through the civil rights movement, evangelical Protestantism among whites and blacks figured centrally in this most compelling drama of southern history.

Notes

Abbreviations

AGA   Flower Pentecostal Heritage Center, Assemblies of God Archives, Springfield, Mo.

DC   Dupree African-American Pentecostal and Holiness Collection, Schomburg Center for Research in Black Culture, New York Public Library, New York, N.Y.

PHCA   Archives of the International Pentecostal Holiness Church, Oklahoma City, Okla.

SCL   Special Collections Library, Duke University, Durham, N.C.

SOHP   Southern Oral History Program, Southern Historical Collection, University of North Carolina, Chapel Hill, N.C.

1. *Christian Index*, March 22, 1883.

2. E. Brooks Holifield, *Gentleman Theologians: American Theology in Southern Culture, 1790–1860* (Durham: Duke University Press, 1978); Larry Tise, *Proslavery: A History of the Defense of Slavery in America, 1701–1840* (Athens: University of Georgia Press, 1988); Mitchell Snay, *Gospel of Disunion: Religion and Separatism in the Antebellum South* (New York: Cambridge University Press, 1993).

3. Quoted in Hunter Dickinson Farish, *The Circuit Rider Dismounts: A Social History of Southern Methodism, 1865–1900* (Richmond: Dietz Press, 1938), 221–22.

4. Carey Daniel, "God the Original Segregationist," John Owen Smith Papers, box 1, Special Collections Library, Emory University, Atlanta, Ga. A note attached, directed to Methodist bishop John Owen Smith, read, "Please read the enclosed and then ask God to forgive you for trying to mix the races."

5. Quotations from Mark Newman, "Getting Right with God: Southern Baptists and Race Relations, 1945–1980" (Ph.D. diss., University of Mississippi, 1993), 93–94.

6. Ibid., 56, 99, 522.

7. Macon's editorials from *Alabama Baptist* quoted in ibid., 520–25.

8. For a fuller development of this point, see Paul Harvey, "Religion, Race, and the Right in the Baptist South," in *Religion and Politics in the Twentieth-Century South*, ed. Glenn Feldman, forthcoming.

9. E. B. Ingram Diary, July 10, 17, 1895, in E. B. Ingram Papers, SCL; Glenda Gilmore, *Gender and Jim Crow: Women and the Politics of White Supremacy in North Carolina, 1896–1920* (Chapel Hill: University of North Carolina Press, 1996), 73; Winfield Henry Mixon Diary, May 1, August 1, 1903, Winfield Henry Mixon Papers, SCL.

10. M. B. Woodworth-Etter, *Signs and Wonders: God Wrought in the Ministry for Forty-Five Years* (n.p.: privately printed, 1916), 98–101.

11. Leon Litwack, *Trouble in Mind: Black Southerners in the Age of Jim Crow* (New York: Alfred A. Knopf, 1998).

12. Charles Joyner, *Shared Traditions: Southern History and Folk Culture* (Urbana: University of Illinois Press, 1999), 25.

13. In recent work, John Boles and Sterling Stuckey have revived the debate, Boles stressing the biracial tradition of southern evangelicalism in the antebellum era and Stuckey grounding black American cultural expression in the African-based ring shout. See Boles, ed., *Masters and Slaves in the House of the Lord: Race and Religion in the American South, 1740–1870* (Lexington: University Press of Kentucky, 1988), and Stuckey, *Slave Culture: Nationalist Theory and the Foundations of Black America* (New York: Oxford University Press, 1987). Mechal Sobel's *Trabelin' On: The Slave Journey to an Afro-Baptist Faith* (Westport, Conn.: Greenwood Press, 1979), if problematic in assuming a monolithic "African cosmos," nevertheless provides a richly detailed portrait of black institutional churches before the Civil War as well as a penetrating analysis of the visionary travels of black conversion experience narratives that juxtaposes the biracial and African sources of black American religion. More recently, William Montgomery has analyzed the mutual interaction of and tension between the African-based religious expressions of the folk church and Protestant notions of respectability in the institutional church in the late nineteenth century. See *Under Their Own Vine and Fig Tree: The African-American Church in the South, 1865–1900* (Baton Rouge: Louisiana State University Press, 1991).

14. Solomon L. M. Conser, *Virginia after the War: An Account of Three Years' Experience in Reorganizing the Methodist Episcopal Church in Virginia at the Close of the Civil War* (Indianapolis: n.p., 1891), 39–40; Myrta L. Avary, *Dixie after the War: An Exposition of the Social Conditions Existing in the South, during the Twelve Years Succeeding the Fall of Richmond* (1906; reprint, New York: Arno, 1969), 203–5; Willis Williams, interview, *Florida Narratives*, vol. 17 of *The American Slave: A Composite Autobiography*, ed. George Rawick (Westport, Conn.: Greenwood Press, 1972), 353. Description of Augusta camp meeting

quoted in Briane Keith Turley, "A Wheel within a Wheel: Southern Methodism and the Georgia Holiness Association" (Ph.D. diss., University of Virginia, 1994), 283.

15. William Hatcher, *John Jasper: The Unmatched Negro Philosopher and Preacher* (New York: Fleming & Revell, 1908), 98, 36.

16. Elizabeth Johnson Harris, "Life Story, 1867–1923," Elizabeth Johnson Harris Papers, SCL.

17. Eli N. Evans, *The Provincials: A Personal History of Jews in the South*, rev. ed. (New York: Simon & Schuster, 1997), 260–62.

18. *Live Coals of Fire*, February 9, 1900. Extant copies of this periodical were consulted at PHCA.

19. *Live Coals of Fire*, October 27, November 3, 1899, January 26, 1900.

20. Florence Goff, *Fifty Years on the Battlefield for God: Being a Sketch of the Life of Rev. J. A. Hodges, Coupled with Some of the Lord's Dealings with H. H. Goff and Wife, Evangelists of the Cape Fear Conference of the Free Will Baptist Church* (Falcon, N.C.: n.p., n.d.), 19, consulted at PHCA; *Holiness Advocate*, September 16, 1901, October 1, 1903.

21. For more on the history of Holiness and Pentecostalism in the South, see Vinson Synan, *The Holiness-Pentecostal Tradition: Charismatic Movements in the Twentieth Century*, 2d ed. (Grand Rapids: Eerdmans, 1997).

22. Ethel E. Goss, *The Winds of God: The Story of Early Pentecostal Days (1901–1914) in the Life of Howard A. Goss* (New York: Comet Press Books, 1958), 34, 42, 56, 113, 129.

23. Ithiel C. Clemmons, *Bishop C. H. Mason and the Roots of the Church of God in Christ* (Bakersfield, Calif.: Pneuma Life Publishing, 1996), 5–20.

24. E. W. Mason, *The Man . . . Charles Harrison Mason* (n.p.: privately printed, 1979), 19; David M. Tucker, *Black Pastors and Leaders: Memphis, 1819–1972* (Memphis: Memphis State University Press, 1975), 87–100.

25. Paul Conkin, "Evangelicals, Fugitives, and Hillbillies: Tennessee's Impact on American National Culture," in *Tennessee History: The Land, the People, and the Culture*, ed. Carroll Van West (Knoxville: University of Tennessee Press, 1998), 287–322; Elsie Mason, ed., *From the Beginning of Bishop C. H. Mason and the Early Pioneers of the Church of God in Christ* (Memphis: Church of God in Christ Publishing House, 1991), 6; *The Whole Truth*, January 6, 1933, consulted in AGA.

26. "Partly—Biography of N. Scippio and Wife," in *A Christian Worker's Handbook* (n.p.: n.p., 1987), 9, 15, consulted in box 1, folder 16, DC.

27. *The Constitution, Government, and General Decree Book of the Church of the Living God, the Pillar and Ground of the Truth, Inc.* (Chattanooga: New & Living Way Publishing Company, n.d.), and materials for the Seventieth Annual General Assembly of the Church of the Living God, the Pillar and Ground of Truth, Inc., both in box 6, folder 8, DC.

28. *Tenets of the Fire Baptized Holiness Church of God of the Americas* (Atlanta: Fuller Press, n.d.), PHCA; *Discipline of the Fire Baptized Holiness Church of God of the Americas* (Atlanta: Church Publishing House by the Fuller Press, 1962), box 7, folder 1, DC. The Dupree Collection constitutes a remarkably rich resource for the history of black Pentecostalism.

29. Bill C. Malone, *Southern Music, American Music* (Lexington: University Press of Kentucky, 1979), 67–68, 76–78.

30. Goss, *The Winds of God*, 129.

31. Bill C. Malone, *Singing Cowboys and Musical Mountaineers: Southern Culture and the Roots of Country Music* (Athens: University of Georgia Press, 1993), 32.

32. For a fuller analysis of Elvis's grounding in his religious upbringing, see Peter Guralnick, *Last Train to Memphis: The Rise of Elvis Presley* (New York: Little & Brown, 1994). For more on sacred passion in religion and music, as well as on the connection between music and struggles for racial justice, see David Chappell, *A Stone of Hope: Prophetic Religion and the Death of Jim Crow* (Chapel Hill: University of North Carolina Press, 2003).

33. Mary King, *Freedom Song: A Personal Story of the 1960s Civil Rights Movement* (New York: William Morrow, 1987), 273.

34. Wilma Dykeman and James Stokely, *Seeds of Southern Change: The Life of Will Alexander* (Chicago: University of Chicago Press, 1962); Jacquelyn Dowd Hall, *Revolt against Chivalry: Jessie Daniel Ames and the Southern Women's Campaign against Lynching* (New York: Columbia University Press, 1979).

35. John Egerton, *Speak Now against the Day: The Generation before the Civil Rights Movement in the South* (New York: Alfred A. Knopf, 1994), 48; Jacqueline Rouse, *Lugenia Burns Hope: Black Southern Reformer* (Athens: University of Georgia Press, 1989), 107.

36. Egerton, *Speak Now against the Day*, 47.

37. Ibid., 425.

38. Tracy K'Meyer, *Interracialism and Christian Community in the Postwar South: The Story of Koinonia Farm* (Charlottesville: University Press of Virginia, 1997).

39. Jim Shumaker, interview, box 6, folder 33–34, Duke University Oral History Program, Durham, N.C.; Virginia French, interview, box 2, folder 1, 13, Duke University Oral History Program; Henry Mitchell, interview, Series F, SOHP.

40. John A. Salmond, "The Fellowship of Southern Churchmen and Interracial Change in the South," *North Carolina Historical Review* 69 (April 1992): 179–99.

41. Howard Kester, *Revolt among the Sharecroppers* (1934; reprint, New York: Arno Press, 1969).

42. Fellowship of Southern Churchmen, "We Affirm," pamphlet, CIO Papers, box 75, SCL; Scotty Cowan to Nelle Morton, August 1, 1949, Fellowship of Southern Churchmen Papers, box 17, Southern Historical Collection, University of North Carolina, Chapel Hill, N.C.; David Burgess, "Preachers, Beware!" *Prophetic Religion* 6 (Summer 1945): 37–38, copy consulted in SCL.

43. Howard Kester to the Field Foundation, December 1952, FSC Papers, box 19, and FSC newsletter, November 1955, FSC papers, box 21, both in Southern Historical Collection.

44. Everett Tilson, interview, Series F, SOHP.

45. John Patrick McDowell, *The Social Gospel in the South: The Woman's Home Mission Movement in the Methodist Episcopal Church South, 1886–1939* (Baton Rouge: Louisiana State University Press, 1986), 144.

46. Ibid., 57–58, quote on 100.

47. Material in the last two paragraphs may found in Rouse, *Lugenia Burns Hope*, 107–15; McDowell, *Social Gospel in the South*, 91, 92, 108; Hall, *Revolt against Chivalry*.

48. Louise Young, interview, February 14, 1972, transcript G-66, SOHP.

49. Thelma Stevens, interview, February 13, 1972, transcript G-58, 19, 34–35, SOHP.

50. Alice Knotts, "Bound by the Spirit, Found on the Journey: The Methodist Women's Campaign for Southern Civil Rights" (Ph.D. diss., Iliff School of Theology and the University of Denver, 1989), 32, 36–39, 68–69, 100, 108, 112; Knotts, "Methodist Women Integrate Schools and Housing, 1952–1959," in *Women in the Civil Rights Movement: Trailblazers and Torchbearers, 1941–1965*, eds. Vicki L. Crawford, Jacqueline Anne Rouse, and Barbara Woods, vol. 16 of *Black Women in United States History*, ed. Darlene Clark Hine (Brooklyn: Carlson Publishing, 1990), 257.

51. Lillian Smith, excerpt from "Killers of the Dream," in *The Oxford Book of the American South*, eds. Bradley Mittendorf and Edward Ayers (New York: Oxford University Press, 1998), 440; Morton Sosna, *In Search of the Silent South* (New York: Columbia University Press, 1977), 197. See also Randall Lee Patton, "Southern Liberals and the Emergence of a 'New South,' 1938–1950" (Ph.D. diss., University of Georgia, 1990), 156–60, and Grace Elizabeth Hale, *Making Whiteness: The Culture of Segregation in the South* (New York: Pantheon, 1998).

52. Myles Horton, interview, 4007-F, SOHP; Everett Tilson, interview, Series F, SOHP; Charles Jones, interview, November 8, 1976, transcript B-41, 3, SOHP.

53. Nelle Morton, interview, Series F, 13–14, 38, 58, SOHP; Anne Queen, interview, box 5, folder 4, 17–18, Duke University Oral History Program; Randolph Taylor, interview, May 23, 1985, transcript C-21, SOHP; Martin Luther King quoted in Lewis V. Baldwin, *There Is a Balm in Gilead: The Cultural Roots of Martin Luther King, Jr.* (Minneapolis: Fortress Press, 1991), 78–79.

54. Fred Hobson, *But Now I See: The White Southern Racial Conversion Narrative* (Baton Rouge: Louisiana State University Press, 1999), 56.

55. Ralph Abernathy, *And the Walls Came Tumbling Down: An Autobiography* (New York: Harper & Row, 1989), 114–15; Susie Weaver, interview, box 6, folder 32, Duke University Oral History Program; John Dittmer, *Local People: The Struggle for Civil Rights in Mississippi* (Urbana: University of Illinois Press, 1994), 231; Charles Payne, "Men Led, but Women Organized: Movement Participation of Women in the Mississippi Delta," in Crawford, Rouse, and Woods, *Women in the Civil Rights Movement*, 5.

56. Dittmer, *Local People*, 258, 196; Bernice Johnson Reagon, "Women as Culture Carriers in the Civil Rights Movement: Fannie Lou Hamer," in Crawford, Rouse, and Woods, *Women in the Civil Rights Movement*, 203–17.

57. Robin D. G. Kelley, "'We Are Not What We Seem': Rethinking Black Working-Class Opposition in the Jim Crow South," *Journal of American History* 80 (June 1993): 88.

58. King, *Freedom Song*, 273.

59. Frederick C. Harris, *Something Within: Religion in African-American Political Ac-*

tivism (New York: Oxford University Press, 1999); Charles Payne, *I've Got the Light of Freedom: The Organizing Tradition and the Mississippi Freedom Struggle* (Berkeley: University of California Press, 1995); Charles Marsh, *God's Long Summer: Stories of Faith and Civil Rights* (Princeton: Princeton University Press, 1997).

60. *New York Times*, March 31, 1996.

61. Lillian Smith to Martin Luther King Jr., March 10, 1956, in *How Am I to Be Heard: Letters of Lillian Smith*, ed. Margaret Rose Gladney (Chapel Hill: University of North Carolina Press, 1993), 193.

For Further Reading

Baldwin, Lewis V. *There Is a Balm in Gilead: The Cultural Roots of Martin Luther King, Jr.* Minneapolis: Fortress Press, 1991.

Boles, John, ed. *Masters and Slaves in the House of the Lord: Race and Religion in the American South, 1740–1870.* Lexington: University Press of Kentucky, 1988.

Chappell, David. *A Stone of Hope: Prophetic Religion and the Death of Jim Crow.* Chapel Hill: University of North Carolina Press, 2003.

———. "The Divided Mind of Southern Segregationists." *Georgia Historical Quarterly* 82 (Spring 1998): 45–72.

Clemmons, Ithiel C. *Bishop C. H. Mason and the Roots of the Church of God in Christ.* Bakersfield, Calif.: Pneuma Life Publishing, 1996.

Crawford, Vicki L., Jacqueline Anne Rouse, and Barbara Woods, eds. *Women in the Civil Rights Movement: Trailblazers and Torchbearers, 1941–1965.* Vol. 16 of *Black Women in United States History*, edited by Darlene Clark Hine. Brooklyn: Carlson Publishing, 1990.

Crespino, Joseph. "The Christian Conscience of Jim Crow: White Protestant Ministers and the Mississippi Citizens' Councils, 1954–1964." *Mississippi Folklife* 31 (Fall 1998): 30–44.

Dykeman, Wilma, and James Stokely. *Seeds of Southern Change: The Life of Will Alexander.* New York: W. W. Norton, 1962.

Egerton, John. *Speak Now against the Day: The Generation before the Civil Rights Movement in the South.* New York: Alfred A. Knopf, 1994.

Evans, Eli N. *The Provincials: A Personal History of Jews in the South.* Rev. ed. New York: Athenaeum, 1973; New York: Free Press Paperbacks, 1997.

Farish, Hunter Dickinson. *The Circuit Rider Dismounts: A Social History of Southern Methodism, 1865–1900.* Richmond: Dietz Press, 1938.

Garrow, David. *Bearing the Cross: Martin Luther King, Jr., and the Southern Christian Leadership Conference.* New York: William Morrow, 1986.

Gilmore, Glenda. *Gender and Jim Crow: Women and the Politics of White Supremacy in North Carolina, 1896–1920.* Chapel Hill: University of North Carolina Press, 1996.

Gladney, Margaret Rose, ed. *How Am I to Be Heard: Letters of Lillian Smith*. Chapel Hill: University of North Carolina Press, 1993.

Goss, Ethel E. *The Winds of God: The Story of Early Pentecostal Days (1901–1914) in the Life of Howard A. Goss*. New York: Comet Press Books, 1958.

Guralnick, Peter. *Last Train to Memphis: The Rise of Elvis Presley*. New York: Little & Brown, 1994.

Hale, Grace Elizabeth. *Making Whiteness: The Culture of Segregation in the South*. New York: Pantheon, 1998.

Hall, Jacquelyn Dowd. *Revolt against Chivalry: Jessie Daniel Ames and the Southern Women's Campaign against Lynching*. New York: Columbia University Press, 1979.

Harris, Frederick C. *Something Within: Religion in African-American Political Activism*. New York: Oxford University Press, 1999.

Harvey, Paul. *Redeeming the South: Religious Cultures and Racial Identities among Southern Baptists, 1865–1925*. Chapel Hill: University of North Carolina Press, 1997.

Hobson, Fred. *But Now I See: The White Southern Racial Conversion Narrative*. Baton Rouge: Louisiana State University Press, 1999.

Holifield, E. Brooks. *Gentleman Theologians: American Theology in Southern Culture, 1790–1860*. Durham: Duke University Press, 1978.

Joyner, Charles. *Shared Traditions: Southern History and Folk Culture*. Urbana: University of Illinois Press, 1999.

Kelley, Robin D. G. "'We Are Not What We Seem': Rethinking Black Working-Class Opposition in the Jim Crow South." *Journal of American History* 80 (June 1993): 75–112.

Kester, Howard. *Revolt among the Sharecroppers*. Reprint, New York: Arno, 1969.

King, Mary. *Freedom Song: A Personal Story of the 1960s Civil Rights Movement*. New York: William Morrow, 1987.

K'Meyer, Tracy. *Interracialism and Christian Community in the Postwar South: The Story of Koinonia Farm*. Charlottesville: University Press of Virginia, 1997.

Knotts, Alice. "Bound by the Spirit, Found on the Journey: The Methodist Women's Campaign for Southern Civil Rights." Ph.D. diss., Iliff School of Theology and the University of Denver, 1989.

Litwack, Leon. *Trouble in Mind: Black Southerners in the Age of Jim Crow*. New York: Alfred A. Knopf, 1998.

Luker, Ralph. *The Social Gospel in Black and White: American Racial Reform, 1885–1912*. Chapel Hill: University of North Carolina Press, 1991.

Malone, Bill C. *Singing Cowboys and Musical Mountaineers: Southern Culture and the Roots of Country Music*. Athens: University of Georgia Press, 1993.

———. *Southern Music, American Music*. Lexington: University Press of Kentucky, 1979.

Marsh, Charles. *God's Long Summer: Stories of Faith and Civil Rights*. Princeton: Princeton University Press, 1997.

McDowell, John Patrick. *The Social Gospel in the South: The Woman's Home Mission Movement in the Methodist Episcopal Church South, 1886–1939.* Baton Rouge: Louisiana State University Press, 1982.

Montgomery, William E. *Under Their Own Vine and Fig Tree: The African-American Church in the South, 1865–1900.* Baton Rouge: Louisiana State University Press, 1991.

Newman, Mark. *Getting Right with God: Southern Baptists and Desegregation, 1945–1995.* Tuscaloosa: University of Alabama Press, 2001.

Patton, Randall Lee. "Southern Liberals and the Emergence of a 'New South,' 1938–1950." Ph.D. diss., University of Georgia, 1990.

Payne, Charles. *I've Got the Light of Freedom: The Organizing Tradition and the Mississippi Freedom Struggle.* Berkeley: University of California Press, 1995.

Rouse, Jacqueline. *Lugenia Burns Hope: Black Southern Reformer.* Athens: University of Georgia Press, 1989.

Salmond, John A. "The Fellowship of Southern Churchmen and Interracial Change in the South." *North Carolina Historical Review* 69 (April 1992): 179–99.

Snay, Mitchell. *Gospel of Disunion: Religion and Separatism in the Antebellum South.* New York: Cambridge University Press, 1993.

Sobel, Mechal. *Trabelin' On: The Slave Journey to an Afro-Baptist Faith.* Westport, Conn.: Greenwood Press, 1979.

Sosna, Morton. *In Search of the Silent South.* New York: Columbia University Press, 1977.

Synan, Vinson. *The Holiness-Pentecostal Tradition: Charismatic Movements in the Twentieth Century.* 2d ed. Grand Rapids: Eerdmans, 1997.

Tise, Larry. *Proslavery: A History of the Defense of Slavery in America, 1701–1840.* Athens: University of Georgia Press, 1988.

Turley, Briane Keith. "A Wheel within a Wheel: Southern Methodism and the Georgia Holiness Association." Ph.D. diss., University of Virginia, 1994.

Kurt O. Berends received his doctorate in history from Oxford University in 1998. He is an assistant professor of history and coordinator of the Christian Scholars Program at the University of Notre Dame. He is completing a book on how the Civil War transformed Protestantism in the South and is the author of "'Wholesome Reading Purifies and Elevates the Man': The Religious Military Press in the Confederacy," in Randall M. Miller, Harry S. Stout, and Charles Reagan Wilson's edited collection, *Religion and the American Civil War* (1998).

Emily Bingham, who received her doctorate in history from the University of North Carolina at Chapel Hill, is an independent scholar in Louisville, Kentucky. She is the author of *Mordecai: An Early American Family* (2003) and the coeditor with Thomas A. Underwood of *The Southern Agrarians and the New Deal: Essays after "I'll Take My Stand"* (2001).

Anthea D. Butler is an assistant professor of theological studies at Loyola Marymount University in Los Angeles, California. She is finishing *Making a Sanctified World: Women in the Church of God in Christ* (forthcoming).

Paul Harvey teaches history at the University of Colorado in Colorado Springs. He is the author of *Freedom's Coming: How Religious Culture Shaped the South from Civil War through Civil Rights* (2004) and the coeditor with Philip Goff of *Themes in American Religion and Culture* (2004).

Jerma Jackson teaches graduate and undergraduate history courses at the University of North Carolina at Chapel Hill. She is the author of *Singing in My Soul: Black Gospel Music in a Secular Age* (2004). Tracing gospel from its beginnings as a mode of worship to its emergence in commercialized culture, Jackson shows how questions about faith and the nature of the sacred influenced twentieth-century African American life. Her essay on Sister Rosetta Tharpe is part of this larger project.

Lynn Lyerly is an associate professor at Boston College. She is the author of *Methodism and the Southern Mind, 1770–1810* (1998) and of numerous chapters and articles on women and gender in southern religion. She is currently working on a cultural biography of Thomas Dixon Jr.

Donald G. Mathews teaches history and exercises modest "deaning" duties at the University of North Carolina at Chapel Hill. He is the author of *Religion in the Old South* (1977) and has written articles and books on religion and southern culture. He is currently working on a book about religion, violence, punishment, and lynching.

Beth Barton Schweiger teaches the history of the early United States at the University of Arkansas. She is the author of *The Gospel Working Up: Progress and the Pulpit in Nineteenth-Century Virginia* (2000) and is completing *Reading Slavery: Literacy, Virtue, and Freedom in the Early United States* (forthcoming).

Jon F. Sensbach teaches early American history at the University of Florida. The recipient of fellowships from the Omohundro Institute of Early American History and Culture and the National Humanities Center, he is the author of *A Separate Canaan: The Making of an Afro-Moravian World in North Carolina, 1763–1840* (1998). He is completing *Rebecca's Revival: Making Black Christianity in the Atlantic World* (forthcoming).

Daniel Woods has taught social and cultural history at Ferrum College since 1982. His primary research area is the evolution of Holiness, Pentecostal, and charismatic spirituality in the South. His essay in this collection is drawn from a book he is completing on the dynamic tension between popular enthusiasm and institutional authority in the development of the International Pentecostal Holiness Church. Woods is also currently studying the influence of railroad travel and metaphors on the Holiness and Pentecostal movements between the 1880s and the 1920s.

Dollard, John, 49

Dombrowski, James, 311

Domestic enlightenment, 71–72, 74–75, 81, 82, 86–87, 91 (n. 18)

Dorsey, Thomas A., 219–20, 239, 304

Double marriage: COGIC on, 212–14

Douglas, Mary, 34, 57 (n. 13), 60 (n. 44), 192

Drane, Arizona, 229

Dreams, 131–32, 138–41, 195

Dress code, COGIC, 205–8

Du Bois, W. E. B., 181–82, 193

Ecstatic worship, 127, 128, 130, 131, 132, 138, 139, 140, 146, 158–59, 195, 209, 210, 211, 222, 293

Edgeworth, Maria, 74, 93 (n. 32)

Egerton, John, 308

Eighteen Original Negro Spirituals, 234–35

Ellington, Duke, 234

Emotion, 127, 131, 134, 135, 167–68, 171, 186 (n. 24), 186–87 (n. 36), 293–94, 295, 296–97; communication from God through, 136–37; as justification for lynching by whites, 158–59, 161. *See also* Ecstatic worship; Lynching: and provocation

Episcopalians, 2–3, 6, 76–78, 85, 86, 110. *See also* Meade, Bishop William

Equality: and communism, 289; dangers of, 286–91; not a Christian value, 286; southern whites attack, 286–91. *See also* White supremacy

Equal Rights Amendment (ERA), 267

Evangelicalism, 2–3, 6–7, 11, 18, 19, 20–21, 24 (n. 13), 34, 44, 73, 76–77, 92 (n. 22), 151 (n. 72), 263, 284–85; female networks of, 79–80, 82; and lynching, 156–66 passim; as narcissistic, 164, 183; and racism, 285–91; and slavery, 100; and southern expressiveness, 293–94, 302

Evans, Eli, 2, 32, 56, 295

Farrow, Lucy, 299

Fellowship of Southern Churchmen, 310–13

Fire-Baptized Holiness Church, 127, 136, 296–97, 302–3

Frey, Sylvia, 13, 52, 153

Friedman, Jean, 45, 260–65 passim

Frontier: and religion, 15

Fuller, William E., 302–3

Funkenstein, Amos: on Jewish identity, 84

Gallagher, Gary, 113

Geertz, Clifford, 155, 193

Gender, 17–19, 260–65; as conservative issue, 290. *See also* Honor; Patriarchy; Sex; Women

Genovese, Eugene D., 41–44, 153

Germans, 12, 17, 24 (n. 14), 31

Girard, René, 115, 156, 181

God: voice of, 126, 128, 131–32, 136–44

Goen, Clarence C., 100

Goff, Florence, 138, 144, 146

Gospel music, 219–45 passim, 303–7; ambiguity of status of, 238–39; and biracial exchange, 304; as business, 230–38, 303, 305–6; and commerce, 219–21, 230–31, 235–36, 244 (n. 63); different from hymns and spirituals, 221–22, 234–35

Great Awakening I, 35

Great Awakening II, 38, 51–52

Great Migration, 195–218 passim

Guelzo, Allen, 35–36, 68

Guilt: and slavery, 100

Guitar music, 221, 222, 224, 225, 226, 229

Ham, story of, 287–89

Hamer, Fannie Lou, 259–60, 318

Hammond, Lily Hardy, 257–58, 268, 313

Hampton Institute, 293

Handkerchiefs, prayer, 301

Haskin, Estelle, 314

Hatch, Nathan, 38

Haygood, Bishop Atticus, 158, 170–71

Healing, 140, 142, 211, 226
Hegel, Georg F. W., 42, 43
Heyrman, Christine, 7–8, 45, 59 (n. 32), 153
Hierarchy: as essential to order, 286
Higginbotham, Evelyn Brooks, 250, 267–68
Hill, Samuel Smyth, Jr., 6, 21 (n. 4), 37, 57 (n. 9), 285
Hobgood-Oster, Laura, 268
Holiness, 135, 160, 163, 291, 295–97
Holmes, Nickels John, 127, 135–36, 140, 142, 143, 145
Holy Spirit, 126, 131, 132, 134, 138, 146, 195, 200, 249, 297, 298
Honor, 104–5, 118–19 (n. 33), 162–63, 168–69; and Christianity, 106–7; and Civil War, 107; and female virtues, 106; and lynching, 160–61. *See also* Patriarchy
Hope, Lugenia Burns, 314
Horton, Myles, 311, 317
Hose, Sam (Thomas Wilkes): lynching of, 161–63, 165–66
Hughes, Sarah Ann, 251

Immaculate protection, canon of: and lynching, 160–61, 169, 171
Indians, 8, 9–11, 15–16, 17, 22–23 (n. 8), 23 (n. 11), 26 (n. 22)
Integration, 315
Interracial connections: and COGIC, 203–4
Interracialism, 307–21
Isaac, Rhys, 6–7, 19, 44

Jackson, Mahalia, 305
Jasper, John, 294
Jenkins, Bee, 320–21
Jesus: as radical, 260; speaks to believers, 129
Jeter, Jeremiah Bell, 107
Jewish assimilation, 67–70, 72–74, 82, 84, 88 (n. 5), 90–91 (n. 15)

Jews, 2, 67–98 passim; and civil rights, 319; and identity, 74, 76, 81, 86–87, 92 (n. 25); Jewish women, 279–80 (n. 109); southern Jews, 89 (n. 6), 90 (n. 11), 93 (n. 39), 97, 98, 269–70; as targets of proselytizing, 78–79
Jim Crow. *See* Segregation
Johnson, Carrie Parks, 314
Johnson, Mother Mary Mangum, 195–96, 199–200, 201–4
Johnson, W. G. "Ting-a-ling," 195, 200, 202, 203
Jones, Charles: and interracialism, 309–10, 317
Jones, Charles Colcock, Sr., 49
Jones, Charles Price: founds COGIC, 196
Jordan, Clarence, 309–10
Joyner, Charles, 292
Judaism, 73, 74, 76, 269; in Charleston, 76. *See also* Mordecai, Jacob

Kester, Howard, 310–13
King, Joseph H., 127, 136–37, 144–45, 150 (n. 39)
King, Martin Luther, Jr., 318, 322
King, Mary, 307, 320
Knight, Marie, 224, 233
Koinonia Farm, 309
Ku Klux Klan, 159, 169, 308

Ladies Congregation of the Children of Mary, 252
Law, William, 51
Lawson, James, 320
Lazarus, Aaron, 74, 80–81, 82
Lazarus, Marx, 75, 81
Lazarus, Rachel Mordecai, 67–98 passim; and child rearing, 75–76; and conversion process, 77–84, 95 (n. 56); as evangelical Christian, 76–80; as Jew, 67–69, 71–72, 75; marriage of, 74. *See also* Domestic enlightenment
Lee, General Robert E., 113–15
Lewis, John, 320

Patterson, Orlando, 41–44
Pentecost, 125, 296
Pentecostal Holiness Church (PHC), 127, 135, 147, 148 (n. 7), 305
Pentecostals, 125–52 passim, 195–218 passim, 295–307; and biracialism, 295–307; ethos of, 126, 127–28, 151–52 (n. 73), 196, 222, 224, 231, 234, 303–4; and racial interchange through music, 300–307; and restoration of old-time religion, 226; uniqueness of music of, 225
Populists, 297–98
Prayer, 125–35 passim, 147
Presbyterians, 5, 7
Presley, Elvis, 303, 306–7
Prohibition, 163
Proslavery religious apologists, 286–87
Purity, 157, 160, 163, 168, 169, 191 (n. 99), 267; sexual and racial, 288–91. *See also* Douglas, Mary
Presbyterians, 5, 7, 47, 108, 113, 155. *See also* Dabney, Robert Lewis

Quakers, 102
Queen, Anne: and interracial action, 317–18

Raboteau, Albert, 40–41, 52, 153
Racial interchange, 284–85, 291–307
Racism: and southern religious thought, 285–91
Ransom, John Crowe, 167
Rape, 160, 161
Raper, Arthur, 156, 193
Red Summer (1919), 307
Reformed theology: changes in during Civil War, 106–7, 108, 115
Religion: as celebration, 226; as culture, 153–57, 220–21, 222; as defined by Geertz, 155; as demoralizing, 101; beyond institutions, 153–57; morale fostered by, 100, 103, 112–13; as multivalent, 249–50, 263–65; as personal

conviction, 101–3; and resistance, 10–11, 13, 18, 19, 40–44, 45, 46, 48–49, 55–56, 251–52, 263–65, 307–21; as social solidarity, 10–11, 13, 14–15, 16, 19–20, 37–39, 49–56, 178–79, 182, 195–98, 222–24; as understanding, 250. *See also* Southern religion
Religious Right, 267
Restoration of Israel, The, 79
Revivals, 32–38, 51–56, 72, 128, 131, 134, 137, 141, 147, 291, 296, 316; in army, 112–13; as ethos, 163
Roberts, Oral, 303
Robinson, Mother Elizabeth Woods, 198, 200, 206–7, 213–14
Roman Catholicism, 10, 12, 14, 15, 16
Roman Catholics, 10, 12, 14, 253, 254, 268–69, 270, 280 (n. 109)
"Royal Telephone, The" (F. M. Lehman), 125
Rustin, Bayard, 310

Sacred-secular dichotomy, 155–57, 227–28, 230, 237–39. *See also* Blues
Sacrifice, 108–9, 115, 167–68, 169, 178, 179, 181–82, 183, 188 (n. 65)
"Saint": as term for sanctified church members, 199
Salem, North Carolina, 18
Scarritt College for Christian Workers, 315
Schweiger, Beth Barton, 21 (n. 4)
Scott, James C., 48
"Second blessing," 129, 135–36, 142
Secularization, 32, 33, 34, 57–58 (n. 13)
Segregation, 3, 4, 17, 187 (nn. 38–40), 284, 285; breached by Pentecostals, 301–2; breached at certain moments, 292–93; folk theology of, 287–88; Lillian Smith opposes, 316–17; as religion, 155, 163–64, 209, 285–91, 292. *See also* Biracial worship; Daniel, Carey
Segregation and the Bible, 312–13
Sex, 159, 160, 161. *See also* Gender

Wesley, John, 51
White, Walter, 156, 158–59, 160–61, 194, 307
White, William Jefferson, 173–74, 175
White Citizens Council, 288
White people, 5–8, 11–13, 19, 31–34, 35–39, 44–48, 53, 56, 67–152 passim, 167, 284, 285–91, 308–18 passim; changes in white women's views on race, 257, 258; and fear of emotion, 297; and interracialism, 307–21. *See also* Segregation; White supremacy
White supremacy, 158–71 passim, 284–91, 295
Whole Truth, The, 301
Williams, Hank, 306
Williams, Mary: and conversations with God, 128–34
Williams, Roger, 102
Wilmington, North Carolina, 297–98
Without Sanctuary, 157
Woman suffrage, 265–66
Women, 17, 44, 45–48, 71–72, 75–78, 91 (n. 18), 95 (n. 55), 106, 247–81 passim; African American women, 195–218 passim, 250, 256–57; and charity, 254–57; and COGIC, 200–201, 204–5, 211, 227; as evangelists, 201, 204, 208, 227, 299, 302; and home missions as expansion of women's work, 255–56; opposition of Methodist women to racism, 313–14; ordaining of among AME and AMEZ, 251; Pentecostal women, 126, 127, 128–34, 195–96; as preachers, 129–30, 143, 179–80, 201, 202, 204–5, 216 (n. 20), 291; religious roles of, 248–50, 252; Roman Catholic women, 12, 17, 18, 252–54; and southern religion, 247–81 passim; and visions, 139, 146. *See also* Church mothers, COGIC; Domestic enlightenment
Women's Christian Temperance Union, 252, 265
Women's Missionary Society, 252
Women's Missionary Union, 252, 254
Wood, Peter, 9–10
Wood, Betty, 13, 52, 153, 262
Woodmason, Charles, 5
Woodward, Comer Vann, 100
Woodworth-Etter, Maria, 291
Wyatt-Brown, Bertram, 168–69

Young, Louise, 315, 320
Young Women's Christian Association, 252